Going
to
Barsetshire

A Companion to the Barsetshire Novels of
Angela Thirkell

Cynthia Snowden

First published in 2000 by
Cynthia Snowden

ISBN 0-9703858-0-3

Library of Congress Control Number:00-92682

Cover art © Sarah M. Waldron, 2000

Additional copies of this book may be ordered
using the form on the last page.

Visit our web page:
http://www.mcn.org/l/thirkell

(For those of our Barsetshire-loving friends dismayed by the
shocking string of letters in this web address
we have given the same sort of ball-park directions
that we use ourselves.)
Using Google, Direct Hit, Lycos, Alta Vista,
or any other good search engine, type in
"Barsetshire," "Angela Thirkell," or "Cynthia Snowden."

Printed in the USA by
Morris Publishing
3212 E. Highway 30, Kearney, NE 68847
800-650-7888

To Kay Lobley and Jim Rogers

Acknowledgements

No work of this sort is accomplished in a vacuum, and my debt is great. For support that wildly exceeded any reasonable expectations, I am deeply grateful to Carol Stone. On the page introducing Comments and Notes I say that I had no Miss Pemberton to goad and guide me, and although that was true at the time, circumstances changed. After she saw the manuscript, Carol kept me sustained with encouraging messages; she corrected errors, and even allowed her brother to borrow the book! Three other members of the Thirkell Society, Edith Jeude, Janet Schmeltzer, and Barbara Houlton, were quick with their appreciation, helpful corrections, advice, and encouragement.

And many are the friends, most of whom had never heard of Angela Thirkell and who thought my endeavor was quixotic in the extreme but were too polite to say so, who read the manuscript or contributed from the areas of their expertise: Bob Anderson, Freddie Brinster, Herb Budden, Edwina and David Compton, Robert Evans, Ian Fraser, Cynthia Gentry, Niall and Maureen Healy, Janet Hubbard, Alan Lynch, Nick Makris, Barbara and Felice Manfredi, Karen Marshall, Nancy and Lewis Owen, Georgia Radford, Jo Ann Ridley, Nathan Thuma, Michael Warlum, and Frank Williams. Sue and Howard Blair made trips to their local library for me, and to Alan Coleman I am grateful for the loan of a beautiful copy of *The Ingoldsby Legends*. Kay Lobley deserves a special mention here for introducing me to the Thirkell novels, for enjoying my book and especially for calling it "indispensable!"

The greatest support was unfailingly provided by my husband, Jim Rogers. His involvement and assistance took many forms: taking the cats to the vet, spraying the hollyhocks, buying a second computer and printer, doing more than his share of errands, sympathizing when I raged at the computer, even moving to another desk—and editing the manuscript (including this paragraph). His help in every way has been of incalculable value.

I am very grateful to the following publishers who have kindly allowed me to quote from their printed works.

For all the selections from the Thirkell novels, I am indebted to Serena Thirkell for her gracious permission and interest, and to Penguin, UK.

Quotations from *Edward Lear—Nonsense Poems and Laughable Lyrics*, 1987, are by permission of Charles H. Frey.

The selections from "A Shropshire Lad" from *The Collected Poems of A. E. Housman*, © 1965, are reprinted by permission of Henry Holt & Co., LLC, and The Society of Authors as the literary representative of the Estate of A. E. Housman.

The excerpt from Lord Kitchener's message to the British Expeditionary Force, which appeared in *The Times* of August 19, 1914, © Times Newspapers Limited, is with permission of *The Times*.

Contents

Introduction

Writing a book when you have to get your facts right is no joke.
— Oliver Marling

Most readers will not go from one Barsetshire novel to another in rapid succession. Even if they did, so dreamlike is the atmosphere that they, like the occasional reader, will need to be reoriented from time to time. It is for these readers, lost in cloud-cuckooland,* that this companion is intended—despite a specific warning to the contrary given in the opening paragraph of *Jutland Cottage*.

We have at times been accused of putting so many people into our books that no one can remember who they are, in which stricture we entirely concur, as we often cannot remember who they are ourself (or selves). We have often been urged to provide some sort of genealogical chart of Barsetshire families, and several kind and gifted young admirers have gone so far as to make a rough table of affinities; but, to tell the truth and shame him that shall be nameless, we have allowed matters to get so far out of hand that it is now almost impossible to reconcile the various discrepancies of dates and ages. For this we have no excuse and shall therefore offer two: the first that we find we get just as muddled about generations and relationships in real life as we do in Barsetshire; the second—in the words of *The Water Babies*—that it is all a fairy story and you must not believe a word of it even if it is true.

Here follows a list of characters, human and animal, and places where they may be found, were you to visit Barsetshire—or to wish to keep all of them straight in your mind. Where possible we have used Thirkell's own words to describe them; what follows may be considered a patchwork of Thirkell's words and ideas with our own.

Readers will be acquainted with the lovely map of Barsetshire by Maurice Weightman, but all must bear in mind that no cartographer could map this country with perfect consistency, as Barsetshire was not created with perfect consistency. Trollope left no map. Barsetshire as we know it came into being haphazardly, over the course of many years, and Thirkell, as we have seen, freely admitted to confusion. Mutability is not only one of Thirkell's major themes, it is a fact in her text.

Many Barsetshire characters appear and reappear in subsequent novels, sometimes as major characters, often as minor ones; frequently they are simply mentioned. Characters are cited below in novels in which they appear, even briefly, if the citation is necessary to avoid confusion; if the characters are only spoken of and news given of them, the citation is in parentheses. The books in which a character plays a major part are indicated in bold type. Minor characters mentioned in easily understood contexts and not referred to again have been omitted. The Trollope characters referred to by Thirkell's characters are named and described in italics.

Everyone is interested in people's ages. Where possible the date of birth is given, calculated by using some interior logic of the text, or the date of publication, or—when all else has failed—by a guess. Even so, any half-awake reader will discern a bit of inconsistency, of age-creep, or perhaps a failure of age to creep, in certain characters. How old was Jessica Dean when she burst on the scene as a glamorous actress in *Private*

---

*Cloud-cuckooland. From Aristophanes' play *The Birds*. As a name for the capital city of the birds a character suggests, "Somewhere, what with all these clouds, and all this air, There must be a rare name somewhere. . . . How do you like Cloud-Cuckoo-Land?"

Enterprise? Was Mr. Oriel really marrying for the first time at eighty-five? How did Lavinia Merton get to be twenty so suddenly? I'll tell you what (to quote Lucy Marling)—it's not very important; don't get out the calculator. The dates are here for fun.

Cultural notes pertain only to Barsetshire, and are not intended as a description of English life in general—although in some cases they may be. These notes may answer some questions or fill out the picture for readers unfamiliar with English culture.

Angela Thirkell read widely all her life, and her novels are so packed with allusions and unidentified quotations that encountering familiar ones and tracking down unfamiliar ones is one of the joys of reading her work. We have tried to simplify that process for you and in many but not all cases have succeeded. We have found that reading the original line or verse greatly expands our appreciation of Mrs. Thirkell's skill. The allusions are often a shorthand way of packing into her work more naughtiness, humor, and intensity than is apparent on the surface. It is not feasible or even necessary to include all of most of the poems quoted from, but we have included enough—more than the line itself, as a rule—to give the complete context of the thought. The result is a trip through the Victorian–Edwardian–classical culture which is, just as she predicted, dying out even as we write. It may be interesting for her readers to have this look back at what we have lost.

Family trees are included for the beginning and end of the series. How these trees have changed since 1961 is for the reader to imagine, but we think these families and their many cousins and grandchildren will have navigated the passage to modern and even post-modern times (whatever that baffling phrase may mean we cannot think) with their usual grace and fortitude.

Where Is Barsetshire?

Anthony Trollope describes in his autobiography the moment he was strolling in the Cathedral Close in Salisbury when suddenly the whole area came alive in his imagination, and he began to plan *The Warden.* As we know, he changed the name of the city to Barchester, and around it he imagined the county of Barsetshire. *The Warden, Barchester Towers, Dr. Thorne, Framley Parsonage, The Small House at Allington,* and *The Last Chronicle of Barset* were published between 1855 and 1867.

If Barchester, with its "most beautiful spire in England" is to be considered Salisbury, then the surrounding county must be, roughly speaking, Wiltshire. A substratum of chalk underlies both Barsetshire and Wiltshire, and both are places with downs where sheep graze, and fertile lowland areas that produce pigs, cattle, and grain. Wiltshire is divided by the Fosse Way, a Roman road running from north to south; Barsetshire is traversed by Gundric's Fossway, a similar relic. Wiltshire's Old Sarum, an ancient site and hill fort, has its parallel in Barsetshire's Old Barum, another ancient fort. In fact, both counties are hotbeds of archeological interest, although it must be said that the finds in Barsetshire are rarely significant. Salisbury is located at the confluence of the rivers Avon, Nadder, and Bourne; Barchester is watered by The River, although it doesn't join the River Rising until far south of the city, just above Southbridge. Both cities have a renowned White Hart Hotel, patronized almost to the exclusion of all others by our Barsetshire friends when they are in town and not dining at the County Club.

Having said all that, we must now say that while Barsetshire is, in many ways, Wiltshire, it also in many ways is not. In general, it is not possible to establish any direct correspondence between the villages of Wiltshire and those of Barsetshire. Angela Thirkell did not live in the country; she lived, except for her ten years in Australia, in London. However, she visited country houses throughout England, drawing on her experiences there for her novels. In the early months of World War II, she removed to Beaconsfield, in Buckinghamshire, and stayed there until early 1945 when crises in the health of her parents necessitated re-opening the house in London so she could care for them there. Beaconsfield provided her with the inspiration for her novels of village life during the war — but Beaconsfield itself was not Northbridge. The town described at the beginning of *Northbridge Rectory* is almost certainly Chipping Camden, in Gloucestershire.

As all Thirkell readers know, the "Barsetshire" series begins with *High Rising,* which introduces Laura Morland, but contains no reference to Barsetshire at all. Barchester is mentioned, and is the scene of the Cathedral episode, in the second novel, *The Demon in the House.* It then goes into hiding, only to reappear two books later in *Summer Half,* set unequivocally in Barsetshire. By the time of *Before Lunch* characters were being reintroduced, and Barsetshire was fully a parallel universe. As time passed and great changes were wrought in England, few or none of them to Mrs. Thirkell's liking, Barsetshire became a refuge for both writer and readers. "Going to Barsetshire" became a relief to Angela Thirkell. In her books she expressed both the sweetness of pre-war times (and in retrospect, even the war times seemed sweet) and the sourness of the grim post-war era. For the modern reader she offers both an education and an escape, which might have surprised her—she knew only about the escape.

Trollope's characters are referred to as early as *Summer Half,* when Mr. Crawley appears as Dean of Barchester Cathedral. And while these ancestors from old Barchester never fall upon the reader thick and fast, they are steady: the Dales, the Sowerbys, the Pallisers, the Grantlys, the Greshams, the Proudies. For readers of both series, this deluge of souls makes a rich experience. For readers of Thirkell only, there's no harm done.

This, then, is where Barsetshire is: it is a place partly to be found in Wiltshire, partly in numerous English villages, partly in the pages of Trollope; it exists in a time that is gone and regretted. But both the time and the place are ours whenever we "go to Barsetshire."

Suggested Itineraries

If a reader, midway through life's journey, should go astray from the straight and narrow, and find himself, or more likely herself, alone in Barsetshire, he (or she) may wish to be guided to a journey shorter than the long hegira represented by all twenty-nine Barsetshire novels. To this traveler we offer the following groups of novels.

Any set will follow a particular family over the course of some years. This should help the reader who has read one Thirkell novel, has developed an interest in the characters, and would like to relate that novel to others.

Lydia Keith, a favorite of many readers, is featured in this series, which gives a picture of life before, during and after the war.

> *Summer Half*
> *Cheerfulness Breaks In*
> *Northbridge Rectory*
> *Growing Up*
> *Private Enterprise*
> *What Did It Mean?*
> *Love at All Ages*
> *Three Score and Ten*

The career of Sam Adams is detailed in this set, which also introduces the Belton and Marling families whose fate is so closely connected with his. Lucy Marling is another favorite.

> *Marling Hall*
> *The Headmistress*
> *Miss Bunting*
> *Love Among the Ruins*
> *The Old Bank House*
> *County Chronicle*
> *Three Score and Ten*

The intertwined stories of Cora Palliser, Margot Phelps, and Tubby Fewling are told in this group, all set in the post-war years.

> *The Duke's Daughter*
> *Jutland Cottage*
> *Close Quarters*

Someone from the Leslie and Graham families appears in almost every Barsetshire novel. Their story is begun and carried through in these. (David Leslie makes cameo appearances in the starred titles.)

Wild Strawberries
Marling Hall
Peace Breaks Out
Love Among the Ruins
*The Old Bank House**
Enter Sir Robert
*A Double Affair**

Mrs. Morland, successful writer of the same novel year after year, is clearly Angela Thirkell herself. She appears frequently in the series, but is a main character only twice (starred); she figures significantly in

*High Rising**
*The Demon in the House**
Cheerfulness Breaks In
Enter Sir Robert
Never Too Late
Three Score and Ten

The politics of the Balkans is explained by the Myxo-Lydian refugees Madame Brownescu and Gradka Bonescu. They appear in several of the books of the series but are most voluble in

Cheerfulness Breaks In
Growing Up
The Headmistress
Miss Bunting

Mrs. Brandon and her son Francis figure significantly in

The Brandons
Private Enterprise
County Chronicle

The very large Dean family, which gave the world the irrepressible, charming and talented Jessica Dean, are featured most prominently in

August Folly
Private Enterprise
Love Among the Ruins
The Old Bank House

The observant reader will have noticed that several of the novels are mentioned more than once—maybe three or four times—and may well be asking, "How is it that just one novel can feature so many predominant characters?" Our answer is: "This is Cloud-Cuckooland! Do not enter this maze without a guide."

Public Figures, 1930 – 1961

Monarchs   Prime Ministers

George V   1910–1936
        Ramsay MacDonald 1929 (National)

        Stanley Baldwin 1935–1937 (Conservative)
        (Stanley Baldwin was Angela Thirkell's second cousin.)

Edward VIII   1936

George VI   1936–1952

        Neville Chamberlain 1937–1940 (Conservative)

        Winston Churchill 1940–1945 (Conservative)

        William Henry Beveridge published the 'Beveridge Report' (*Social Insurance and Allied Services*) in 1942. This formed the basis of the welfare state.

        Clement Attlee 1945– 1951 (Labour)
        Stafford Cripps, Chancellor of the Exchequer 1947
        Aneurin Bevan, Minister of Health 1945

Elizabeth II   1952 –
        Winston Churchill 1951–1955 (Conservative)
        Sir Anthony Eden 1955–1957 (Conservative)
        Harold Macmillan 1957–1963 (Conservtive)

Part One

A List of Characters

Will you have tea, Mr. Carton? You have come at just the right moment, because we can't quite make out how Mr. Oriel and old Lady Pomfret were connected and you are so good at families.

Your great uncle the bishop, Oriel, married some time in the 'sixties one of Squire Gresham's daughters whose name for the moment escapes me. His wife's brother, Frank Gresham, the present man's great-grandfather, married Mary Thorne who was the illegitimate niece of the Dr. Thorne who married Miss Dunstable whose money came from a patent Ointment of Lebanon. Dr. Thorne was only a distant cousin of the Ullathorne Thornes, to whom old Lady Pomfret belonged, but the connection is there all right, though I couldn't give the precise degree.

— Mrs. Belton and Sydney Carton, *The Headmistress*

Aberfordbury of Wapford, Baron. The Cedars, Muswell Hill.

A man of unknown origins who was thought to have made his fortune in shipping, he came into our lives as Sir Ogilvy Hibbard. Presumably he had been knighted by Lloyd George—he was definitely considered an upstart, and known to be a liberal. In 1950 he was elevated to the peerage, and as Lord Aberfordbury he was no better liked. According to Sam Adams, Aberfordbury was "straight as a corkscrew, and no gentleman." Besides, as Lord Stoke said, "his ties are disgusting." Even his dog was a menace. He didn't utter a single word that we have ever heard, but his dreadful actions have spoken loudly enough.

(BL), (MB), (PBO), (OBH), (LAR), (JC), (LAA), (TST)

Accompanist. London.

The unnamed pianist who accompanied the Clovers whenever music was needed. He played quite divinely and always hurried back to his mother after a show. WDIM

Adams family:

Adams, Sam. Hogglestock. The Old Bank House, Edgewood.

Self-made ironmaster, owner of a large rolling mill in Hogglestock. He had been born in Hogglestock in squalid circumstances which he never tried to conceal. A talented businessman, he was wealthy and successful in 1943, but he was then a rank outsider, an unmitigated vulgarian, and not liked. He was a widower with an adolescent daughter, and though he may not have known he was gauche, he knew he had a lot to learn. Because of his fundamental integrity, and his balance of brain and heart, he was befriended by Mrs. Belton, under whose benign influence he began to acquire polish and to advance socially. As he said of himself, he "was always a one to learn something from his betters," and he was open minded, but he retained his own personality. The nature of his accent has never been mentioned, but his speech is suggested partly by repetition of clichés, and partly by mispronunciations. These he modified to some degree, and he toned down his dress. He was a J.P., elected to the Barsetshire County Club in 1943, and elected Labour Party MP for Barsetshire from 1945 to 1950. In 1950 he left the Labour Party and joined the Conservatives. Generous in spirit, he was a frequent quiet benefactor here and there. In appearance he was large and heavily built and had a certain appeal to women. He married Lucy Marling, stunning the county, in 1948. They had three children: Amabel, born in 1950, a son named William, then a daughter, Leslie. Sam acquired directorships of several other companies and continued for many years as a Justice of the Peace.

H, MB, PBO, (PE), LAR, **OBH,** CC, DD, HaRe, (JC), WDIM, TST

In Sam Adams, Thirkell created, whether intentionally or not we cannot say, a New Man, that immigrant from the working class who rises to mingle with the Old Elite and who acquires enough power of various sorts to set political, cultural, and social agendas. Even the name—Adams—is suggestive. Sam was not her only New Man—Donald Macfadyen, Ted Parkinson and Aberfordbury were others—but he was the most important. From one point of view, the series can be said to be about Sam Adams, although that almost certainly was not Thirkell's intention. Sam, who came from a laboring family, typified what AT deplored in the rising class: having no "background"—no education, no training in any of the social graces and no desirable social context. Yet by proverbial hard work, good sense, decency, intelligence and some good luck, he acquired first money, then power, then at last a degree of polish and status. Although these achievements would indicate considerable ambition, raw ambition never seemed to be part of his make-up. Rather, the wealth, power and status were by-products of his daily decisions and energy. He also gradually changed his religion from chapel to church, and his politics from Labour to Conservative, becoming the type of New Man who adopts the values of the old guard, rather than imposing his own. His ascendance to a high position in Barsetshire was not rapid nor was it total. But he was liked, he was accepted, and he had influence.

The rise of the New Man and the eclipse of the Old Elite was a major social change of the age. It was represented in C.P. Snow's series, *Strangers and Brothers,* by Lewis Eliot, a character similar to Sam but milder, and in Anthony Powell's novel cycle, *A Dance to the Music of Time,* by Kenneth Widmerpool, a very different character indeed.

Adams, Lucy Emily Marling. Marling Hall, Marling Melicent. The Old Bank House, Edgewood. The youngest of the Marlings, born in 1916, she was 25 in 1941. Lucy was rough and ready, energetic and enthusiastic, known by her constant "I'll tell you what." At the beginning of the war she was a VAD, but gradually she took over most of the management of the Marling Hall farming, and later raised vegetables for Sam Adams. She and Sam were married in 1949 and lived at the Old Bank House in Edgewood.

$\qquad$ **MH**, (H), MB, PE, LAR, **OBH**, CC, DD, HaRe, (JC), WDIM, ADA, TST

Adams, Heather. *See* Pilward, Heather.

Adams, Amabel Rose. The Old Bank House.
Daughter of Sam and Lucy Adams, born in 1950. Attended Barchester High School in 1960.

$\qquad$ DD, HaRe, TST

Addison. The Priory School, Lambton.
A friend of young Dean's. $\qquad$ LAR, (OBH), DD

Albert. Rising Castle.
Footman. Brother of George Knox's Annie and cousin to Mrs. George Panter at Hatch End. By 1955 Albert had risen to become Lord Stoke's butler and valet. $\qquad$ DH, ESR, NTL, TST

Alcock, Mrs. Staple Park.
The Bonds' cook. $\qquad$ BL

Alf. High Rising.
An amiable half-wit who was available for odd jobs, particularly any having to do with animals. $\qquad$ TST

Allen, Nannie. Number 1, Ladysmith Cottages, Lambton.
Mother of Selina and former nanny for the Waring family, the Leslies, and the Luftons. After retiring on pension from the Warings, she took in lodgers, and helped in the kitchen at The Priory School and later at Harefield House School. By nature fierce and snappish, she became a rather overbearing old lady, presuming on her age and her many ex-nurslings. $\qquad$ GU, LAR, (OBH), DD, HaRe, JC, CQ

Annie. Low Rising.
The Knoxes' parlormaid in the early 30's. HR

Annie. The Rectory, Northbridge.
The Villars' second housemaid, 1940. NR

Arabin, Francis. *From Trollope.*
He attended Lazarus College, Oxford and was vicar of St. Ewold's, then Dean of the Cathedral at Barchester. He married Septimus Harding's daughter, Eleanor. He is most prominent in Barchester Towers *and* The Last Chronicle of Barset.

Arbuthnot family:

Arbuthnot, Mrs. Colonel (deceased).
A colonel's lady with whom Captain Brandon had been involved while in India in 1876. He was transferred to another station and she became the possessor of a handsome diamond bracelet—and an infant son. (B), (PE)

Arbuthnot, name and rank unknown (deceased).
The aforementioned son of the above Mrs. Colonel Arbuthnot and Frederick Brandon, born in 1877. He was the nephew of Amelia Brandon and the father of Captain Frederick Arbuthnot. (B)

Arbuthnot, Captain Frederick (deceased).
Grandson of the above Mrs. Arbuthnot. It was to him, the mystery heir, that Amelia Brandon left £10,000 when she died in 1938. He was the husband of Peggy and brother of Effie Arbuthnot; he was killed in Burma in 1945. Fred was a serious womanizer who frequently strayed—he loved gaiety, women, horses and society. He was no better a brother than he was a husband—charming, to be sure—but he extracted large amounts of Effie's capital from her, leaving her only £150 a year. (B), (PE)

Arbuthnot, Florence Edith, "Effie". *See* Crofts, Effie.

Arbuthnot, Peggy. *See* Brandon, Peggy.

Archdeacon of Plumstead. Plumstead Episcopi.
Author of *A Short Survey of the Religious and Lay Aspects of Glebe Land,* not a best seller. He was a keen Dickens enthusiast, an ardent fox hunter, and widely acknowledged to have no sense of humor.
PT, CBI, (PBO), CC, DD, HaRe

Archdeacon's daughter. Plumstead Episcopi.
Unnamed daughter of the above. Her mother had been related to George Rivers. In 1940 she organized the Land Girls for Western Barchester. She and Guy Barton were married in 1941. PT, CBI, (MH)

You will like Mrs. Dean, mama. She is rather like you, only a little more intelligent because her husband is alive.

— Francis Brandon

Babs. Silverbridge.
Owner of Babs's Buttery, a favorite village place for lunch in 1950. Babs, perhaps more properly known as Mrs. Lefevre, was a middle-aged woman, red-faced and jolly, with a fierce mop of grizzled hair that sprang out in all directions.   DD

Badger, Miss. London.
John Leslie's efficient secretary in his London office.   WS

Baker. Beliers Priory.
Elderly kitchen maid who broke the Sèvres, the Dresden, and the Crown Derby with punctuality and dispatch. The china was saved by the advent of Selina, and Baker's feelings soothed by the tact of Lady Waring.   GU

Baker, Mrs. Rushwater.
By 1933, Mrs. Baker had retired from her position as housekeeper at Rushwater House and lived in Folkstone. She invited Conque for a visit every year.   WS

Banks, Miss. Southbridge School, Southbridge.
A Latin mistress at Southbridge school. She was small and slight, with bad skin and short hair brushed flatly back from her forehead, like a man's. Her left-leaning ideas and poor educational background finally resulted in her being sacked. She went to work for UNESCO in Paris for a while after the war, and had the misfortune to be professionally involved with Geoffrey Harvey, who also sacked her.

SH, (PBO), (PE), (LAR), (CC)

Bannister, Mr. Rushwater.
Vicar at St. Mary's, Rushwater, 1933. Like so many others, he was sorely beset by the vagaries and machinations of Lady Emily Leslie, but he adored her. He left St. Mary's to become a canon, and moved to the Close.   WS, (CBI), (MH), (PBO), (LAR)

Barclay, Tom. Marling Melicent. Yorkshire.
A young captain stationed near Marling Hall who had somehow become a friend of Lucy Marling. From a good Yorkshire family, he was distantly related to Lord Stoke. He married Lettice Watson in 1942; they lived on the Barclay property in Yorkshire. Tom and Lettice had two sons.

MH, (GU), (LAR), (OBH), CC

Barclay, Lettice. Marling Hall, Marling Melicent. Yorkshire.
Elder daughter of William and Amabel Marling. In 1941 Lettice was a widow with two small daughters and a comfortable income. She lived with the children and their nurse in a large flat over one wing of the stables at Marling Hall. Early in 1942 she married Thomas Barclay. **MH**, (LAR), (OBH), CC

Barton family:

Barton, Walter. Mellings, Nutfield.
Successful and busy architect, a partner in the firm of Barton & Wicklow. He was the author of *Minor Domestic Architecture of East Barsetshire.* PT, (BL), (CBI), (MH)

Barton, Susan. Mellings, Nutfield.
Wife of Walter. Author of several learned historical novels about the more obscure bastards of Popes and Cardinals. Because of her continual researches and writings, she tended to live in the past. As a result she became adept at assuming a pleasant air of attention which veiled her wandering thoughts—a skill perfected by several Barsetshire women. PT, (MH), (CBI)

Barton, Guy. Mellings, Nutfield.
Son of Walter and Susan, in his mid-twenties in 1937, and a junior partner in his father's firm. He was breezy, smug, and affably self-centered. In the RAF during the war, he married the daughter of the Archdeacon at Plumstead. He became an authority on church architecture. **PT**, (CBI), (JC)

Barton, Alice. See Wicklow, Alice.

Bateman. Southbridge.
Once Colonel Crofts' batman. Yes, it's confusing, but there it is. When Colonel Crofts became the vicar at Southbridge, Bateman became his gardener, general helper, and sexton. He married the lovely blonde Eileen from the Red Lion. PE, JC, NTL

Bateman, Eileen. Southbridge.
A niece of Mrs. Dingle's, Eileen was the incredibly blonde and genuinely pretty barmaid at the Red Lion. She wore a Victorian black satin bust but despite that, stood no nonsense. In 1947 she married Colonel Crofts' former batman, Bateman, and became the cook at the Vicarage. CBI, (GU), NTL, CQ, TST

Beasley, Commander. Tork Cottage, Northbridge.
A grumpy fellow who had occasionally been heard to say "Bah!" He was retired from the Navy and was a member of the British Needlers Society, to whose members the Past and Present were as one. He participated enthusiastically in the Coronation Pageant held in Northbridge in 1953. The stencils used to pattern the fabric for costumes were made by Commander Beasley. NR, WDIM

Beedle family:

Beedle, Mr. Winter Overcotes.
Station master, a descendant of a long line of railway men who had been proud of the prewar service, and deeply regretted the deterioration in equipment and amenities brought about by the war. He had served in the 1914–1918 war under Sir Harry Waring, who was then General Waring. Mrs. Thirkell claimed that his character was based on an amalgamation of various station masters in the Beaconsfield area, and that his attitudes were not based on wishful thinking. GU, OBH

Beedle, Mrs. Winter Overcotes.
His good and kindly wife, who bravely endured during the captivity of their son. He had been taken

prisoner before Dunkirk. As a girl Mrs. Beedle had been nursemaid at Beliers Priory under Nannie Allen. GU

Beedle, Henry. Winter Overcotes.
Son of the above. Henry was with the Barsetshire Yeomanry in Dunkirk, and was captured just before the evacuation. During five years as a POW in Germany he learned all there was to know about raising vegetables. In 1948 he went to work for Lucy Marling at Adamsfield.
(GU), OBH, LAA

Beedle. Beliers Priory. Pomfret Towers.
The nephew of stationmaster Mr. Beedle. He was an upper servant at Pomfret Towers and before that had been in service with Sir Harry and Lady Waring. LAA

Beeton, Mrs. Rising Castle.
Lord Stoke's cook. She was distinguished by Having a Leg, and so far is known is not related to the original Mrs. Beeton. TST

Belton family:

(Note: Trollope wrote about a Will Belton in *The Belton Estate,* but the estate in question was in Somerset, and there is no apparent relationship, except in the use of the name.)
Belton, Frederick. Arcot House, Harefield.
A Wykehamist, a landowner, and a member of the county set. Well into middle age by 1943, Mr. Belton had clear eyes and skin and an upright, spare figure. He was owner of Harefield House, which he was obliged to rent to the Hosiers' Girls' Foundation School. His pride was deeply wounded, for after five generations in Harefield House, he, in the sixth, would have to leave it. But, except for occasional atavistic outbursts, he bore this grief reasonably well.
H, (PBO), LAR, CC, DD, HaRe, CQ

Belton, Lucy Thorne. Arcot House, Harefield.
Wife of Frederick; born in 1882. She struggled to deal with her adult children in ways that would not inflame their touchy sensibilities, and as she had a kind heart and quick sympathy with the young, she was most often successful at this. Mrs. Belton had a beauty of spirit as well as of bone and a kind of inner light like mother of pearl. Tactful and wise, she had a benign influence on Sam Adams after they met in 1943, guiding his transition from crass *arriviste* into Barsetshire gentleman. She oversaw the decorating of the Old Bank House in 1948, and later helped him with his office at Pomfret Towers in the late 1950's. **H**, (MB), LAR, OBH, CC, DD, HaRe, CQ

Belton, Charles. Arcot House. The Priory School. Harefield House School.
Youngest of the Beltons, Charles was born in 1921. He was in the Royal Artillery during the war and afterwards came home to Harefield where he lived until he began teaching at the Priory School. Although he might not have been quite aware of it, mothers liked him on sight, for he was fresh-faced, fair-haired, blue-eyed, and had a naturally nice disposition. After a troubled engagement, he and Clarissa Graham were married in 1952. They had lovely quarters at Harefield House when the Priory School moved there shortly afterwards. **H, LAR**, OBH, CC, DD,**HaRe**, JC

Belton, Clarissa Graham. Holdings, Little Misfit. Harefield House School, Harefield.
The third of the Graham children, born in 1929. Like a porcelain shepherdess, Clarissa was dainty and proud, with a pretty, insolent face, dark eyes and hair, fair skin, and small bones. Her hands were elegant and her fingers tip-tilted. Affected and spoilt, yet clever and talented, she earned a degree from Cambridge in engineering draftsmanship, taking a good second, but by then she had lost

from Cambridge in engineering draftsmanship, taking a good second, but by then she had lost interest in that or any other work. She was always in demand to arrange flowers for weddings and celebrations. Alas, Clarissa was a bit of a minx; her sharp tongue hurt several people. It can therefore be no surprise that her engagement to Charles Belton was long and difficult; yet when they were finally wed, the marriage was surprisingly very happy. It was said that having finally been tamed by Charles, Clarissa was blissfully content. They had four children.

WS, MH, (MB), PBO, LAR, OBH, CC, DD, **HaRe**, (ESR), TST

Belton, Freddy. Dowlah Cottage, Harefield.
Elder son of the Beltons, as much a gentleman as his father. Born in 1900, Freddy as a young man had deep-set very blue eyes, and was slender and dark. Having attended the Royal Naval College at Dartmouth, he embarked upon a naval career and was a captain during the war, serving at the Admiralty afterwards. He and Susan Dean were married in 1947, and lived in Dowlah Cottage for a while before leaving the area.

H, **LAR**, OBH, CC, DD, HaRe JC

Belton, Elsa. *See* Hornby, Elsa.

Belton, Susan Dean. The Dower House, Worsted.
Only 16 in 1935, Susan was a typical hoydenish teen-ager. During the war she worked for prisoners of war while studying at Oxford. By 1946 she was the Depot Librarian of the Red Cross Hospital Library in Barchester, and had become a capable, pleasant, attractive young woman, although not introspective. She had good business sense, which always comes in handy. In the summer of 1947 she was wooed and won by Freddy Belton. After their marriage they lived for a time with the senior Beltons in Arcot House, but after Mrs. Hoare's obligingly timely death they moved to Dowlah Cottage. Their first child, a son, was born in the summer of 1948.

AF, PE, **LAR**, OBH, CC, DD, HaRe

Bent, Miss. Adelina Cottage, Wiple Terrace, Southbridge.
Miss Bent lived with her friend Miss Hampton. Chubby and fly-away, she wore supernumerary beads and other peasant get-up. Her looks were, as they say, deceiving, as she looked incompetent but wasn't. She was the business half of the relationship, and the driver of their little car. Both she and Miss Hampton were notable drinkers and held crowded, noisy drinks parties. Always together, they were on hand for many activities during the war, and afterwards were perennially helpful and hospitable.

CBI, GU, MB, (PBO), PE, CC, JC, NTL, CQ, TST

Bertha. Rushwater House, Rushwater.
A housemaid of long standing, still with the family in 1947.

PBO, LAR, ADA

Bertha. Pomfret Towers.
This Bertha was one of those rare and precious creatures who had never been disabused of the belief that service at the Towers was preferable to a tiresome job as a waitress or counter girl.

ADA

Bessie. Rushwater House, Rushwater.
Third housemaid in the 20's and 30's.

WS, (PBO), LAR

Betty. *See* Topham, Betty.

Bingham, Lady Dorothy.
A cousin of Lady Emily Leslie, and second daughter of the Duke of Towers. She was the mother of three sons, all in the Army, and the twins, Hermione and Rose.

WS

Bingham, Hermione.   Tadcaster.
Daughter of Lady Dorothy, and twin of Rose. She married Lord Tadpole.   WS, (ADA)

Bingham, Rose.   See Leslie, Rose.

Birkett family:

Birkett, William Henry.   Southbridge School. Dower House, Worsted.
Headmaster first of the prep school, then of the senior school at Southbridge, and author of *Determination of Logical Causality*. He was described as a "Fine Old English Gentleman," though at the time, 1936, he was barely middle-aged. He was invariably wise, civilized, and patient, although sorely tried by the wartime experience of having the Hosiers' Boys' Foundation School at Southbridge School. Oddly, however, Mr. Birkett felt that neither he nor Mr. Bissell had learned anything from each other in the six years they spent together. He retired in 1946 and moved with Mrs. Birkett to the Dower House, Worsted, where he worked on his edition of the *Analects* of the Procrastinator, published by the Oxford University Press in 1948.

HR, DH, **SH**, BL, CBI, GU, MB, PBO, PE, LAR, OBH, CC, HaRE, JC

Birkett, Amy.   Southbridge School, Southbridge.   Dower House, Worsted.
Wife of Mr. Birkett, known as "Ma Birky" to the generations of boys who knew her as the capable wife of the headmaster. One of the truly professional women of Barsetshire, she arbitrated quarrels among the staff, organized countless teas and dinners, and tirelessly dispensed sage advice to generations of boys and their parents.

HR, DH, **SH**, BL, GU, MB, PBO, PE, LAR, OBH, CC, HaRe, JC, TST

Birkett, Geraldine.   *See* Fairweather, Geraldine.

Birkett, Rose.   *See* Fairweather, Rose.

Bishop of Barchester.   Cathedral Close, Barchester.
The Bishop had few friends in the Close or in the county. He was known to be Low in his preferences, Left in his sympathies and mean in his outlays. Many were the epithets he attracted: "Puss in Petticoats," "The Pompous Prelate," or, leftover from his college days, "Old Gasbags."   Former guests at the Palace told horror stories of dim lights, hard beds, thin blankets, scanty food, poor drink, and perpetual chill. For large entertainments the Palace would engage Scatcherd & Tozer at the lowest possible tariff. If the Bishop insisted on attending a ceremony at the Cathedral, a cold draught over his throne could be arranged. He and his wife are literary descendants of Bishop and Mrs. Proudie, Trollope's famous Cathedral couple. The Bishop of Barchester and his wife had one depressing son who worked before, during and after the war in a Westminster office. The bishop is referred to in almost every novel, but appears, with his wife, only in one, WDIM. His wife also appears briefly in CC.

Bissell family:

Bissell, Mr.   Maria Cottage, Wiple Terrace, Southbridge.   27 Condiment Road, E 48, London.
Headmaster of the displaced Hosiers' Boys' Foundation School which was evacuated to Southbridge School in 1939.   At that time he was a lean middle-sized man of thirty-five, of working-class background and therefore very class-conscious. Initially, he was hostile to the effete (his thought, not ours) educational system represented by Southbridge School, and to "Capittleism" in general. Despite his numerous misgivings he did his best, and made a decent adjustment that gradually evolved into the formation of lasting friendships with many of his Southbridge neighbors and colleagues, so much so that he and Mrs. Bissell rented the Red House from Joyce Smith in 1948.

CBI, (PBO), PE, (CC)

Bissell, Elaine. Maria Cottage, Wiple Terrace, Southbridge. 27 Condiment Road, E 48, London. Wife of Mr. Bissell. She was a small plumpish woman with very neat hair and a singularly sweet and placid expression, smoothly gracious, and possessed of real goodness. She was socialist, but calmly so. Before her marriage she had been a teacher and psychologist. **CBI**, (PBO), PE, (CC), TST

Bissell, Edna.
Mr. Bissell's great niece, who looked like, and was, an idiot. The Bissells had adopted her and genuinely cared for her. Despite some apparent progress in her early years with the Bissells, Edna regressed after the war and was institutionalized. CBI, (PE)

Bodger, Percy. Starveacre Hatches
Ratcatcher to the rich and famous—but not just any rich and famous. Bodger refused a commission from Sir Ogilvy Hibbard, saying that he worked against rats, not for rats. He also had a sideline in well cleaning.
H, OBH

Bohun, Thomas. Cathedral Close, Barchester.
Canon of Barchester from 1657 to 1665, in which year he traveled to London to observe the effects of plague on human bodies, and never returned. Author of "The Worme of the Flesh and the Worme of the Spirit," "To his Mistress, on seeing Sundrie Worme-castes," and other curious poems. In his will he left money to establish Boone's Benefit in Winter Overcotes. Oliver Marling worked for several years on a biography of Bohun.

Boncasson, Isabel. *From Trollope.*
A wealthy and beautiful American heiress who married Lord Silverbridge, eldest son of the Duke of Omnium and his wife, Lady Glencora. Isabel Boncasson is a principal character in The Duke's Children.

Bond family:
Bond, Alured, Lord. Staple Park, Skeynes.
Descended from Jedediah Bond, a Yorkshire manufacturer of woolen goods who received his title in 1902. A little round-faced man with a white moustache, he managed to seize what happiness he could from those feared twin despots, his wife and his butler. And while he was at it, he feared his pig man, but conquered his fear in the interest of raising Cropbacked Crunchers. During the war he let Staple Park to a school; he and Lady Bond lived in the White House and the butler was at last let go. Lord Bond died in the early 1950's. (AF), **BL**, (MH), (GU), MB, LAR

Bond, Lucasta, Lady. Staple Park, Skeynes.
Half-sister of Lord Stoke and wife of Lord Bond. She looked like an escapee from the cast of *The Importance of Being Earnest.* Lady Bond freely made arrangements for her friends and family without the faintest regard for their plans or their feelings, and she bullied the tenants for what, had they but known it, was their own good. She was on every committee, and was, in short, a benefactress to the entire county. It must be said that she was also sensible and well-organized. In 1955, after being widowed, she left the area and took a house in Bath, or perhaps it was Cheltenham.
AF, **BL**, (MH), (GU), MB, (LAR), (ESR), (NTL), TST

Bond, C.W. (Cedric Weyland.) Staple Park, Skeynes.
Son of Lord and Lady Bond and a pleasant young man. After attending Hocker's preparatory school, Eton, and Oxford, he entered a business that had a branch in New York. In addition to being his father's heir, he was heir to Lord Stoke's property (though not the title). C.W. married Daphne Stonor in 1939 and came into the title after the war. AF, **BL**, (LAR), TST

Bond, Daphne Stonor. The White House, Skeynes; Staple Park, Skeynes.
Spirited young step-daughter of Lilian Stonor, born in 1918. She married C.W. Bond in 1939. In 1947 they entered the names of their two sons, ages six and four, for the Priory School.

BL, LAR, TST

Bonescu, Gradka. Barchester. London.
Bog! Which pleasure! Which joy! Gradka was a Myxo-Lydian refugee of great intelligence and moxie, though of a lumpish and dwarfish stature. At first her manners struck an odious note between cringing and arrogance. She worked as a cook for the Fieldings in 1944, and took advantage of being near Miss Bunting to be tutored, with marginal success, in English. After taking a degree by correspondence, she returned to Myxo-Lydia and founded a women's school, Bunting College. Such a triumph was this that she was made first a member of a trade delegation to England,and then Myxo-Lydia's ambassador. Brash, assertive, and full of good will, she exploited to the maximum any power or prestige that this position afforded her—usually to deflate prigs and bores who were threatening the happiness of her friends. She was a member of the "syndicate" that bought Wiple Terrace in 1960 and gave it to SouthBridge School. *See* **Wiple Terrace** in the **Places** section.

MB, LAR, CC, DD, ADA, CQ, TST

Bostock, Mr. Rushwater.
Vicar at St. Mary's following the departure of Mr. Bannister. In addition to performing his pastoral duties in a thoroughly satisfactory way, he could mend bicycle tires in a trice, was willing to play squash with Emmy Graham, and suffered himself to be blown upon horribly by Rushwater Romany.

PBO, LAR, OBH, DD, ADA

Boulle family:

Boulle, M. Henri.
French professor who, with his family, rented The Vicarage at Rushwater for the month of August, 1933. He was tall, good-looking, and silent, with a melancholy face and courteous manners.   WS

Boulle, Madeleine.
Wife of Professor Boulle. Mme. Boulle was stout and authoritative, with masses of grey hair. She keenly felt the superiority of everything French.   WS

Boulle, Pierre.
In his early 20's, he was one of those young men who fell in love with Agnes Graham. During the war he was at the French embassy in London. Later, like his father Henri, he became a professor. In Paris, 1960, he and his wife were hosts for a few months to Lavinia Merton.   WS

Boulle, Ursule.
Stout and giggling daughter of the Boulles.   WS

Boulle, Jean Claude.
Sixteen-year old son of the Boulle family; a passionate royalist.   WS

Brandon family:

Brandon, Amelia—Aunt Sissie. Brandon Abbey, near Chaldicotes.
Born circa 1850, Aunt Sissie had grown up in Brandon Abby and had never changed one whit of its ghastly Victorian decor. During her prolonged solitary old age she tormented Mrs. Brandon and her children with threats and enticements relating to her will. Almost her sole joy in life was reading, or having someone read to her, the letters from India of her brother Frederick. Miss Brandon's eldest brother was the father of Henry Brandon. She died in the summer of 1938.   B, (PE)

Brandon, Delia. *See* Grant, Delia Brandon.

Brandon, Francis. Stories, Pomfret Madrigal.
Born in 1915, Francis was the son of Mrs. Brandon and the evanescent Mr. Brandon. He was tall and good looking, with an easy assurance; he was clever and selfish, but with unsuspected depths. Francis did not go to University, but became a chartered accountant with a genius for making money, which we have always felt to be one of the nicest kinds of genius. Francis worked in the office of a Barchester company. During the war he served with the Army in the Near and Middle East, and was awarded a Military Cross. He married Peggy Arbuthnot in 1946, and they quickly had three children and in 1952 a fourth. Francis' business affairs prospered; by 1946 he was a director in the company. He and his family lived at Stories.   **B**, (CBI), **PE**, LAR, OBH, CC, HaRe

---

Brandon, Captain Frederick (deceased).
Beloved older brother of Amelia. While stationed in India in the 1870's he had carried on a dalliance with Mrs Arbuthnot and had given her a diamond bracelet. This attracted the notice of, among others, her husband. Captain Brandon was transferred to a hill station where he was killed while on a boar hunt. The child born as a result of the liaison with Mrs. Arbuthnot grew to be the father of Captain Fred and Effie Arbuthnot.   (B), (PE)

Brandon, Henry (deceased).
Departed and scarcely mourned husband of Lavinia Brandon. The son of the elder brother of Frederick Brandon, and the nephew of Amelia Brandon, he was thus heir to a considerable fortune. He had been a pleasant, if unexciting, husband, with no county connections other than his aunt. He very amiably died of pneumonia while he and Lavinia were on holiday in France. They had been married six years.   (B)

Brandon, Lavinia. *See* Joram, Lavinia.

Brandon, Peggy Arbuthnot. Editha Cottage, Wiple Terrace, Southbridge. Stories, Pomfret Madrigal.
Peggy was born around 1921 to an Indian judge and an admiral's daughter, people of minor Devonshire stock. She was the widow of Fred Arbuthnot, living after the war with her sister-in-law in Wiple Terrace. She seemed appealingly helpless, but in reality was efficient and capable. She took life lightly as a protection and tended to use men in the nicest possible way. She and Francis Brandon were married in 1946. They lived at Stories, first with Lavinia Brandon, and later by themselves with their children. Peggy had to recall her ability to be long-suffering, for Francis went through a spell of being rather beastly.   PE, LAR, OBH, CC, HaRe

---

Brown.
Head gardener at Rushwater, 1932.   WS

Brown, Mr. High Rising.
Owner of the garage.   HR, DH

Brown, Mr. Southbridge.
Proprietor of the Red Lion, churchwarden, and occasional taxi driver.   CBI, GU, PBO, TST

Brown, Abner. Southbridge.
A grazier and carter of wood.   CBI

Brown, Henry. High Rising.
Cousin of Sid who rented his bicycle to Tony Morland for a few days, until it was damaged in an accident.

DH

Brown, Haig. Southbridge.
The local constable, nephew of the proprietor of the Red Lion.

JC, TST

Brown, Mrs. Southbridge.
Wife of Haig Brown. She came in every morning to help old Admiral Phelps and Mrs. Phelps.

CQ

Brown, Sid. High Rising.
Porter at the railway station.

HR, DH

Brownescu, Mme. Southbridge.
A formidable Myxo-Lydian refugee housed near Southbridge during the war. She was even more disagreeable, selfish, and ungrateful than the other Myxo-Lydians who had been given asylum in England, and thus she assumed a kind of royal dignity. She was small and wiry, with a mop of frizzled dark hair and a leopardskin coat. It was thought that she had been a dancer. Her disdain for England and the English transcended her difficulties with the language and made her the ambassador from her group. In 1942 she and Gogo arranged an interesting exhibit of Myxo-Lydian atrocities at the museum in Winter Overcotes. After the war the Brownescus ran a school of peasant weaving and folk dancing at Bathwater Cold in the Cotswolds.

CBI, GU, H, (MB), DD,CQ

Brownescu, M. Gradko. "Gogo." Southbridge.
Presumed to be the husband of Mme. Brownescu. He was a melancholy yellow-faced poet, always huddled in a sheepskin coat and wearing a skin-tight beret. After the war he had been given a position in the Mixo-Lydian Embassy but had been dismissed for speculating in currency. After that episode the Brownescus began their folk-art workshops. He was never—well hardly ever—heard to say anything except, "czy provka, provka, provka!"

CBI, GU, H, (MB), DD

Bunce family: A pure Anglo-Saxon survival, celebrated for never changing their clothes by day or night. They are probably descended from Mr. Bunce, the oldest and worthiest of the men in Hiram's Hospital in Septimus Harding's day. Mr. Bunce is described in *The Warden*. Phineas Finn's London landlords were Mr. and Mrs. Bunce as well.

Bunce, "Old". Northbridge.
The ferryman who lived on the river near the Keiths. He had a large, exuberant family and might have been but probably wasn't married to their mother. He died in the mid-1950's.

SH, (CBI), PE, OBH

Bunce, Effie. Northbridge.
Housemaid at Punshions for Miss Pemberton. Later in the war she was a Land Girl near Hallbury, returning to Miss Pemberton when the war ended. After Miss Pemberton's death, she worked as housemaid for Nurses Ward, Heath, and Chiffinch when they retired to Punshions. Effie was the mother of several children of shame, all healthy, who in the fullness of time did well in school, got jobs, and married.

NR, (MB), PE, WDIM, NTL, LAA

Bunce, Ruby.   Northbridge.
Another disastrously good-natured daughter of old Bunce, and occasional housemaid at Northbridge Manor. She contributed her fair share of children of shame to the little house beside the river, and they, too, throve and prospered.   NR, WDIM, LAA

Bunce. Northbridge.
The son of Old Bunce. He was the Mertons' cowman.   PE

Bungay, Mr.   London.
A publisher with the firm Bungay, Bacon, and Pendennis, an amalgamation of three firms. According to Mr. Johns, the firm liked anything to do with Russia, or anything at all if it were bad enough. Mr. Bungay had the rights to every State-published book in Mixo-Lydia, which comprised all the books there published. Bungay did well from this contract and bought large country houses. The name Bungay, Bacon, and Pendennis is possibly an allusion to *The Honorable Historie of Frier Bacon and Frier Bongay,* a comedy by Robert Greene, performed in 1594, and to Thackeray's *Pendennis.* Mr. Bungay might have been a take-off of Victor Gollancz, publisher and active member of the Left Book Club.   Then too, the Duke of St. Bungay is a significant character in Trollope's parliamentary series.   PT, (LAR)

Bunting, Maud. Marling Hall. Hallbury.
Retired governess living with the Marlings during the war, and acting in a ladylike and non-committal way as housekeeper, secretary, occasional governess to Diana and Clare Watson, and supervisor of Red Cross stores. A short, spare, grey-haired elderly woman she wore nondescript clothing and often tied a piece of black ribbon around her faded neck. She had a little front of false hair.   The authority she exercised was considerable. Her wisdom, kindness and infallible taste made her much loved and also rather an *éminence grise.* She was later lured out of retirement to coach Anne Fielding for a year. She became ill and died while with the Fieldings in Hallbury in 1944. Her character and appearance were very closely based on a retired governess, Miss Bennet, whom Mrs.Thirkell had met at Bere Court in Hampshire. Miss Bunting stood for all the old values so dear to gentrified Barsetshire; her death marks a turning point in the series.
                                                                             MH, MB, (PBO), (LAR)

Burden. Barchester.
Headwaiter at the White Hart in Barchester, who had been there since before human memory. As a master of his art, Burden felt that without him the White Hart would sink into a second-class hotel. Not the least of his virtues was that he could be counted on for the latest local gossip.
                                                             LAR, OBH, ESR, HaRe, JC, ADA, LAA, TST

C

Cameron, Alister. London.

An architect, the junior partner in Mr. Middleton's firm. He was hard-working, patient, and forbearing, taking on much of the drudgery of the firm's work. He enjoyed reading the classics and wrote reviews of books on classical subjects. An agreeable turn of fate left him with a hefty legacy from his parents. He was two years older than Mrs. Stonor, whom he married in 1939. They lived in London in one of the Inns of Court. **BL**

Carter. Nutfield.

The Bartons' chauffeur. PT

Carter family:

Carter, Everard. Southbridge School. The Old Rectory, Northbridge.

Born in 1907. Housemaster, senior housemaster, and eventually headmaster of Southbridge School. A Cambridge man, calm and capable, he was the obvious heir when Mr. Birkett retired in 1946. Everard married Kate Keith in 1936. They had three children: Bobbie (b.1937), Angela (b.1938), and Philip (b.1939). In 1958 he retired and he and Kate moved to Northbridge. He was the author of a book about Lord Eldon. **SH, CBI**, GU, (MB), PBO, PE, OBH, CC, JC, NTL, CQ, LAA

Carter, Kate. Marling Hall. Southbridge School. The Old Rectory, Northbridge.

Kate, born in 1915, was the relentlessly domestic elder daughter of the Keiths of Northbridge Manor. Never happier than when she had a sock to darn or a button to sew on, she made a perfect headmaster's wife. Though it pains us to say it, she was more than a bit dull.
SH, (B), CBI, GU, PBO, PE, OBH, CC, JC, WDIM,NTL, CQ, LAA, TST

Carter, Richard. A., Esq. The Old Manor House, Hatch End.

A "kind of cousin" of Everard Carter, he had been in the artillery in the war. He married Lord Crosse's daughter and moved to Hatch End late in 1954. NTL

Carter, Mrs. The Old Manor House, Hatch End.

Lord Crosse's daughter, wife of Richard Carter. Her excellent taste made the restoration of the Old Manor House such a success. The Carters had a small son, almost three, and a daughter of nine months when we met them in the summer of 1955. NTL

Carton, Sidney. Assaye House, Harefield.

A scholar, born around 1888, whose work on Fluvius Minimus made his reputation. Although he had a house in Harefield, he was during term time a don at St. Jude's, Oxford. He was the very pattern of a don: tall and thin, rather untidy, with spectacles and receding hair, capable of vitriolic rancor in the field of scholarship. Secretly, however, he was very kind to his pupils, if they were male, for as a rule he disliked educated women. He had no known ties except for an old mother of 80, and his Oxford friend Mr. Fanshawe. A tie did develop between him and Madeleine Sparling; they were married in 1946.

H, (PBO), (PE), LAR, HaRe, CQ

Carton, Madeleine Sparling. Harefield Park, Harefield. Assaye House, Harefield.
Headmistress of the Hosiers' Girls' Foundation School, which was evacuated to Harefield Park in 1943. Born in 1897, she had been brought up by her grandfather, old Canon Horbury, who had given her the run of his library. She was tall, attractive, and well-built, with dark wavy hair, large brown eyes, good teeth and neat feet—a not unbecoming majesty of figure, as perhaps of an uncrowned queen. Miss Sparling was awarded an honorary doctorate in 1944 and married to Mr. Carton upon her retirement from the school in 1946.

H, (MB), (PE), LAR, OBH, HaRe, CQ

Caxton. Hatch House, Hatch End.
Estate carpenter for the Hallidays, a man of few words but those few far too often repeated. His father had been one of Lord Pomfret's keepers. A spare, elderly man, he wore to great effect a square hat of folded paper, the badge of his trade. On the door jambs of the carpenter shop he kept a record of the heights of George and Sylvia Halliday. He was sexton at the church and also played the church organ.

PBO, ESR, NTL, ADA

Caxton, Mrs. Pomfret Towers.
Housekeeper in 1937.

PT

Champion, Pvt. Northbridge.
A member of the Barsetshire Regiment who in civilian life had been a nurse. He worked in the office at the Villars' during the war.

NR

Chapman, Mrs. Northbridge.
The Villars' cook, and aunt of Effie Bunce. Her husband Bob Chapman had been a sort of flash in the pan, who had left her with Bert.

NR, (WDIM)

Chapman, Bert. Northbridge.
Son of the Villars' cook and the elusive Mr. Chapman. However, he and his father had become acquainted when both were mess waiters in the same regiment in 1941.

NR, (WDIM)

Chiffinch, Nurse; "Chiffy". London. Punshions, Northbridge.
Very capable nursing sister always on hand for a new baby, sick relative, or ageing parent. Nurse Chiffinch was never short of oblique ways of inserting her opinions. She was a friend and room-mate of Nurse Ward and Nurse Heath, "Wardy" and "Heathy." When Punshions became available after Miss Pemberton's death, Miss Ward and Miss Heath took it over, painted it and spruced it up. Miss Chiffinch joined them there.

DH, PT, CBI, NM, MH, (GU), H, MB, PBO, CC, DD, (HaRe), CQ, LAA, TST

Chives. Southbridge
Loquacious jobbing gardener who provided services for the residents of Wiple Terrace. Unfortunately he had been a corporal in the Barsetshires, which gave him yet another tiresome topic to blather on about.   PE

Choyce, Herbert. The Vicarage, Hatch End.
A gentleman and a vicar, Mr. Choyce came to Hatch End in 1933, after having served a rather rough parish in Liverpool. He was an old friend of Mr. Halliday's, who had given him the living. A Christian in the best sense of the word, Mr. Choyce was initially rather self-effacing and ingratiating, but he grew into a stronger

and more appealing fellow. To please Mr. Halliday, he developed various techniques for a rapid Sunday service, and, somewhat along those lines, he invented a number of devices useful to the householder, such as a cat flap. A thoughtful aunt of the sort who abound in Barsetshire left him a considerable sum of money in 1955. Inspired by that he married Miss Merryman in 1956. PBO, ESR, **NTL**, ADA, LAA, TST

Choyce, Dorothea F. Merriman. Pomfret Towers; Holdings, Little Misfit; The Vicarage, Hatch End.
For years, Merry was the indispensable personal assistant to Edith, Lady Pomfret. Her role in life, it seemed, was to shelter the upper classes from the burdens of their complex obligations. She was therefore a blend of guide, philosopher, and friend, keeping always a mysterious barricade between herself and her employers. Or, as Mr. Wickham said, one wondered what the hell she really thought about things. Like Maud Bunting, she was to some degree an *éminence grise* because her counsel was always wise and her actions always right. After Lady Pomfret's death, Miss Merriman went to Holdings, as a sort of keeper for Lady Emily Leslie. When Lady Emily died in 1948, Merry went back to Pomfret Towers to assist the young Lord Pomfret. In 1956 she and Mr. Choyce, vicar at Hatch End, were married.
PT, MH, H, (PBO), LAR, OBH, DD, JC, HaRe, WDIM, ESR, **NTL**, **ADA**, TST

Clifford, Mr. Northbridge.
A schoolmaster with a passion for notoriety, though it seems odd that a schoolmaster would need more notoriety than he had already. NR

The Close Upper Servants' Club. Barchester.
Simnet was the leader of this organization, and Mrs. Hicks was given membership when she arrived at the Close in 1958. It was through the Servants' Club that a close surveillance could be kept on developments in the Bishop's Palace by using such MI5 techniques as examining the contents of wastepaper baskets.

Clover, Aubrey. London.
Aubrey Clover's real name was Caleb Lover. He was an immensely talented actor, writer, and producer. After he was wounded at Dunkirk and invalided out of the army, he and Jessica Dean, his leading lady and partner, went on tour during the war. Cultivating a nondescript appearance, and having a genius for protective coloring, he looked to everyone like someone they had met somewhere. In social settings he was gifted at playing exactly the right role at precisely the right time. Although he was at first presented as probably homosexual, he and Jessica were married in 1948. Several times they gave a short play or sketch for some sort of "do" being mounted by amateur groups in Barsetshire. Their daughter, Sarah Siddons Clover, was born in 1949, and a son Henry, born in October, 1953. PE, LAR, OBH, CC, DD, WDIM, TST

Clover, Jessica Dean. The Dower House, Worsted. London.
In *August Folly* Jessica was the small child who was saved from a bull by Richard Tebben. During the war, too young for conscription, she attended the Royal Academy of Dramatic Arts. By the time the war was over, thanks to a magic wrinkle of time, she had emerged from her chrysalis as a glittering butterfly, a glamorous and successful actress, the partner of the brilliant actor, writer, and producer Aubrey Clover. Wisdom, charm, confidence, and generosity had been meted out to her in impressive abundance. In 1948 Jessica and Aubrey were married; they became the parents of two children. AF, **PE, LAR, OBH**, CC, DD WDIM, TST

Clover, Sarah Siddons. London.
The daughter of Aubrey and Jessica Dean Clover, born in 1949. She was to be a bridesmaid in the wedding of Lord Mellings and Lavinia Merton, in 1962. CC, (TST)

Coates, Adrian. London.

The young publisher of Mrs. Morland's novels (perhaps a stand-in for James Hamilton, the actual publisher of AT's novels). He married Sybil Knox in 1933. They had a daughter, Laura, born in June 1934, a son, Richard, born in March, 1938, and a third child born early in 1939.

HR, DH, (PT), (CBI), (LAR), LAA, TST

Coates, Sybil Knox. Low Rising Manor, Low Rising. London.

George Knox's daughter, born in 1912. Although sweetly devoted to her widowed father, she was somewhat ill-assured. She was struggling to be a writer when she met the publisher Adrian Coates in 1933. They were married later that year.

HR, DH, (CBI), LAA, LAA, TST

Cobbold. Gatherum Castle.

The bailiff. He was good with cows.

CC, DD

Conque, Amelie. Rushwater House, Rushwater . Folkestone.

Lady Emily Leslie's French maid, from Vache-en-Étable. Despite having spent forty years in England she could barely speak English. After Lady Emily's death, she lived with the retired housekeeper, Mrs. Baker, at Folkestone, and for a while was invited for an annual week's visit to Holdings.

WS, MH, PBO, LAR, OBH, ESR

Cowshay, Miss. Barchester.

During the war she was a cashier at Pilchard's Stores, and later worked in the Regional Commissioner's Office. After the war she became Mr. Adams' secretary at the Hogglestock Rolling Mills, and in his office at Pomfret Towers. In 1958 she was working as Lord Pomfret's private secretary.

MH, LAR, OBH, ADA, LAA

Cox, Mrs. Marling Melicent.

A village woman who had been in service to good families. Upon retirement, she acquired a house and rented rooms to "ladies," one of whom, in 1941, was Joyce Smith.

MH

Coxon. Lambton.

A garage owner and cab driver in 1942.

GU

Coxon, Geoffrey. Lambton.

Son of the above. He became engaged to Marigold Smith in the summer of 1950.

(DD), (HaRe)

Crawford, Mr. Oxford.

Mr. Birkett's predecessor at Southbridge School. He left Southbridge and went to Lazarus College, Oxford.

CBI

Crawley, The Rev. Josiah. From Trollope.

It was he, the poor perpetual curate of Hogglestock, having gotten entangled in the moral dilemma about the stolen check, who was at the center of The Last Chronicle of Barset. He had a wife, Mary, and three children, Bob, Grace, and Jane. These are the forebears of the present Mr. Crawley and his family.

Crawley family:

    Crawley, Josiah. The Deanery, The Close, Barchester.

    Dean of Barchester Cathedral, and father of eight children. During his entire professional life he resented and defied the Bishop, who was, we must say, resented and defied by everyone else among our Barsetshire friends as well. In youth, Dean Crawley had shared rooms at Oxford with George

Knox; he had toured the capitals of Northern Europe before the first war. In mid- and later life he was rather formidable, with huge eyebrows that grew progressively wilder, which he used to great effect. Even so, he was skilled at baptisms. In company, he was perhaps a wee bit bombastic. However, he knew more about wine than anyone else in the Close. In 1949 he published *A Foreigner in Finland.* The Crawleys are mentioned in *O, These Men, These Men!,* which is not part of the Barsetshire series.

SH, BL, CBI, (GU), MH, (H), MB, PBO, PE, LAR, OBH, CC, HaRe, JC, ADA, CQ, LAA, TST

Mrs. Crawley.   The Deanery, TheClose, Barchester.
The eighth child of a country parson, she was wife and helpmeet to Josiah Crawley, and mother of his eight children. A skilled hostess, she entertained often, but was not too caught up in activities to reflect on life. For years she had carried on the subterranean feud between the Palace and the Deanery. Of all the eight Crawley children, we have only met Octavia, but we do know that two of the sons were in the Church, and two of the daughters had married clergymen.

SH, BL, CBI, (MH), H, PBO, PE, LAR, CC, HaRe, JC, DA, CQ, LAA, TST

Crawley, Grace.
One of the Crawley's numerous grandchildren, named for one of the daughters of old Josiah Crawley, although she herself was very modern in her outlook. She was fair, with a lovely oval Victorian face. While visiting her grandparents in 1956 she became engaged to John–Arthur Crosse. They were married that autumn.   **ADA**

Crawley, Jane.
Sister of Grace, younger by one year. Like Grace, she was a graduate of Barchester High School for Girls. Dark and pretty, she had been working on her brother's farm and was just becoming interested in pigs when she met George Halliday in 1956. They got engaged the same night that Grace and John–Arthur did and were married in a double ceremony in the Cathedral that autumn.

ADA

Crawley, Octavia.   *See* Needham, Octavia.

Crockett, Selina.   *See* Hopkins, Selina.

Crofts, Lieutenant-Colonel the Reverend Francis Edward.   The Vicarage, Southbridge.
He had been a colonel in the war and came to Southbridge as its recently ordained new vicar in 1946, when the previous vicar had left to become Principal in St. Aella's Home for Stiff-Necked Clergy. Colonel Crofts was tall and middle-aged, with a moustache, a beard, and very blue eyes under shaggy eyebrows. He was a widower with grown sons in the Indian Army. Another fetching thing about him was that he had rather a lot of money. His honest simplicity and unselfconsciousness won him new friends quickly, but it was an interest in birding that drew him and Effie Arbuthnot together. They were married in 1946.

PE, CC, HaRe, JC, CQ, TST
Note: An earlier Crofts, Dr. James Crofts, lived in Barsetshire in the 1850's. He married Bell Dale.

Crofts, Effie.   Editha Cottage, Wiple Terrace, Southbridge. The Vicarage, Southbridge.
Sister of the deceased and not much mourned Fred Arbuthnot. She was a devoted birdwatcher and skilled painter of birds. No beauty and likewise no spring chicken, her steadfastness and simplicity were nonetheless noted by a worthy Barsetshire man; she married the Reverend Colonel Crofts in 1946. As the vicar's wife she was a success, and she continued to paint lovely watercolors of birds and landscapes, bringing out a book, *Coot and Hern,* in 1949.   **PE**, (OBH), CC, HaRe, JC, CQ

Crosbie, Adolphus. *From Trollope.*
The cad who jilted Lily Dale, in The Small House at Allington. *No sooner had he proposed to Lily than he went on a visit to Courcy Castle. There he proposed to, and was accepted by, Lady Alexandrina de Courcy, who was anxious to marry because of her two previous broken engagements. Their marriage was a pronounced failure.*

Crosse, John Morton, Crosse Hall, East Barsetshire.
Third Baron Crosse, father of John Arthur. As a child he had been in love with Lady Emily Leslie, and as a lonely widower he proposed to Mrs. Morland. (Initially his name was spelled without the final "e", but an actual Lord Cross took it ill and threatened a lawsuit—so the spelling was changed.)   ESR, NTL, ADA

Crosse, John–Arthur. Old Manor House, Hatch End. Crosse Hall, East Barsetshire.
Lessee of the Old Manor House in Hatch End, where he was manager of the bank that had been occupying the property. He was about 30 in 1954, and altogether charming and affable. He was the only son of Lord Cross, which made him a significant heir and contributed to his appeal. He and Grace Crawley were married in 1956.   **ESR, ADA**

Crowder, Miss. "La Petite". Glycerine Cottage, Northbridge.
She and her special friend Miss Hopgood had lived on the Riviera and considered themselves spiritually French. She also considered herself a linguist, though she despised dictionaries—which no one found hard to believe, considering the strange mix-up in naming the cottage. Every summer Miss Crowder and Miss Hopgood visited Mentone and stayed at the Pensione Ramsden.   NR, WDIM, ADA

Crump, Mr. Allington.
A builder who understood the old Barsetshire houses better than anyone around. He was frequently called in when renovations were to be done; he was the consultant when The Cedars was restored.   DD

Curwen. Pomfret Madrigal.
The Brandon's chauffeur. The back of his neck spoke to them eloquently, registering every nuance of disapproval and umbrage.   During the war he was employed in an aero-engine works, but after the war he returned to Mrs. Brandon for a few years.   B, PE, (CC)

Dale family: From Trollope. *They are principal characters in* The Small House at Allington *and* The Last Chronicle of Barset.

Bernard Dale *was the nephew and heir of Squire Dale. He wished to marry Isabella, who refused him. Later he married Emily Dunstable, cousin of Martha Dunstable. There was no great fault in him, but no great virtue either.*

Christopher Dale *was an old squire, uncle of Lily, Isabella, and Bernard.*

Isabella (Bell) Dale *was Lily's older sister, the favorite of their uncle. Although intended by her uncle for his heir, Bernard Dale, she married Dr. James Crofts .*

Lily Dale *was the heroine of* The Small House at Allington. *After being jilted by Adolphus Crosbie, she, though otherwise intelligent and sane, swore she'd never marry. And she never did, despite being importuned by Johnny Eames. Somehow she managed to make sense of this decision. Few readers ever could.*

Dale family:

Dale, Doctor. The Rectory, Hallbury.

Rector of St. Hall Friars. Born in 1862, a great nephew of Lily Dale, Dr. Dale was married late and widowed early. He was left with the small child, Robin, when he himself was fifty-six. A man of private means, he was able to keep a good cellar and remain comfortable. He was scholarly, contributing learned articles which were models of precise thought to *The Journal of Classical Studies.* His life's work was devoted to a study of the prophet Haggai and his era. He died in August 1945.

MB, PBO

Dale, Anne Fielding. Cathedral Close, Barchester. Hallbury. Allington.

Only child of Sir Robert and Lady Anne, born in 1927. Because she had suffered from delicate health during her childhood and into her teens, much of her education took place at home. Though slight, she was elegant, with large dark eyes. Having been quietly brought up, she was not a slave to the spirit of that restless age. Anne and Robin Dale were married in the summer of 1947. Their twin daughters, Roberta and Dora Maud, were born in 1949, and a son arrived a few years later. The family lived at Southbridge School for a few years and then moved to Allington.

MB, PBO, PE, LAR, OBH, CC, HaRe

Dale, Isabel. See Silverbridge, Lady.

Dale, Priscilla. The Great House, Allington.

Mother of Isobel, and, in 1948, a widow of many years' standing. We are sorry to say that she was not good to Isabel, and wouldn't allow her to marry during the war. She would not even give Isabel more than pocket money and sometimes when Isabel wanted to take a job, Mrs. Dale would throw a heart attack. Only when her infirmities forced Mrs. Dale to get a companion did Isabel feel free to move to the Marlings' for a few months. Mrs. Dale very obligingly died in 1949.   (CC)

Dale, Robin. The Rectory, Hallbury. Southbridge School, Southbridge. The Great House, Allington.

The only child, born in 1918, of the Reverend Dr. Dale. Robin's foot was shot off at Anzio during the war and he wore a pretence one. After his discharge he kept a preparatory school for small boys for several months and then returned to Southbridge School and his pre-war job as a classics master. Later he became headmaster of the Junior House. Charming and clever, he married Anne Fielding in 1947. They had twin daughters, born in 1949, and later a son. With the death of Mrs. Dale, Isabel's mother, Robin inherited the Great House at Allington; in the 1950's he and Anne started a pre-preparatory school there.   **MB**, PBO, PE, LAR, OBH, CC, HaRe

---

Danby, Mr. and Mrs. The Vicarage, Southbridge.

Mr. Danby was vicar in 1939.   CBI

Dean family:

Dean, Frank. The Dower House, Worsted. Winter Overcotes.

Brother-in-law of Mr. Palmer and husband of Palmer's sister, Rachel Dean. He was an Old Southbridgian, of good middle-class stock from somewhere in the north of England and was a very successful engineer, often engaged on overseas projects. He served in the Observer Corps during the war.   AF, GU, PE, LAR, OBH, WDIM, (TST)

Dean, Rachel. The Dower House, Worsted. Winter Overcotes.

Lovely ox-eyed wife of Frank, sister of Mr. Palmer, and mother of nine children. During the war Mrs. Dean supervised the Land Army in the Winter Overcotes area. She suffered a curious form of narcolepsy and over the years came to resemble the dormouse; why no one tried to stuff her into a tea pot it is impossible to say.   **AF**, PE, LAR, OBH, WDIM

Dean, Betty. *See* van Dryven, Betty.

Dean, Gerald. Dean, the twins.

Three of the Dean sons who never appear in the narrative. All three had military careers. At the time of *August Folly*, Gerald was serving in India and the twins at sea somewhere.

Dean, Helen. *See* Fanshawe, Helen.

Dean, Jessica. *See* Clover, Jessica Dean.

Dean, Laurence. The Dower House, Worsted.

Eldest son of the Deans, an engineer in his father's firm. Laurence was jaunty and full of moxie at 25 or so in 1935, when he met Margaret Tebben. They were married and lived in Scotland during the war, with their children. Laurence was heir to the Manor House at Worsted, which after the war they inherited and lived in.   AF, (PE), LAR

Dean, Margaret Tebben. Lamb's Piece, Worsted.

Margaret, born in 1917, was the sweet, gentle and, we regret to say, overlooked daughter of the Tebbens. Two years younger than her brother, Margaret was good at languages, but not much consideration had been given to her education, beyond a year in France and Germany. She and Lawrence Dean fell in love in the summer of 1935 and were married soon thereafter. By 1946 they had a little brood of four children.   **AF**, (GU), (MB), (PE), LAR, WDIM

Dean, Robin. The Dower House, Worsted.

As a child of 10 or 11 in *August Folly,* 1935, he was jolly and bright. At twenty, he was interested in farming and attended an agricultural college. In 1946 Robin became the father of twins. He worked under Martin Leslie and Mr. Macpherson at Rushwater for six months in 1949.   AF, LAR

Dean, Susan. *See* Belton, Susan.

Dean, young. Priory School, Lambton.

The son of Lawrence and Margaret Dean, young Dean was a pupil at the Priory School. He was one of a trio of eager and polite little boys, the others being Addison and Pickering. After leaving the Priory School he entered Southbridge School.   LAR, DD

Deanna. Rushwater House, Rushwater.

A village girl who helped in the kitchen in 1950.   LAR, DD, TST

---

de Courcy family: From Trollope.

A haughty family living at Courcy Castle. One or another appears in Barchester Towers, Doctor Thorne, The Small House at Allington, *and* The Prime Minister.

Earl de Courcy *and his wife* **Countess Rosina** *were parents of a large family.*

Alexandrina, *a daughter, beguiled Adolphus Crosbie, with the result that he jilted Lily Dale and married her.*

George *was her brother who married a plain but wealthy woman.* **John** *was the youngest son.*

Amelia, Rosina, *and* **Margaretta** *were other daughters.*

---

de Courcy, George.

As a young man, George de Courcy was a clumsy lout who smelt of wine. Later he was in prison "for something to do with money matters." His relationship to Lady de Courcy is never made clear.

(ESR), (ADA)

---

de Courcy, Lady. London. Villa Thermogene, Mentone, France.

An acquaintance of Mrs. Halliday, and the aunt of Tommy Greaves. She divided her time between her house in London and the Villa Thermogene in the south of France.   ESR, ADA

Dingle, Mrs. Southbridge.

The sister of Eileen at the Red Lion, she "obliged" for residents of Wiple Terrace, appearing at each cottage once or twice a week to clean.   CBI, (PE)

Dorothy. *See* Simnet, Dorothy.

Downing, Harold. Punshions, Northbridge. The Hollies, Northbridge.

Wretched, downtrodden lodger of Miss Pemberton's; she so conscribed his life that he was nearly a prisoner. Mr. Downing was a scholar, an authority on Provençal Poetry, and author of *The Biographical Dictionary of Provence,* though apart from that he seemed barely *compos mentis.* Miss Pemberton housed him and fed him, not comfortably but for very little, and also helped him relentlessly with his book, which was in progress for years. He had been at Oxford with Gregory Villars and in the Navy from 1914 to 1916, when he was invalided out. By 1940 he was meek, stooped, and grey, and so poor that he feared estranging Miss Pemberton and being evicted from his lodging. He gradually lost that fear, and in 1953, very late in life, he married Mrs. Turner.   **NR**, CC, NTL, JC, **WDIM**, ADA

Downing, Poppy Turner.   The Hollies, Northbridge.

A jolly and pretty widow of a certain age, with lots of enticing tendrils in her coiffure. As was so often the case in the county, where live husbands were as a rule exemplary, her deceased husband had been a wastrel and a drunkard. A benign providence took him from her after only one year of marriage, before he had run through all the money. When her nieces were orphaned by influenza, she adopted them both. It was she who, when evacuees began arriving in Northbridge in 1939, organized the communal kitchen and worked there at least four hours a day. As if that were not enough she kept a welcoming open house for all the family's many friends. Mrs. Turner left Northbridge after the war to live in Norfolk near Betty and her husband but returned in 1953 when the lease on her Norfolk cottage was up.   She and Mr. Downing were married in 1953.   **NR**, CBI, (PE), **WDIM**, ADA

Dubois, M.   Southbridge School, Southbridge.

French master.   HR, DH

Duchaux, Mlle.

Former governess of Frances and Geoffrey Harvey. She visited them in 1941when they lived in the Red House in Marling Melicent.   MH

Dudley, Poppy. *See* Matron.

Dumka.   Old Manor House, Hatch End.

A Myxo-Lydian refugee working as a housemaid in the home of the Richard Carters. She was a distant relative of Gradka: "Her mother is cousin to my father's sister."   NTL

Dunsford, Mrs.   Hovis House, Northbridge.

The widow of a general, Mrs. Dunsford was middle-aged in 1940, and occupied the house that Eleanor Halliday's mother had lived in as a girl. Occasionally Mrs. Dumsford offered her back drawing room for various community activities. In later life she began spending long periods of time with Lady de Courcy at the Villa Thermogene in Mentone.   NR, (PE), WDIM, ADA

Dunsford, Barbara.   Hovis House, Northbridge.

Mrs. Dunsford's unmarried daughter. They lived together, they were wont to say, like sisters. Eventually Barbara decided that she would like a bit more from life, and, in a move of great daring, she visited Mentone. Here she found a slave-friend named Wendy, who called her Friendy, and as far as we know she made her home in the south of France forever more.   NR, WDIM, ADA

Dunstable, Martha. *From Trollope.*

She was introduced in Doctor Thorne, *the daughter of a self-made millionaire whose considerable fortune derived from patent medicine. She managed the business after his death, and yet had time for extended country house visits. Miss Dunstable was vivid and outspoken. With all her money, her passable good looks, and her remarkable curls, she attracted the attentions and suits of several men. She was very aware that her fortune was her main attraction, and not until she met James Thorne did she find a man she could love and trust. They were married in the late 1850's. Both were relatives of the present day Edith, Lady Pomfret, and of Mrs. Belton, who had both been Thornes.*

Dutton, Lieutenant.   The Rectory, Northbridge.

One of the officers billeted on the Villars in 1940. He was a former don with leftist leanings.   NR

Duval, Jacques.

Nephew of Mlle. Duchaux, who visited briefly in Marling Melicent on Christmas Day, 1941. He was trying to pass himself off as an officer, but was quickly identified by Tom Barclay as a corporal.   MH

It's ladies trying to put fuse wires in that keep the electric industry going.

— George Empson

Eames, Johnny. *From Trollope.*
Johnny was a hobbledehoy widow's son, of small means and modest expectations. By virtue of saving Lord de Guest from a bull, in The Small House at Allington, *Johnny became his friend, and Lord de Guest became Johnny's mentor. This gave Johnny certain advantages in his career, but none at all in his pursuit of the hand of Lily Dale, who had sworn never to marry. Johnny was a cousin of Grace Crawley and helped the Crawley family during their troubles in* The Last Chronicle of Barset. *He is thought to be a depiction of the young Trollope.*

Edie. *See* Jackson, Edie.

Edward. Southbridge School, Southbridge.
Odd-job man at Southbridge School. He struck up friendships with the boys and in general had no use for the masters and matron. He could do absolutely anything, from cooking to first aid. When Simnet left Southbridge in 1948, Edward became the headmaster's butler.   HR, DH, (GU), CBI, PE, CC, JC, NTL, CQ

Eileen. *See* Bateman, Eileen.

Ellangowan–Hornby, Mrs. Admiral. Deceased.
The aunt of Christopher Hornby. The daughter of a Scottish peer, she had the lease of Arcot House, which came to Christopher after her death. Mrs. Admiral Ellangowan–Hornby had a taste for white walls, good furniture, and ferocious cleanliness. The Beltons were able to take possession of the house furnished and move there with very little trouble.   (H)

Empson, George, "Sparks." Southbridge.
Matron's eldest nephew, an electrician. It was he who did the wiring at Editha Cottage when Mrs. and Miss Arbuthnot moved into it in June 1946. When not amusing himself by such private enterprise, George worked as head wireless operator on the newest and largest Atlantic liner.   PE, (JC), (HaRe)

Ethel. Laverings, Skeynes.
The Middletons' housemaid.   BL

Ethel. Stories, Pomfret Madrigal.
The Brandons also had a housemaid named Ethel, in 1946.   B, PE

Everleen. Camberly.
The Bill Marlings' undernurse. She came to them from an orphanage.   (CC)

Well I must say it sounds quite foully shattering, but just as you like. I suppose you are going to talk about stars. I must say I think stars are perfectly pretentious, if you see what I mean.

— Rose Birkett Fairweather

Fairweather family:

Fairweather, Edith.   *See* Keith, Edith.

Fairweather, Geoffrey.
Older of the Fairweather brothers. He attended Southbridge Preparatory School, and after Rugby joined he Barsetshire Yeomanry. Geoffrey married Geraldine Birkett at the outbreak of the war.   DH, SH, CBI

Fairweather, Geraldine Birkett.   Southbridge School, Southbridge.
The Birketts' younger daughter, born in 1921. Geraldine was intellectual and rather dull compared to her spectacular older sister, but she had a clever face and was always pleasant. She married Geoffrey Fairweather, then a captain in the Army, a few months after the wedding of her sister to his brother. The arrival of their first son, John, interrupted her nursing career; she was not happy about it.   (HR), SH, CBI, (GU), (PE)

Fairweather, John.   The Laurels, Greshamsbury.
Younger brother of Geoffrey. After Southbridge and Rugby, he entered the navy, and appeared as a *deus ex machina* to relieve the Birketts of their lovely but maddening daughter, Rose. John was a willing and very suitable husband. How he managed to keep his temper and love on an even keel over the many years of Rose's vacuity and foolishness we do not know. But he did, and she continued to love him. During and after the war John was stationed in various places outside England, but eventually he was assigned to the Admiralty. He and Rose were able to lease The Laurels in Greshamsbury, which made it possible for him to be home on weekends. John and Rose had four children, Amy, John, and two other daughters whose names we fear will forever elude us.
SH, CBI, PBO, CC, HaRe, **JC**, CQ NTL, ADA, CQ

Fairweather, Rose Birkett.   The Laurels, Greshamsbury.
Elder daughter of the Birketts. Gorgeous and addle-pated, Rose drove everyone mad. She had been witlessly engaged several times before finally marrying John Fairweather, then a Navy lieutenant, in July 1939. Unaccountably successful, this marriage flourished at various foreign postings. After the war the Fairweathers took a house in Greshamsbury, where Rose, still lovely and still a bit slapdash, concerned herself generously with local affairs and made for her family a comfortable and welcoming home.
(HR), **SH, CBI**, (GU), PBO, CC, HaRe, **JC**, NTL, ADA, CQ

Fanshawe, Charles.   Oxford.
Scholar; dean of Paul's College, Oxford. He had been Winifred Tebben's tutor in her Oxford days, and was a close family friend of the Deans whom he visited in the summer of 1935.   Despite his being twice the age of Helen Dean, Charles and she became engaged that August and were later married. During the war Fanshawe was seconded from Oxford for special work in the Censor's Office, and then for an assignment in some hush-hush department where he was known as X74. When Tom Grantly was at Oxford in 1948, Mr. Fanshawe was his tutor. Among Fanshawe's publications was a book on the Roman elegaic poet Tibullus.
AF, SH, CBI, (H), PE, LAR, (OBH)

Fanshawe, Helen Dean.   The Dower House, Worsted.
Helen was twenty-five in 1935, and a driver of racing cars. During the summer of 1935 she realized her love for Charles Fanshawe; they were married later that year. During the war she was in London overseeing some of the motor transport. By 1946 Helen and Charles had three children.   **AF,** (H), (PE), LAR

Featherstonehaugh.
Captain of Rowing while a student at Southbridge, and in love with Matron, to whom he wrote odes. Before the war he went into the Nigerian police and later was on a ship that was torpedoed while he was en route home on leave. He did not survive.   SH, (CBI), (GU), (PE)

Feeder, Mr. Louisa Cottage, Wiple Terrace, Southbridge.
Assistant master at Southbridge School. Mr. Feeder had a wireless, and played it at such a volume and with such frequency that it generated many complaints from Mr. Traill. (There is a teacher named Mr. Feeder in Dickens' *Dombey and Son.*)   PE, CC, JC, CQ, NTL, TST

Feeder, Mrs.   Editha Cottage, Wiple Terrace, Southbridge.
Feisty old mother of Mr. Feeder. She moved into Editha Cottage in 1946, when the Arbuthnots left it. Ever more aged and bony, she dressed in black, drank enthusiastically when there was a party, and willingly when there wasn't. Occasionally Mrs. Feeder enlivened her life by taking a little trip to Monte Carlo. She was outspoken to a degree that kept her listeners on the edges of their chairs.   CC, JC, CQ, TST

Feilding, Miss. Stories, Pomfret Madrigal.
Teacher of the infants evacuated to Stories. She stayed on with a few of them after peace was declared, until they were all transferred to Sussex with its delightful view of the Chanctonbury Ring.   (CBI), PE

Ferdinand, Isabella. Hosiers' Girls' Foundation School, Harefield Park, Harefield.
A stage-struck student in 1943.   H

Ferguson. Staple Park, Skeynes.
Lord and Lady Bond's chauffeur.   BL

Ferris, Mr. Southbridge School, Southbridge.
Tony Morland's housemaster at Southbridge Preparatory School. Known as "The Ferret."   (HR), DH

Fewling, George "Tubby." St. Sycorax, Northbridge.   Greshamsbury Rectory, Greshamsbury. Acacia
House, The Close, Barchester.
Ex-naval officer who took holy orders after the First War, during which he had risen to the rank of commander. He also was distinguished as one of the last men to go around the Horn in a sailing

ship. Contrary to his wishes and expectations, he was not tall, gaunt, and ascetic, but short and comfortably rounded. During the second war he was priest-in-charge of St. Sycorax in Northbridge, where he felt persecuted by the adoration of the local spinsters who liked his high church services. He was transferred to Greshamsbury early in 1952 and modified his services to accommodate local wishes. About that time he inherited a comfortable sum from an aunt, which enabled him to buy and cherish with guilty love a snappy sports car. He was given to entertaining harmless and romantic fantasies, one of which was a secret wish to drive in the auto races at Goodwood. Playing the piano was one of his joys. Tubby loved to entertain, and in return his welcome extended throughout the county; he dined out often. In 1952 he fell in love with Margot Phelps and married her in 1957. His honors included an honorary Doctorate of Divinity. He was made an Honorary Canon in 1951 and moved to the Close as a Resident Canon in 1957.

NR, (PE), CC, **JC**, ADA, **CQ**, TST

Fewling, Margot. Jutland Cottage, Southbridge. Framley Court, Framley. Acacia House, The Close, Barchester.

Born in 1910, Margot was the hard-working, selfless, and—though we hate to say it—shapeless and dowdy daughter of Admiral and Mrs. Phelps. In 1952 she was taken in hand by her friends, who arranged a haircut, new clothes, and suitable shape-giving underwear. All these measures had the desired outcome: she married Donald Macfadyen in 1953. This was a happy marriage cut short by his death in 1957. Within a few months she had agreed to marry Tubby Fewling; they were married in the autumn of 1957.

CBI, GU, PE, **JC, CQ,** LAA, TST

Fielding, Sir Robert. Number Seventeen, The Close, Barchester.

Chancellor of the Diocese, Sir Robert was a lawyer with a large leonine head. Gardening was one of his favorite pastimes, and gossip one of his delights. He was a member of the Conservative Club, standing for election to Parliament in 1945. Sir Robert was also a Governor of Southbridge School.

MB, PBO, PE, LAR, OBH, HaRe, WDIM, ADA, LAA

Fielding, Lady Dora. Number Seventeen, The Close, Barchester.

Sir Robert's wife. Born in 1900, she was brought up in the Close. Although she was kept busy with half the women's organizations in Barchester, she maintained an unruffled confidence.

MB, PBO, PE, LAR, OBH, CC, HaRe, WDIM, ADA, LAA

Fielding, Anne. *See* Dale, Anne.

Fillgrave, Abel. Barchester.

Physician and surgeon. His name follows in the tradition of Trollope and other Victorian writers, who often gave minor characters unsubtle and heavily humorous names. Mr. Quiverful, the father of fifteen, Dr. Pullbody, Farmer Greenacre and William Brisket (the butcher), are examples.

(CBI), (GU), (H)

Finch. Pomfret Towers.

A footman. It was he who was derelict in the matter of Alice Barton's shoes. He later became an odd-job man on the estate.

PT, LAA

Fletcher, Eva. The Lodge, Silverbridge.

The solid and reliable and middle-aged cook for Lord and Lady Silverbridge in 1950.

DD

Fletcher, Gloria. The Lodge, Silverbridge.

Eva's niece. She tried to be the parlormaid, but labored under the handicap of an entire want of social sense.

DD

Flo. Low Rising.

The adenoidal, half-witted younger sister of Annie, the Knoxs' parlormaid. She helped out now and then at Low Rising Manor, and occasionally, under great protest from Stoker, at Mrs. Moreland's in High Rising.   HR

Ford, Dr. James. High Rising.

A country doctor known and loved throughout the county. A perennial bachelor, he had been engaged to Sylvia Gould in 1934, but she had doubts, perhaps because of the twenty-year difference in their ages, and called off the marriage. Although always professionally discreet, Dr. Ford was a great gossip, and carried news around the county with him on his rounds. Years later, in 1960, he and Sylvia drifted back together and decided to marry after all.

HR, DH, B, (CBI), GU, MB, PE, LAR, OBH, DD, JC, NTL, CQ, **TST**

Foster family:

Foster, Major. Deceased.

The odious nephew of the seventh Earl of Pomfret. His death in a hospital in Cape Town at a relatively young age precipitated his son, Giles Foster, into the role of direct heir while in his early twenties.   (PT)

Foster, Giles. *See* Pomfret.

Foster, Lady Emily. Pomfret Towers.

Born in 1940, she was the younger sister of Ludovic. Much more "pure Pomfret" than he, she was also very like her mother, robust and vigorous with a love of riding and hunting. She attended Barchester High School as a weekly boarder and was designated Girl of Honor in her last year. In 1960 Emily was planning a career in market gardening, and looking forward to being one of the bridesmaids in Ludo's wedding.

H, LAR, OBH, WDIM, ESR, LAA, TST

Foster, the Honorable Giles. Pomfret Towers.

Born in 1942, Giles was the youngest child of young Lord and Lady Pomfret. Very like his sister in being glib and active, he took an intense pleasure in all forms of athletics. From an early age he was a confident and able rider, and was active in the local pony club. No student, he left school at sixteen and planned to work for a while at a stud farm, and then take a course in estate management.   (H), LAR, OBH, WDIM, ESR, LAA, TST

Foster, Ludovic, Viscount Mellings. *See* Mellings, Viscount.

Foster. Northbridge.

Foster had been the second housemaid at Northbridge Manor, but by 1940 she was the Villars' very capable parlormaid. As the years passed she kept up their standard of living in a most exhausting way.   NR, PE

Fothergill, Mrs. Hatch House, Hatch End.

The Hallidays' cook. She had started at Hatch End in 1911 as a scullery maid, and was thus, by 1955, elderly and suffering from My Feet. She could read tea leaves.   PBO, ESR, NTL, DA

Fothergill, Mr. Gatherum Castle.

Agent for the Duke of Omnium. In 1937 he had persuaded the Duke to make over to the National Trust two miles on either side of the River Rising near Hallbury, thus preventing it from being developed.   MB

Freeman, Ernie. Hallbury.
Driver of the baker's van.   MB, (LAR), CQ

Freeman. Hallbury House.
Admiral Palliser's elderly parlormaid.   MB

Freeman. Hallbury.
The verger at St. Hall Friars, Mr. Freeman was also a part-time journalist whose articles appeared occasionally in the *Barchester Chronicle*.   MB

I wonder what's the longest a cow ever lived.
— Emmy Graham

Gale, Nurse.   Beliers Priory.
Nurse to Philip and Leslie Winter's children.   LAR

Gawky, Professor.
A communist, the intellectual rival of Mr. Downing on the subject of Provençal history. She was the author of *Gaily the Troubadour*.   (NR), (WDIM)

Gissing family:

Gissing, Fritz.   Wiple Terrace.
The son of the pestilential Gissings. He had escaped war service by being in a reserved occupation: films. He was arrogant, callow, and, like his parents, utterly selfish.   CBI
Note: Originally the Gissings were named Warburg and were Jewish, but when Alfred Knopf, Thirkell's American publisher, objected, the name and identity were changed.

Gissing, Gloria.   Wiple Terrace.
Wife of Oscar. In looks she was dark and ravaged; in behavior she gave offense at every turn. Naturalized Germans, she and Oscar had no sympathy for England or the war effort, and had no intention of making any sacrifices. She openly patronized the black market. They emigrated to America before many weeks had passed, bringing relief, the keenest form of joy, to their Southbridge neighbors.   CBI

Gissing, Oscar.   Wiple Terrace.
He was employed by Dante–Technicolor Films, which had been evacuated to a location near Southbridge.   CBI

Goble.   Home Farm at Holdings, Little Misfit.
The Grahams' bailiff, he whose heart was in pigsties. His life held no greater joy than to take a fine pig, such as Holdings Blunderbore, to the Barsetshire Agricultural Show and win the occasional first prize. He raised White Porkminsters.   LAR, (OBH), DD, ESR, NTL, ADA

Goble, Mrs.   Edgewood.
The fat postmistress.   OBH

Goesler, Madame Max. From Trollope.
A wealthy Viennese widow whose charm, beauty and worldly wisdom made her a success in London society in the 1860's. Madame Max, as she was known, appears in the parliamentary series, most notably in Phineas Finn, Phineas Redux, The Prime Minister, *and* The Duke's Children.

Gorman, Jennifer. Barchester.
A school chum of Grace Gantly and later assistant to Madame Tomkins. (OBH), LAA

Gould family:

Gould, Mr. and Mrs. The Vicarage, High Rising.
Mr. Gould was the vicar of High Rising. Together he and Mrs. Gould were the parents of the four Gould girls, but other than that we fear that they were rather dull. At least Mrs. Moreland came to find them so, though a list of their good works would be long. DH, NTL, LAA, TST

Gould, Rose; Gould, Dora. The Vicarage, High Rising.
The younger daughters of the Goulds. They were Tony Morland's friends while he was in High Rising in 1934, when he was thirteen. Twenty-seven years later they were still there, working at jobs in Barchester and gallivanting with their many unmarried friends. DH, TST

Gould, Ruth.
The second eldest of the Gould daughters. On a farm outside Barsetshire, she raised chickens assisted by a friend-that-I-live-with. (DH), (TST)

Gould, Sylvia. The Vicarage, High Rising.
Eldest daughter of the Goulds. A trained games mistress, she was briefly engaged to Dr. Ford in the summer of 1934. Later, when out of the country, she decided that the twenty-year age difference was too great, and broke the engagement. She returned to High Rising in the late 1950's, and began working for Sam Adams at Pomfret Towers. She also began to see Dr. Ford again. They were engaged in 1960 and no doubt married later that year. **DH**, TST

Govern, James. Cottage, Marlling Hall.
The Marlings' estate carpenter. He was a widower when he met Hilda Plane at the Red House in 1941. They were married in 1942. MH

Grace. Stories, Pomfret Madrigal.
The Brandons' second housemaid in 1938. B

Gradka. *See* Bonescu, Gradka.

Graham family:

Graham, General Sir Robert, KCMG. Holdings, Little Misfit.
Relative newcomers to Barsetshire, the Graham family had been at Holdings only since Waterloo. Following family tradition, Sir Robert was a professional soldier; he was also the principal heir of his Aunt Florence. He refused with unflagging firmness ever to bother about his wife's many relatives, and in any case his army career kept him away from his family most of the time, in London or at various overseas postings. He was on the Honors List in 1941 and knighted in 1942. After his retirement he was at home more often, but by no means much, as he continued to serve on yet more high-level political missions. In 1955 he was standing for East Barsetshire County Council. In appearance he was of slight wiry build, with grey hair and dark piercing eyes; he dressed in good well-worn tweeds.
(WS), (MH), (H), (MB), (PBO), (LAR), (OBH), CC, (DD), (HaRe), (ESR), NTL, ADA, (TST)

Graham, Lady Agnes. Holdings, Little Misfit.
Wife of Sir Robert, daughter of Henry and Lady Emily Leslie, sister of Giles (dec.), John, and David Leslie, and mother of James, Emily, Clarissa, John, Robert and Edith Graham. Described by her

brother David as a "divine idiot," Agnes, as a young matron with a cooing manner, was vague in the extreme, with interest primarily in her children. Her conversation engulfed her hearers in clouds of imbecility. The passage of time brought out other qualities; she became a charming hostess, and was capable of ably managing her many community activities, her needlepoint embroidery, or unforeseen situations.

WS, (BL), MH, (GU), H, (MB), PBO, LAR, OBH, CC, DD, HaRe, **ESR**, NTL, ADA, LAA

Graham, Clarissa. *See* Belton, Clarissa.

Graham, Edith. *See* Harcourt, Lady William.

Graham, Emily. *See* Grantly, Emily.

Graham, James. Holdings, Little Misfit.
The eldest of the Graham children, born in 1927. Although he was the most like his Uncle David Leslie, he followed the traditional Graham family pattern of Eton, Sandhurst, and the Brigade of Guards. As Sir Robert was unable to attend Clarissa's wedding, it was James who gave away his sister on January 1, 1952. James was Edith's favorite brother, despite always beating her at chess.

WS, MH, (MB), LAR, CC, HaRe, ESR, NTL, LAA

Graham, John. Holdings, Little Misfit.
The fourth child, second son, of the Grahams, born in 1934. Like his older brother, he too went to Eton, Sandhurst, and then joined the Brigade of Guards.

MH, (GU), H, (MB), LAR, OBH, CC, DD, HaRe, (ESR), NTL, ADA

Graham, Robert. Holdings, Little Misfit.
Born in 1935, Robert was the youngest of the Graham sons and fifth of the six children. He was his grandmother's favorite. He was fun to be with and somewhat poetical. Like the others, he went to Eton, Sandhurst, and then entered the Brigade of Guards. In 1958 he was asked by his sister Edith to be godfather to her first born, Gwendolyn Sally Harcourt.

WS, MH, H, (MB), PBO, OBH, CC, DD, HaRe, NTL NTL, ADA, LAA

Grant family:

Grant, Felicia. Italy.
Widow of Edward Grant and mother of Hilary, whom she distressed by being, he said, "so confoundedly in the spirit of things." She lived mostly in Italy and was a self-proclaimed authority on rustic Italian life. For some reason this inspired her to dress in loose homespun garments, the effect exacerbated by many strings of rattling and clacking beads. Mrs. Grant was in Italy studying Calabrian folklore when the war broke out. The Italian government allowed her to remain for a while, but eventually the war drove her back to England. With the onset of peace she moved to Sicily.

B, (CBI), (GU), (H), (PE), (OBH), CC

Grant, Delia Brandon. Stories, Pomfret Madrigal.
Born in 1919, daughter of Mrs. Brandon, and younger sister of Francis. Delia was a frank and lively girl with curly brown hair and bold brown eyes. After leaving Barchester High School, she spent a year in Paris, which did nothing to destroy her keen wish to see mutilated accident victims. She and Hilary Grant were married in 1940; during the war she worked in Barchester General as a VAD. Later they lived in London with their children, the twins, Felicia and Freddy, we think. Delia's children were among those who experienced the greatest mutability as to their ages, names, and sexes.

B, CBI, (NR), (MH), (H), (PE), HaRe

Grant, Hilary.   The Vicarage, Pomfret Madrigal. Chelsea, London.

A cousin of Francis and Delia Brandon, born in 1915. His father was the son of Amelia Brandon's youngest aunt, which makes the relationship perfectly clear. He was a pleasant and thoroughly decent young man, though somewhat intimidated by life—perhaps from having lived so unconventionally and his mother's being half-crazed. An Oxford graduate, he was reading for the bar in 1938, though he said he would have preferred a career in publishing. Hilary and Delia Brandon were married in 1940. Hilary was the author of *A Diabolist of the Restoration*. During the war he was in the Intelligence Corps and made occasional trips to Washington, D.C. After the war he developed an interest in archeology and wrote a book about his discoveries.

B, (CBI), (MH), GU, (H), (PE), (OBH), HaRe

Grant, Captain Jerry.   Near Marling Melicent.

A young man who was a friend of Lucy Marling's in 1941.   MH

Grantly family: *From Trollope.*

This family is central to Trollope's Barsetshire series.

Bishop Grantly was beloved. Upon his death his son Theophilus, the Archdeacon of Barchester, was passed over as next bishop, and Bishop Proudie was appointed.

The Reverend Theophilus Grantly was the son of Bishop Grantly. He was the Archdeacon of Barchester and Rector of Plumstead Episcopi. He was married to Susan Harding, the daughter of Septimus Harding. They had several children, of whom the following are of particular interest:

Henry Grantly, who had a military career and in middle age took Grace Crawley as his second wife.

Griselda Grantly, who was beautiful but cool and passive. Both mothers wished her to marry Lord Lufton but she married Lord Dumbello, who later became the Marquis of Hartletop. Plantaganet Palliser, the Duke of Omnium, found her especially attractive, and letters passed between them.

Grantly family:

Grantly, Septimus. The Vicarage, Edgewood.

The vicar of Edgewood, named for his great-grandfather, Septimus Harding. He was tall and handsome, with the same kind and gentle expression as the one in the portrait of another great-grandfather, Bishop Grantly.   **OBH**, DD, HaRe, (TST)

Grantly, Mary Carter.   The Vicarage, Edgewood.

Wife of Septimus, and mother of Tom, Eleanor, Henry, and Grace. Lily Dale was her old aunt.

OBH, DD, HaRe, TST

Grantly, Tom. The Vicarage, Edgewood.   Agent's cottage, Rushwater.

Born in 1920, Tom was the Grantlys' eldest child. In 1949 he was a war veteran who, as a major, had given honorable service, but once home was unable to settle to a career. Thinking he'd rather like farming, he was invited by Martin Leslie to learn what he could at Rushwater, where he went for a prolonged stay. After a bit of trial and error, he decided that farming was indeed his true vocation, and that Emmy Graham was his true love. They were married in 1950 and he became the agent for the estate. They had several children and lived in the very fine house left vacant by Mr. Macpherson's conveniently-timed death.   **OBH**, DD

Grantly, Eleanor.   *See* Keith, Eleanor.

Grantly, Emily Graham.   Holdings, Little Misfit. Rushwater.

Wife of Tom. She was the eldest Graham daughter, born in 1928. Emily grew up to be robust and rather stout, with a mop of light brown curls, blue eyes, and sunburnt skin. She took great interest in the farming side of life at Holdings, and became energetically and tiresomely cow-minded. After a stint as a Land Girl, she went to Rushwater to help her cousin Martin Leslie manage the farm there after he came home from the war with a leg injury. Emmy was hard-working, straightforward, and utterly reliable. While at Rushwater she met Tom Grantly. They were married in 1950, lived in the former agent's house, and raised a large family.

WS, MH, (MB), **PBO**, LAR, OBH, CC, **DD**, ADA, TST

Grantly, Henry Arabin. The Vicarage, Edgewood.
The Grantleys' younger son, born in 1931. In 1949 he was desperate to be posted to the Barsetshire Yeomanry for his military service, and haunted the post office until his notice came. When it finally did he went off joyfully to his assignment in the Far East. He returned two years later, one of the few to come home with no parasites or tropical disease. He decided to read law, and was articled to the Barchester firm of Keith and Keith.

OBH, HaRe

Grantly, Grace. *See* Lufton, Lady.

Greaves, Thomas Crosby. The Rectory, Northbridge.
A jovial youth, the life and soul of any party, Tommy was one of the officers billeted on the Villars in 1940. It turned out that he was a nephew of Lady de Courcy. Early in 1941 he got engaged to Mrs. Turner's other niece; they married after the war. They lived in London, where Tommy, or Bing as he was known then, was a successful stockbroker. They led the pleasant affluent life of those who have no children. NR, (WDIM)

The Greens. Greshamsbury.
Their travel plans enabled them to rent their house for a few years to Captain and Mrs. John Fairweather in 1952.

JC

Gresham family: From Trollope.
An influential Barsetshire family in the mid-nineteenth century.
> *John N. Gresham was MP for Barsetshire in his time. He was the grandfather of Frank Gresham.*
> *Francis N. Gresham, son of John and father of Frank, was also an MP for East Barsetshire. He married **Lady Arabella De Courcy**. They lived at Greshamsbury Park in Greshamsbury, where they had serious financial troubles.*
> *Frank Gresham was the son of Francis, and heir to the estate and all its debts. His parents intended him to marry a wealthy woman and recoup the family fortune, but instead he fell in love with **Mary Thorne**. When, as luck would have it, she turned out to be a wealthy heiress, they were free to marry.*

Gresham family:
Gresham, Mr. Greshamsbury.
Mr. Gresham was a distant relative of the contemporary Francis Gresham. He was for years the MP for East Barsetshire, and permanent honorary chairman of the Barsetshire Conservative Association. In 1949 Mr. Gresham was a middle-aged bachelor of old county stock, liked and respected by everyone. He was often a best man but never a groom. LAR, OBH, (CC), (ESR), ADA

Gresham, Francis. Greshamsbury House, Greshamsbury.
A career Navy man, Francis was a prisoner of war in the Far East; he was released in 1943. Once home, he was unfit for active duty and continued his career at the Admiralty. He and his wife, the former Jane Palliser, already the parents of Frank, had two more children, both daughters. The family lived with Admiral Palliser during his remaining years, and then occupied one wing of Greshamsbury House, which was owned by the National Trust. (MB), PBO, JC, ADA, CQ

Gresham, Francis Junior. Hallbury House, Hallbury. Greshamsbury House, Greshamsbury. Born in 1936, Frank was the irrepressible son of Francis and Jane. He attended Robin Dale's pre-preparatory school in Hallbury and later went to Southbridge School.   **MB**, PBO, HaRe, JC, CQ

Gresham, Jane Palliser. Hallbury House, Hallbury. Greshamsbury House, Greshamsbury. Wife of Francis Gresham. During the time he was a prisoner during the war, she lived with her father, Admiral Palliser, in Hallbury. She very bravely carried on, not knowing if Francis were dead or alive, and was a good mother to Frank.   **MB**, PBO, (CC), JC, ADA, CQ

Gresham, Jane Beatrice "Batty," and Gresham, Mary. Greshamsbury House, Greshamsbury. The two daughters born to the Greshams after Francis Gresham's return.   (ADA), CQ

Grey, Una. Low Rising Manor, Low Rising.
Possessive and semi-mad secretary to George Knox in 1932. She was lovely to look at, but far from delightful to know, combining cunning, hysteria, and deceit in a sinister personality. When finally prevailed upon to leave Low Rising, she went to London to be a companion to Mr. Knox's mother, and left Mrs. Knox to marry a naval man.   **HR**, (DH), (B)

Grobury. Silverbridge.
Gardener at the Lodge, he was descended from an old Barsetshire family, and liked to say that Grobury was his name, and Growberry was his nature. This made his employers laugh sycophantically.   DD

Gudgeon. Rushwater House, Rushwater.
Butler in the days before the elder Leslies moved to Holdings. He concealed within his tall and dignified presence the soul of an artist, poet, soldier, explorer and mystic. He released all of these essences four times a day in sounding the gong for breakfast, lunch, tea, and dinner. By 1945 Gudgeon had retired and had gone to live with his sister in Bovey Tracey.   WS, (PBO)

So you keep a boys' school; and in London; interesting; much vice?
— Miss Hampton

Hacker, Percy. Southbridge School, Southbridge.

Hacker (as we shall always think of him) was a classics student who kept a chameleon named Gibbon while at school; he was a pale boy with untidy hair, a vacant look, and a slouching gait. Hacker won the Montgomery Open Scholarship for Lazarus College, Oxford. After the war he held the chair of Latin at Redbrick University, later transferring to Uppings. He was the author of works on classical subjects and was famous for exchanging venomous letters on the subject of Aulus Gellius with every Latin scholar in Europe. All his life, Hacker kept a chameleon. In 1958 he spoke at the opening of the new wing at Southbridge School.

SH, (GU), PE, HaRe

Halliday family:

Halliday, Leonard. Hatch House, Hatch End.

An esteemed squire and Lord of the Manor at Hatch End. The Halliday family had owned land in Barsetshire since before the Domesday Book. Mr. Halliday had been active all his life, but by 1953 his health was declining, and after some bitterness he accepted his failing powers with unselfish self-discipline. He became ever more weak and his mind wandered; he died in 1955. PBO, ESR, NTL

Halliday, Eleanor. Hatch House, Hatch End.

Wife of Leonard. Mrs. Halliday was one of Barsetshire's excellent woman; originally she was from Northbridge. She exhausted herself caring for her husband during his last illness. After her husband's death she went for a prolonged stay with her daughter Sylvia at Rushwater, but she was ever less welcome because she had become egocentric and annoying. Her son George was not eager to have his mother living with him at Hatch House. Luckily, Eleanor renewed acquaintance with two old friends and developed an entirely new life, living part of each year with one or the other.

PBO, ESR, NTL, ADA

Halliday, George. Hatch House, Hatch End.

Son of Leonard and Eleanor, born in 1921. Young George came home to Hatch House from serving with the Barsetshire Regiment during the war, and helped his father run the farm. Gradually, with kindness and practicality, he assumed all the responsibilities. After Leonard's death George led a rather grim and lonely life, leavened by his friendship with John–Arthur Crosse and the Grahams. When he renewed his acquaintance with Jane Crawley after many years, he fell in love. On the first date he proposed and was accepted. They were married in 1956. A son, Martin, was born in 1960.

PBO, ESR, NTL, ADA, TST

Halliday, Sylvia. *See* Leslie, Sylvia.

Hamp, Mr. Worsted.

The local tailor. In India during the first war he had suffered sunstroke, and to add injury to insult, had been kicked in the head by a mule. The result was a morbid intolerance of cold and a set of cranial disfigurements that fascinated his clients. As he knelt to make some adjustment they could stare at his bald, bulging, livid skull.

GU, (DD), JC

Hamp, Mrs. Lambton.

Sister-in-law of Mr. Hamp. She kept the village shop.

GU, (LAR), HaRe

Hampton, Miss. Adelina Cottage, Wiple Terrace, Southbridge.

An author whose subject was vice. A list of her titles includes *Crooked Insect, Chariots of Desire, A Gentle Girl and Boy, Ways to Be Foul, Temptation at St. Anthony's,* and *My Daughter Is My Son.* She and her friend Miss Bent were long-term residents of Wiple Terrace and were known for their drinks parties. They had a standing weekly order with the Red Lion for six bottles of gin, two of French vermouth, two of Italian vermouth, and two of whiskey. During the first war Miss Hampton had driven an ambulance in France and Myxo-Lydia. She was the sole support of four nephews. Rather handsome, with short, neatly curled grey hair, she dressed in gentlemanly style, in black coats and skirts, with white blouses, her slim legs in silk stockings and her feet in brogues. Her cigarettes were held in a very long black holder. Miss Hampton and Miss Bent were active locally and were on hand for every celebration or good cause, usually accompanied by their small black elephant-headed dog. **CBI**, (NR), GU, MB, (PBO), PE, (OBH), CC, JC, NTL, CQ, TST

Harcourt family: Harcourt is the family name of the Dukes of Towers. This family is described in Peter Ibbetson. *At the turn of the century a rather degenerate duke had died of hard living, leaving a sickly heir, who also died. The title then passed to the father of the present Duke of Towers, the deceased husband of the Dowager Duchess. Elaine, Gwendolyn and William Harcourt were the Duke's other children.*

Harcourt, Lady Elaine. Harcourt.

A sister of Lord William. She had had one fling at love, with Dobby Fitzgorman, who had broken his neck in a riding accident. In any case she would never have been allowed to marry him, because he was a Liberal and shot foxes. Elaine seemed to be fated to a lifetime of living with her mother and doing chores that in earlier times would have been done by a parlormaid, but a chance invitation to America gave her hopes of a zippier life.

ADA, **LAA**

Harcourt, Lady Gwendolyn. Harcourt. The Vicarage, Harefield.

Elder sister of Lord William. Her interest in celibate clergymen kept her single until middle age, when Mr. Oriel, one of the celibate clergymen, asked her to marry him. They were wed in 1958 and lived in Harefield.

ADA, **LAA**

Harcourt, Lord William. The Parsonage, Harcourt.

Younger brother of the Duke of Towers. William, a tall and pleasant young clergyman, was Dean Crawley's chaplain. Like the Dean, he had attended Lazarus College, Oxford. His interest in Edith Graham grew quickly when he met her while she was living with the Crawleys. They were married in 1957, and moved to Harcourt where William's brother, the Duke, gave him living. Their daughter, Gwendolyn Sally, was born the next year and another child was expected a few years later.

ADA, **LAA**

Harcourt, Edith Graham, Lady William. Holdings, Little Misfit. The Vicarage, Harcourt.

Almost as difficult as Clarissa, and the last of the Graham children, Edith was born in 1937. As a child she had been a determined poet, and had even then a selfish charm. In her early teens she was away at a boarding school, and by the time she was eighteen she liked books, had pretty manners, and knew how a farm was run. She had the dark hair and eyes of the Fosters, and a peculiar quiet elegance, as well as greater capacity for loving and being loved, for hurting and being hurt, than her elder sisters. At nineteen she described herself as a grown-up daughter at home, but everyone felt she should be more than that, and finally she completed an estate management course. However, she still had to struggle to control her temper, and was unsure of her way in life. These problems were resolved when she married William Harcourt, younger brother of the Duke of Towers, in 1957. In 1958 they had a daughter, Gwendolyn Sally, and by 1960 were expecting another child.

MH, H, (MB), PBO, LAR, OBH, DD, HaRe, WDIM, **ESR**, **NTL**, **ADA**, LAA

Harding family: From Trollope.

The Reverend **Septimus Harding** *was a precentor of the cathedral and warden of Hiram's Hospital, an almshouse for old men near Barchester.*

Susan Harding, *his daughter, was married to* **Theophilus Grantly**, *Archdeacon of Barchester. Among their children were Griselda and Henry Grantly.*

Eleanor Harding, *Septimus' younger daughter, was married to* **Francis Arabin**, *Vicar of St. Ewold's and Dean of the Cathedral. They had two daughters, also Susan and Eleanor.*

Harker, Mr. Northbridge.

A curate. He was described as uninteresting, and he must have been, because he was never heard of again.

NR.

Hartletop. From Trollope.

This refers to the Marquis of Hartletop, who had been Lord Dumbello before his father's death. His wife was **Griselda (Grantly)**, *and his seat was Hartleltop Priory. The family was wealthy and the property abundant.*

Harvest, Lionel. London.

Epicene colleague of Joan Stevenson at the BBC in 1933. Happily, he was heir to £4000 per annum. On the strength of this knowledge Joan inveigled him into a companionate marriage; they lived in Bloomsbury. When the inheritance was realized, Lionel retired from his profession and wrote a scathing exposé of Broadcasting House, called *Cast Me Abroad*. It was not a great success, despite the clever title.   WS

Harvey, Frances. The Red House, Marling Melicent.

Independent young woman—though we cannot say how young—perhaps not very—who had been posted as secretary to Oliver Marling at the Regional Commissioner's Office in Barchester in 1941. As her brother Geoffrey was working in the same office, they decided to take the Red House together. Frances was fair in complexion and determined in character. She was described by Mr. Marling as looking like "an educated rocking horse." Frances and Geoffrey left Marling Melicent after a few months; she went into the Censor's office for much of the war, then to Gatherum, to the Ministry of General Interference. The rest of her career took her from agency to agency. She enjoyed being important and ordering people about, and her bureaucratic assignments gave her ample opportunity to exercise her unpleasant influence for years to come. She never married, but was a great friend of Lord Aberfordbury.

MH, (H), (PBO), (LAR), CC, DD, WDIM, TST

Harvey, Geoffrey. The Red House, Marling Melicent.

Geoffrey brought a taste of Bloomsbury to Barsetshire—and it was a taste which nobody liked. A Cambridge graduate, he had worked before the war in London at the Board of Red Tape and Sealing Wax, and was known to, but not enjoyed by, David Leslie. He was seconded to the Regional Commissioner's Office and got to know Oliver Marling there. Geoffrey was dark and tall, with a longish lock of hair in front that he kept flipping back in a self-consciously poetic way. He and Frances were cousins of young Lady Norton. He was the author of a novel about Pico della Mirandola, had published some poetry, and was working on a study of Jehan le Capet. After leaving Barsetshire Geoffrey returned to Bloomsbury and shared a flat with his friend Peter, continuing his work at the Board of Red Tape. At some point during the war he was decorated for giving a couple of talks behind the Maginot line—that was the extent of his wartime heroism. He was a good official, almost brilliant, but it must be said that he had an unfortunate manner.

MH, (H), (PBO), (LAR), DD, WDIM

Hastings, Dr. Barchester.
The best surgeon in Barsetshire, luckily on hand when Sir Cecil Waring was rushed to the hospital in the summer of 1950.

DD

Heath, Nurse. Punshions, Northbridge.
One of the trio of nurses consisting of Ward, Heath, and Chiffinch. Toward the end of their careers they joined in redecorating Punshions and all made their home there.

(PBO), DD, (HaRe), WDIM

Hepplethwaite and Crowther. London.
A highly distinguished firm of wine merchants.

Herdman. Rushwater.
Cowman at Rushwater House farm, an independent fellow who followed his own inclinations. We are sorry to learn that he suffered from lumbago and boils in his later years.

(PBO), LAR, OBH, (CC), DD

Hettie. The Vicarage, Pomfret Madrigal.
In 1938 Hettie was Mr. Miller's housemaid. She was the daughter of Turpin, the Brandons' gardener. She enjoyed a mild yet satisfying renown for her very good parsnip and dandelion wine.

B

Hibberd. Northbridge.
Sexton. He sported a Newgate frill, *q.v.* Before the war he took care of all the gardens at the rectory, but during the war he confined his efforts to the vegetables.

NR

Hibberd, Doris. Northbridge.
Mrs. Turner's maid of all work.

NR, WDIM

Hibberd, Sir Ogilvy. *See* Aberfordbury, Baron.

Hibberd, Mr.
Son of Lord Aberfordbury. He was a director of the National Rotochrome–Polychrome Universal Picture Postcard Company, and as such managed to stir up resentment with divers unwelcome schemes. He stood for Parliament in 1945 but we are pleased to say was defeated by Sam Adams.

NTL, TST

Hicks, Mrs. Northbridge. The Vicarage, Greshamsbury.
As a girl Mrs. Hicks had been in service at Gatherum, and later was the mother of the head housekeeper at Northbridge Rectory. Mr. Fewling lodged with Mrs. Hicks when he was in Northbridge, and took her with him to Greshamsbury, and later to Barchester, as his housekeeper. She was a member of the Close Upper Servants' Club.

(NR), NTL, JC, ADA, CQ

Higgins. Beliers Priory, Lambton.
The gardener.

LAR

Highmore, Harry Peel. Northbridge.

A pleasant-faced young curate who became priest-in-charge at St. Sycorax when Canon Fewling left to go to Greshamsbury in 1952. In Northbridge's Coronation Pageant, he played Beckett, and made himself a clever tonsured wig using the hair of a red setter. WDIM, ADA

Hilda. *See* Plane, Hilda.

Hoare, Mr. Pomfret Towers.

Estate agent in the time of the 7th Earl of Pomfret. PT

Hoare, Mrs. Dowlah Cottage, Harefield.

Widow of the above. On the one hand, her family made almost unbearable demands on her, but on the other hand they died and left her things. Her house was full of furniture, paintings, and other legacies of which she was very proud. She died in 1951. H

Hobb, Mr. London.

Hermione Rivers' literary agent. PT

Miss Hobb. Marling Melicent.

Miss Hobb came to take care of the kennels at The Cedars in 1952, when Oliver and Maria Marling's baby was born. The dogs fawned around her legs, which were permanently encased in a kind of chauffeur's black hard leggings, so the arrangement was a success. HaRe

---

Hoggett, Giles. From Trollope.

> *In* The Last Chronicle of Barset, *Giles Hoggett is a Hogglestock bricklayer who gives good advice to the Reverend Josiah Crawley during the miserable affair of the stolen check.*

Hoggett, Miss. Hogglestock. The Old Bank House, Edgewood.

Sam Adams' hideous but faithful housekeeper. She adjusted well to the move to Edgewood, and to the addition of a wife and children to Mr. Adams' life. OBH, CC, DD, HaRe TST

Hoggett, Frank. Framley.

Brother of Miss Hoggett, and Mr. Macfadyen's second-in-command at Amalgamated Vedge Ltd. DD

Hoggett, Grace. Hogglestock.

The nurse hired by Heather and Ted Pilward for their baby in 1949. Grace was the niece of Frank Hoggett. DD

Holden. Rushwater.

Sexton at St. Mary's Church. WS

Holden, Lieutenant. The Rectory, Northbridge.

One of the youngish officers billeted on the Villars in 1940. It turned out that he was a cousin of one of Mr. Villars' assistant masters, when Mr. Villars had been a headmaster. Before the war Mr. Holden had worked for the publisher Adrian Coates. He was well educated, a student of history, with a somewhat more than sentimental attachment to Mrs. Villars. After the war he became a partner in the Coates firm. He married and had three children. NR, WDIM

Holinshead. Southbridge School, Southbridge.

A senior student desperate to get into the war in 1939. CBI

Holly, Cicely.   Hosiers' Girls' Foundation School, Harefield.
In 1943 Miss Holly was the very capable assistant to Madeleine Sparling, the school's headmistress, and was, incidentally, a first-class billiard player. She was roly-poly and brisk and had small black eyes—rather like the Plum Pudding Flea—but there was no nonsense about her. When Miss Sparling retired, Miss Holly became the headmistress.   H, MB, LAR, OBH

Holt, C.W.
In 1933, Mr. Holt was that poor creature, a social parasite. He lived by going from house to house, being obliging, and was both a bore and a snob. He knew Burke's *Peerage* and *Landed Gentry* by heart, but was none the better for it. In addition to other kinds of snobbery, he was a garden snob, and thus there was a mutual attraction between him and Lady Norton. He was one of the few people disliked by Lady Agnes Graham, whose father had described Mr. Holt, rather mildly, really, as an infernal bore. Among the Leslie young Mr. Holt was called a toad eater. In 1947, his books were sold by Sotheby's.   WS, (PE), (LAR), (ESR)

Hooper.   Brandon Abbey.
One of Miss Brandon's chauffeurs.   B

Hooper, Lieutenant.   The Rectory, Northbridge.
Another of the Villars' officers, a chap with very broad opinions. He left Northbridge to continue his service in Lambton, where he was conscientious but, though he had passed for a captain, he couldn't pass for a gentleman. He was admirable as an officer, irksome as a man.   NR, GU, (MB)

Hopgood, Miriam.   Glycerine Cottage, Cow End, Northbridge.
Miss Hopgood lived with Miss Crowder, her special friend, whom she called "La Petite" and to whom she was "Chère Amie." They were Francophiles who except in wartime spent part of every year in Mentone, on the Riviera. They took part in all the good works of the Northbridge community.   NR, PE, WDIM, ADA

Hopgood, Helen "Florrie".   The Milky Way, Northbridge.
Miss Hopgood's aunt. Mrs. Hopgood was the broad and tall widow of an astronomer who had discovered a new star, Porter Sidus, while working at the Matthews Porter Observatory in Texas. She too was interested in astronomy, in a serious amateur way, and in bird watching.   NR, PE, JC, WDIM, ADA

Hopkins, Mr.   Southbridge School, Southbridge.
A left-leaning science master who came to Southbridge in 1939 with the Hosiers' Boys' Foundation School when it was evacuated from London. He despised the milieu of the school as effete and unconscionable, and left at the end of the first term to take a position in Monmouth. In 1940 he was interned as a Fifth Columnist.   CBI, (PE)

Hopkins, Selina Allen Crockett.   Beliers Priory, Lambton.
A widow in her late 40's, the daughter of Nannie Allen. During the war she came to Beliers Priory as useful maid to Lady Waring. Selena had a sensitive nature, set off by dimples, lustrous eyes, and lots of curly hair wreathing her pretty face with quivering tendrils to a most beguiling effect. At the least provocation she would weep and her curls would tremble. Many men admired her, but she chose Sgt. Ted Hopkins as her next husband. They were wed in 1943, and remained at the Priory when it became a school, he as gardener and she as cook. When the school transferred to Harefield they went with it.
                                                    GU, LAR, DD, HaRe, JC, (CQ)

Hopkins, Ted. Beliers Priory, Lambton.   Harefield House School, Harefield.
In 1942 Sgt. Hopkins was at the convalescent hospital at Beliers Priory with an eye injury. He had served under Captain Colin Keith, who had been a great comfort to him when his wife had died. It was his good fortune, several months later, to win the heart of Selina Crockett. Before the war he had been in the vegetable trade and he and Selina, as cook and gardener, were the backbone of the staff of the Priory School, and moved with it when it became the Harefield House School.   **GU**, LAR, DD, JC, CQ

Hopper. Northbridge.
The less popular of Northbridge's two cobblers in 1939. He was for some reason a seeker of notoriety. There are people like that.   NR., WDIM

Hornby, Christopher.   Harefield.
Born in 1903, he was nephew and heir to old Mrs. Ellangowan–Hornby who had the lease of Arcot House in Harefield. In 1943, a Naval captain, he came to Harefield to make arrangements with the Beltons about the sub-lease. Captain Hornby was tall, dark-complexioned and quiet. His mother, who had died when he was a child of one year, had been related to Sir Robert Graham. While in Harefield he deepened his acquaintance with Elsa Belton. They were engaged, and married in 1944. They lived mostly on his family property near Aberdeathly, Scotland, where they raised their daughter, Catriona, and son, Freddy. By autumn 1944, Christopher was a Rear Admiral. He was knighted and made Admiral by 1951.   **H**, (MB), LAR, DD

Hornby, Elsa Belton.   Harefield, Aberdeathly, Scotland.
Second of the three children of Frederick Sr. and Lucy Belton, born around 1917. She was a graduate of Barchester High School, where she had been a particular chum of Octavia Crawley. As a young adult she was capable and handsome, though her face had a certain hardness; she was rather spoilt. During the war she worked at a hush-hush job at an undisclosed location, thought to be London, and often visited Harefield. She married Christopher Hornby in 1944 and moved with him to his family home in Scotland. They had two children, Catriona, born in 1945, and Freddy.   **H**, LAR, DD

Horniman, Miss. Lambton.
Sister of the vicar of Lambton, who died in 1942. Her niece, also a Miss Horniman, had been a mathematics mistress at Barchester High School.   GU

Horton. Mellings, Nutfield.
The Bartons' butler. He died in 1943.   PT, (H)

Horton, Dunstan.   The Vicarage, Southbridge.
The vicar at Southbridge, whose departure left the vacancy filled by Colonel Crofts. He was a tall, elderly, bony man, with ecclesiastical grizzled side-whiskers and rather stooped shoulders. Life was enlivened for him by continual bickering with his aunt, who was his junior by some years. He had left Southbridge to become Principal at St. Aella's Home for Stiff-necked Clergy.   PE, JC

Horton, Monica. Editha Cottage, Southbridge.
The younger aunt of Dunstan Horton. Like her nephew, she too was tall and gaunt, with a long face and bony ankles. The most interesting thing about her was that she was prescient, and saw color auras. Nobody seemed very impressed by this, however.   PE, JC

Hubback. Hatch End.
Maid of all work for the Hallidays. By 1945 she had been there for years and years.   PBO, ESR, NTL, ADA

Hubback, Mrs.   Hatch End.
Proprietor of The Shop, and a relative of Halliday's maid. She was 91 in 1956.   (PBO), (LAR), ESR, ADA

Hubback, Aggie.   Holdings, Little Misfit.
In 1954 Aggie was working on approval as a parlormaid. She was a great-niece of Mrs. Hubback at The Shop.   ESR

Hubback, Mr. and Mrs.
Proprietors of the Bridge Inn, located in a small village outside Barchester in 1947. The Hubback's interpretation of rules and regulations was markedly creative.   PE

Humble, Ellen.   Hosiers' Girls' Foundation School, Harefield.   The Vicarage, Harcourt.
In 1947, Ellen had been private body servant to Miss Holly, and in 1949, nurse to the twin daughters of Robin and Anne Dale. She became nanny to the infant Gwendolyn Sally Harcourt in 1958. Ellen was the niece of the Beltons' maid Wheeler, and of the shopkeeper in Harefield.   H, LAR, CC LAA

Humble, Faithful.   Hallbury.
Proprietor of a tobacco shop that also housed a small circulating library.   H

Humble, William.   Harefield.
The Beltons' cowman.   H, DD

Hunter, Mrs. Harefield.
A woman visiting Harefield and invited to a wartime work party. Her tactless remarks and failure to provide her own milk and sugar for her tea ensured that she would never be invited again.   H

Oh yes, my lady. Quite air-minded as they say Dorothy and Henry are. Quite little travelers. And over in America they say the baby food's lovely and I daresay the Americans will make quite a fuss of them.

— Ivy

Icken: Harefield House, Harefield.
According to Mr. Belton, the best estate carpenter in the county.   H

Ivy.
In 1933, Ivy was second nursemaid to the Graham children. She became nannie to the children of David and Rose Leslie in 1947.   WS, MH, (PBO), LAR

J

Jackson, Arthur Fishguard, Corporal. The Rectory, Northbridge.
Originally from Nutfield, Jackson was an electrician. During the war he was billeted at the Villars', where he had a room over the stables in which he kept several rabbits. While there he married Edie. They had no children.
NR, CQ

Jackson, Edie (Alice Edith Pover). Northbridge Rectory, Northbridge.
Edie was the Villars' half-witted kitchen maid during the war, rather a slave to Mrs. Chapman, the cook. Despite looking like the March hare, she was alluring to Corporal Jackson. They were married in 1944.
NR, CQ

Jenks, Private. Beliers Priory, Lambton.
The son of Lord Pomfret's head keeper, Tom Jenks, and the nephew of Mrs. Phipp's sister. Jenks is the soldier who shot Matron's cat while convalescing from appendicitis at Beliers Priory in 1942. While not shooting, he occupied himself with mending every bit of machinery on the place. By 1943 he was engaged to a girl in the Land Army.
GU, H

Jessie. Southbridge School, Southbridge.
For years she was a valued but hideous housemaid at the school. She ruined her eyesight by not wearing her spectacles—but that kept her from being called up during the war.
SH, CBI, GU, (PE), CC, CQ

John. Manor House, Worsted.
The Palmer's cowman.
AF

Johns & Fairfield. London.
A London publishing house that published Lord Pomfret's memoir, *A Landowner in Five Reigns* and the work of George Knox, Mrs. Rivers, Mrs. Barton, and Lisa Bedale. It also brought out Philip Winter's Latin grammar, Margot Phelps' pamphlet on goat care, and Mrs. Crofts' book of bird pictures, *Coot and Hern.* On occasion Johns & Fairfield would try to lure Laura Morland away from Adrian Coates.
(HR), (SH), (PT), (CBI), (MH), (PE), (LAR)

Johns, Mr. London.
Senior partner in the above firm, a stout, successful fellow. As the representative of Mrs. Rivers' publishers, he was often required to sustain trying little social episodes with her. He was Mr. Wickham's uncle, a very fortunate connection for Barsetshire writers and artists.
PT, (PE), LAR, (OBH), (CC)

Joram, William, Canon.   Barley Street, Barchester.   The Vinery, The Close, Barchester.
A former Colonial Bishop in Mngangaland, where he had great success.   He came to Barsetshire at the beginning of the war, doing locum work first at Little Misfit and later at Rushwater, where he oversaw the care of evacuees.   For a long time he had rooms with Mrs. Tompkins.   He held a canonry in Barchester in 1945 and moved to the Close as a resident Canon in 1948, taking the house that Canon Thorne had vacated. For years he was an admirer from afar of those local lovelies, Agnes Graham and Lavinia Brandon.   He and Mrs. Brandon were married in 1949.

CBI, MH, MB, PBO, PE, LAR, OBH, **CC**, DD, HaRe, WDIM, ADA, LAA, TST

Joram, Lavinia Oliver Brandon.   Stories, Pomfret Madrigal.   The Vinery, The Close, Barchester.
Born in 1894, by 1938 Mrs. Brandon had been for many years the widow of Henry Brandon.   She was delightfully hen-brained, or so it seemed.   With large near-sighted blue eyes, soft pale skin and gently waving hair, she was still lovely in early middle age—so much so that enamored men were one of the banes of her life.   But she was content to be single and live quietly.   During the war, she was rather surprisingly in charge of the local Land Girls, and her house was used as a nursery for a dozen or so evacuated infants.   She shared her home with Francis after he married, but this was not a success.   She married Canon Joram, whom she had met in the first winter of the war, in 1949.

B, CBI, (GU), PBO, **PE**, LAR, OBH, **CC**, DD, HaRe, WDIM, ADA, LAA, TST

I'm not much good at sewing myself, but I can cut out, which is more than most people have the sense to do. And if you want a needle and cotton, or pins, or anything, you'll find one in the basket on the table, unless Mrs. Gissing has taken them all.

— Lydia Keith

Keith family:

Keith, Henry. Northbridge Manor, Northbridge.
Successful solicitor from an undistinguished family of Barsetshire landowners, in partnership with his son Robert. They had offices in Barchester, and handled many of the affairs of the cathedral. In this they were carrying on a tradition of three generations. In the first months of the war, Mr. Keith was struck by a lorry in Barchester and killed. SH, B, CBI

Keith, Helen. Northbridge Manor, Northbridge.
A pleasant woman, the wife of Mr. Keith. She developed heart trouble at the beginning of the war, and went to stay with her daughter Kate Carter in Southbridge, going later to be with her sister in Bournemouth. She died there, apparently. At any rate she was never heard from again.
SH, B, CBI, (NR), (GU)

Keith, Colin. Northbridge Manor, Northbridge: London.
Colin was the Keiths' second child, born around 1913. In 1936, before studying law, he spent a term as junior classical master at Southbridge School. That autumn, following a reading holiday in Europe, he read law in the London chambers of Noel Merton and eventually became a barrister-at-law in the Inner Temple. His specialty was railway law. During the war he was a captain with the Territorials. After a long career as an eligible bachelor, he married Eleanor Grantly in 1950. They lived in London with their children. He was the author of *Keith's Commentaries upon Lemon on Running Powers,* better known as *Keith on Lemon,* published in 1947.
SH, CBI, GU, **PE**, LAR, **OBH**, (HaRe), WDIM

Keith, Edith Fairweather. Northwest of Barchester.
The older sister of Geoffrey and John Fairweather. She was a graduate of Barchester High School, where she had been Head Girl and one of Miss Pettinger's prime favorites and was thus very dull. She was married to Robert Keith; they had two children, Henry and Catherine. It was her connection with the Keiths that brought her brothers into the circle of the Birketts in the summer of 1936.
SH, (CBI), WDIM

Keith, Eleanor Grantly. The Vicarage, Edgewood. London.
Wife of Colin. She was the Grantlys' elder daughter, born in 1925. She had done a secretarial course after leaving school, and in 1948 was secretary to Susan Dean at the Red Cross Hospital Library in Barchester. After Susan's marriage, Eleanor became the Depot Librarian. She and Colin Keith were married in 1950 and lived in London. LAR, **OBH**, (HaRe), WDIM

Keith, Kate. *See* Carter, Kate.

Keith, Lydia. *See* Merton, Lydia.

Keith, Robert. Northwest of Barchester.
The eldest of the four Keith children. By the summer of 1936, he was married to the former Edith Fairweather and a junior partner in the family firm. After his father's death he managed the business successfully and established his home in Nutfield. By 1939 he and Edith were the parents of three children; Henry, born in 1931, Catherine, born in 1934, and an unnamed other child. SH, (CBI), (NR), OBH, CQ

Klobber, Mr. London.
A Viennese refugee who had established a tailoring business in London. He made clothing for the Deans, including Susan's Red Cross uniform. He broke his heart over the skirts which, owing to the hoydenish ways of English women who would put things in the pockets and sit down without pulling them up, were always baggy behind. PE

Knox, George. Low Rising Manor, Low Rising.
Great friend of Laura Morland, and her neighbor at High Rising. In 1903 he had taken a first in Greats, and by a pleasant twist of fate had been left independent by his wealthy father. He was the author of historical biographies, and was a vigorous talker. Tony Morland admired him for the generous tips he gave. Mr. Knox was a widower of 54 in 1933, when he married Anne Todd. It has been suggested that he was patterned on AT's friend, the author E. V. Lucas. **HR**, DH, MB, PE, DD, NTL, LAA, TST

Knox, Anne Todd. High Rising. Low Rising Manor, Low Rising.
Born in 1892, Anne spent her quiet life in the village of High Rising, as a dutiful daughter to a mother who became slightly mad in her old age. She was both friend and part-time secretary to Mrs. Morland. After her mother's death in 1933, she married George Knox as his second wife. It was thanks to her that Low Rising Manor was modernized. **HR**, DH, (GU), MB, LAA, TST

Knox, Sybil. *See* Coates, Sybil .

Knox, Mrs. London.
George Knox's old mother. She was French, and famous for ill-nature and senile crabbedness. HR

Koska, Madame. London.
A *couturière*, the heroine of all Mrs. Morland's thrillers, set in the treacherous world of high fashion. HR

Krogsbrog, Petrea. Sweden. *See* Tebben, Petrea.

*Do you know, Mother, the girls and I always
thought Grandpa had written the Bible.*
— Lord Lufton

Lefevre, Babs. *See* under Babs.

Lee. The Towers.
Lee, a half-gypsy whose mother had been a Margett, was employed as a useful man at the Towers. He had a variety of duties; sometimes he was a woodsman and sometimes he sold tickets to people wishing to tour the house.   LAA

Leslie family:

Leslie, Henry. Rushwater House, Rushwater. Holdings, Little Misfit.
A wealthy but untitled landowner. In early manhood he had been an active, tall, fresh-faced, heavy-built man. In 1933 he was the father of adult children, established in his country house and well on his way to becoming a curmudgeon. He was crusty; he objected to foreigners and education for women, and was outspoken in his other opinions. At the onset of the war his health declined rapidly and he and Lady Emily moved to Holdings, the home of their daughter Agnes Graham. He died there in 1945.   **WS**, (AF), (PT), (B), (BL), MH, (H)

Leslie, Lady Emily Foster. Rushwater House, Rushwater. Holdings, Little Misfit.
Daughter of the sixth Earl of Pomfret and sister of the seventh, Lady Emily was born in 1867, married in 1889, and came to Rushwater with her husband in 1897. Lady Emily had a charm that captivated everyone, a brilliant smile and beautiful dark, keen, loving hawk's eyes. She seemed to her family to be an iridescent, opal-changing, wind-blown rainbow fountain, a spirit of love, who saw only the best in anyone. They adored her; all of them were amused by her continual efforts at managing everything, her ongoing chaos of artistic whims, her conversational flights of fancy, the whirlwind of disorganized activity that surrounded her. She died at Holdings in 1948 and was sadly missed.   **WS**, (PT), (BL), MH, (GU), (H), (MB), PBO, LAR, OBH, (HaRe), (ESR)

The character of Lady Emily is considered to be based upon that of Mary Wyndham Charteris, Countess of Wemyss. Lady Wemyss and her parents, Percy and Madeleine Wyndham, were family friends of Edward Burne–Jones, AT's grandfather. The Wyndhams were the owners of Clouds, a Wiltshire country house, a favorite of the group known as the Souls. Mary, their daughter, lived with her husband Hugo Charteris, later Lord Elcho and still later Lord Wemyss, at Stanway in Gloucestershire. Lady Wemyss was the mother of seven children. One son died in childhood and two were killed in the First War; the eldest left a young heir. One of her daughters was Cynthia Asquith. Lady Wemyss had a very long and very close friendship with Arthur J. Balfour, and another briefer romantic interlude with Wilfrid Blunt, who had been her mother's lover many years before. Blunt was the father of one of Lady Wemyss' daughters. Lord Wemyss too had at least one child outside the marriage. These details form an interesting contrast to the virtuous nature of all the relationships in AT's novels. According to Margot Strickland, AT's biographer, Lady Wemyss was not disturbed by her portrayal, but some of the Charteris family took offense.

Leslie, Agnes.   *See* Graham, Lady Agnes.

Leslie, Clive (Minimus).
Third son of the John Leslies. He was named after a maternal uncle who had been killed in the 1914 war. Like the others, he was a Southbridge student, a quiet boy with the easy grace of the born athlete.   LAR, CC, JC, NTL, (ADA), CQ

Leslie, David.   London, Paris, New York.
Youngest of the children of Henry and Lady Emily, born in 1907. David was handsome, debonair, independently wealthy, and selfish. By 1933 he was the author of a novel, *Why Name,* and he tried out for a position with BBC but was not accepted, rather to his relief. He was then free to spend a year or so in Argentina looking after the family's beef interests. During the war he was a non-flying flight lieutenant; after the war he was in an unknown but charmingly lucrative business. David feared boredom of all things and was often assailed by a wish to be somewhere else and with someone else. Women of course adored him, and he did make occasional offers of marriage, but they seemed calculated to be wisely rejected. He seemed to avoid commitment, looking, as he said, for a woman who was funny as hell all the time. He left the proverbial trail of sadder but wiser hearts—until Rose Bingham, to whom he had occasionally proposed, decided in the summer of 1945 that the time had come. He and Rose led a nomadic life, but seemed by the 50's to spend most of their time in New York. Their two children, Dorothy and Henry, were named after grandparents.
                              WS, MH, (GU), (MB), **PBO,** LAR, OBH, ESR, ADA

Leslie, Eleanor.   Rushwater.
Eldest child of Martin and Sylvia Leslie, born in 1946. Eleanor got an early start as a social activist in 1960, when she took a leading part in trying to save Wiple Terrace.   LAR, OBH, TST

Leslie, Giles.
Eldest son of the Henry Leslies. He was killed at Arras in the First War, leaving a son and heir, Martin. His widow remarried and moved to the United States.   (WS), (LAR), (OBH)

Leslie, Henry (Major).
Eldest of the three sons of John and Mary Leslie. He attended Southbridge School, where his dullness was gradually recognized as a façade. He later went to Oxford and took a good First in 1957.   DA, PBO, (PE), LAR, CC, JC, ESR, NTL, ADA, CQ

Leslie, John.   London.   Rushwater House, Rushwater.   Old Rectory, Greshamsbury.
The Henry Leslies' second son, born in 1899. In the navy in the First War, John was left a widower when his wife Gay died shortly after the war; they had been married only one year. He was in business in London when he met Mary Preston during a visit to Rushwater in the summer of 1933; they were married later that year. During the war he and Mary and their children lived at Rushwater while John worked in Barchester as head of the Regional Commissioner's Office. After the war they moved to Greshamsbury and remained active in county affairs, although we are sorry to report that to younger people he and Mary seemed uncommonly dull.
                              WS, BL, MH, (PBO), LAR, OBH, CC, JC, NTL, ADA, CQ

Leslie, John (Minor).
Second son of John and Mary. As is the case with many second or third sons, he was blessed with charm which he was able to lay on in unnecessarily lavish quantities. He loved to climb trees and scale roofs and steeples. After leaving Southbridge School he entered Oxford on a scholarship. He was a member of the Oxford Alpine Club.   PBO, LAR, CC, JC, WDIM, ESR, ADA, NTL, CQ

Leslie, Martin. Rushwater House, Rushwater.

Born in 1916, son of Giles Leslie, and heir to the Rushwater estate. After his father's death he continued to live with his grandparents at Rushwater; his mother and stepfather lived in the United States. He attended Oxford, coming into his inheritance in 1945 when his grandfather died. During the war, he sustained a serious leg injury at Anzio, was awarded the George Medal, and finished the war in the War Office. Martin was not remarkably quick-witted, but of a very kind nature. In 1945 he married Sylvia Halliday and they made their home at Rushwater. Their children were Eleanor, George, and two others.   **WS**, (MH), (MB), **PBO**, LAR, OBH, DD, ADA, LAA, TST

Leslie, Mary Preston.   Rushwater House, Rushwater.   Old Rectory, Greshamsbury.

Daughter of Robert Graham's eldest sister, born in 1910. Her father had been killed in the 1914–18 war, and her mother was not well—or so it seemed. This accounted for Mary's being rather at loose ends when she was invited to Rushwater in the summer of 1933. She married John Leslie as his second wife later that year, and became the mother of three sons. The entire family, John, Mary, Henry, John Jr., and Clive, have been so often described as dull that we fear it might be true. But they have all been happy and led blameless lives.

WS, MH, (PBO), LAR, OBH, CC, JC, NTL, ADA, CQ

Leslie, Rose Bingham.   Paris. New York.

Lady Dorothy's other daughter, the twin of Hermione. Rose was in the Foreign Office during the war. Stunningly suave and attractive, tall, and with dark sleek hair, a seductive husky voice and enough charm to make her loved everywhere, she corralled David Leslie into a marriage in 1945 that was surprisingly happy. They had two children, Dorothy and Henry, born a year apart.

WS, PBO, (PE),LAR, WDIM, ESR, ADA

Leslie, Sylvia Halliday.   Hatch House, Hatch End.

Sylvia was the golden daughter of Leonard and Eleanor, and two years younger than her brother George. She had fair wavy hair, cornflower-blue eyes, long lovely legs, and an easy grace. She reminded some of the Winged Victory, a Viking, or an Amazon. She had hoped to be a dancer, not being at all bookish, but the war put an end to those ideas, and she served in the WAAF. On a visit to Rushwater House in 1945 she met Martin Leslie. They were married in September, 1945, and made a success of the farm at Rushwater. They had four children, of whom Eleanor was the eldest.

PBO, LAR, OBH, DD, ESR, NTL, ADA, TST

Lily. Gatherum Castle.

A cook who had been with the family of the Duke of Omnium since she was a girl. By 1949 she was elderly, dressed in black, with her gray hair strained back off her forehead, and wore steel-rimmed spectacles. She suffered from sciatica.   CC

Lorimer. Southbridge School, Southbridge.

Classics master during Colin Keith's short tenure at the school in the summer of 1936. Mr. Lorimer had the gait and appearance of a tortoise, and had an uncanny gift for forcing his pupils into scholarships. He kept extremely good sherry and port. He died in the summer of 1936.   SH, (PE)

Louisa. High Rising.

The maid of all work at the home of Mrs. Todd and Anne Todd, in 1932.   HR

Lufton family: *From Trollope.*

Lady Lufton was a well-to-do widow with a son, Ludovic. She lived at Framley Court.

Ludovic was her son. Lady Lufton had wanted him to marry Griselda Grantly, but he had fallen in love with **Lucy Robarts**, *the sister of his friend* **Mark Robarts**, *and, to cut out all the details, he married her. Mark and Lucy lived in Framley parsonage.*

Lufton family:

Lufton, Mary, Dowager Lady. Framley Court, Framley. Old Parsonage, Framley.
Born in 1889, Lady Lufton was the widow of one Lord Lufton and mother of another. She had sad and stormy eyes, a sensitive mouth, and an air of helplessness, for it was difficult for her to adjust to her husband's death and her new role as widow. The family was not well off, and she had had to let part of her house to Mr. Mcfadyen, the market gardener. However, she made this adjustment and many others with increasing grace and confidence. She was godmother to Ludovic, Lord Mellings.

(GU), DD, HaRe JC, CQ, TST

Lufton, Lady Grace. The Vicarage, Edgewood.
Wife of young Lord Lufton. The youngest Grantly, Grace was born in 1932. In 1949 she was a student at Barchester High School, and given to hanging on the arms of attractive men in a very irksome way. Once she had graduated she remained at home and commuted (dreadful word, but we have no choice) to a secretarial course in Barchester. Later she took a job at the Barchester Central Library. As a young adult she was pretty and quick on the uptake, entirely unpretentious, comfortable and fun to be with. In 1951 she became engaged to Ludovic, Lord Lufton. They lived at Franley Court and had several children.

OBH, **HaRe**, JC

Lufton, Justinia. *See* Swan, Justinia.

Lufton, Ludovic, Baron. Framley Court, Framley.
Born in 1923, Ludovic was the son and youngest child of Lady Lufton. Thinking to learn more about agriculture, he attended an agricultural college for a while in 1946 after his release from the army, and worked under Roddy Wicklow at Pomfret Towers. In 1950 he was a very tall young man who looked as if everything to do with life was a trial and anxiety to him. Although he appeared to be vague and shambling, he conscientiously learned the ropes of being a lord after his father's death. He tried to be sensitive to his mother's needs and when the House was sitting, he bravely lodged in London with their very parsimonious and unpleasant relative Juliana Starter, who took his ration book and then starved him. He was disarmingly ingenuous, with a truly kind nature. He married Grace Grantly in 1951 and they moved into Framley Court.

DD, HaRe

Lufton, Maria. *See* Marling, Maria.

I wonder why one always thinks other people will love things? I am sure if some of my friends heard I was going to hell they would say 'I am sure Laura will like it immensely and think of all the interesting people she will meet.' But really, I daresay one would find friends. I have found people very nice on the whole, wherever I have been, except, of course, for the really horrible ones.

— Laura Morland

M., Miss. *See* Mowbray, Miss.

Macfadyen, Donald. Framley Court, Framley.
A native of Fife, born around 1900, who rose from a working class family to become a great success as a market gardener; he was president of Amalgamated Vedge. A pleasant and sympathetic man, Mr. Macfadyen had a good forehead and lines of work and purpose in his face. It was his good fortune to win the love of Margot Phelps, whom he married in 1952. The marriage was happy but short, for Mr. Macfadyen died in 1957. **JC**, HaRe, (CQ)

Macfadyen, Margot Phelps. *See* Fewling, Margot.

Macpherson, Mr. Rushwater House, Rushwater.
Scottish agent who came to Rushwater in 1896, the same year that Lady Emily arrived as the bride of Henry Leslie. He loved Lady Emily and served the Leslie family for fifty-four years, until his death in 1950.
(MH), LAR, OBH, DD

Macpherson, Miss. Marling Melicent.
Matron of the cottage hospital. LAR

Mallow, Mr. High Rising.
The station master at Stoke Dry. (DH), TST

Mallow, Mrs. High Rising.
Dr. Ford's worthy housekeeper, and aunt both of Mr. Knox's Annie and of Mr. Mallow at the station.
HR, (DH), TST

Mallow. Skeynes Agnes.
John Middleton's cowman. He was the cousin of Mr. Mallow, the stationmaster at Stoke Dry, and thought to be the best cowman in the county. BL

Manners. Southbridge School, Southbridge.

Son of a greengrocer and furniture remover on the Isle of Dogs, Manners was considered to be one of the nicest of the London schoolboys evacuated to Southbridge School during the early years of the war. He was kept on at Southbridge when the rest of his school returned to London, and won a scholarship in history to Lazarus College, Oxford. He became a professor at Upping College.   CBI, NTL

March, Dr. Marling Melicent.

A neighbor of the Harveys when they lived at the Red House in 1941.   MH

Margett, Alf. Worsted.

Younger brother of Bert Margett. He worked in the village shop.   (AF), (GU)

Margett, Burt. Worsted.

A porter at the train station in the 30's. Shortly after the war he married Doris Phipps, and when Mr. Patten retired, Bert became station master.   AF, GU, (LAR)

Margett, Jasper. Beliers Priory, Lambton.

Keeper on the Waring estate, although he turned up at Pomfret Towers from time to time. The grandson of a half-gypsy witch and son of a known poacher, Jasper was vaguely sinister, a poacher, trapper, and source of forest lore. He was considered by some to be a Romany king. He was skilled at his job, adored Sir Harry, and was grieved at the demise of his craft as the big estates began falling under the load of death duties.
                                    GU, OBH, DD, LAA

Margett, "Old." Near Skeynes.

Old cottager who lived on Pooker's Piece.   BL, WDIM

Marigold. Lambton.

A maid employed by the Winters at the Priory School. She was the village problem girl whose very unoriginal ambition was to be a film star. Her entire being was modeled on Glamora Tudor, and she was abetted in this by having the kind of hair that stays where it is put, and a neutral skin on which she was able to perform cosmetic fantasies. Marigold's last name was Smith, if anyone is interested.   DD

Marlene. Holdings.

Kitchen maid and general utililty in 1949.   DD

Marling family:

Marling, William. Marling Hall, Marling Melicent.

A country squire, born in 1880. As a veteran of the Boer War, Mr. Marling was much respected in the community. Often he played the part of Ye Olde Country Squire to the fullest, speaking in jerky fragments of sentences and dropping his g's. His Aunt Lucy had been married to the old Duke of Omnium's youngest son. Both had been drowned on the *Titanic*, and he would regale his children with this stirring tale from time to time. Mr. Marling was very interested in county families. He was on several county committees and struggled to maintain his property and morale as he saw his world crumble and realized that he would have little to leave to his children. As time passed he became increasingly, but selectively, deaf.   **MH**, MB, LAR, **OBH**, **CC**, DD, HaRe

---

Marling, Amabel. Marling Hall, Marling Melicent.

Wife of William and daughter of Lord Nutfield. Though not beautiful, she had the good looks that come with breeding, and an intelligent, unselfish mind. In 1941 she was coping masterfully with her somewhat difficult husband and many local affairs. She combined self-confidence and insensitiveness with a capacity for taking pains and a tradition of service. Her approach to life was to pull everyone who entered the house into her orbit and to plan their activities regardless of their wishes. As times changed and her burdens grew heavy she was more reflective, but refused to let herself brood or give way to self-pity.　　　　　　　　　　　　　　　　　　　　　**MH**, OBH, **CC**, DD

Marling, Bill. Camberly.
The eldest of the four Marling Children. In Miss Bunting's opinion, Bill represented the ideal product of Barsetshire. He had been brought up by a nannie; he had been to the right preparatory school and the right public school. He was in the right regiment and was the husband of a very suitable wife and father of four very suitable children. In 1941 he had not yet been sent abroad; his wife, Dierdre, and their children were living with her parents in the north of England. After the war they lived at Camberly. Bill was a keen rider and was absorbed in local sporting events.　　MH, CC

Marling, Dierdre. Cambrerly.
Usually referred to as "Mrs. Bill," Dierdre was Bill's nice dull wife. She was a bishop's daughter and always knew what she ought to do, wherever she was. Her heart was kind and luckily she was so stupid in some ways that she was never embarrassed at all, and never guessed that her use of the most tiresome and outdated catchwords gave great pain.　　　　　　　　　　MH, CC

Marling, Lettice. *See* Watson, Lettice.

Marling, Lucy. *See* Adams, Lucy.

Marling, Maria Lufton. Framley Court, Framley. The Cedars, Marling Melicent.
Born in 1916, eldest child of Lord and Lady Lufton, and wife of Oliver Marling. In 1950 Maria was a typical county woman, tall, going slightly grey, with off-hand good looks and an athletic figure. Her great interests were the Young Conservatives and raising cocker-spaniels. She had an air of undamaged confidence in herself and the world, and had a quick, decisive mind. She and Oliver were married in 1950.　　　　　　　　　　　　　　　　　　　　　　DD, HaRe

---

Marling, Oliver. Marling Hall, Marling Melicent. London. The Cedars, Marling Melicent.
Born in 1914, Oliver suffered eye problems that began when he was a student at Eton. During the war he was exempt from military service because of his poor eyesight and severe headaches. He had been in business in London, but during the war was with the Regional Commissioner's Office in Barchester. After the war he returned to his London occupation but was often at Marling Hall, and was so long an eligible bachelor that the shine wore off his eligibility. He worked for several years on an opuscule about the life and work of Thomas Bohun. Tall and thin, Oliver was self-centered and was once referred to by Mr. Wickham as "a bit of cold fish," although he was anything but cold in his unrequited love for Jessica Dean. In 1950 Oliver married Maria Lufton. They lived at The Cedars on the Marling estate, the gift of Oliver's father. As Maria was not at all domestic, Oliver decorated the house with results so good that most people didn't know how good it was.
　　　　　　　　　　　　　　　　　　MH, PE, LAR, OBH, CC, DD, HaRe, TST

Masters. Hallbury.
A local farmer for whom Effie Bunce worked as a Land Girl in 1944.　　　　　　　　　　MB

Matron (Poppy Dudley). Southbridge School, Southbridge.

For many years, the capable and hard-working matron in Everard Carter's house. From time to time various boys, such as Featherstonehaugh, were in love with her. As it turned out, she and Sister Chiffinch had been probationers together at Knight's.   SH, (CBI), GU, PE, NTL, CQ

Matron. Beliers Priory, Lambton.

A veteran of the first war, Matron was in charge of the convalescent center at the Priory during the second war.   GU

McBean. Southbridge School, Southbridge.

Head gardener, 1940.   CBI

Mellings, Viscount (Ludovic Neville Eustace Guido Foster). Pomfret Towers.

Eldest of the Lord and Lady Pomfrets three children, born in 1939 and heir to the title. Ludo was named for Lord Lufton; Lady Lufton was his godmother. Like his father, he too was quiet, thin, shy, and sensitive, and he quickly grew quite tall. To everyone's surprise, including his own, it happened that he could sing well. From his prep school he went to Sandhurst and from there to the Brigade of Guards. As a young adult he was charming, conscientious, and courteous. He became engaged to Lavinia Merton in 1960; they planned to marry at Easter, 1961.   (BL), MH, H, (MB), OBH, PE, **WDIM**, ESR, NTL, ADA, **LAA**, TST

Merriman, Dorothea. *See* Choyce, Dorothea.

Merrivale, Mrs. Valimere, Hallbury.

Owner of the house in which Heather Adams lodged in the summer of 1944 while being tutored by Miss Holly. Mrs. Merivale was a widow and mother of four daughters—Elsie, Peggy, Evie, and Annie—all away on various war duties.   MB

Merton family:

Merton, Noel. London. Northbridge Manor, Northbridge.

Noel was born in 1903 into a family of good provincial legal stock; he was the son of a Barchester solicitor. He had grown up in London, but was well-acquainted in Barsetshire, where, as a London barrister, he was known as a rising young man with pleasant manners. Tall and elegant, and an accomplished flirt, he preferred to amuse himself with charming married women. He became friendly with Lydia Keith in 1936, and for her sake gave up his plan to be a permanent uncle; they were married while he was on a three days' leave in May, 1940. He returned to active duty just in time to take part in the evacuation of Dunkirk. Noel spent his remaining years of service in Intelligence. After the war he returned to his chambers in the Inner Temple, but was in Barsetshire on weekends. He and Lydia had three children. He became a KC in 1946 and was knighted in 1953.

SH, B, **CBI**, **GU**, PE, OBH, CC, HaRe, **WDIM**, CQ, **LAA**, TST

Merton, Lydia Keith. Northbridge Manor, Northbridge.

Lydia, born in 1918, was the youngest of the Keith children. As a student at Barchester High School for Girls she was a bit overflowing—in fact, a loud-voiced amazon—but lovable, and though somewhat rebellious, a passionate student of history and literature. After graduation she spent a year in Paris and returned a bit more sedate, although still outspoken and capable of wrenching handshakes. In appearance she was tall, dark-haired, and good looking, with a kind and understanding expression. At the outbreak of the war, she devoted herself to the care of her parents and the property, and still found time for numerous war activities. Her indiscriminate good nature became more sober, and her views were shaped by her conversations with Noel Merton. They were married in May, 1940. She was a VAD for some of the time during the war, and also did a stint in the Land Army. She and Noel had three children, Lavinia, Harry, and Jessica. They were able to buy

Northbridge Manor from Robert Keith near the end of the war, and made it their home, although they had a flat in London as well. Lydia and Noel remained happy and important citizens of Barsetshire. Lydia is considered by some to be almost as much a representation of AT as is Mrs. Morland. **SH**, B, **CBI**, **GU**, (H), (MB), **PE**, OBH, CC, HaRe, **WDIM**, CQ, NTL, **LAA**, TST

Merton, Lavinia. Northbridge Manor, Northbridge.
Eldest child of Noel and Lydia, born in 1943. She was brash and outgoing, with dark shining hair and kind eyes. She loved to play the piano. In 1960 she spent six months in France with the family of Pierre Boulle, returning to pick up her friendship with Ludo, Lord Mellings. They were engaged in the autumn of that year and planned to marry at Easter, 1961.
PE, H, (MB), OBH, WDIM, **LAA**, **TST**

Merton, Harry. Northbridge Manor, Northbridge.
Second child of Noel and Lydia, born in 1946. He planned to go to Cambridge when last heard from. HaRe, WDIM, LAA

Merton, Jessica. Northbridge Manor, Northbridge.
Youngest child of Noel and Lydia, born in 1948. She was to be a bridesmaid at the wedding of Lavinia and Ludo in 1961. (HaRe), WDIM, LAA, TST

Middleton, John. Laverings, Skeynes.
A London architect who took up the role of gentleman farmer when he rented the Laverings property from Lord Bond in the early 30's. He was irascible, egocentric, and verbose—a bit of a windbag, according to Lord Stoke, and we think anyone would agree, except that it was more than a bit. He was the brother of Lilian Stonor and, not that there is any connection, raised Norfolk Nobblers. **BL**, (MH), (GU), MB, LAR

Middleton, Catherine. Laverings, Skeynes.
Wife of John, fifteen years his junior. She was patient and loving to her essentially unlovable husband. She was sensible in practical matters, but often lonely and somewhat saddened by her own strength. She longed for a shoulder to lean upon, but did not avail herself of one when it appeared, although she occasionally had the faraway look of someone hearing secret harmonies. She was content to be needed. **BL**, MB, LAR

Miller, Justin. The Vicarage, Pomfret Madrigal. The Parsonage, Ullathorne.
Mr. Miller had served as a chaplain during the First War, and by 1938 was vicar in Pomfret Madrigal. An educated man, he now and then took in a student to coach in the classics. He was of a definitely High tendency in his church, and very popular with his parishioners. He married Ella Morris, a lost love of his youth, in 1938. In 1951 he transferred to St. Ewold's in Ullathorne, and was replaced by Mr. Parkinson.
B, CBI, GU, PE, LAR, CC, HaRe, ADA

Miller, Ella Morris. The Vicarage, Pomfret Madrigal. The Parsonage, Ullathorne.
Miss Morris was descended from a long line of vicarage ancestors. The thoughtlessness of her vicar father had made it necessary for her, upon his death, to take semi-menial positions as paid companion to elderly ladies, and she endured many years of bleakness. As the long-suffering companion of Miss Brandon, Miss Morris in 1939 was tired-looking and worn. Therefore, it was the happiest of days when she and Mr. Miller were reunited and later married. She became the perfect vicar's wife. **B**, CBI, PE, CC, HaRe, ADA

The Chief and Prince of Mngangaland. Ease Africa.
The Chief was head of Mngangaland when Mr. Joram served there as Colonial Bishop in the 30's. Mr Joram kept up with the Chief when he returned to England, and took special interest in the career of the Chief's eightieth son. The Prince took a third in P.P.E., *q.v.*, at Lazarus College, Oxford, read a bit of law, and then returned home and conducted a ritual slaughter of most of his relations, to the tune of the Eton Boating Song

accompanied by native drums. He proclaimed himself Chief and declared Mngangaland a Republic. He was automatically elected President, and his knowledge of P.P.E. came in handy. Every year he sent Mr. Joram a Christmas card. Neither the Chief nor the Prince appears in the action of any novel; we learn about them from Mr. Joram's interesting reminiscences.

Morgan, Dr. Harefield.

A woman who caused suspicion and derision by attempting to use her ideas of psychoanalysis on her patients. Apart from having a face like a marmoset, she was insignificant in appearance and uncertain in temper. Dr. Morgan spent a good deal of her earnings on clothes, mostly unsuitable to her particular type of dowdiness and profession. After she left Harefield she went to work for the Ministry of Nutritional Hygiene.

H, DD, HaRe

Morland, Laura. High Rising. London.

Author of the happily very successful Madame Koska series of detective thrillers. About their literary value she had no illusions, calling them "good bad books" and being quite content with them and with her increasing fame as their author. Born in 1897, she married early and had become the mother of Gerald, John, Dick and Tony, when a stroke of rather good fortune left her a widow in the late 20's. She began writing and by 1932 she was successful enough to provide Tony with an education at Southbridge School, maintain a flat in London and a cottage in High Rising, employ a full-time cook-housekeeper, run a small car, and include a fur coat in her wardrobe. Although vague and wandering in conversation—in fact referred to as a "heavenly fool" and other such affectionate epithets—she was popular with her many friends. Most readers take her for the alter ego of AT. Mrs. Morland was known to say that her books were all alike, and to admit that she couldn't tell them apart herself, and was always getting them mixed up. She led a very active life, turning up at every event and invited frequently for tea, to dine, or perhaps to speak to some more or less suitable group. She in her turn was a gracious hostess. Although she was not county and never pretended to be, the county would have been dimmer and poorer without her.   HR,DH,(AF),(PT),B, CBI, (NR), MH, GU, MB, PBO, PE, LAR, OBH, CC, DD, HaRe, JC, **ESR**, **NTL**, ADA, LAA, **TST**

Morland, Henry (deceased).

Mrs. Morland's unlamented husband was described by those who had known him, such as George Knox's mother, in various unflattering ways—as, for instance, a suet pudding. She herself said of him, "He was quite easy to get on with, and then he died." It is true, however, that he had been a drain on his wife's finances, and it was much more convenient altogether when a kind fate removed him in the most acceptable way several years before the series begins.

Morland, Robin.

Tony Morland's eldest son, born in 1949. He was a jolly and enterprising little boy, very like his father at the same age.

TST

Morland, Tony. Southbridge School. High Rising. London.

Mrs. Morland's youngest son. Born in 1920, he was by age twelve an irrepressible talker, and obsessed with trains. He was a boarder at Southbridge School, attended Paul's College, Oxford, on a scholarship, and served in the tank corps in the war. After being demobilized he worked in the Office of Red Tape and Sealing Wax in London, where he lived with his wife and three children.

HR, DH, (AF), **SH**, B, CBI, GU, NTL, TST

Morple, Bill. Winter Overcotes.

At the beginning of the war, Bill was a porter at the Winter Overcotes station. He had a permanent set of grievances and leftist leanings, convinced on no evidence at all that everything was better in Russia. He went into the army early in 1943. While there, certain of his skills were an asset to covert operations, but after the war, using the same skills, he fell in with a bad lot and in 1947 was serving a long prison term for robbery and assault.   MH, GU, (LAR), (OBH)

Morris, Ella. *See* Miller, Ella.

Mowbray, Miss (Miss M.). London.
Miss M. was the daughter of a doctor in the East Riding of Yorkshire. She asked no more of life than to stand between Jessica Dean and the world in every possible way. It was one of those delightful quirks of fate that she was a first class cook.   CC, WDIM, TST

Moxon, Mr. Worsted.
Mr. Thomas' curate, he was a breezy young man with a great belief in words, especially his own. A scoutmaster, he was devoted to Boys in the abstract. At the least opportunity he very tiresomely extolled his belief in fellowship. To everyone's relief he left Worsted late in 1935 to accept a curacy at Clacton-on-Sea.
AF, (GU)

*You show me a man as is in Parliament
and I'll show you a liar.*

— Mr. Nandy

Nannie. *See* Ivy.

Nandy, Henry.   Marling Melicent.
Ancient nihilistic pensioner whose face was seamed with the dirt and wrinkles of a long disgraceful life. Mr. Sandy had a Newgate frill, *q.v.* He drank whenever he could and smoked a very nasty pipe all day long, and lived in one stinking room. He was rumored to be rolling in money, but was in fact living on a pension that had been provided by Mr. Marling's father—and thus by Mr. Marling.   MH, LAR, OBH, (WDIM)

Needham, Tommy.   Cathedral Close, Barchester.   The Vicarage, Lambton.
In 1939 Tommy was a young cleric, a graduate of Oxford and secretary to Dean Crawley. He had a pink and cheerful face, fair hair, and no particular ability. Before entering the army as a chaplain, Tommy became engaged to Octavia Crawley. He served in Iceland for a time, and then was transferred to North Africa, where in 1942 he was injured in battle and lost an arm. When Sir Harry Waring offered him the living at Lambton, he accepted on the spot and immediately made plans to marry. Tommy and Octavia had eight children.   **CBI**, (MH), **GU**, (PBO), LAR, HaRe TST

Needham, Octavia Crawley.   The Deanery, The Close, Barchester.   The Vicarage, Lambton.
The Crawley's eighth and youngest and dullest child. Octavia and Lydia Merton attended Barchester High School together and remained good friends over the years. A plain and uninteresting girl with a dull but self-satisfied face, Octavia was not her best in blue or indeed in any other color. During the war she worked as a nurse, and married Tommy Needham in 1943. As Octavia was competent and responsible to the highest degree and was a tireless worker, she was a wonderful vicar's wife, likely to land Tommy a Bishopric. Indeed, as she grew older she bore an increasing likeness to the wife of the Bishop of Barchester in dress and manner. In the late 1950's she was bringing up her many children to be cheerful and self-reliant citizens of the Brave New World.   MH, **CBI**, **GU**, (H), (MB), PBO, PE, LAR, HaRe, ADA, LAA, (TST)

Norton family:

Norton, Lady Victoria.   Norton Hall.
Lord George Norton, an ex-Governor, had been made a peer by Lloyd George. After his death in 1936, Lady Norton was known as "The Dreadful Dowager" except within her family, where she was called "Moggs." She had been a Lady in Waiting to Queen Alexandra and was impervious to every kind of discomfort. She had a face like a cab horse and was almost more tedious than humanly possible. Her passion was gardening, and she was author of a horrid little anthology about gardens called *Herbs of Grace,* and another irritating booklet, *Along My Borders,* both published by a vanity press. Lady Norton had been introduced to the Leslies by Mr. Horton. She was a cousin of William Marling. In her later dowager years she had a private suite in a very comfortable hotel in Cheltenham.   WS, B, (MH), (H), PE, (LAR), OBH, CC, DD, CQ

Norton, Lord George. Norton Hall.
The son of Lord and Lady Norton. He had been at school with Oliver Marling. He was nearly as insufferable as his mother—a pompous ass, according to Sam Adams. Nonetheless, young Lord Norton was on some of Mr. Adams' boards.   MM, DD

Norton, Lady Eleanor. Norton Hall.
The most human of the Nortons, young Lady Norton took over the Red Cross Hospital Library in the autumn of 1948 when lady Pomfret resigned. Eleanor was a cousin of Geoffrey and Frances Harvey, which is why the Harveys lived for a few months at Norton Park in 1941, and returned for occasional visits.   (MH), PE, DD

Nurse Peters. *See* Peters, Nurse.

Nurse (Miss Vance). Stories, Pomfret Madrigal. Beliers Priory.
A major force to be reckoned with at the Brandons'. Originally, she was the nurse of Francis and Delia, but after they grew up, Nurse remained in the household, doing all the sewing and mending and looking after the linen—and after Mrs. Brandon. Nurse had a running feud with Rose, which kept an undercurrent of tension going, although it was nice, in a way, because each tried to serve Mrs. Brandon better than the other. She remained with the house when Mrs. Brandon, by now Mrs. Joram, moved to The Vinery, and took care of the three children of Francis and Peggy Brandon. In 1952 Nurse was more than usually the cause of friction in the household, and Lady Cora Waring saved the day by persuading her to go to the Priory and take care of the nursery there. Later Nurse Vance organized a sort of Small Child Hotel in a seaside town where parents could send children for a supervised vacation.   **B**, PE, CC, HaRe

You know, or you will know when you are older, that when you lose money, or don't get the money you had hoped to get, the best way to comfort yourself is to spend some.
—The Duke of Omnium

Odeena. *See* Panter, Odeena.

Omnium. *From Trollope.*
*The old **Duke of Omnium** was the uncle of Plantaganet Palliser; he was a man of vast wealth.*
Plantaganet Palliser, *known as Planty Pal among his intimates, was his heir, a somewhat stuffy but worthy man who fulfilled his duties fully and honorably when he himself became Duke of Omnium.*
The Duchess of Omnium, Glencora Palliser, *was the wife of Plantaganet, a spirited and beautiful woman.*

Omnium, Duke of.   Gatherum Castle, West Barsetshire.
The Duke, whose name was Plantaganet Palliser, was the descendant of the most famous member of the family, Trollope's Plantagenet Palliser. The Duke was a veteran of the First War. By the late 1940's the family, struggling to maintain Gatherum Castle, was living in the servant's quarters. The Duke was a tall, middle-aged man with a drooping moustache and a gentle, bewildered manner; one thinks of the White Knight. He seemed kind but rather vague, and passed the evenings weeding the borders.
(MH), (MB), (PBO), (PE), **CC**, DD

Omnium, Louise, Countess of.   Gatherum Castle, West Barsetshire.
The Duke's wife, and mother of Glencora, Jeffrey, and Gerald (deceased). She kept a Grade A dairy herd and belonged to the Friends of Barchester Cathedral Embroidery Guild.   (MH), **CC**, DD

Oriel, Caleb. *From Trollope.*
Rector at Greshamsbury, handsome and well-bred enough to marry Frank Gresham's sister Beatrice.

Oriel, Caleb.   The Vicarage, Harefield.
A descendant of the above. It seems he was born in 1873, but we cannot be too rigid about that, for mutability is in operation here. He attended Balliol College. In 1943 he was seventy, fine-boned and silver-haired, with a large and flexible Adam's apple which fascinated the rash beholder's eye, but he had been considered a handsome man in his youth. As Mr. Carton said of him, he was drying up nicely. He had been the vicar at Greshamsbury before moving to Harefield. Apparently he had never wished to marry until, in 1958, he summoned the courage to intimate his feelings to Lady Gwendolyn Harcourt; she led him down the path to all the right sentences so that a proposal was accomplished. He was at that time working on a study of the General Epistle of St. Jude.
H, LAR, OBH, CQ, LAA

Packer.
Owner of Packer's Universal Royal Derby, the roundabout that was a feature of all the local fêtes.

B, LAR, (CC), TST

Packer. Hallbury.
Owner and driver of a taxi.

MB

Palfrey. Laverings, Skeynes.
Lilian Stonor's maid, in 1938.

BL

Pallisers. *From Trollope.* See *Omnium.*

Palliser family:

Palliser, Admiral. Hallbury House, Hallbury.
A widower, Admiral Palliser was the father of Jane Gresham, who lived with him during the war, and another daughter and two sons, all adult and living away from Barsetshire. He was a distant connection of the Duke of Omnium. During the war he was on the board of a large engineering works and was treasurer of the Barsetshire branch of the Soldiers' and Sailors' Families Association.

MB, LAR

Palliser, Lady Arabella. A daughter of the family, mentioned in *Miss Bunting* and never again.

Palliser, Lady Glencora. *See* Waring, Lady Cora.

Paliser, Lady Griselda. Another ephemeral daughter of the family, mentioned in *Marling Hall* and never again.

Palliser, Jeffrey. *See* **Silverbridge.**

Palmer, Fred and Louise. The Manor House, Worsted.
One of the landed gentry, Mr. Palmer was the brother of Rachel Dean. He was considered a good landlord and owned a fine herd of cows. Mrs. Palmer, very much the female squire, took her duties seriously but tempered her authority with generosity and kindness. As the hectoring producer of unsuitable plays she used casts cobbled together from local volunteers of dubious talent. As Mr. and Mrs. Palmer had no children, Laurence Dean was their heir.

AF, BL, (GU), (LAR)

Palmer. Northbridge Manor, Northbridge.
The Keiths' unpleasant parlormaid in the 30's. She remained with the house when the Mertons settled there after the war, and was still there in 1953.

SH, CBI, PE, WDIM, LAA, TST

Panter family:

Panter, George.   #6, Clarence Cottages, Hatch End.
Mr. Halliday's carter. In the First War he had lost an arm in the Ypres salient, but by 1945 could handle horses as well as any man in the neighborhood.   PBO, ESR, NTL, ADA, TST

Panter, Mrs. #6, Clarence Cottages, Hatch End.
Wife of George. She did her ironing just inside her front door, and thus knew everything about what was happening in Hatch End. She did laundry for Lord Stoke, the Richard Carters, and others of the local gentry.   PBO, (LAR), NTL, ADA

Panter, Fred.   Marling Melicent.
He made the coffin for Job Harrison's infant in 1941.   MH, (ESR)

Panter, Geo.   Hatch End.
Cousin of the above, proprietor of the Mellings Arms. It was sometimes believed that the place acted as a clearing house for poachers.   PBO, HaRe, ADA

Panter, Jimmy.   Hatch End.
Son of George the carter and grandson of Mrs. Hubback at The Shop.   PBO, ESR

Panter, Odeena.   Holdings, Little Misfit.
Daughter of George the carter and Mrs. Panter, and named after the Barchester Odeon. She was a maid at the Grahams' in the 1950's.   ESR, NTL, ADA

Pardon, Mrs. Marling Hall.
Wife of the gardener. She obliged in the house in 1950.   CC, DD

Parfitt. Holdings, Little Misfit.
The Grahams' butler in the 1930's and 1940's.   MH

Parkinson, Theodore.   The Vicarage, Pomfret Madrigal. The Vicarage, Greshamsbury.
In 1946, Mr. Parkinson was a weedy, pale young curate with no background and a poor education; he barely succeeded in becoming ordained. He assumed the living at Pomfret Madrigal, transferring later to New Town, Greshamsbury. He was another of the New Men, of a working class family, educated first at a Theological School and later by his own continuing efforts. He was decent and hard-working, with a thin, lined face. He won, sometimes grudgingly, the affections of those who knew him. PE, **CC**, **HaRe**, **CQ**, LAA

Parkinson, Mavis Welk.   The Vicarage, Pomfret Madrigal; The Vicarage, Greshamsbury.
An undertaker's daughter, Mavis was pretty, with an air of authority. She was capable and affectionate, and so shiningly and unselfconsciously good that any man would have been the better for her company. It was at least partially due to her help that her husband made such a success in his work. She was capable of any sacrifice and was a hard-working mother to their three children, Harold, Connie, and Josiah.
(PE), **CC**, **HaRe**, **CQ**, LAA

Parry, Mr. Barchester.
Head librarian at the Barchester Central Library.   HaRe, JC

Passmore, Colonel.   The Rectory, Northbridge.
One of the officers billeted on the Villars' in 1940. He was a veteran of the 1914–1918 war, and in peace time was a solicitor.   NR

Patten. Worsted.
Second gardener at the Manor House. AF

Patten, Mr. Worsted.
Station master in 1935. AF

Pattern, Mr. Hallbury.
Surviving partner of Pattern & Son, local developers and builders, in the 1940's. MB

Paxon, "Minnie." Northbridge.
A youngish matron for whom the war was her shining hour. She was involved in every conceivable useful activity and thus had many uniforms. She was flirtatious and a frequent laugher—thus the nickname "Minnie Ha-Ha." She had large violet eyes and a snappy personality. **NR**, WDIM

Paxon, Mr. Northbridge.
Husband of Minnie. He managed a bank in Barchester during the day and at other times patiently endured the multiple inconveniences of his wife's ardent wartime duties. NR

Pemberton, Ianthe. Punshions, Northbridge.
A literary woman, a scholar, and thereby one of Northbridge's crowning glories. Well into middle age by 1940, she had never been a beauty, and certainly was not then. Stodgy, with the face of a depraved cardinal, she suffered from complete absence of charm, yet she could on occasion summon a certain toad-like dignity. She dressed in homespun sacking and stout boots. She had a lodger, Mr. Downing, over whom she exercised a grim control. The fare was meagre and the temperature low, but she offered high and reasoned thinking. Miss Pemberton gave Mr. Downing her tireless editorial assistance with his *Biographical Dictionary of Provence.* In return she wanted his unwavering fidelity to her wishes. To do her justice, she was capable of generosity, and tried to be fair when she realized it was the right thing to do. She was an authority on the Langue d'Oc, secretary of the English Word-Lover's Association, and author of a biography of the queen of Edward IV. Despite her very straitened circumstances, she was an excellent cook and in 1941 wrote a successful cookery book. She died in 1955. **NR**, JC, **WDIM**

Perry family:

Perry, Mr. Plassey House, Harefield.
A stout, jovial little man, he and his father before him had been doctors in Harefield. They had been the family physicians of the Beltons, and the two families had traditionally been friends. The Perrys were the parents of three sons, who all became doctors. **H**, LAR, DD, HaRe, CQ

Perry, Maud. Plassey House, Harefield.
Wife of Mr. Perry. She was given to enthusiasms and causes in a very tiresome way. During the war she was active on many fronts, and especially championed the cause of the Myxo-Lydians. **H**, DD, HaRe, CQ

Perry, Augustus (Gus). Harefield.
The twin of James, distinguished in adulthood by his bushy eyebrows. Although his first love was skin afflictions, he settled down as Harefield's general practitioner and seemed destined to take the place of Dr. Ford in the county's trust and affection. H, (LAR), DD, HaRe, CQ, LAA

Perry, James. London.
Younger than his brother Gus by fifteen minutes, James was a surgeon at Knights. He was distinguished from his twin brother by his long nose. H, (LAR), HaRe, LAA

Perry, The Honourable Mrs. Bob. London.
Wife of Robert and the daughter of a titled Harley Street consultant. She dressed with expensive simplicity, her hair, legs, hands, stockings, and shoes all of a striking correctness worth a thousand a year to any husband. Her too, too kind condescension made Robert's parents think they had lost their son forever.   HaRe

---

Perry, Robert. London.
Eldest and rather starchy son of the Perrys. Thanks to the skilled pushing and string-pulling of his wife, he became a successful Harley Street consultant.   H, (LAR), DD, HaRe, LAA

Peters. Pomfret Towers. Crosse Hall.
Butler at Pomfret Towers in 1937. After leaving the Towers he went into service with Lord Crosse, and was there in 1954 when Edith Graham began visiting at Crosse Hall. After his move to Crosse Hall Peters had married a very nice-looking woman who worked there every day.   PT, ESR, ADA, NTL

Peters, Nannie. Pomfret Towers.
Also known as Nurse, Nursie, or Nanny, Nannie Peters had come to Pomfret Towers as a young woman to take Ludovic from the month in 1939, and there she had stayed ever since, partly because no one had the heart to send her away. Lavinia Merton solved that problem by asking her to come into the new home she and Ludo planned to establish. Nurse Peters was the sister of Peters, the butler.   OBH, LAA, WDIM, TST

Pettinger, Bertha. Barchester.
Headmistress of Barchester High School. She was renowned for her keen status-consciousness, her insufferable ignorance and insolence, her mincings and amblings, and painted coconut-like face—also for her thin, mean hospitality. She had been hostess to Madeleine Sparling when the Hosiers' Girls' School was evacuated to Barchester in 1939; it was an experience that haunted Miss Sparling's thoughts for years afterward. Not surprisingly, Miss Pettinger was one of the few friends of the Bishop's wife, and as such was considered no better than an agent of the palace. To the horror of many of her ex-pupils, she was awarded an OBE in 1944. When not actively on duty at the school Miss Pettinger felt that she was almost as others, though better educated and more important.   SH, CBI, H, MB, PBO, (PE), (DD)

Phelps family:
Phelps, Admiral. Jutland Cottage, Southbridge.
In 1939, Admiral Phelps was a small, spare, dry-faced man, a retired Rear Admiral. He lived with his wife and daughter on a small property in Southbridge. While his health permitted he was active in local affairs, and the door was always open to any visiting Navy man. Whether Navy or not, visitors would be regaled with the story of the Battle of Jutland, during which Admiral Phelps had had his most glorious hour. His health slowly deteriorated after the war, and he died in 1957, shortly after the death of his wife. The Phelpses had a son who had died before their daughter Margot was born.   CBI, GU, PE, **JC, CQ**

Phelps, Mrs. Jutland Cottage, Southbridge.
A great, bouncing, masterful woman who, as an admiral's wife, had lived in all sorts of unlikely places and was equal to anything. During the war she focussed her energetic enthusiasm on the Southbridge ARP and the Red Cross; she and Margot started the cottage hospital for the evacuee children and ran a canteen for their parents. She wore trousers that were quite unflattering. After the war, as her husband's health declined, Mrs. Phelps began to dwindle as well, and to rely more and more on Margot. After Margot married, Mrs. Phelps seemed rejuvenated for a while, but then collapsed and died of a heart attack in 1957.   CBI, GU, PE, **JC, CQ**

Phelps, Margot. *See* Fewling, Margot.

Phipps family:

Phipps, Mrs.   Worsted.
In 1935, Mrs. Phippps was the Tebbens' none too talented cook.   During the war she worked Tuesdays and Fridays at Beliers Priory.   AF, GU, (LAR)

Phipps, Mr.   Worsted.
Husband of the above. He was the Tebbens' gardener and odd job man, and had been the local sexton since 1902.   AF

Phipps, Ernie.   Worsted.
Son of the Phipps.   AF

Phipps, Doris.   Worsted.
Daughter of Mr. and Mrs. Phipps. In 1935 she helped her mother occasionally, but during the war she worked full time as a porter at the Winter Overcotes station.   After the war she married Bert Margett and worked in an airplane factory.   AF, GU

Phipps, Palmyra.   Worsted.
Another member of the family. For years she was the telephone operator and postmistress in Worsted, then at Skeynes, and eventually in Barchester. She was later transferred again to Lambton as head of the exchange. As she knew everyone in the area she was often of invaluable assistance, at least to those she liked.   (AF), BL, GU, OBH, DD, HaRe, CQ, TST

Pickering. Priory School, Lambton.
One of the trio of schoolboys that included Addison and young Dean.   CC, DD

Pickthorn, Miss.   Hogglestock.
Mr. Adams' extremely competent Secretary-in-Chief.   LAR, OBH, CC, DD, (TST)

Pie, Sir Omicron.   *From Trollope.*
Well-known London physician, mentioned in several of the Barsetshire novels.

Pie, Omicron.   London.
Grandson of above. A brilliant orthopedic surgeon.   MB, (CQ)

Pillman, Mr. London.
Oculist much favored by Oliver Marling.   (MH), (MB)

Pilson, Gertie. Harefield.
Local telephone operator in 1944. She obligingly passed on messages when the need arose.   H

Pilward family:

Pilward's Entire, later Pilward and Son's Entire.
A beer delivered in a dray pulled by two very well-trained Suffolk-Percheron-cross cart horses.

Pilward, Bert. Hogglestock.
Owner of the very successful Pilward brewing company. He went into a partnership with Sam Adams and Donald Macfadyen in the 1950's.   LAR, OBH, HaRe, TST

Pilward, Heather Adams. Hogglestock.
Daughter of Sam Adams. In 1942 she was a bright but podgy and spotty pupil at the Hosiers' Foundation Girls' School, where she cherished dreams of glory and hated everyone. Gradually this ugly duckling turned into a swan of sorts, first being compared to Anne of Cleves, and finally, after graduating from her engineering course at Cambridge, described as poised and definitely good-looking. Almost a genius at mathematics, she retained a substantial interest in her father's business after her marriage to Ted Pilward in October, 1948.   **H, MB,** (PBO), LAR, OBH, CC, DD

Pilward, Ted. Hogglestock.
Scion of the Pilwards Brewing family, the eldest of six. He had finished his degree in physics and chemistry at Cambridge when the war broke out. Ted and Tom Grantly served together in Iceland, where they amused themselves by putting their soap ration down the geysers. He married Heather Adams in 1948. They had two children, the first, a son, Edward Belton, born in 1949.

MB, LAR, OBH, (CC)

Plane, Hilda. The Red House, Marling Melicent.
Maid-of-all-work at the Harveys'. She had begun her career as under-nurse when Frances and Geoffrey were babies and had never got around to leaving them. By 1941 she was middle-aged, with short, straight grey hair and interesting clothing. She married Mr. Govern early in 1942.   MH

Podgens. Framley Court.
The Luftons' ancient retainer, an ex-coachman. When Maria Lufton went to The Cedars, he went along to help with the dogs.   DD, HaRe

Podgens, Mrs. Framley Court.
Lady Lufton's cook. She was one of the many Podgens who gave good service at Framley Court.   HaRe

Pollett family:

Pollett. Skeynes.
Ed Pollet's brother and the Middletons' driver in 1938.   BL

Pollett. Nutfield.
Commissionaire at Pomfret Towers in the 1950's for the Adams, Pilward, and Macfadyen group.

ADA

Pollett, Miss. Number Seventeen, The Close, Barchester.
The Fieldings' parlor-maid, a distant and very despising cousin of Ed Pollett.   PBO, LAR

Pollett, Ed. Skeynes; Marling Hall
Half-witted but good natured, Ed was the illegitimate son of Lord Pomfret's keeper and a virago mother. He was also the nephew of Mr. Patten at the railroad station, and to him Ed gave such extra help as zeal unsupported by intellect could afford. The passage of time exposed a streak of mechanical genius in Ed, and he became Lord Bond's chauffeur; then he went to Marling Hall where he managed the tractor and did odd jobs. In 1942 he married Millie Poulter, also decidedly wanting. They had several children. A further passage of time revealed a gift of water-sense in Ed and he was in demand for well work.   AF, BL, MH, MB, LAR, OBH, DD

Pollett, George. Worsted.
Proprietor of the Sheep's Head.   GU

Pollett, Mrs. George.   Worsted.
She gave assistance at the Sheep's Head as a great and resourceful cook.   GU

Pollett, Jim.   Worsted.
Driver of the bus that ran between Worsted and The Ram and Twins; a second cousin of Ed.   AF

Pollett, Lily Annie.   Worsted.
War-time railway porter at the station in Winter Overcotes.   She was strong as a man.   GU, LAR

Pollett, Millie Poulter.   Marling Melicent.
A red-haired village girl, vacant but pleasant, who lived with her aunt, Mrs. Cox.   During the time in 1941 when Frances and Geoffrey Harvey were living at the Red House, Millie came in on some mornings to help.   She and Ed Pollett were married in 1942 and she speedily became the mother of several vacant but cheerful, handsome, and healthy children.   MH, (MB), LAR

Pollett, Sid.
A railroad employee, cousin of Ed.   AF

The Pomfrets:

Pomfret, Lord.   Pomfret Towers.
The seventh earl was, by 1937, elderly and dispirited, for his only son, Harry, had been killed in a frontier skirmish in Northern India some time after the end of the First War.   A man of immense size, even in his eighties, and bald, with bushy eyebrows and fierce little eyes, he continued to ride horseback all over the county.   Lord Pomfret was the author of *A Landowner in Five Reigns*.   His last great act was to save Pooker's Piece in 1938.   He died a natural and peaceful death in May, 1940, and was succeeded by his designated heir, Giles Foster, the son of his nephew.   He was the brother of Lady Emily Leslie.   (WS), **PT**, BL, (CBI), (NR), (MH), (LAA)

Pomfret, Edith Thorne, Lady.   Pomfret Towers.
Lady Pomfret was descended from Trollope's Dr. Thomas Thorne, who had married the admirably wealthy Martha Dunstable.   Lady Pomfret never fully recovered from the death of her son and spent most of her time in Italy as a semi-invalid.   She died in 1938.   **PT**, (MH), (H), (NTL), (TST)

Pomfret, Lord, Giles Foster.   Pomfret Towers.
Eighth Earl of Pomfret and Lord Lieutenant of Barsetshire.   Heir to the Pomfret title and property, he succeeded to both upon the death of the 7th Earl of Pomfret in 1940.   He had been brought up almost entirely in Italy, and then had worked in London for a firm of art dealers until he became aware of his future responsibilities; eventually he moved to the Towers at the invitation of the old earl.   Unfailingly dutiful, courteous, honorable, and pleasant, but plagued with a naturally delicate constitution, a sort of *neuraesthenia gravis*, he fulfilled his role with success but at some cost to his personal health and happiness.   It was his great good fortune to marry Sally Wicklow in 1938.   She protected and helped him throughout their marriage.   They had three children.   Without in the least intending it, Lord Pomfret was attractive to women, to whom his charm, good manners, and air of fatigue exercised a stirring appeal.   **PT**, (B), (CBI), (MH), H,
MB, PBO, PE, LAR, **OBH**, HaRe, JC, **WDIM**, ESR, ADA, CQ, LAA, TST

Pomfret, Lady. Sally Wicklow.   Nutfield.   Pomfret Towers.
In 1937, Sally was a vigorous, outdoorsy girl.   She loved dogs and horses and feared nothing; she was forthright, and capable.   When she married Giles Foster in 1938, these good qualities and many others made her a great success as Lady Pomfret.   Sally made it her business to take care of Giles, who was not strong but was very conscientious, and to faithfully execute all the duties expected of

her as his Countess, and as the mother of his three children. She was a member of the St. John Ambulance Brigade and in 1946 was made a Lady of Grace. **PT**, (B), (BL), (CBI), MH, H, MB, PBO, PE, **OBH**, HaRe, JC, **WDIM**, ESR, NTL, ADA, CQ, LAA, TST

Porter, Walden Concord.   Porterville, Texas, USA.
A wealthy American manufacturer so interested in Provençal literature that he underwrote Mr. Downing during the last years of his writing *The Biographical Dictionary of Provence*. Mr. Porter had also endowed the observatory at which Helen Hopgood's husband did his work.   (NR), (WDIM)

Poulter, Millie.   *See* Pollett, Millie.

Poulter, Nurse.   Beliers Priory, Lambton.
Served in the convalescent hospital in 1942, and did private duty nursing thereafter.   GU, CC

Powell-Jones, Captain.   The Rectory, Northbridge.
Another of the officers billeted at the Villars' in 1940. In civilian life he had been a young professor of Cymric (Welsh) at one of the colleges in Bangor, Wales.   NR.

Powlett, Mrs.   The Vicarage, Harefield.
Mr. Oriel's housekeeper and cook. She had ruled him with a firm hand from the day, just before the war, when his sister had died and left him in her care.   H, HaRe, CQ

Preston, Mary.   *See* Leslie, Mary.

Pridham, Sir Edmund.   Pomfret Madrigal.
A baronet, born in 1872 of a venerable county family. He suffered off and on from an old leg injury sustained during service in the Boer War. Sir Edmund was middle-aged in 1938. He was Mrs. Brandon's friend and the trustee of her estate, active in county affairs, a churchwarden, and a responsible landlord.
B, CBI, (MH), (MB), PBO, PE, LAR, OBH, CC, HaRe, JC, ESR, ADA, LAA

Propett.   Southbridge.
The church sexton. Mr. Propett lived in a 16ᵗʰ century cottage shiny with grime. He was a malevolent old man, living with a malevolent old woman, thought to be his wife. They died within a few hours of each other in August, 1946.   PE

Propett, Young Mrs.   Southbridge.
Niece-in-law of the sexton's wife. She was a robust grandmother with sound views on scrubbing and on polishing the brights. Every morning she came in to help Colonel Crofts.   PE

Protheroe.   Southbridge School, Southbridge.
A classics master in 1933.   DH, (SH)

Proudie, Bishop.   *From Trollope.*
*Small and insignificant Bishop of Barchester in the 1850's and 60's. **Mrs. Proudie** was the domineering, penny-pinching, scheming, and ruthless wife of the bishop. She had inaugurated a fine tradition of stinginess and inhospitality at the palace.*

Prsvb. Myxo-Lydia.
An admiral in the Myxo-Lydian navy, and/or a Myxo-Lydian dramatist, an intellectual of the first run, dead at age 20. We will leave the pronunciation of his name to the Myxo-Lydians.   H, CQ

Pucken family:

Pucken, "Old."

Tom's father. He had died when he fell into a ditch while drunk and suffocated under a load of hay that capsized on him during the night.   BL

Pucken.   Framley.

The Luftons' cowman.   DD, HaRe

Pucken.   Marling Hall.

The Marlings' pig man.   LAR, (OBH)

Pucken.   Northbridge Manor.

The Mertons' cowman.   (WDIM)

Pucken, Irene.

Daughter of Tom and Sarah. She worked as kitchen maid for Mrs. Palmer at Worsted.   BL

Pucken, Lou.   Skeynes.

Youngest of the five Pucken girls. Like her mother, she helped in the Laverings or White House households.   BL

Pucken, Tom.   Skeynes.

Mr. Middleton's cowman. He also drove the cart horse.   BL

Pucken, Sarah Margett. Skeynes.

Tom's wife. She was the sister of the Margett who kept the shop in Worsted. Sarah had been kitchen maid at Staple Park before her marriage. She was always willing to come in and oblige as occasional household help for the Middletons or the occupants of The White House.   BL

Come and sit somewhere where there is a fire.
I want to talk to you about myself.
— Julian Rivers

Reid, Mr. High Rising
Keeper of the shop in 1932.   HR

Rivers family:

Rivers, Hermione. Herefordshire or Shropshire. Duke's Close, London.
Overbearing and insufferable author of numerous exotic-locale romances featuring middle-aged women adored by younger men. She was, according to Lord Pomfret, "always gadding about being literary." Certainly, as the wife of a distant connection of Lord Pomfret, she presumed upon the relationship and gadded his way for several weeks every year.
                                      PT, (H), PE, (LAR), HaRe, (ESR), (TST)

Rivers, George. Herefordshire or Shropshire.
Hermione's husband, the cousin of the seventh earl. George was devoted to his estate and nothing —certainly not his wife—could drag him away from his farming and county pursuits.
                                               (PT), (PE), (LAR), (ESR)

Rivers, Phoebe.
Daughter of George and Hermione. She was a friendly and decent though somewhat unhappy young woman, and an aspiring actress. She eventually married Lord Humberton and lived in Shropshire.   **PT**, (CBI), (MH), (HaRe), (ESR)

Rivers, Julian. London.
The Rivers' spoilt artistic son, born around 1916. He had deep-set dark blue eyes, and black locks flung recklessly above his marble brow. As a corollary to this, he was entirely self-centered. He was involved in an avant-garde artists' group, the Society of Fifteen, sometimes known as the Set of Five. As time passed he aspired to ever greater outrageousness and thus in 1951 he was appointed by Lazarus College to a Professorship of Culture at a salary of £800. He is thought to be modeled on AT's son Colin MacInnes, whose values were very different from hers.
                          PT, (MH), (H), (MB), (PBO), (HaRe), (CQ), (TST)

Robarts family: from Trollope.
Dr. Robarts *died leaving little money; his two unmarried daughters had to live with relatives.*
Lucy Robarts *lived at Framley with her brother* **Mark.**
Mark Robarts *was the young vicar of Framley Church, and lived at Framley Parsonage (in modern times called the Old Parsonage). He was a good friend of young Lord Lufton; it was through that connection that he had been given the living.*
Fanny *was Mark's wife, and* **Jane** *was his second sister, who lived with their married sister, Mrs. Crowdy.*

Rose.   Stories, Pomfret Madrigal.   The Vinery, The Close, Barchester.

Rose had been Mr. Brandon's parlormaid since before his marriage to Lavinia, and she was still with the family in the 1950's. Her ruling passion was her competition with Nurse in a silent struggle for the soul, or at least the love and approbation, of Mrs. Brandon. She moved into Barchester to The Vinery when Mrs. Brandon married Canon Joram in 1949.   B, PE, CC, HaRe

---

Ruth. Harefield.

The Perry's housemaid. She had every defect of sulks, complaining, and tactlessness, but was faithful and devoted.   H, DD, HaRe

The curious thing is that one never hears people squabbling about who should not pay, which really would be far more reasonable.

— Eric Swan

Samson.   Greshamsbury.
Owner of the local garage. Occasionally he would help out by acting as driver for someone.   CQ

Sartoria, Mme. London.
Lady Graham's very talented dressmaker—the one who described Emmy and Clarissa as *"cheval de charrue et cheval pur sang," q.v.*   CC, ADA

Saunders.   Northbridge Manor, Northbridge.
The Keiths' chauffeur in 1936.   SH, (CBI)

Scatcherd, Sir Roger.   *From Trollope.*
A stonemason who was imprisoned for several years for murdering Henry Thorne, his sister's seducer. Upon his release he became a successful contractor, amassed a fortune, and was made a baronet. He increased his income by making loans at high rates. He was not a pleasant character, and died of alcoholism. His son also died of alcoholism, and the estate went to Mary Thorne, who was then rich enough to be acceptable as a wife of Frank Gresham.

Scatcherd family:

Scatcherd, Mr.   Rokeby, Hatch End.
Artist of the Rising Valley, a descendant of the old working-class Scatcherd family, and a remarkable relic of the past. His habitual working costume was an old Norfolk jacket, knickerbockers buttoned below the knee, a deerstalker hat, a silken scarf and a heavy tweed Inverness cloak. In fair weather the cloak was left at home and there were other seasonable adjustments, but in all weathers he appeared in his drooping walrus moustache. Not content with his remarkable appearance, Mr. Scatcherd's conversation abounded in florid and excessive locutions.
PBO, (WDIM), ESR, NTL, DA, TST

Scatcherd, Hettie.   Rokeby, Hatch End.
Mr. Scatcherd's niece and housekeeper, whose father, Mr. Scatcherd's brother, owned Rokeby. Her ceaseless scolding and carping did not bother Mr. Scatcherd, who asked only that his meals be regular. In 1945 she was middle-aged, cut her hair short with the kitchen scissors, and refused to go to the dentist. Religion was the pillar of her life.   PBO, ESR

Scatchered, Mr.   Northbridge.
Brother of the above Mr. Scatcherd. Although he had been bedridden for years, he was the proprietor of Scatcherd's Stores all through the 30's and 40's.   NR, PBO, ESR

Scatcherd, Mr.   Barchester.

Another member of the family, who was in the catering business with Mr. Tozier as his partner.

OBH, CC

Selina.   *See* Hopkins, Selina.

Shergold, Mr.   Southbridge School, Southbridge.

Everard Carter's replacement as housemaster of the Senior House in 1946. Mr. Shergold was ex-Navy, a very good fellow with an intelligent, active mind; he was a gentleman, sufficiently good at cricket and an enthusiast for winter sports; he had some money of his own, but wasn't married. While stationed in the Mediterranean he had raced jerboas.

PE, CC, JC

Sid.   Stories, Pomfret Madrigal.

The Brandons' garden boy.

B

Siddon, Mrs.   Rushwater House, Rushwater.

The housekeeper, who knew Rushwater House better than any of the family. She had started her career as the stillroom maid before the First War, and was at Rushwater in 1960.

WS, PBO, LAR, OBH, NTL

Silverbridge. *From Trollope.*

Silverbridge was the second title of the Duke of Omnium, and the courtesy title of his heir. It was also the name of a town and borough connected with the estate.

Silverbridge family:

Silverbridge, Lord, Jeffrey Palliser. Gatherum Castle, West Barsetshire. The Lodge, Silverbridge. Oldest son of the Duke of Omnium; a pleasant young man discouraged by changes that made his hereditary role problematic. During the war he had served with the Barsetshire Yeomanry, and in 1949 he was working on a history of the unit. At that time he worked in London for the publishing house of Johns and Fairfield. Jeff could play the piano, and was one of those pianists gifted with the velvet touch and impeccable rhythm that is so often given to those entirely nonmusical in the classical sense. He married Isabel Dale in 1949. She had recently inherited a respectable amount of money, and he was able to leave his job and run for Parliament. Their first child, a boy, was born in 1950, and the second, also a boy, in 1952.

CC, DD, (JC)

Silverbridge, Lady. Great House, Allington. The Lodge, Silverbridge.

Born Isabel Dale in 1919. In 1948, although she was heir to the remains of the Dunstable and Scatcherd fortunes, she was keeping busy. She was secretary to Eleanor Grantly at the Red Cross Hospital Library in Barchester, while under her *nom de plume*, Lisa Bedale, she wrote thrillers. She went to the Marlings' to help organize things before Lucy's marriage. Isabel had a pure oval face, blue eyes, fair hair, and a Juno-like figure. She was sensible, forthright, honest, and dutiful to but distant from her very unpleasant mother, who had the good grace to die in 1949.   Isabel married Jeffrey Palliser, Lord Silverbridge, later that year; they were fortunate in being able to lease The Lodge, in producing a male heir right away, and in having enough money to enable Jeff to stand for election. Isabel continued writing mysteries.

CC,DD,HaRe,(JC)

Simnet family:

Simnet.   Southbridge School, Southbridge.   The Vinery, The Close, Barchester.

Butler first for the Birketts, then for Canon Joram. Simnet had seen service in France from 1915–1917. In the mid-30's he became a scout at Lazarus College, Oxford, but resigned because he didn't hold with the Master's political and social views. He was capable, discreet, and helpful—indeed, his handling of large parties was famed throughout the county. He married Florrie, sister of Eileen at the Red Lion in Southbridge, which accounted somehow for his wish to change his situation. Unless under stress he spoke in a satisfying Jeevesian way.

SH, CBI, PBO, PE, LAR, CC, HaRe, LAA, TST

Simnet. London.
Brother of the above. He held the position of Apparitor of Worship for the Hosiers, but wasn't above helping his brother on such occasions as the Jorams' sherry party in January, 1952. The Simnet brothers had an old mother living in Barchester.

H, HaRe

Simnet, Dorothy. The Vicarage, Hatch End. London.
Mr. Choyce's maid during the war. Despite being rather superannuated and markedly wanting, she and the London Mr. Simnet were married in 1945.

H, LAR, HaRe

Simnet, Florrie. The Close, Barchester.
The sister of Eileen at the Red Lion in Southbridge pressed into duty as Simnet's walking-out partner when Eileen abandoned Simnet to marry Bateman. One thing led to another, as it so often does, and Florrie and Simnet married and left Southbridge to come to Barchester. Florrie served as cook-housekeeper to Canon Joram (as he was then) and her husband as butler.

CC, HaRe

Simpson. London.
A junior member of Noel Merton's law firm, Simpson was a youngish middle-aged man who looked as if he spent his life carrying out instructions to the letter. He was used to overseeing funeral arrangements.

B

Smith, Joseph, "Holy Joe." Southbridge School, Southbridge.
The school chaplain in 1936. He was a Cambridge man, very interested in athletics, and after leaving university had been in India for six months as secretary to a perambulating bishop.

SH, CBI, PE, LAR, JC, CQ

Smith, Joyce Perry. The Red House, Marling Melicent.
In the early years of the war she was a recent widow, whose late husband had died of DT's. Circumstances forced her to put the Red House up for rent in the autumn of 1941, and she became the most trying of landladies to her tenants, the Harveys. She was thin and dressed in black, showing some remains of former prettiness in her fine eyes. As Miss Perry, she had been a teacher at the infant school in Rushwater. In 1948 she rented the Red House to the Bissells, and in 1950 she sold it, moved to Torquay and, some years later, remarried, or so it was said.

MH, (LAR)

Snow, Jim. Southbridge School, Southbridge.
School carpenter who helped Miss and Mrs. Arbuthnot prepare Editha Cottage for their occupancy. He was a merciless craftsman, demanding to the last drop of blood the full weight of his employers' attention.

PE, JC, NTL, (CQ)

Sowerby, Nathaniel. *From Trollope.*
A well-to-do MP who lost a great deal of money gambling.

Sowerby, Miss. The Old Bank House, Edgewood; Worthing.
The last of the family of Nathaniel Sowerby. The Sowerbys had been Rangers of the Chaldicotes Chase for a hundred years or so before it was deforested. The family had slowly descended, and her funds were depleted. In 1947 she was forced to sell her home, The Old Bank House, to Sam Adams for £8,000, and to go to Worthing to live with her widowed sister.

OBH, DD, (TST)

Spadger. Winter Overcotes.
The cowshed specialist.   OBH

Sparks. Brandon Abbey.
Miss Brandon's maid.   B

Sparling, Madeleine. *See* Carton, Madeleine.

Sparrow. The Manor House, Worsted.
The Palmers' butler. He was a good fast bowler for the village cricket team.   AF

Spencer. Staple Park, Skeynes.
The Bonds' insubordinate and intimidating butler. Lord Bond was able to let him go when he and Mrs. Bond
moved to the servants' wing of the house during the war.   BL

Spender, Major Robert.
One of the officers billeted on the Villars in Northbridge in 1940. A master of circumlocution, his dreaded
conversational gambits consisted almost entirely of reports of his wife and children, Billy, Jimmy and
Clarissa.   NR, GU, DD

Spender, Mrs.
Wife of Major Spender. Not only was her talk ceaseless, it pertained exclusively to herself, and contained
numerous catch phrases and maddening affectations.   Altogether, she drove everyone to despair. She was
plump, forty-ish, markedly auburn-haired and astonishingly dressed in clashing colors   NR, GU, DD

Spindler. Pomfret Madrigal.
Proprietor of the Cow and Sickle. Mrs. Spindler cooked.   B

Stanhope family: *from Trollope.*

> **The Reverend Vesey Stanhope** *held a prebendial stall in the diocese, and was vicar of three parishes. He had
> a lovely house in the Close. However, on the excuse of having a sore throat, he had lived in Italy with his family for
> several years, leaving his pastoral duties to curates.*
> **Mrs. Stanhope** *was beautiful and well dressed. That said, there was nothing more to tell about her.*
> **Charlotte Stanhope**, *was the eldest child. She made it her goal in life to preserve the dignity of the family.*
> **Ethelbert Stanhope** *was the son. His goal was to marry a wealthy woman, as he had no intention of working.*
> **Madeleine Stanhope Neroni** *was the married daughter. However, she had left her husband, who had every
> vice, including cruelty. Although she was a cripple, she was still very beautiful. Her small daughter was* **Julia
> Neroni.**
> **Paolo Neroni** *was the husband of Madeleine. He had married her expecting to be supported; he was without any
> redeeming qualities.*

Starter, the Honourable Juliana.
A guest at Staple Park in 1939. Juliana was the daughter of Lord Mickleham, and the youngest of eighteen
children. She had been Lady-in-Waiting to Princess Louisa Christina of Cobalt-Herz-Reinigen, and after the
Princess' death she had little to think about but the interesting subject of her digestion.   In 1950 she took
Lord Lufton as a lodger in London during House sessions and gave him Kornog for breakfast, while using
his ration book to extend her larder.   **BL**, (HaRe), (LAA)

Stevenson, Joan.   London.

An irksomely competent employee of the BBC, and an alarmingly free-thinking friend of David Leslie's. She married Lionel Harvest as soon as possible after learning he was heir to a tidy £4000 per year; they lived in Bloomsbury.   **WS**, (DD)

Stoke, Lord.   Rising Castle, High Rising.

The thirteenth baron, born Algernon Courcy in 1876, but called "Tom" by his half-sister, Lucasta Bond. His mother, old Lord Stoke's first wife, had been a Miss Hooper, daughter of Squire Hooper of Rumpton in Somerset. In 1932 Lord Stoke was on his way to becoming a crusty old bachelor, and by 1960 he had definitely become one. In conversation he had the advantages of a loud voice, a complete belief in his own judgment, and increasing deafness. A great farmer and stockman Stoke was often driven here and there in the county in a dog cart or brougham. He was the keenest antiquarian, the most ardent pig-raiser, and the nosiest invader of kitchens in the county.

HR, DH, PT, BL, CBI, GU, MB, PBO, (PE), LAR, OBH, DD, JC, ESR, **NTL**, ADA, LAA, TST

Stoker.   High Rising;   London.

Mrs. Morland's cook and helper, from the early 30's onward. Stoker was fat, brusque, good-natured and a good cook. She had come from Plaistow, and was "Mrs." by courtesy.   HR, DH, ESR, NTL, LAA, TST

Stonor family:

Stonor, Lilian.   The White House, Skeynes.   London.

Youngish widow of the much older and retired Colonel Stonor, and stepmother to his two children. She was John Middleton's sister, and rented the White House from him for the summer of 1938. Lilian was a well-defended person, selfless and caring, an amateur painter, and a spinner of scattered thoughts into web-like sentences. Later in 1938 she married Alister Cameron, John's junior partner in their architectural firm.   **BL**

Stonor, Daphne.   *See* Bond, Daphne.

Stonor, Denis.   The White House, Skeynes;   New York.

Born in 1914, Denis was the stepson of Lilian Stonor. Like C.W. Bond, he had spent two years at Hocker's preparatory school. His health was delicate, and, until he smiled, his features were ugly and monkey-like. Musically talented, he became a success in New York as a composer of ballets and light but heart-rending musical plays. Occasionally he returned to England on visits. He was a good friend of the Clovers.   **BL**, (MB), LAR, (CC), DD, TST

Strelsa, Guido.   Italy.

Italian cousin of the Earls of Pomfret and the Fosters. He was famous for having been turned out of every gambling hell in Europe. The Strelsas had a villa outside Florence; the Earl of Pomfret and his family were always welcome there.   (PT), (PBO), (LAA)

Stringer, John. From Trollope.

Proprietor of a public house in Barchester. He paid his rent with a stolen check which ended up in the possession of Mr. Crawley, who was later accused of having stolen it.

Stringer.   Barchester.

A second-rate law firm used by the Bishop of Barchester. This Stringer was descended from the Stringers at the Dragon of Watley, who were involved in the affair of the Reverend Josiah Crawley and the check.   CQ

Sumter, Lee. USA.
One of Edith Graham's American admirers. As luck would have it, his cousin Franklin was married to the Duke of Towers, and became Edith's sister-in-law. LAA

Sutton, Mr. Rushwater.
Sexton at Rushmere Abbey in the early 1930's. WS

Sutton, Lottie. Rushwater.
Lottie was Mr. Sutton's daughter, who turned peculiar and had to be put in the county asylum. But then, all her mother's family were queer. It if hadn't been for Henry VIII breaking from the Church, and destroying the abbeys, the monks might have been able to do something for her—or so Lady Emily thought. (WS)

Swan, Eric. Southbridge School, Southbridge. Harefield House School, Harefield.
Born in 1920 to a Scottish mother and an English father. As a cool and intelligent student at Southbridge School, Swan unnerved his masters by looking at them through his spectacles. He went to Cambridge and was in Africa during the war, returning to spend a year reading with Mr. Fanshawe at Paul's, Oxford. His friendship with Philip Winter drew him to the Priory School in 1950. As an adult, Swan was clever, thoughtful, and charming to the point of being silver-tongued. He was an inveterate quoter of lines or phrases of prose or poetry. He married Justinia Lufton in 1952 and became a master at Harefield School. In 1959 he returned to Southbridge School as Headmaster upon the retirement of Everard Carter. He was the author of a book on Fluvius Minucius. **SH**, (PE), DD, **HaRe**, **JC**, (TST)

Swan, Justinia Lufton. Framley Court, Framley. Old Parsonage, Framley. Harefield House School, Harefield.
The younger of the two Lufton daughters, both of whom were older than their brother Ludovic. In 1950, Justinia worked in the Close as secretary to the Dean. She was small and very elegant, with soft brown hair and a head set beautifully upon her pretty neck and shoulders. In 1952 she married Eric Swan.
DD, HaRe, JC, TST

Swift-Hetherington. Southbridge School, Southbridge.
Tony Morland's friend. HR, DH

*When I eat green stuff I understand
why cows have four stomachs.*
— Gilbert Tebben

Tacker.   Rushwater.
The sexton at St. Mary's Church in the 30's and 40's.   PBO

Tacker, Mrs.   Rushwater.
Mr. Tacker's wife. In her youth she had been a housemaid at Rushwater House   PBO

Talbot family:

Talbot, Amorel.   Northbridge.
One of a trio of cranky octogenarian brothers, the others being Tufnel and Alwyn. They were united in their rancorous disagreements. Amorel had been a professor of religion, and was the father of Marjorie and Dolly; he died in 1956 at the age of 95.   NR

Talbot, Dorothy, "Dolly."   Northbridge.
Professor Talbott's younger daughter, who, by 1940, was also elderly. Like her sister, she was leading a hard-working and blameless life, devoted to working for the Red Cross and to caring for her father. She adored Mr. Fewling.   NR, (PE), WDIM

Talbot, Marjorie.   Northbridge.
Always known as Miss Talbot, her proper designation as elder daughter of Professor Talbot. During the war years she was a pillar of the Northbridge Red Cross.   NR, (PE), WDIM

Tebben family: The Tebbens came to Lamb's Piece in the mid-1930's.

Tebben, Gilbert.   Lamb's Piece, Worsted.
A civil servant during the week, Mr. Tebben was, for the rest of the time, a leading scholar of the heroic age of Norway and Iceland. As such he was a mainstay of the Snorri Society. So absorbed was he in 16th century Scandinavia that he was somewhat overrun by his wife's plans and domestic machinations. Mr. Tebben retired in 1946, after which the family lived full time at Lamb's Piece.
                                    AF, BL, (GU), MB, (PE), LAR

Tebben, Winifred Ross.   Lamb's Piece, Worsted.
Mrs. Tebben had taken a first at Oxford in economics, and was the author of several useful and uninteresting textbooks. She had a passion for dismal thrift and domestic fuss. This manifested itself in ways which, though admirable in themselves, were irksome and embarrassing to her family. Her hair in its straggling disorder, her homespun, peasantlike dress, the donkey intended to provide serious transportation, and her ceaseless preoccupation with cheap and leftover food made life a trial for them all. She adored her son and took her daughter for granted. **AF**, BL, (GU), MB, LAR, OBH

Tebben, Petrea Krogsbrog. Stockholm.
Daughter of Swedish writer and industrialist Anders Krogsbrog. Petrea provided strong social guidance for Richard, of which he was badly in need. They were married in 1948 and lived in Sweden.

LAR

Tebben, Richard. Lamb's Piece, Worsted. Sweden.
The Tebbens' son, born in 1915. Richard had just come down from Oxford with a third in Greats in the summer of 1935. He despised and was embarrassed by his parents, and depressed by his home. A lucky fluke landed him a good job in Mr. Dean's engineering firm. During the war he was in the Army, but was discharged in 1944 with a tropical disease—or perhaps it was a stiff knee. He became an overseas agent for Sam Adams, and in 1947 married a Swedish heiress named Petrea Krogsbrog. We hope he bought his mother a new raincoat. **AF**, (BL), (H), (MB), (PE), LAR

Tebben, Margaret. *See* Dean, Margaret.

Tempest, Canon. Lambton.
Temporary vicar for the Lambton parish after the death of Mr. Horniman. He was angry and elderly and hustled the congregation through the service. He had been the incumbent at St. Ewolds before Mr. Miller arrived there in 1949. GU, (HaRe)

Thatcher family:
Thatcher, Mr. Grumper's End, Pomfret Madrigal.
A confirmed gambler who dispensed upon the dogs money that would otherwise would have gone to his wife and large brood of deserving children. He was a loyal patron of the Cow and Sickle.

B, CBI

Thatcher, Mrs. Grumper's End, Pomfret Madrigal.
A handsome, draggled woman, she was the unfortunate wife of Mr. Thatcher and the mother of his eight children. She was a markedly easygoing housekeeper, which may explain why the Thatcher's house was considered the most desirable by the evacuee children in 1939. Mrs. Thatcher was charwoman for several local families. The Thatchers' children that we can name were Edna, Doris, Bessie, Herb, Jimmy, and Teddy. B, CBI, HaRe

---

Thatcher, Alf. Grumper's End.
Cousin of the Thatcher family, Alf had a brilliant army career, having been awarded the George Cross for bravery and devotion to duty. By 1950, however, he was serving seven years for a peculiarly brutal attack upon an elderly pawnbroker in Limehouse. (CC)

Thatcher, Bessie. Grumper's End, Pomfret Madrigal. Stories, Pomfret Madrigal.
A young woman who came to Stories to take charge of the Brandons' nursery after Nurse left in 1952 to go to Beliers Priory. HaRe

---

Thatcher, Doris. Grumper's End, Pomfret Madrigal. The Rectory, Edgewood.
Younger than her sister Edna. During the war both sisters worked as daily helps at the Cow and Sickle. It must not have been all work and no play, for by 1947 when she went to work for the Grantlys in Edgewood, Doris had four children of shame: Gladys, Sid, Stan, and Glamora, all of whom made themselves useful about the house and garden. B, (CBI), **OBH**, DD, HaRe

Thatcher, Edna.   Grumper's End, Pomfret Madrigal. The Rectory, Edgewood.
The older sister. She had contented herself with just the one child of shame, Percy. He was 12 in 1947, when this strange family, the two sisters and their five children, moved to Edgewood to provide domestic help for the Grantlys. Edna was a very good cook.

B, (CBI), **OBH**, DD, HaRe, WDIM

Thatcher, Herb.   Grumper's End, Pomfret Madrigal.
Brother of Jimmy. Delia Brandon made a splint for his broken arm.   B

Thatcher, Jimmy.   Grumper's End, Pomfret Madrigal.
A child who had the chicken pox in 1938. He was one of eight children in a poor and disorganized family, but he won a scholarship in 1947 to one of the new redbrick universities.   B, (CC)

Thatcher, Percy, "Purse." Edgewood.
The son of Edna, Purse was not good at school but had mechanical aptitude. In 1951 he won a scholarship to the County Technical School and planned to study electricity.   B, OBH, HaRe

---

Thatcher, Sid. Edgewood.
The son of Doris Thatcher. He helped out about the house and garden of Edgewood Rectory, where he lived with his mother, brother, sisters, cousin, and aunt. He developed an affinity for plants and took *Palafox borealis* under his special protection when it came to live at the rectory. By putting it on a sunny kitchen shelf and treating it to a massive daily dose of popular tunes from the wireless, he made it thrive and flower in half the expected time. He was allowed to sell the seeds and bank the proceeds. In 1960 Mr. Adams was planning to take him on at Adamsfield.

OBH, TST

Thatcher, Teddy. Grumper's End, Pomfret Madrigal.
Brother of Jimmy and Herb.   B

Thomas, Dr.   The Rectory, Worsted.
Rector of the Worsted church. He was a friend of the Palmers', a classics scholar, and father of two unmarried daughters.   AF

Thomas, Phyllis.   The Rectory, Worsted.
Known as Miss Thomas, she was the pleasant, 30-ish, weather-beaten daughter of an ageing and deaf father.

AF

Thomas, Dolly.   The Rectory, Worsted.
Dr. Thomas' younger, equally devoted daughter.   AF

Thorne family: From Trollope.

   Thorne, Doctor Thomas. He was from a family of respectable, middle-class people—except for his brother, Henry. Dr. Thorne married Martha Dunstable.
   Thorne, Henry. Brother of Thomas. Henry fathered an illegitimate daughter, Mary, and was killed by Roger Scatcherd, her uncle.
   Thorne, Mary. The daughter of Henry Thorne and Mary Scatcherd. Thomas adopted Mary, who eventually married Frank Gresham.
   Monica Thorne lived with her bachelor brother Wilfred, the Squire of St. Ewold's and Ullathorne. They were cousins of Thomas and Henry.

Thorne, Canon. The Close, Barchester.
Elderly descendant of the Thorne family, he was popular in the Close. He was very deaf.   (MB), (PBO)

Todd, Anne. *See* Knox, Anne.

Tomkins, Madame.   Barley Street, Barchester.
A French dressmaker who arrived in Barchester around 1937 She had had a romantic war marriage in 1917 to the son of the cathedral gardener, who was then the boot and knife man at the Bishop's Palace. By 1937 he had vanished. To make ends meet, she took in lodgers, of whom Bishop Joram was one. In a few years Mme. Tomkins had become known as quite the best cutter, fitter, and arbiter of taste in the county. Sir Robert Fielding described her as "a sphinx without a secret."   MB, (PBO), LAR, OBH, HaRe, LAA

Tomkins, Sr.   The Close, Barchester.
Sexton at the Cathedral.   LAR, CC

Tomkins, Jr.   The Close, Barchester.
Verger at the Cathedral.   ESR

Tomkins.   Pomfret Towers.
A woodman.   LAA

Tompion, Mr.   Little Misfit.
Vicar in the late 1930's.   (CBI), MH

Topham, Captain.   The Rectory, Northbridge.   Norfolk.
One of the officers billeted on the Villars in 1940. Before the war he had been a sporty sort, interested in horse racing and the stage. He had lowbrow tastes in drink, and was hearty and unsubtle. When in 1941 he inherited a house in Norfolk, he proposed to Betty, Mrs. Turner's niece. They were duly married and lived in the house, where they raised a family.   NR, (WDIM)

Topham, Betty. The Hollies, Northbridge.
Mrs. Turner's elder niece. Orphaned in childhood by influenza and adopted by Mrs. Turner. She was very close to her apparently nameless sister, known only as "Mrs. Turner's other niece." Betty was a keen birder, and a pleasant and helpful young woman. She and Captain Topham were engaged in 1940, married after the war, and lived at his family property in Norfolk.   **NR**, (PE), (WDIM)

Tory, Mrs.   Hallbury House, Hallbury.
Admiral Palliser's cook. She kindly believed that to hear Master Frank Gresham conjugate Latin verbs and decline Latin nouns was as good as going to chapel.   MB

Tory, Greta.   Hallbury.
Niece of Mrs. Tory, she carried the mail during the war. In 1947 she was a waitress at the White Hart in Barchester.   MB, LAR, (CQ)

Towers: *(For more information about the Harcourt family see the note at the Harcourt entry.)*
　　Towers, Duke of.   Harcourt.
　　Since the dukedom to which he was heir consisted of very little, the Duke was content to lease Harcourt Towers and live in the village in a house of reasonable size. He had an American wife and two or three nice children.   LAA

Towers, Duchess of.   Harcourt.

Born an American named Franklin, she was a Southern beauty with Southern charm from Lumberville, which we think must be much like Laurel, Mississippi. Like Laurel, it apparently was a hotbed of Southern charm and beauty. Frankie had spent time in New England as well. As it turned out, she was a cousin of Lee Sumter, one of Edith Graham's American beaux.   **LAA**

Towers, Dowager Duchess of.   Harcourt.

Dorothea, referred to in the family as "Dow," was known in her youth as "The Plunger." She became the mother of the Duke, and of William, Elaine, and Gwendolyn Harcourt. She cultivated a slight eccentricity, was markedly forthright, and used a *face-à-main*.   DA, **LAA**

Note: The Duchess of Towers is one of the two main characters of George du Maurier's *Peter Ibbetson.*

Tozer, Mr..   Barchester.

Having been a mess waiter in the Salisbury Plain encampments during the First War, Mr. Tozer considered himself qualified to enter the catering business in partnership with Mr. Scatcherd. He was a non-stop talker.

CBI, CC, HaRe, ADA, LAA, TST

Note: In Trollope's Barsetshire, John and Tom Tozer were moneylenders who held the promissory notes of Mark Roberts and Lord Lufton.

Traill, Donald.   Maria Cottage, Wiple Terrace, Southbridge.

An assistant master at Southbridge School, who arrived there in 1946 after being demobilized. He had grown up in a large house in South Kensington and couldn't adjust to life in a small cottage, where his gramophone bedeviled Mr. Feeder, and Mr. Feeder's wireless bedeviled him.

PE, LAR, CC, JC, NTL, CQ, TST

Note: A Mr. Traill was one of the main characters in Hugh Walpole's 1911 novel based on his experiences as a teacher at Epsom College, *Mr. Perrin and Mr Traill.*

Trapes, Mrs. London.

Jessica Dean's dresser.   CC

Turner, Poppy.   *See* Downing, Poppy.

Turpin, Mr. and Mrs. Pomfret Madrigal.

Mrs. Brandon's gardener in 1938, and the only person we have heard of who could walk venomously. The Turpins continued to live near Stories; Delia and Hilary Grant and their children stayed with the Turpins while on visits to Francis and Peggy.   B, HaRe

---

Twicker, Nanny.   Northbridge Manor, Northbridge.

As a young woman from Westmorland, she had been nanny to all the Keith children. She and her husband lived on the Manor property.   SH, (GU), PE, (LAR), OBH, WDIM

Twicker.   Northbridge Manor, Northbridge.

The Keith's gardener, and husband of Nanny Twicker. He died in 1955.   SH, GU, WDIM

> *I only do some housework and cooking and gardening
> and the family mending, but I must have a thing
> about getting knocked about.*
>
> — Betty Updike

Umbleby, Yates. *From Trollope.*
An inept lawyer who mismanaged the estate of Frank Gresham and had to be replaced.

Umbleby, Mr. and Mrs. The Laurels, Greshamsbury.
Local solicitor. His family had been property owners in the county for over a hundred years. After the war they had let their house to the Greens, who in turn sub-let it to the John Fairweathers in 1952. They had three young children in 1957. (JC), CQ

Updike family:

Updike, Philip. Clive's Corner, Harefield.
The Belton's solicitor in 1943, and later, Mrs. Macfadyen's. He was of middle height, with gray hair and a quiet voice and manner. His family had been Harefield solicitors for several generations, and handled the affairs of many of the area's large landowners, as well as the local interests of Lord Pomfret. H, LAR, DD, HaRe, CQ

Updike, Betty. Clive's Corner, Harefield.
The accident-prone wife of Philip. A tall, thin, fair woman looking, in 1943, ridiculously too young to be the mother of four children between 15 and 25. In a rather tiresome way she had a "sort of a thing" about so much that brought her some sort of injury, that one cannot help thinking she might better have been drowned at birth. **H**, LAR, DD, HaRe, CQ

Updike, Miss. Clive's Corner, Harefield.
The nice, rather dull elder daughter of the Updikes. During the war she was a WAAF, and after the war ran a large domestic science school. Also, unless this was her sister, she was head of the Barchester Public Library for a while. In 1955 she went to Pomfret Towers as a fill-in secretary and assistant when Miss Merriman went to Holdings for a rest.

H, (LAR), (DD), (HaRe), (NTL), ADA

There was a good deal to be said for the war. One made so many friends that one would never have met under normal conditions.
— Gregory Villars

Valoroso, Ruby and Marleen.
Child evacuees living near Rushwater in 1941. They were tap dancers, pleasant looking but bold faced. Their father was an acrobat and their mother an alcoholic who had been reformed by Bishop Joram.　　MH

Vance, Miss. *See* Nurse.

van Dryven, Woolcott Jefferson. USA.
American husband of Betty Dean, the son of a career diplomat. The family's wealth derived from peanut exports. He was interested in archeology and architecture, among many other things. He adored to pontificate, but was so enthusiastic that he was rather lovable　　(BL), LAR, WDIM, LAA

van Dryven, Betty Dean. The Dower House, Worsted. USA: New York and Texas.
Eighteen during the summer of 1935, she was intensely interested in her future as a classics scholar at Oxford, where she took a first in Greats. She then went to New York and planned to do graduate work at Bryn Mawr. Somehow this led, as things so often do, to marriage a wealthy American, Woolcot van Dryven. She was his right-hand man in the peanut trade. They had three children, and except for long visits, lived in the U.S.　　**AF**, BL, (PE), LAR, WDIM

Verger. The Close, Barchester.
The Crawleys' butler in 1953.　　WDIM, ADA

Vidler family:

　　Vidler, Mrs. Rushwater.
　　A woman who did odd jobs.　　WS

　　Vidler, Mrs. Northbridge.
　　Proprietress of The Mitre.　　WDIM

　　Vidler, Dorothy. Hatch End.
　　Mr. Crosse's servant at the Old Manor House in 1954.　　ESR

　　Vidler, Percy.
　　The illegitimate brother of Vidler the fish.　　WS

　　Vidler. Northbridge.
　　The poulterer.　　NR

Vidler the fish. Hatch End.
The man who drove the fish van. WS, PBO, NTL

Villars family:
Villars, Gregory. The Rectory, Northbridge. The Close, Barchester.
A veteran of the first war, Mr. Villars began his career as headmaster of Coppin's school, and then, in 1937, he took holy orders and went to Northbridge as rector. In 1957 he became a canon at the cathedral and he and Verena moved to Barchester. **NR**, (GU), PE, JC, WDIM, CQ

Villars, Verena. The Rectory, Northbridge. The Close, Barchester.
Wife of Gregory. Before the war she had been ill. In 1940 she was about forty-five and had two grown sons. She was not from a clerical family, and felt she wasn't a good parson's wife. She sat on few committees and rather limited her wartime activities, but she did all that she could to provide a comfortable and pleasant home for her husband, helped in this by a private income. Mrs. Villars had a perfect social façade, and behind it a lively interior life. She was a cousin of Sir Harry Waring.
NR, (GU), PE, JC, WDIM, ADA, CQ
Note: Mrs. Villars' first name was taken from *The Heir of Redclyffe*, in which it was a special endearment used by Guy Morville for his wife Amy. Verena was one of the names Amy gave her infant daughter. This source of her name is specifically mentioned by Mrs. Villars in Chapter II of *Northbridge Rectory.*

Villars, Gregory.
The Villars' older son. In 1940 he was twenty-six and was required to stick to his job as a professor of engineering. (NR), (CQ)

Villars, John.
The Villars' younger son. In 1940 he was a Wing Commander, entirely engaged with instruction.
NR

Walter.   Rushwater.
Footman at Rushwater House.   WS, (LAR)

Ward, Nurse.   London.   Punshions, Northbridge.
One of the trio of nurse friends that included Nurse Chiffinch and Nurse Heath.   They were known among themselves as Wardy, Heathy, and   Chiffy.   When they reached retirement age, Nurses Ward and Heath refurbished Punshions, the former home of Miss Pemberton. Nurse Chiffinch joined them there later, and although all were retired one of them would take an occasional baby or nursing case if she knew the family well.   (HaRe), NTL, TST

Waring family:

Waring, Sir Harry, Bart. Beliers Priory, Lambton.
Born in 1866, Sir Harry had attended Oxford. Although he was 76 in 1942, he worked in London on the board of a regimental charity and at home in the garden. In addition he had several county jobs.   He looked just right for a retired general who was a country gentleman, with a fierce appearance—due perhaps to his grizzled moustache, high forehead and piercing blue eyes—yet he was obviously very kind. Not as obvious was the way he hated making decisions, and the way he loved to impart bad or portentous news. He was a cousin of Verena Villars and godfather to Henry Beedle. He died early in the winter of 1948–49.   **GU**, PE, LAR, (DD)

Waring, Lady Harriet.   Beliers Priory, Lambton.
One of the excellent women of Barsetshsire, Lady Harriet was good looking, fastidious in her tastes, and pleasant in her manners. She was conscientious, sensible, and hard-working, active in the Red Cross, the Girl Guides, the WVS, and several wartime working parties. In 1942 she was over sixty. The Warings' only child, their son George, had been killed in 1918 just before the armistice; Cecil Waring was their heir. Lady Harriet died just a few weeks after her husband, in the winter of 1949.
GU, PE, LAR, (DD)

Waring, Sir Cecil.   At sea. Beliers Priory, Lambton.
Nephew of Sir Harry Waring and heir to his title and estate. He served in the Navy during the war, first as Lieutenant, then as Captain. Following his discharge from active service, Sir Cecil founded a school for naval orphans at Beliers Priory.   He married Cora Palliser in 1950.
(GU), LAR, **DD**, HaRe, JC, WDIM

Waring, Lady Cora.   Gatherum Castle, West Barseshire. Beliers Priory, Lambton.
The daughter of the Duke and Duchess of Omnium, born in 1919. During the war she drove an ambulance. She was dashing, charming, confident, commanding, and sensible but high-spirited, with a bracing social honesty. Added to all this, she had great good looks, with sleek dark hair, dark eyes

and exquisite legs.   She loved to drive at high speeds through the county. She married Sir Cecil Waring in 1950. Their first child was a son, Plantaganet Cecil.   **CC, DD**, HaRe, JC

Waring Leslie. *See* Winter, Leslie.

Watson, Lettice. *See* Barclay, Lettice.

Watson, Roger (Deceased).
Husband of Lettice. Killed at Dunkirk in 1940.   MH

Watson, Diana and Claire.   Marling Hall, Marling Melicent.
Young daughters of Roger and Lettice Watson. In 1941 Diana was five and Claire turned four.   They later attended a boarding school and became rather boring.   MH, (CC)

Watson family:
    Watson, Charles.   Hallbury.
    A Hallbury solicitor.   MB

    Watson, Molly.   Hallbury.
    Of good sub-county stock, jolly and rather fat, with a loud voice, Mrs. Watson assumed the leadership of all the Hallbury wartime activities. It was she who provided the space for meetings and work parties in an extra building on their property. She and Miss Holly had been students together at Fairlawns.   MB

    Watson, Tom.   Hallbury.
    The eight-year-old son of the Watsons.   MB

Weaver, Sir Hosea. London.
Master of the Hosiers' Company in 1944. He was a Cambridge man who had the root of the matter in him. During the war he did not rise above the level of lieutenant, but was employed on the hush-hush mission near Beliers Priory, where he met Philip Winter.   H, DD

Welk, Harold.   Barchester.
An undertaker, and as such, someone who knew a lot about wood. The widowed father of Mavis Parkinson, he became very helpful to her and her family, once his duty was pointed out to him. Mr. Welk was said by Sir Edmund Pridham to be a direct descendant of Cedric the Saxon.   (PE), HaRe, CQ

Wendy.   France.
The Slave Friend made by Barbara Dunsford in Mentone in 1956, and who called Barbara "Friendy."
                                                                                                                          (ADA)

Wesendonck, Robert.
Speechless school friend of Tony Morland's, who visited High Rising in 1932 and 1933 when he was a shrimp-like little boy in spectacles. He grew up to be an Olympic swimmer.   HR, DH, (TST)

Weston.   Rushwater.
The Leslies' chauffeur in 1933.   WS

Wheeler. Pomfret Towers.
The farmer at the home farm.   OBH

Wheeler. Pomfret Towers.
A housemaid in 1937. PT

Wheeler. Pomfret Towers.
A groom in 1948. OBH

Wheeler, Bill. Harefield.
A first-class chimney sweep—the only one who really understood the chimneys at Pomfret Towers.
(H), (OBH), (CC), (CQ)

Wheeler, Florrie. Harefield.
In 1942, when she was sixteen, she was part of the domestic staff at the Beltons', just after they moved into Arcot House. H, HaRe

---

Wheeler, Sarah. Arcot House, Harefield.
The Beltons' formidable and capable house-parlormaid and cook. She had been with them since serving as Freddy's nurse. H, LAR, CQ

Wheeler, Sid. Harefield.
Proprietor of the Nabob, the local pub. H, (LAR), HaRe

Wickens, Mr. & Mrs. Assaye House, Harefield.
An ex-scout from St. Jude's, Oxford, Mr. Wickens had a game leg. His wife was very deaf and was thus contented. Together they kept Mr. Carton comfortable when he was in Harefield, and looked after the house when he was absent. H, HaRe

---

Wickham, Mr. Northbridge Manor, Northbridge.
The Mertons' agent. An ex-Navy man from the First War, he also served in the second. Wicks was of an ancient Barsetshire family who had lived over Chaldicotes way. He was genial and welcome everywhere among his many friends in the county. Innumerable wonderful pals kept him supplied with every variety of drink; he reciprocated with game birds he had shot while on vacation. By 1946 he was driving about in a disgraceful little clanking car on visits and bird-watching expeditions. He was the sort of man who would show up at a party with several extra bottles of something good, so that though he was never married he made a great contribution to society. (GU), **PE**, OBH, CC, HaRe, **JC**, WDIM, CQ, LAA, TST

Wicklow family:

    Wicklow, Roddy. Nutfield.
    Son of a partner in the architectural firm of Barton and Wicklow. In 1937 he went into the office of Mr. Hoare, the agent at Pomfret Towers and became the sole agent upon Mr. Hoare's death. In 1939 he married Alice Barton, daughter of his father's partner. A leg injury during the war got Roddy invalided out of the army in 1943 and he returned to work. Always dependable and good, he did his job well for many years.
        PT, B, BL, (CBI), (GU), (H), MB, (PBO), PE, OBH, WDIM, ADA, LAA, TST

    Wicklow, Alice Barton. Mellings, Nutfield.
    The daughter of Walter and Susan Barton. Extremely shy and delicate, Alice had led the life of a semi-invalid until her late teens. She had wanted to be an architect, but, discouraged in this by her family, had turned to painting. She was thin and sallow, with dark lank hair and large brown eyes.

When she gained confidence, she became quite pretty, and attracted the attention of her old friend, Roddy Wicklow. They were married in 1938 and lived in his family home in Nutfield, where Alice enjoyed a quiet success as a painter. The Wicklows had three children, Guy, Phoebe, and Alice.

PT, (BL), (CBI), (PE), OBH, ADA, LAA, TST

Wicklow, Sally. *See* under Pomfret.

Winter, Philip.　Southbridge School, Southbridge.　Dower House, Lambton.　Beliers Priory, Lambton. Harefield.

In 1936 Philip was an over-sensitive, self-important, left-leaning classics master at Southbridge School, just bringing out a small book on Horace. When war broke out he entered the Territorials, and during the war served with the Barsetshires. In 1942, markedly matured, and a colonel working in intelligence, he was stationed at the Dower House in Lambton, where he met the Warings. He and Leslie Waring were engaged in 1943 and married in 1945. After the war they founded the Priory School at Beliers Priory, and Philip began work on a Latin grammar. The school, renamed Harefield House School, was moved to Harefield House in 1952, after the Hosiers' Girls' Foundation School vacated the property.

SH, CBI, GU, (MB), PE, LAR, CC, DD, HaRe, JC, CQ

Winter, Leslie. Beliers Priory, Lambton.　Harefield House, Harefield.

Niece of Sir Harry, and Cecil Waring's sister, Leslie was normally a competent and well-organized young woman. However, during the war she had worked in London for a naval charity, and on an Atlantic crossing her ship had been torpedoed. She had been rescued after two days adrift in a lifeboat. This and other stresses necessitated a complete rest, and she was invited by her aunt to Beliers Priory to recuperate. Here she met Philip Winter; they were engaged in 1943 and married in 1945. After the war they started the Priory School at Beliers Priory. Their first child, Noel, was born in 1946 and their daughter Harriet in 1948. The school moved to Harefield House in the summer of 1952. As headmaster's wife, Leslie became an accomplished sock-darner, button-sewer, tea-giver, parent-greeter, and was, in short, the perfect helpmeet for Philip.

GU, (PE), LAR, CC, DD, HaRe, JC, CQ

Winthrop, Mr. Silverbridge.

Sir Cecil Waring's local solicitor. Mr. Winthrop had a post-office mouth, a description we are sure will need no explanation to anyone who has ever read *Great Expectations*—or dropped a letter in a slot.　　　DD

Part Two

A List of Animals

Horses are all the wrong shape.
— Julian Rivers,
Pomfret Towers

Animals

We've had hens for ages, so I don't really mind doing the food. I just wish they weren't so ungrateful.

— Margot Phelps

Bramble.

A pony at Rushwater House in 1945. He scorned his employers but was always willing to humor them and always set off for home at a brisk cheerful trot—then when he clattered into the stable yard he would stand still with such violence that he nearly knocked their teeth out against the bar the reins go over.   PBO

Brisket.

Hallidays' pony at Hatch House.   PBO

Chips.

Sally Wicklow's fox terrier. It was one of a trio, including Chloe and Wuffy, of exuberant and undisciplined dogs.   PT

Chloe.

Sally Wicklow's lurcher bitch. (A lurcher is a cross, properly between a sheepdog and a greyhound, often used by poachers.)   PT

Crumpet.

The Warings pony, which they used during the war to pull a cart. He had a small head and was stout, yet at the slightest opportunity he would tear at any scanty blades of grass along the way in a manner expressive of starvation and ill treatment.   GU

de Gaulle.

Conque's French poodle. He had been abandoned by one of the Free French, and had mange.   LAR

Flora.

John Middleton's ageing brown spaniel. She was long-suffering, as was everyone else in the household, but was skilled in the types of defiance acceptable in dogs. She may well not have liked him referring to himself in the third person as "Master."   BL

George.

A cat belonging to the Leslie family when David Leslie was a child. With great resourcefulness, George, when shut into the nursery dollshouse, flung all the furniture out the windows.   WS

Gibbon.

Hacker's chameleon. Formerly named Greta Garbo, and finally called Philip Gibbon, this reptile led an eventful life. It featured in the flooding of the bathroom at Southbridge School; it appeared during class in a red costume; and it was placed on a pink cake to test its color-changing abilities— to name just a few of its life's dramas. One of the world's best-educated lizards, it not only attended Southbridge School, but also spent some years at Oxford studying, or at least lying upon, the great classics of the Western World.   SH

Giulia.
An overweight King Charles spaniel belonging to Edith, Countess of Pomfret.   PT

Gunnar.
The Tebbens' tabby cat. Gunnar led a rich and interesting private life that his humans knew nothing about, and was quite possibly the most contented individual in the family.   He died at 16, and though much missed was never replaced with a kitten because, as Mrs. Tebben said, Gunnar didn't like kittens.   AF, LAR

Holdings Blunderbore.
A fine boar. He was the focus of hopes for a first at the Barsetshire Agricultural Show in the summer of 1955.   ESR

Holdings Goliath.
The Holdings entry in the Barsetshire Pig Breeders' Association show at Staple Park in 1946. Without the presence of Sir Robert to hearten him up, or perhaps because of the malevolence that came from his small evil eyes, Goliath came in second among the porcine competitors.   LAR

Holdings Hangover.
A boar that took second place at the Barsetshire Agricultural in 1953.   ESR

Lily Langtry.
A Jersey cow, much beloved by John Middleton. During the summer of 1939 she produced a heifer calf named Daphne, in honor of Daphne Stonor.   BL

Marling Magnum.
Champion boar, winner of the Challenge Cup at the Barsetshire Pig Breeders' Association show in 1946. So immense was his bulk one could see nothing of his feet except by bending double. A White Porkminster turning the scale at over fifty score, he was a very Churchill of a beast.   LAR

Mickey.
 Large half-caste dog belonging to the Thatchers in Gumper's End.   The only comb in the house seemed to belong to him.   B

Modestine.
A donkey bought by Mrs. Tebben to save the expense of keeping an automobile, the idea being that he ould pull a small cart. He was somewhat pretentiously named after the donkey that accompanied Robert Louis Stevenson on his *Travels with a Donkey,* but was re-christened Neddy by the younger Deans in 1935. In 1936 Modestine was sold to the Dean family, and made himself useful in the garden. At some point during the war he was sold to an evacuated nursery school, and, in 1947, despite rumors to the contrary, was thought to be still among the living.   AF, (LAR)

Pelléas.
A gentleman goat brought by Miss Hampton and Miss Bent to be sold at the Bring and Buy sale benefiting the New Town Cottage Hospital in Hallbury in 1944. Pelléas ended up stabled on the hospital grounds, and spent the rest of his life occasionally pulling a small cart for the benefit of child patients.   MB

Penny.
An old Scotch terrier with an elephantine face. He belonged to Mrs. Barton, who took the view that he should be destroyed because of his strong personal odor.   PT

Phaedra. (FEE.dra)

Mr. Palmer's prize cow. According to the Greek legend, Phaedra was the wife of Theseus and step-mother of Hippolytus, with whom she was in love.   BL

Pilgarlick, Pilbox, and Pilbeam.

Three of the grey Suffolks that pulled the dray carrying barrels of Pilward and Son's Entire. Pilgarlick could pull twenty-five hundredweight, standing. These horses were crossed with Percherons, which might explain their color. Suffolks are normally chestnuts.   OBH

Pillicock.

A small determined pony provided for the Honorable Giles Foster by Jasper Margett. He had a rough coat and a forelock that he tried constantly to toss away from his eyes, but he was harmless and had the wisdom only a good children's pony has.   OBH

Poniatowski.

The Marlings' pony, used for pulling a cart. It was named for any of several members of the great Polish family of that name, perhaps especially André.   MH

Puss.

Mr. Choyce's cat. When he married, Puss was glad of another, better, lap to sit on.   NTL

Rushwater Churchill.

One of the prize bulls belonging to the Leslies, named in honor of Sir Winston while he was standing for re-election in 1945, the year of Rushwater Churchill's birth. Although in a thoughtless moment he tried to gore the cowman, this bull knew a lady when he saw one, and was quite receptive to Virgil recited in a Romany-like murmur by Tom Grantly.   PBO, LAR, DD, ESR

Rushwater Romany.

The bull of the year in 1945. He used his simple arts to frighten the vicar.   PBO

Rushwater Rubicon.

He was the bull that changed Richard Tebben's life. Everyone thought that Richard's courage and presence of mind when the bull was loose in the lane saved little Jessica Dean from being trampled, tossed, gored—who knows? Her father was suitably appreciative.   AF

Note: (This is very like the scene from *The Small House at Allington* in which Johnny Eames saved Lord de Guest from a bull and was thereafter a favorite of his.)

Seraph.

A dog belonging to Maria Lufton. Seraph was a languishing cocker spaniel that looked like a canine edition of Elizabeth Barrett Browning.   DD

Smigly-Rydz.

A small black dog with hearth–rug hair belonging to Miss Hampton and Miss Bent. Smigly-Ridz was of a hopeful disposition but was unremarkable except that he, like Penny, had an elephantine head and mournful eyes. His behavior was at all times exemplary; he was in fact, little more than an animated bolster. He is of interest mainly because his name changed to honor the political hero of the moment. His many names included Zog, Beneš, Amethyst, Eisenhower, Mannerheim, Churchill, and Schusnigg. As these were all gallant men, his name was finally changed to Gallant.   CBI, GU, PE

Sylvia.

A pretty cocker spaniel belonging to Amy Birkett. Tony Morland adored her.   HR

Turk.

The Marlings' large, shaggy, exuberant, and disobedient dog.   Turk was of no particular breed, with a very large face which he was apt to push at strangers, and was exhaustingly faithful and affectionate.   Although Lucy thought he was more attached to the house than he was to her, he always slept in a basket outside her room after she left home. He died in 1950 at fifteen, not long after Lucy married and left Marling Hall.

MH, DD

Winston.

The kitten given by Mrs. Phipps to the Warings, and immediately appropriated by Matron, whose cat had just that day been shot by a convalescent soldier who thought it was a squirrel. Or so he said.   GU

Wuffy.

An Airedale, one of the terrible trio of Sally Wicklow's rowdy dogs.   PT

Part Three

A List of Places

"The road to Brandon Abbey was through
some of the loveliest scenery in Barsetshire. Leaving
PomfretMadrigal it went through Little Misfit, with a glimpse
of the hideous pinnacles of Pomfret Towers in the distance, and then
followed for several miles the winding course of the Rising, among water
meadows that looked greener than ever in contrast with the sun-parched country."

— Angela Thirkell, The Brandons

Barsetshire Places

Aberdeathly. The home in Scotland of Admiral Christopher Hornby and his family. It was of unparalleled hideousness, built of granite with pepper-pot turrets and located on the slopes of Ben Gaunt just above Loch Gloom. It was about ten miles from Inverdreary, where the train stopped twice a week. The main house was a hospital during the war. Christopher and Elsa Hornby lived there in the reconditioned factor's house.

Acacia House. Located in the Cathedral Close, this was where Canon Fewling took his bride. It was of red brick, three-storied, with a stone parapet at the top. The rear of the house sloped away toward the river. On the ground floor were a dining room that gave a view of the Close, and the Canon's study. On the first floor an L-shaped drawing room ran the length of the house and looked out over the river. The master bedroom was above that on the second floor, with a dressing room, smaller bedroom, and a good bathroom.

Adamsfield. A three-acre piece of property originally on the Marling estate and farmed in the eighteenth century by Adam Nandy, the great-grand-father of Henry Nandy. It was bought by Sam Adams in 1947 to be used for raising vegetables for the canteens in his factories.

Aloes. The Northbridge home of Miss Talbot and Miss Dolly Talbot.

Arcot House. A handsome house owned by the Beltons in the village of Harefield. They moved into it in the autumn of 1942, when it became too expensive to maintain the much larger Harefield House. Although it was not the large country house that they were used to, it was by no means meager or pitiful. The drawing room looked out onto the village street in front and onto the garden in back. A large cedar in the lawn provided a fine place for tea on pleasant days.

Assaye House. The house in Harefield belonging to Sidney Carton. It was older and smaller than the Beltons' house, having at one time been part of the Abbey. It had two stories, a massive oak staircase, and a large room, formerly a barn, which Mr. Carton used as a study, library, sitting room, smoking room and work room.

Barchester High School. A girls' school accommodating both boarding and day pupils. It occupied a late Georgian house in Barchester. After the war a preparatory school was attached to the High School, which the ten-year-old Lavinia Merton was attending in 1953.

Barsetshire. The county is described from the heights of Hangman's Hill. It was a charming country of rolling downland and fertile fields. Water meadows lay to the west and southwest along the River Rising. In the distance the roofs of Barchester and the high steeple of Barchester Cathedral could be made out. Valleys watered by meandering streams and threaded by roads were in the farthest distance, just before a line of real hills.

Beliers Priory. The home of Sir Harry Waring and his wife, built by his grandfather in 1872. It was being used by the military as a convalescent hospital during the Second War, when central heating and adequate plumbing were installed. In 1945 Philip Winter and Leslie Waring Winter, with Sir Harry's approval, turned it into a boys' preparatory school called The Priory School. Later, Beliers Priory was inherited by Cecil Waring. Built on the site of a pre-Reformation abbey in the 1870's, it was large, inconvenient and uncomfortable to an impressive degree.

Bishop's Palace. The Bishop's residence in the close, referred to by custom as the Palace. We do not have a description of the building, as we have never been invited inside it, but those who have returned from visits say that their experience was unpleasant in the extreme, valuable only for vivid memories of hunger, cold, discomfort, and darkness.

Bolder's Knob. Thought to have been once dedicated to Baldur, it was a steep green lump between Pomfret Towers and Hatch End, one of the higher elevations in the county.

Bostock & Plummer's. A Barchester department store. The Bishop's wife patronized the ladies' ready to wear department.

Boxall Hill. Another hill, located east of Barchester and west of Greshamsbury. It featured in Trollope as the site and name of Scatcherds' home. This house later passed back to the Greshams when Frank Gresham's wife, Mary Thorne, turned out to be the heir to the property.

Brandon Abbey. A mid-Victorian pile built in "Scotch baronial" style on the site of a ruined religious house. Miss Brandon's father built it when she was a small child in the 1860's and it had never been redecorated. It was left to a charity at her death, but while it was being renovated by Walter Barton, the war erupted and the Ministry of General Interference took it over, only vacating it in December of 1947.

Cap Ferrat. Located on the French Riviera. Lord and Lady Pomfret had a villa there.

Casa Strelsa. The home in Florence of the Strelsas.

Cathedral. Assuming that the Barchester Cathedral is, in fact, Salisbury Cathedral, we can turn to any one of a number of books for a description or information. The Cathedral was begun in the 13th century and the spire, completed in the 14th, is the highest in the country at 404 feet. The interior underwent a savage "restoration" in the 18th century, which left it rather bare, as various monuments, screens, and other features were removed. The cloisters have an arched roof and are said to be the largest and oldest of any cathedral in England. The Cathedral sits in the center of large lawns studded with immense trees, which are themselves surrounded by the Close, creating a space of unusual beauty, tranquility, and interest.

Cathedral Close. The Close is just that, streets that surround the Cathedral on four sides. The houses are from varied architectural periods, of varying sizes, and all beautiful, and all give a view across the park to the Cathedral. Only pedestrian traffic is allowed, and the atmosphere is serene.

The Cedars. A property given to Oliver Marling by his father in 1950. It was a small house of two stories, with three bedrooms upstairs, a brick-paved stable yard, and a small, well-laid-out garden. Oliver and Maria lived there after their marriage, and she kept her cocker spaniels in the stables.

Chaldicotes. From Trollope. A heavily mortgaged estate belonging to Nathaniel Sowerby. Martha Dunstable bought it and she and Dr. Thorne lived there after their marriage.

> Chaldicotes is a house of much more pretension than Framley Court . . . it is a place
> of very considerable pretension. There is an old forest . . . attached to it, called the
> Chase of Chaldicotes. . . . The house of Chaldicotes is a large stone building, probably
> of the time of Charles the Second. It is approached on both fronts by a heavy double
> flight of stone steps. In the front of the house a long, solemn, straight avenue through
> a double row of lime-trees, leads away to lodge-gates, which stand in the centre of the
> village of Chaldicotes; but to the rear the windows open upon four different vistas,
> which run down through the forest . . . four open green rides, which all converge together

at a large iron gateway, the barrier which divides the private grounds from the Chase. The Sowerbys, for many generations, have been rangers of the Chase of Chaldicotes. . . .

(Framley Parsonage)

Clive's Corner. The house in Harefield belonging to the Updikes. It was of time-softened red brick decorated in front with stonework, pleasant but not astonishing. It had stables and a small paddock.

Cockspur Theatre. The London theatre where Aubrey Clover and Jessica Dean were based.

County Club. Located in Barchester, a popular meeting place for the county landowners, professionals, and other men of note. During the war, the dining room and one drawing room were open to members of both sexes, but in 1948 the government offices that had occupied the Women's County club vacated them and both clubs reverted to their original policies of being limited to members of one sex, and their guests. Some of the members were Sir Harry Waring, Lord Pomfret, Frederick Belton, Lord Stoke, Sam Adams, Sir Robert Fielding, Donald Macfadyen, and Septimus Grantly.

Cow and Sickle. The inn and public house in Pomfret Madrigal; Mrs. Grant stayed there in *The Brandons*. Mr. and Mrs. Spindler were the proprietors.

Crosse Hall. The home of Lord Crosse, situated between Boxall Hill and Greshamsbury Hall. It was a medium-sized brick house, well-proportioned on the lower floors but low-ceilinged on the top floor.

Cross Keys. A Barchester pub suitable for informal lunches.

Deanery. The of Dean and Mrs. Crawley, located in the Cathedral Close. It housed the family though the number of grandchildren grew past twenty. It was early Georgian in age and design, beautiful and inconvenient in equal proportions. The rooms on the ground floor were low, and made good studies, libraries, and offices. The first floor had high ceilings and overlooked the Close, but on the floors above the house became a warren of corridors, staircases, bedrooms and bathrooms. Olivia had a biggish bedroom on the second floor that offered a view of the garden with its herbaceous border and the river at the bottom of the slope.

Dipping Ponds. A series of small ponds, located on the site of the little abbey of Beliers, two miles from Worsted. They were thought to have been stew ponds (ponds used for keeping fish until ready for use) in the middle ages. The largest of them, although shallow and muddy, was used for swimming.

Dowlah Cottage. The Harefield cottage of Mrs. Hoare, furnished and decorated with the many special things bequeathed to her. It was a pleasant two-storied house with a passage that ran from the front door straight through to the garden. After the war, Freddy and Susan Belton and their son Freddy lived there in great happiness and comfort.

Drill Hall. A large wooden building in Greshamsbury used for such community activities as bazaars. In winter draughts came in through the walls, and in summer the heat beat down on its corrugated iron roof. A small wash-house was attached that had one cold-water tap.

Edgewood. A West Barsetshire village, the home of the Grantlys at the Rectory, along with their domestic staff Edna and Doris Thatcher and their four children; Miss Sowerby (and later the Sam Adamses) at the Old Bank House; Mrs. Goble at the post office; and other villagers. The Cross Keys was its public house, and the church St. Michael and All Angels. The wood for which the town was named had all but disappeared by the 1940's, and other unlovely effects of modernization had occurred. Shops were made from fine old houses, new buildings were constructed of hideous, harsh new brick that clashed with the mellowness of the old brick, an old church had become a cinema, plate glass had replaced small panes, and altogether Edgewood was losing its character.

Edgewood Rectory. The home of the Grantlys in the 1940's. It was near the church on a slight rise at the north edge of town. The grounds were too large for any recent rector to afford to keep up properly; they included a croquet lawn and a tennis court that had been used as a vegetable garden during the war. The kitchen was large, warm, sunny and welcoming.

Fish Hill. A lovely steep eminence on which sheep grazed, trees were gnarled, rare birds nested, and the vistas induced soul-searching monologues.

Fleece. The pub and inn in Skeynes. It had been a free house, selling several kinds of beer and ale, until in 1946 an urgent need for beer arose to provide for the increased custom occasioned by the Barsetshire Pig Breeders' Association show held nearby. At that point the innkeeper yielded his principles and became tied to Pilward's Entire—and had enough beer.

Framley Court. The seat of the Lufton family, in northwest Barsetshire. By 1949, it had become too costly to maintain properly, and the widowed Lady Lufton had let part of it to Mr. Macfadyen of Amalgamated Vedge. When her son married, he lived in their part of Framley Court and Dowager Lady Lufton moved with her unmarried daughter to the Old Parsonage.

> [Framley Court] was a low building of two stories, built at different periods, and devoid of any
> pretensions to any style of architecture; but the rooms, though not lofty, were warm and
> comfortable, and the gardens trim and neat beyond all others in the county. Indeed, it was
> for its gardens that Framley Court was celebrated. (*Framley Parsonage*)

Framley Parsonage (Old Parsonage). The home of Mark Robarts in the mid-nineteenth century, and home to some generations of parsons afterwards. But as time passed and servants were fewer and standards changed, the Parsonage became secular and was used as a dower house by the Lufton family.

> . . . nothing in the parsonage way could be more perfect than [Framley] parsonage. It had all
> the details requisite for the house of a moderate gentleman with moderate means, and none of
> those expensive superfluities which immoderate gentlemen demand. . . . And then the gardens
> and paddocks were exactly suited to it; and everything was in good order. . . . (*Framley Parsonage*)

Gatherum Castle. Home of the Palliser family: the Duke and Duchess of Omnium, Jeffrey and Cora Palliser. It had been built at great expense in the early 1820's, with an entrance hall reminiscent of Euston Station. The usual complement of marble statuary, old masters, brocade draperies, and heavy furniture failed to mask its essential monstrousness. During the war the Ministry of General Interference had occupied the Castle, converting bedrooms and corridors into a hive of small offices, and using the large rooms as recreation centers. In the basement were kitchens and canteens for employees of differing social ranks. The Duke and Duchess lived in what had been the servant's quarters.

Glycerine Cottage. The Northbridge cottage occupied by Miss Crowder and Miss Hopgood The name was inspired by a small wisteria-covered villa near Mentone, in the south of France, called "Les Glycines." (*Glycine* is the French word for wisteria.) It was a tiny place but it suited the two dear friends; they lived in it for years.

Golden Valley. This is an elusive geological feature, subject to the mutability that has affected some of the residents and other locales of Barsetshire. It is visible from the windows of Beliers Priory, no doubt because it is near Beliers Priory. Later, however, it is part of the estate at Pomfret Towers. We think it is most memorable as the lovely spot on the last page of *Three Score and Ten* where Ludo and Lavinia walk hand in hand and plan their future together, a long crescent-shaped valley with beeches on one side and grazing cattle on the other. There is an actual Golden Valley in Gloucestershire, but if it has any connection with this one, we cannot say.

Great House at Allington. This was the west Barsteshire home of Squire Dale, the benevolent uncle of Isabel and Lily Dale, in *The Small House at Allington*. (The nearby small house was one he owned which he offered to the Dales rent-free.) By 1949, the Great House was owned by Isabel Dale's widowed mother, who left it to Robin Dale when she died that year. Robin and Anne moved into it and started a pre-preparatory school for small boys.

> . . . the house itself was very graceful. It had been built in the days of the early Stuarts, in that style of architecture to which we give the name of the Tudors. On its front it showed three pointed roofs, or gables . . . and between each gable a thin, tall chimney stood, the two chimneys thus raising themselves just above the three peaks . . . the beauty of the house depended much on those two chimneys . . . and on the mullioned windows with which the front of the house was closely filled. . . . (*The Small House at Allington*)

Greshamsbury. Village in East Barsetshire that was home to the Fairweathers, the John Leslies, the Parkinsons, the Captain Francis Greshams, the Umblebys, and the vicar, Tubby Fewling. The new part of town remained mostly separate from the old part, so the original character of Greshamsbury was retained.

Greshamsbury Park. The hereditary seat of the Gresham family. As with so many other large houses, Greshamsbury House had become a property of the National Trust by the mid-twentieth century. The owners lived in a part of the house, the great rooms were on display, and cousins, the Francis Greshams, lived in a small wing. We must again turn to Trollope for a description.

> [The Park and House are] a fine old English gentleman's seat . . . built in the . . . purest style of Tudor architecture. . . . The gardens . . . have been celebrated for two centuries. . . .
>
> (*Doctor Thorne*)

Grumper's End. The unsalubrious slum of Pomfret Madrigal. Once a collection of small, mean cottages, it had been transformed by 1956 into a large estate of council houses.

Gundric's Fossway. An old Roman road or chalk track, running north and south through Barsetshire. It skirted the Halliday property, mounted the downs and gave a panoramic view of all Barsetshire from the summit of a steep green hump known as Bolder's Knob. The Fosse Way, which is an old Roman road linking southwestern with northeastern Roman Britain, runs along the western edge of Wiltshire.

Hallbury. A village in west Barsetshire. Technically on the estate of the Duke of Omnium, it was now largely a limited company. It was home to Admiral Palliser, Mr. and Mrs. Watson, and Mrs. Merivale. Sir Robert and Lady Fielding owned Hall's End and stayed there occasionally. The Rectory was occupied until 1945 by Dr. Dale. The church in the Old Town was St. Hall Friars. This town, as was the case with others, was struggling to retain its particular character, but had been subjected to the depredations of speculative builders and an influx of London commuters. The town became divided into the Old Town on the hill and the New Town in the outlying areas, each with its distinctive style.

Hallbury House. The home of Admiral Palliser. It had a large garden, a small horse paddock, and included a field that was usually let out for grazing.

Hall's End. The small house in Hallbury owned by Sir Robert and Lady Fielding.

Hangman's Hill. A very considerable eminence in west central Barsetshire. Once thick with beeches and thorn trees, it was planted in the 1940's with larches and firs which grew quickly and could be harvested frequently. What was lost in the beauty of the trees was made up in the beauty of the views, for the loss of the trees gave increase in the panorama of downs, fields, water-meadows, rivers, and villages.

Harcourt Abbey. This seems to have been a red herring, in a sense. It was mentioned once at the end of ADA and then never again.

Harcourt Towers. The ancestral seat of the Duke of Towers. It had been built around the same time as Pomfret Towers, and was considered a remarkable survival of mixed architecture, being part seventeenth century chateau, part mid-Victorian railway station, and part Natural History Museum. The walls were of particularly ghastly purple-red brick combined decoratively with yellow stone, and the roof was a miracle of pepper-pot turrets, peaked turrets, and iron frills. By 1958 it had been made into a kind of country club and was open to the public at half a crown apiece, with teas in the servants' hall. The local hunt had leased the stables, and the grounds had been laid out as a golf course, so that altogether it was economically viable.

Harcourt. The village near the Towers. It contained the reasonably-sized home of the duke and duchess, a somewhat smaller house for the dowager duchess and her two daughters, a rectory in which Lord and Lady William lived, the church, the Harcourt Arms and the customary shops and services.

Harefield. A village northwest of Barchester. It was home to the Beltons, Updikes, Perrys, Sidney Carton, Mr. Oriole, and, at Harefield House, the Hosiers' Girls' Foundation School. When the Hosiers' School moved nearby after the war, the building, formerly the handsome home of the Belton family, was used to house the Harefield House School. The Nabob's Head was the local pub; Sid Wheeler was the proprietor. Madras Cottages housed the poor. It lay in the upper valley of the River Rising, where the river in its juvenile form flows hither and thither through the meadowlands north of the village. The High Street slants across this scene; the houses on the south command a view of the hills, and the houses on the north having gardens that slope toward the water meadows.

Harefield House. The family home of the Beltons, bought in the late eighteenth century by an ancestor who had burst into affluence with the help of the Honorable East India Company. It was a large property with a handsome Palladian house, a folly, and extensive gardens. Two curved arcades led from the center block to small houses at either end. Inside the main house, one entered through a paneled vestibule paved with black and white squares of marble into a hall from which doors led into various gracious reception rooms. A wide staircase with shallow steps led upward; a domed skylight above gave an airy feeling. On the parapet of this block a row of plaster urns made a stately impression.

Hatch End. A village near Little Misfit on the River Rising, home of the Hallidays at Hatch House; the Panters; Mr. Scatcherd and Hettie Scatcherd at Rokeby; the Vidlers; Mrs Hubback; and the Richard Carter family at the Old Manor House. The Mellings Arms was the local pub, George Panter, proprietor. There was a church, of course, and a vicarage in which Mr. Choyce lived. The town was spread out along the River Rising, separated from it by the water meadows and the road. Most of the houses were constructed of the local grey stone which with time had been embroidered with lichens of gold and green, and the cottages were made of stone, old brick, or wattle-and-daub, many with thatched roofs. There was no Great House nearby, Pomfret Towers being the center of interest. As it lay so close under the downs, Hatch End was in shade for much of the day, whatever the time of year.

Hatch House. A house built in 1721 for the Halliday family, outside the village of Hatch End. It was larger and situated on more land than the Old Manor House in the village; when it was built, the Old Manor House was let and the family removed to Hatch House.

High Rising. The village where Mrs. Morland came to live permanently after the war, bringing with her the worthy housekeeper, Stoker. High Rising was attractive and unpretentious, with only one street of houses most built in the Georgian style. Laura Morland's house was at one end, and described as "uninteresting," but as it was never described in any detail, we will never know if we agree. There was also a shop, a garage run by Mr. Brown, a church, a vicarage in which the Goulds lived, and the Rising Arms. Dr. Ford lived at High Rising with his housekeeper Mrs. Mallow, and nearby at Low Rising was Low Rising Manor, the home of George and Anne Knox where Adrian and Sybil Coates were frequent visitors. By the late 1950's High Rising had grown to be a town.

Hiram's Hospital. From Trollope

A charity established in 1434 on a pleasant property just outside Barchester. The purpose of it was to provide for the old age of twelve indigent men who were no longer employable. Each was given his own room, all meals, and a small daily stipend. The Hospital of St. Nicholas, founded in 1227, situated near the Close in Salisbury, and dedicated to housing and supporting the poor, is said to be the original of Hiram's Hospital.

Hogglestock. A working-class community in the north of Barsetchire, which became the location of Sam Adams' rolling mills. Trollope describes Hogglestock.

> Barsetshire, taken altogether, is a pleasant green tree-becrowded country, with large bosky hedges, pretty damp deep lanes, and roads with broad grass margins running along them. . . . Just up in its northern extremity this nature alters. There it is bleak and ugly, with low artificial hedges and without wood; not uncultivated, as it is all portioned out into new-looking large fields, bearing turnips and wheat, and mangel. . . . There is not a gentleman's house in the parish of Hogglestock besides that of the clergyman; and this . . .can hardly be said to be fit to be so. It is ugly, and straight, and small. There is a garden . . . but this garden, like the rest of the parish, is by no means ornamental. . . . It produces cabbages, but no trees: potatoes . . . but hardly any flowers, and nothing worthy of the name of a shrub. . . . The Hogglestock farmers were a rude, rough set, not bordering in their social rank on the farmer gentle.
>
> *(Framley Parsonage)*

Holdings. The home of the Grahams. A large country property built during the Regency Stucco era, located near Little Misfit, it had a large reception room known since the eighteenth century as the Saloon, with four long windows looking out over the garden and beyond to the river.

The Hollies. Home of Mrs. Turner and her two nieces, it was a pleasant stone Georgian house standing back a little from the street. During the war it was a social center, always a place for a warm welcome.

Hoopers Platt. A derelict area on which was built the Air Raid Wardens' shelter in Northbridge.

Hop Pole. The public house in Marling Melicent.

Hosiers' Girls' Foundation School. A school for girls supported by the Hosiers, a City Livery Company. Originally it had been situated in London but was evacuated to Barchester under a working arrangement with Barchester High School. Its London buildings had been almost completely demolished in 1940 and it was looking for a new permanent home. An intermediate location which allowed the school autonomy was the site at Harefield Park. After the war the Hosiers acquired a nearby piece of land from Mr. Belton and built an entirely new school and campus.

Hovis House. The Northbridge house of Mrs. Dunsford and Miss Dunsford. Work parties were held in the large back drawing room during the war. Before the Dunsfords occupied the house, Eleanor Halliday's parents had lived there. The name was thought to derive from Offa or Hoven, the names of the putative original owners.

Jasper Margett's Cottage. *See* Pear Tree Cottage.

Jutland Cottage. The Southbridge home of Admiral and Mrs. Phelps and their daughter Margot. Originally called The Hollies, the house was renamed by the Phelps for the Battle of Jutland, one of the Admiral's keenest memories. The small house was two-storied, and there was enough in the way of grounds to provide space for a vegetable garden, a chicken run, and a few goats. Naval men of all ages were always welcome there.

Ladysmith Cottages. Lambton Home of Nannie Allen. These had been built by the father of Sir Harry Waring, and were unattractive but comfortable, solid, and warm. Dark grey slate roofs, absolutely rain-proof, sloped down to walls of grey brick decorated with a diamond pattern in red brick. Each cottage was let at a nominal rate to a retired servant or pensioner, and with each came the right to coal. The end units were most desirable, having bow windows in front upstairs and down, and built-out halls, thus making the sitting room in front reach the width of the house.

Lamb's Piece. A modest house caused to be built in the 1920's by Mrs. Tebben. It was situated on a steeply sloping lot near Worsted. The rooms were cramped, especially the dining room, half of which had as an afterthought been turned into a very inadequate study for Mr. Tebben. The stairs creaked. Originally a country retreat, the Tebbens lived there year round after Mr. Tebben retired.

Lambton Vicarage. This became the home of Tommy and Octavia Needham in 1943.

The Laurels. One of the two good houses in Greshamsbury. It was owned by the Umblebys and leased to the Greens, who in 1952 sub-let it to the John and Rose Fairweather and their family.

Laverings. An old farm owned by Lord Bond and rented to the architect John Middleton and his wife. It was down a little lane half a mile east of Skeynes. Over the years the house had been altered, burnt, and rebuilt, but still retained its essential character. It had been derelict for ten years when Lord Bond bought it to prevent its being sold to and possibly lived in by Sir Ogilvy Hibberd. Included in the property were the White House and four large fields. This became Mr. Middleton's country retreat for about ten years, but when he married, his wife lived in it full time, and he was there every weekend.

Little Gidding. This was the arresting name of a lane in Hallbury, mentioned in *Miss Bunting*, set in 1945. The original Little Gidding was a religious community in Huntingdonshire, established in 1625 and broken up by Cromwell in 1646. T.S. Eliot's poem, *Little Gidding*, appeared in 1942. We are left to draw our own conclusions about what meaning, if any, there is in this.

Little Misfit. A very small village near Hatch End. Holdings, the home of the Grahams, was located there.

The Lodge. A house in Silverbridge inherited by Cecil Waring when his uncle Sir Harry Waring died. He rented it to Lord and Lady Silverbridge in 1950. It was hidden by a low brick wall behind which was a row of rhododendrons; two brick pillars supported the wrought iron gate. A short drive led to a red brick house sitting tidily among its gardens and lawns. A terrace offered a view of a line of tall lime trees that led to the river. Inside, the hall was paneled in white wood, running the length of the house to open through glass doors to a large lawn. The drawing room ran the length of the house and had elegant mantelpieces. Four bedrooms were on the first floor, and above that, many more.

Low Rising. A hamlet about a mile from High Rising, near which was to be found the home of the George Knoxes. The tiny village consisted only of a church and vicarage, a farm or two, and some cottages.

Low Rising Manor House. The home of George Knox and his wife and, before her marriage, his daughter Sybil. It was out of the village, and reached, after leaving the road, by a willow avenue that ran along beside the brook. The house was at the end of this lane, solitary, mist-shrouded, perhaps a bit scarey. It looked in the early 1930's like the farmer's house it had been for many hundred years. That is the way Mr. George Knox liked it, and he was slow to bring in improvements, but bring them he did, for after he married for the second time, wives being what they are, improvement was inevitable.

Lufton Park. The previous seat of the Lufton family, it was "ancient and ramshackle" (Anthony Trollope, *Framley Court)* even in the nineteenth century, and was only a memory by 1949.

Macpherson's House. Home of the agent at Rushwater House. It was a small Regency house, somewhat of the *cottage orné* persuasion, with improbable stucco battlements and a porch that seemed to have been intended for a church. Inside, a wide hall, a drawing room overlooking the veranda, a small conservatory, a dining room, three bedrooms and a modern bath made this a very desirable home for Tom and Emmy Grantly when they married after Mr. Macpherson's death.

Marling Hall. The home of William and Amabel Marling and, until their marriages, their children Lettice, Oliver and Lucy. It was a fine old home that showed the sad signs of attrition brought about by death duties and other modern improvements. Trees had been sold for timber or had died for lack of care. The home farm was barely surviving. The property had been in the Marling family for generations, and the house was over two hundred years old. One wing had been added in 1780. There was an avenue of limes from the house to the river, and a two-story pavilion called the stone parlor had been built against the south-west corner of the house. During the war the family appropriated the servants' hall for a dining room, and the principal rooms were closed, except the drawing room which was used for Red Cross stores.

Marling Melicent. The village near Marling Hall. Its most notable resident was Joyce Smith, owner of the Red House. The favorite local pub was the Hop Pole. A cottage hospital was in the village, in addition to the usual shops and services.

Melicent Halt. The train station for Marling Melicent and Marling Hall.

Mellings. The Nutfield home of the architect Walter Barton, his wife and children. Once a dower house of the Pomfrets, it stood between a turn in the road and the river. Part of it was an original Jacobean structure with a south front that had been added in 1760. The gardener's cottage had been converted to a small scale model of the Parthenon. Mr. Barton rented the property from Lord Pomfret, and had wrested an agreement from his Lordship's agent that allowed him to install central heating. From this property Lord Pomfret's second title came.

Mellings Arms. The pub in Hatch End.

The Milky Way. The Northbridge cottage belonging to Miss Hopgood's aunt, Helen Hopgood.

The Mitre. An inn in Northbridge where a good lunch was served.

Mngangaland. The East African country in which the Colonial Bishop Joram served with such relish for many years until he retired to Barsetshire in 1940. It was an anthropologist's dream, for there many curious rites and customs had survived for years beyond the demise of Colonialism.

Myxo-Lydia. A small Balkan country from which numerous refugees came to England during the war. The Myxo-Lydians had an ancient, intense, and murderous hatred of their neighbors, the Slavo-Lydians.

Nabob's Head. The inn and public house in Harefield.

Northbridge. The home of the Villars, Mrs. Turner, Miss Pemberton and Mr. Downing, Mrs. and Miss Dunsford, Miss Hopgood and Miss Crowder, Miss Hopgood's aunt, Commander Beasley, and, not too far away, the Keiths, and later the Noel Mertons. Miss Ward, Miss Heath and Miss Chiffinch settled there when they retired from their most active years. Much of the town was Cathedral property. Because the law firm of Keith & Keith represented the Cathedral in much of its business, and because Mr. Keith had been a local property owner, the town was protected from much modern development. Life in the town during the war was based on Mrs. Thirkell's experience of Beaconsfield, where she spent several months of the war, but in looks it is thought that Northbridge is very like Chipping Camden in Gloustershire.

Northbridge Manor. The home of the Keiths, a small property. A short lime avenue led up to a square red brick house, about a hundred and fifty years old. The rooms were well proportioned, with a wide central passage running through the ground floor from the front door to french windows that opened at the further end onto a gravel walk between grass plots. During the war the house was used by an insurance company. Robert Keith inherited the house, but was comfortably established near Nutfield, so after the war it was sold to Lydia Keith Merton and her husband Noel.

Northbridge Rectory. The Northbridge home of the Villars. During the war it was used to house part of the staff of the Barsetshire Regiment, at which time central heating and various improvements were added by the government. The house was large, with ten bedrooms, a large coach house, and stables. The garden, like so many in Barsetshire, sloped down to the river. When the Villars moved to the Cathedral Close, the Rectory was taken by Everard and Kate Carter as a retirement home after they left Southbridge School. As it was then no longer literally a rectory the name was changed to "Old Rectory."

Norton Hall. The home of Lady Norton. Her mere existence had turned the place, built by John Wood and decorated by the Adam brothers, into a drear and dismal shell of its true beauty.

Number Seventeen. The home of Sir Robert and Lady Fielding, located in the Close. It had at one time belonged to Canon Robarts, and was one of the most handsome of houses where all houses were handsome. Three stories high, built of red brick, it had a gracefully curved shell-shaped projection over the front door. The hall was paved with stone flags, and the spiral staircase wound gracefully to the upper floors.

Nutfield. A town on the estate of Lord Pomfret. The architect Walter Barton lived there with his family, and the Wicklows lived down the street. It was the prettiest town in that part of England, still much the same as it had been in the eighteenth century. Because it was so much the property of the Earl of Pomfret, there had been no speculative building because he wouldn't have it, and no cinemas or chain stores had been allowed. Nutfield High Street, lined with elms, ran down to the river. The houses were Georgian, set back and protected from the street within walls or iron fences, some with gardens behind that ran down to the river.

Old Bank House. The Edgewood home of Sam Adams and his family, which he bought in 1948 from Miss Sowerby. Like Number Seventeen, it was three-storied and had a shell canopy. The drawing room ran the length of the house, and after Mr. Adams' renovation (done with the assistance of Mrs. Belton) was hung with Chinese paper and draperies of pre-war silk. An elegant Chinese-Chippendale sofa, three large Chinese vases filled with fountains of flowers, and gilded mirrors gave an impression of noble contentment. The small library contained the Sowerby collection of books, sold with the house. In the dining room were silver-striped paper, Regencystyled mahogany furniture, and some good silver and crystal. Glass doors led from the stone-paved hall into the garden, with its green lawn and colorful herbaceous border.

Old Barum. Located in West Barsetshire between Hallbury and Barchester, it was an ancient hill fort, described as triple-tiered, grass-grown and mysterious in that no one knew very much about it.

Old Begum. An ale-house in Harefield.

Old Manor House. The house in Hatch End lived in by the Halliday family before they built Hatch House in 1721. It was still owned by them in 1954 and used as a rental property. The Richard Carters were the occupants in 1955.

Old Parsonage. *See* Framley Parsonage.

Old Rectory. The Greshamsbury home of the John Leslies, a late Georgian house standing in grounds belonging to the house and not the church. Mr. Oriel had lived in it when he was at Greshamsbury.

Parsley Island. An island in the river opposite Northbridge Rectory. It belonged to Farmer Brown, who often rented campsites, and was a favorite picnic spot of the Keiths'. Beech trees grew there right down to the water; there were grassy clearings and thickets. A path led to an abandoned gravel pit.

Pear Tree Cottage. The home of Jasper Margett. On the Beliers Priory property, the cottage got its name from the large pear tree that towered over it. On the outside, it was like a picture from the height of the Romantic school, with its thatched roof, wattle and daub construction, small lattice windows, stone-rimmed well, ancient pigsty, and bench beside the door. Inside, however, the picture was not so romantic. One grimy room downstairs comprised all the functions of home, kitchen, sitting room, and dining room; there were wall-to-wall vermin skins tacked up, and bunches of dried animal corpses hung about like strings of onions do in other kitchens. A little stairway in the hall led to his bedroom above.

Pension Ramsden. This is where Miss Hopgood and Miss Crowder stayed during their annual visits to Mentone, on the Riviera. It was kept by the French widow of a major in the British army, and therefore had a comforting somewhat-English atmosphere—though some of the rooms had bidets.

Pilchard's Stores. A Barchester department store.

Plassey House. The home in Harefield of the Perrys. It was smaller than the Belton's Arcot House, but perfectly pleasant. Mrs. Perry was one who followed the country custom of keeping the front door open during the day; there was a glass door inside it through which the visitor could see down the hall to the glass doors at the other end, which revealed the garden beyond which contained the biggest elm tree in that part of the country. As Plassey was a doctor's house, patients arrived during office hours. They came into a cobbled yard through the carriage gate and crossed to the surgery in what had once been the orangery.

Pomfret Abbas. The small church near Brandon Abby at which Miss Brandon's funeral took place.

Pomfret Madrigal. A village in central Barsetshire, built on the site of a former abbey. Mrs. Brandon lived there at Stories, the vicarage was a short walk away, and the local watering spot, the Cow and Sickle, offered food and rooms. The church was ancient, being part of the old abbey. Sir Edmund Pridham lived nearby. Grumper's End was the dismal area on the outskirts of town that housed the village poor, including the large Thatcher family.

Pomfret Towers. Built by the sixth Earl of Pomfret in the early 1870's. While at Oxford he had come under the influence of the Gothic revival, and had been tremendously impressed by his first sight of St. Pancras Station in London, as indeed who is not. Therefore, he decreed that his own home should be built along the same imposing lines to a design by Sir Gilbert Scott. What resulted was the huge conglomeration of turrets, steep roofs, gables, chimney stacks, and clock tower commonly referred to as a "pile." The interior vied with the exterior for extravagant application of decoration and design, with carved marble, carved plaster, and walls painted to resemble tapestries or hung with heavy silks. Miles of corridors guaranteed weary servants and tepid meals. It was here that Lady Emily Leslie had grown up with her brother, the seventh Earl of Pomfret, who lived in it nearly eighty-five years. After the seventh Earl's death, and the eighth Earl had inherited, the cost of upkeep finally became too great, and the main part of the building was leased to a conglomerate headed by Sam Adams, Donald Macfadyen and Bert Pilward.

Pooker's Piece. A wooded field near Skeynes. It had been bought in the 1830's by the Reverand Horatio Pooker, the vicar of Skeynes Agnes, and bequeathed by him to the Charity Commissioners. For nearly a hundred years this field had lain there quietly until in 1939 it was bought by Sir Ogilvy Hibbard, who planned to use the site for a garage and a teashop. Old Lord Pomfret resolved the ensuing flap by forcing Sir Ogilvy to sell the land to him. This property is referred to by Lucy Marling as Pook's Piece in *Marling Hall.* No doubt she was confused.

Porridges. A play on Claridge's, a fine London hotel.

Puckles. A Northbridge linen-draper, whose old-fashioned establishment was a sort of unofficial Ladies Country Club, serving tea and buns.

Punshions. A charming but gloomy and uncomfortable old stone cottage occupied by Miss Pemberton and her lodger, Mr. Downing. It had been restored in 1919 by Mr. Barton after it had been condemned, but despite Mr. Barton's work it remained draughty, exuding damp from the stone floor and ensured a high degree of discomfort. The living room was somehow on two levels, having been cobbled together from two smaller rooms. Noise traveled easily up the uncarpeted stairs and down the thin floors of the second story rooms.

After Miss Pemberton's death Punshions was taken by the Misses Ward, Heath, and Chiffinch, who redecorated and made it much more cheerful and warm. Carpets were laid over the stone flags and wooden staircase; cream paint was applied to the entire interior, including the ceilings; gas radiators were installed and draught-excluders imported; the open fireplace was boarded up, painted pink, and a gas fixture was put in.

Punshions was half-way down the High Street, just beyond the Mitre.

Ram and Twins. A small public house on the edge of the forest outside of Worsted.

The Red House. The house in Marling Melicent owned by Joyce Smith and rented to Frances and Geoffrey Harvey in the winter of 1941. It was a particularly revolting specimen of Edwardian villa, built of purple-red brick patterned with contrasting grey brick. The upper story was painted to resemble timber, there were overlapping tiles with scalloped edges, and there were various gables, leaded glass windows, and a Swiss chalet type of porch. With its blue door, garden gnomes, fake rocks, witch balls, a concrete rabbit, and, finally, a monkey puzzle tree, the Red House represented a high and depressing form of middle-class kitsch.

Red Lion. An inn and public house in Southbridge, operated by Mr. Brown and strongly supported by Miss Hampton and Miss Bent. It was one of those relics of coaching days with a handsome brick front and an arched gateway leading to the paved yard and stable wing.

Regional Commissioner's Office. In 1941 John Leslie was the Regional Commissioner for the Barchester area. Oliver Marling and Frances and Geoffrey Harvey also worked in the office, the purpose of which was to organize services for the county if the central government were unable to do so. It was housed in a very hideous building that had been a failed commercial college, and had every drear quality such an arrangement could be expected to produce.

Rising Castle. The ancestral home of Lord Stoke, whose heir was young Lord Bond at Staple Park. In fact, the castle was a ruin, and Lord Stoke's home was a comfortable mansion constructed from the stones of the ruins. What parts of the old castle still held together were open to the public at sixpence apiece. Its situation was on a hill above the confluence of the River Rising and Rushmere Brook. Under the castle was a cave known as the Stokey Hole that had an opening on to the banks of Rushmere Brook and, according to legend, a series of tunnels connecting it to the Tower of London.

Rokeby. Mr. Scatcherd's well-built hideous little house just outside the village of Hatch End. It was owned by his brother, who allowed him to live there for a nominal rent. *Rokeby* is a long narrative poem by Sir Walter Scott. Rokeby was both the name of a castle and the name of one of the principal characters. All of them were involved in considerable to-ing and fro-ing, attacking and taking prisoner, slaying and being slain and other components of high drama.

Rushmere Brook. A tributary of the River Rising.

Rushmere Pool. A favorite picnic spot on the banks of Rushmere Brook. The pool had been created by the damming of the brook at a low and narrow point in the valley by a Lord Stoke of bygone days. The long shallow pool was overhung with beech trees, and at its upper end was a small grassy slope on which the picnickers sat to enjoy the view as they ate their sandwiches.

Rushwater House. The home of Henry Leslie and Lady Emily Leslie, built by Mr. Leslie's grandfather. It was large and comfortable, Gothic in style, but not hideously so. Inside it was welcoming, unpretentious, and spacious; it was the scene of many happy gatherings. All the ground floor rooms opened onto a graveled terrace that had steps leading down to the gardens and lawns. Upstairs, a broad corridor ran the length of the top story and made an area for children, where they could play neither seen nor heard.

Another feature of Rushwater House was "The Temple," a Palladian folly, part pyramid and part pagoda. Mr. Macpherson's house was on the estate, as was St. Mary's Church, and a thriving home farm. The Prince of Wales had come for the shooting in 1900, and it had been used as an Officers' Hospital during the First War.

St. Ewolds. The church in Ullathorne to which Mr. Miller was sent in 1951. This parish is frequently mentioned in Trollope. It was in close touch with the Close and traditionally had been a stepping stone to a Canonry.

St. Mary's. The small church on the Rushwater estate.

St. Michael and All Angels. The church in Edgewood, begun in 1473, and continued over the course of more than a hundred and fifty years. The Reverend Septimus Grantly was its pastor.

St. Sycorax. The Anglican church in Northbridge, where Father Fewling was priest-in-charge, and conducted services in accordance with his high church beliefs.

Scatcherd's Stores. Scatcherds were purveyors of groceries and general provisons, established since 1824 in Northbridge on the High Street.

Sheep's Head. The public house in Lambton.

Silverbridge. A village in west Barsetshire. It is frequently mentioned in Trollope's political novels, also in *The Small House at Allington*. Sir Harry Waring owned a house in Silverbridge which was inherited by Cecil Waring.

The town was on the river and had once been a bustling port in the days of the wool trade. It was home to the regional office of the Department of Red Tape and Sealing Wax, and to a nice little restaurant, Babs' Buttery. It was renowned for its steep High Street, lined with handsome stone and brick houses, which ran right down to the river, which at that point was spanned by a humped bridge built in the eighteenth century. A wharf with all its attendant equipment in the form of cranes, pulleys and bollards edged the river along with a row of high warehouses.

Skeynes Agnes. A little Saxon church with a round tower and shingled spire located between Worsted and Skeynes. On a hill overlooking the downs, it occupied a hidden spot behind large yew trees and farm buildings.

Southbridge.   A village on the river, southwest of Barchester. Its chief landmark was, of course, Southbridge School, but it was also home to Wiple Terrace and a nice public house, the Red Lion. Among its residents were the Phelps at Jutland Cottage, Miss Hampton and Miss Bent at Adelina Cottage, Mr. Traill in Maria Cottage, Mr. Feeder in Louisa Cottage and his mother Mrs. Feeder in Editha Cottage. Mr. and Mrs. Crofts were in the Vicarage. The Birketts and the Carters were at Southbridge School, Eileen at the Red Lion and numerous members of the Brown family were occupied in useful ways throughout the community.

Southbridge School. Located in the river valley just outside the village of Southbridge, the school was both a pre-preparatry and a preparatory school for boys up to seventeen or eighteen. The chapel had been built by Sir Gilbert Scott, the same architect who designed Pomfret Towers, to the same standards of mid-Victorian Neo-Gothic hideousness. Its peaks and spire were landmarks among the other school buildings set amidst the lawns and playing fields with the river in the distance. The school was enlarged by the addition of a new wing in 1951, and another wing housing a library was added in 1958.

Southbridge Vicarage. Home of the Vicars of Southbridge, most recently the Rev. Crofts and his wife. It was a triumph of Neo-Gothic architecture, with lancet windows, scrolled fret-work, many gables, and abundant shade-giving conifers and shrubbery. On the other hand, it was well-built on solid foundations and had a modern bathroom. Some of the ground floor rooms afforded views of the church and, in the distance, the school.

Sowerby Arms. The public house in Edgewood.

Staple Park. The seat of Lord and Lady Bond. It was an imposing mansion in a walled estate, situated on a slope overlooking an ornamental water, spanned by a Palladian bridge. During the war it was let to a school, and Lord and Lady Bond lived in a small house on the property. After the war the Bonds resumed their residence in the big house.

Starveacre Hatches. A series of floodgates put across the River Rising in the early eighteenth century. A lovely one-arch bridge spanned the river there.

Stoke Dry. The railway halt for Rising Castle and the Rising villages.

Stories. The early Georgian house in Pomfret Madrigal where Mrs. Brandon lived with her children. It was pleasantly situated and very comfortable, with a garden containing a large Spanish chestnut tree, under which the family and their guests often had tea. During the war, Stories housed ten evacuee infants and their two nurses.

Villa Thermogene. The Rivera home of Lady de Courcy. Thermogene is also the name of a patent remedy for various chest ailments; it was a pre-treated wrap designed to generate heat, somewhat like a mustard plaster.

The Vinery. A house in the Close lived in for years by Dr. Thorne and after his death by Canon Joram. The source of the name was a mystery, for the only vine on the property was a passionflower on the south wall of the house. It was a rather small house, pleasantly furnished in good but not exciting taste. On the ground floor were the white-paneled dining room and the Canon's study. On the stairwell walls were paintings of landscapes framed by painted columns, and on the ceiling, painted clouds upon which reposed modestly positioned gods and goddesses.

The White Hart. An old and revered Barchester hotel; its dining room was favored by the local gentry. It was listed by the RAC and AA, and given four stars by each, for the meals, though unexciting, were well-cooked and carefully served. In a private room behind the bar the Precincts Club met.

The White House. A house on the Laverings property more elegant than Laverings itself. Mrs. Stonor rented it from her brother Mr. John Middleton in the summer of 1939.

Wiple Terrace. Long a Southbridge landmark, Wiple Terrace consisted of four joined cottages of two stories each, above which was a stucco pediment bearing the words "Wiple Terrace 1820." The Terrace had been erected as a monument to the four daughters of Mr. Wiple, and each cottage bore the name of one daughter: Maria, Adelina, Louise, and Editha. In the early 1940's the property belonged to Paul's College, but was administered in a benign and friendly way.

Miss Hampton and Miss Bent were the inhabitants of longest standing, having lived in Adelina Cottage since the early 1930's. Two masters from Southbridge School, Mr. Feeder and Mr. Traill, occupied Maria and Louisa. Editha had been lived in by a variety of residents: the vicar's aunt, Mrs. and Miss Arbuthnot, and Mr. Traill's mother. In 1960 the property was bought by a syndicate of friends and presented to Southbridge School, thus assuring "one of the rummest places in England" would be safe from the unkind intentions of developers.

Winter Overcotes. An East Barsetshire community; it was a major railway center for the area. The Beedles lived there. The Deans, also, lived at or near Winter Overcotes in a house never named or described, though it must have been large, and it was probably very pleasant; it included some fields and pastures and barns because Mr. Dean was interested in farming "a bit," and his son Robin was decidedly keen. After the war the Deans' was a popular gathering place for the young and not-so-young of Barsetshire.

Wishing Well. A picnic spot near High Rising. Here a natural stone arch overhung a little bubbling sandy-bottomed spring. Wishes were granted to those who would sacrifice a coin or even a pin to the spirit who dwelt in the depths.

Woolpack. A very popular pub in Worsted. It was considered the most dashing of the local watering holes by the young masters at the Priory School.

Part Four

Comments and Notes

*I think Shakespeare must have had an extraordinary mind. I mean
he has such a wonderful vocabulary. When you think of all the
words you have to look up in the glossary, it just shows.
But I don't look up the words as a rule because I
think Shakespeare didn't mean you to. I mean
he expected you to know them, and
if you didn't, he didn't mind.*

— Lydia Keith, *Summer Half*

When working on these notes we felt very much like Mr. Downing writing his *Biographical Dictionary of Provence,* if we may make so bold a comparison. The more we did the more we found to do, and the work seemed to stretch away into an infinite regression of permanent incompletion as we sifted through the twenty-nine novels again and again and months passed away.

But we are not Mr. Downing, nor do we have a Miss Pemberton to goad and aid us. We give you a reasonable list that should help you understand much, but probably not all, that needs explaining or warrants further understanding.

A

Between the acts, darling, one does truly love one's real friends.
—Jessica Dean

Abbreviations

AA	Automobile Association
ABC	Aerated Bread Company.
ARP	Air Raid Precautions; also ARPS, Air Raid Precaution Services.
ATS	In World War II, the Women's Auxiliary Territorial Service; it is now known as the Women's Royal Army Corps.
CBE	Commander of the British Empire.
ID	Criminal Investigation Department: a plainclothes police branch based at Scotland Yard.
DBE	Dame of the British Empire.
DTs	Delirium tremens, an affliction suffered by severe alcoholics.
JP	Justice of the Peace.
KBE	Knight of the British Empire.
KC	King's Counsel: an honor for barristers.
KCB	Knight Commander of the Order of the Bath: an award for service in public service, the military, the diplomatic service, or home civil service.
KCMG	Knight Companion of the Order of St. Michael and St. George: an honor often awarded by the Foreign Office.
LCC	London County Council.
MCC	Marylebone Cricket Club.
MFH	Master of Fox Hounds: an important person in the local Hunt, who housed the pack of about forty hounds.
MBE	Member of the Order of the British Empire
MC	Military Cross: a military award.
MGI	Ministry of General Interference.
MP	Member of Parliament.
OBE	Order of the British Empire.
OM	Order of Merit.
PG	Paying Guest.
PPE	Politics, Philosophy, and Economics.
QC	Queen's Counsel: an honor for barristers.
RA	Royal Academy of the Arts.
RAC	Royal Automobile Club.
RC	Roman Catholic.
RIBA	Royal Institute of British Architects.
RSPCA	Royal Society for the Prevention of Cruelty to Animals.
VAD	Volunteer Aid Detachment.
VC	Victoria Cross: the highest military award.

WAAC   Women's Army Auxiliary Corps, known since 1949 as the WRAC, Women's Royal Army Corps.

WAAF   Women's Auxiliary Air Force, known since 1949 as the WRAF, Women's Royal Air Force.

WI   Women's Institute: an organization that brought culture and education to rural areas.

WRNS   Women's Royal Naval Service, often referred to as Wrens.

WVS   Women's Voluntary Services, more recently WRVS, Women's Royal Voluntary Service. Originally formed to organize non-uniformed women into various wartime duties, the WRVS has increasingly included services to civilians such as the aged, the ill, the handicapped and children.

Abbé Faria. A character from *The Count of Monte Cristo,* by Alexandre Dumas *père*. See **Dantes, Edmund.**

Absit omen. *Latin.* May the omen be missing; God forbid.

Acharné. *French.* Merciless, fierce, stubborn.

Ack emma. A jolly colloquial way of saying A.M. or *ante meridian,* meaninng "before noon." See **pip emma.**

Actaeon. According to the Greek myth, the hunter Actaeon happened to come upon Diana while she was bathing in the forest. As punishment for seeing her nude body he was turned into a stag, whereupon his own hounds tore him to bits.

Adam. More particularly, "the old Adam." This refers to the unregenerate sinner in one's character.

Adam, Robert (1728–1792). Scottish architect who worked with his brother and partner, James. They were influential in changing house design from Palladian to a neo-classical style. Robert was also well-known as a designer of furniture and as a decorator. His rooms were characterized by shallow plaster motifs and meticulous attention to detail.

Ad lib. *Latin.* Short for *ad libitum,* meaning at pleasure, as one wishes, to any extent: freely.

Adscriptus glebae. *Latin.* Attached to the soil.

Adultery. Not in Barsetshire. Not that we know of, at least. It is true that Mr. Henry Leslie disappeared on a prolonged visit to the capitals of Northern Europe when Lady Emily had introduced a kiln into the service room, and what he did while away we cannot say. Noel Merton, John Middleton, and Sir Robert Graham were all husbands who spent a great deal of time away from home, especially the latter, and we don't know what they did, either. Noel Merton is the only man we know to have allowed his eye to wander and his thoughts to stray. Then, some years later, his wife Lydia cast sensitive glances at Lord Pomfret. Although both episodes were observed by others, we think no lasting harm was done.

Angela Thirkell has been taken to task for being unrealistic or perhaps naïve in matters of sex. Certainly her England is not the England of Anthony Powell or Evelyn Waugh. But we think she knew her public very well, and gave it what it wanted. Her own life was very much unlike that of any of her heroines; she was acquainted with various forms of domestic grief. But as she herself described Barsetshire as "Cloud Cuckooland," we don't think she was fooling herself; we think she knew the value of a good escape.

Advocaat. A heavy Dutch cordial sometimes known as "egg brandy" because it is a mixture of brandy, eggs, and sugar.

Aeneas. A famous Trojan leader immortalized by Virgil in the *Aeneid.* Legend has it that during his wanderings Aeneas, while in Carthage, had an audience with the beautiful young Queen Dido. She immediately fell in love with him. After a ceremony that he allowed her to believe was a binding marriage (O these men, these men!), Aeneas tarried for a few blissful months by her side. Then the gods sent Mercury to remind Aeneas of his duty to his men, so he collected them and provisioned his ships. As they were preparing to sail, Dido appeared and made a scene. Aeneas heard her out, but of course left anyway. She gathered together a huge funeral pyre, lighted it, and threw herself on it, thereby teaching him a valuable lesson.

Aertex. An open-weave knit fabric, used primarily for underwear and sport shirts. Aertex was originally a brand name that has become generic for this type of fabric.

Aged P. From Dickens' *Great Expectations.* The Aged Parent was the father of the law clerk John Wemmick, Junior. The old man was clean, cheerful, quite well-cared for, and almost totally deaf. He liked to be nodded to; guests were instructed to nod and keep nodding. This lent a surreal touch to all discourse.

"Mr. Aggs, Mr. Baggs, Mr. Caggs, Mr. Daggs. . . ." A line from Dickens' *Our Mutual Friend.* Mr. Lightfoot's clerk read these names to Mr. Boffin from his appointment book in the hope of making him believe that Mr. Lightfoot had a busy schedule. In fact, at that time Mr. Boffin was Mr. Lightfoot's only client.

Aguecheek, Andrew. A character from Shakespeare's *Twelfth Night.* Sir Andrew was a knight who, though foolish, arouses sympathy when he says, "I was adored once too."

Alea jacta est. *Latin.* The die is cast. This was supposedly said by Julius Caesar when he had crossed the Rubicon River and felt he could not turn back. If you feel that this would add to your conversational repertoire, the "j" is pronounced as if it were "y."

Allen, Ben. From Dickens' *Pickwick Papers.* Ben was a medical student, the brother of Arabella. After her marriage to the sporty Winkle, Ben had to be placated.

"All her days were trances." A line from "To One In Paradise," by American poet Edgar Allen Poe (1809–1849).

> And all my days are trances,
> And all my nightly dreams
> Are where thy gray eye glances
> And where thy footstep gleams
> In what ethereal dances,
> By what eternal streams.

"Âme déchiré, / Jusqu'à mourir." *French.* A soul tormented almost to death.

Amurath. The name of several Turkish sultans. In Henry IV, Part II, Act 3, scene 2, Henry says to his brothers, "Not Amurath an Amurath succeeds, but Harry Harry."

The Amazing Marriage. These words were used by Noel Merton to describe the marriage of Aubrey Clover and Jessica Dean, presumably because everyone had considered Clover a homosexual. In using the phrase Noel alluded to a novel of that title by George Meredith, published in 1895. *The*

Amazing Marriage has no similarity at all to the Barsetshire marriage, but the title provided an apt description of what the Clovers' friends couldn't help thinking.

Amitié carée. *French.* Friendship squared.

Amos Barton. From George Eliot's *Scenes from Clerical Life.* Amos Barton was a clergyman who wasn't much liked by his parishioners until his sweet and of course uncomplaining wife died from exhaustion and her seventh confinement.

Analects. Writings selected from among the best by a classical author.

"And if God will. . . . " A slight misquotation from Elizabeth Barrett Browning's Sonnet XLII. For the entire poem see the entry under **Every day's most quiet need.**

"And leaves the world to darkness. . . . " *See* **Gray, Thomas.**

"And so to bed." A frequent end to the day's entry from Samuel Pepy's *Diary.*

Annals of the Parish. A novel by John Galt, published in 1821. It is a humorous account of life in a Scottish parish during the five decades between 1760 and 1810.

Anselm, St. (1033–1109). Archbishop of Canterbury from 1093 until his death. He had conflicts with the Crown and was temporarily exiled by both William II and Henry I.

Anti-Jacobin. A journal founded in 1797 by George Canning. During its brief life of not quite two years it published parody and satire with a Tory slant. *The Loves of the Triangles* first appeared in its pages. Jacobin in this sense means a political reformer, especially one advocating complete equality.

Anubis. A dog-headed Egyptian god, the son of Osiris. He was connected with death, and came to be considered as guarding the entrance to the infernal regions, escorting the souls of the dead to the place of judgment. *So* appropriate for the name of the ship on which the Bishop and his wife almost certainly might meet their doom.

Anzio. An Italian seaport, 33 miles southeast of Rome. It was the site of an Allied landing on January 25, 1944. It was here that Robin Dale suffered the injuries that cost him his foot.

Aperçu. *French.* An overview or intuitive grasp.

Apollyon. From Greek mythology: the king of hell.

Apple. *See* **Paris.**

Arachne. From Greek mythology. Arachne had the effrontery to challenge Athena to a spinning contest, and when Athena broke Arachne's web, Arachne hanged herself. Athena then changed her into a spider.

Arbiter eleganatarium. *Latin.* An authority in matters of taste.

Arcadians. A reference to those ancient Greeks who lived in Arcadia, a rural mountainous region. It was thought of as a place of innocence and beauty, a sort of Eden or even a paradise. For the reader who has made her or possibly his way to the final chapters of *Three Score and Ten, The Arcadians* refers to an

122

exuberant Edwardian musical, first performed in 1908, and "Oh Naughty Naughty One, Mayfair" was the telephone number of a much sought-after gentleman.

Argle-bargle. (Somemtimes argy-bargy.) Wrangling argument.

Argus. From Greek mythology. Argus was a being who had one hundred eyes. He was appointed by a jealous Juno to watch Io. In this Argus failed, having been killed by Mercury. Juno set his hundred eyes in the tail of the peacock.

Arianism. Of or pertaining to, as they say, the beliefs of Arius. Arius (250–336) believed that Christ was not the equal of God, nor of His essence, although first and finest among mortals—an explanation that will be clear to the meanest intelligence.

Arnhem. A city in the Netherlands that was captured by the Germans in 1940. It was the scene of terrible fighting in 1944; allied forces were trapped in the city and only a few escaped. In 1945 it was recaptured.

Army and Navy stores. Located on Victoria Street, London: a cooperative store begun in 1864 to sell to members of the military forces at a discount. In 1918 it was opened to the public.

Arnold, Matthew (1822–1888). English poet and literary critic, professor of poetry at Oxford from 1857–1867. His poem "Baccanalia, or the New Age" is often quoted from in Barsetshire—*see* **So the silence was.** His sonnet "Shakespeare" begins

> Others abide our question. Thou art free.
> We ask and ask—Thou smilest and art still,
> Out-topping knowledge.

Arras. A small city in northern France which was the scene of several intense battles during the 1914-18 war. It was virtually destroyed by shelling.

Arrière pensée. *French.* Mental reservation, ulterior motive. In contemporary jargon, hidden agenda.

Articled. Bound under articles (a contract) of apprenticeship.

Aunt Sally. A grotesque female figure set up at carnival stalls as a target at which to throw balls.

Area. A small paved yard outside the basement entrance of an urban house, approached by a flight of steps.

Armida. A voluptuous enchantress, from the 16th century poet Tasso's *Jerusalem Delivered.*

The Ashes. The Ashes are—or is—a mythical prize awarded to the victor in the annual England vs. Australia cricket match. The story behind the name is that when England was defeated by Australia in the first match in 1882, a humorous epitaph described the "death of English cricket" and said, "The body will be cremated and the ashes taken to Australia."

Ashton, Lucy. A character from Scott's *The Bride of Lammermoor.* Lucy loved and pledged herself to a man her parents despised. Her mother in particular schemed to get her to marry another. Lucy obeyed, but lost her reason and killed him on their wedding night. Then, as luck would have it, she died too, for those were the days when derangement caused almost instant death.

"At one stride comes the dark. . . ." A line from Part III of *The Rime of the Ancient Mariner*.

> The sun's rim dips, the stars rush out:
> At one stride comes the dark;
> With far-heard whisper o'er the sea
> Off shot the specter bark.

Audit ale. A special and especially good ale made by certain colleges at Oxford and Cambridge to drink on the day of their annual audit. This tradition goes back to the end of the eighteenth century.

Au fond. *French*. At bottom; fundamentally.

Austen, Jane (1775–1817). Renowned English novelist, the author of *Pride and Prejudice, Sense and Sensibility, Mansfield Park, Northanger Abbey, Emma, Persuasion,* and some shorter works.

Avanti. *Italian*. Forward, ahead.

Why haven't I a rich aunt with fixed basins?
— Charles Belton

Baal. Any of several local Semitic gods; baal is a Semitic word for god.

Bab Ballads. Humorous verses written and illustrated by W.S. Gilbert, of Gilbert and Sullivan fame. They were published between 1866 and 1877. *See* separate listings for individual poems: **Captain Reece, tea tasters,** *Nancy* **Brig, West India Sugar Broker** *and* **The Two Ogres.**

Baboo (Babu). A Hindu title of respect, sometimes used pejoratively of an Indian whose education and facility in English was ambitious but superficial. To readers of Edwardian popular fiction, Baboo referred to Baboo Jabberjee, a comic character created by F. Anstey (Thomas A. Gutherie) in a popular series of stories published in *Punch* in the late 1890's. They were later collected into a book.

Badajoz. A city in northwest Spain. Over the centuries it has been the subject of sieges, most recently during the Napoleonic Wars. It was re-taken by Wellington in 1812.

Baedeker. Karl Baedeker (1801–1859), a German, originated a popular series of detailed travel guides.

Bags. Men's slacks. They became especially popular in the 1920's, when Oxford bags were stylish; they had pleats and wide legs. It may be recalled that the Bishop in his college days was known as "Old Gasbags."

The Baliff's Daughter. The full title is *The Baliff's Daughter of Islington,* an anonymous ballad which Sir Thomas Percy included in his collection of 1765, *Reliques of Ancient English Poetry.* The ballad tells the story of lovers separated by circumstances and happily reunited after seven years.

Bands. Strips hanging down the front of the robes of those in the legal, clerical, or academic professions. *See* **Geneva bands.**

Bangs, Molly. A stand-in for the famous Regency courtesan Harriette Wilson. AT wrote a biography of Wilson called *The Fortunes of Harriette,* published in 1936. Lord Byron was one of Harriette Wilson's patrons.

Banns. Banns were announcements of an intended marriage read from the pulpit of the parish church on the three successive Sundays within three months of the wedding. Anyone knowing of any impediment to the union was supposed to rise right there and say so.

Mr. Baptist. From Dickens' *Little Dorrit.* Mr. Baptist's real name was John Baptist Cavaletto. He was a cheerful Italian who lived in Bleeding Heart Yard. Residents there responded to his friendliness as he passed and would rush out to teach him the English names of things.

Bardell *vs.* Pickwick. From Dickens' *Pickwick Papers*. Mrs. Bardell, a widow, brought a breach-of-promise suit against Mr. Pickwick. As the jury was being seated, a chemist named Thomas Groffin protested that if he had to serve in the jury his shop would be staffed only by his messenger boy, and people would be murdered by wrong prescriptions. The judge dismissed the complaint as of no consequence, and Mr. Groffin took his place in the jury box with a pleasant and comfortable attitude.

Barkis. From Dickens' *David Copperfield*. Mr. Barkis shamelessly used David as a go-between, asking David to tell Miss Peggoty that "Barkis is willin'."

"Barnes' gander was stole by tinkers." From Dickens' *Little Dorrit*. This line was uttered at dinner, à propos of nothing, by Mr. F's aunt. She was given to such pronouncements; they dampened the enthusiasm of the other diners.

Baroque. When used to describe pearls, this means irregularly shaped.

Barratry. The purchase or sale of an ecclesiastical position.

Barrister. A trial lawyer who is retained by a solicitor to represent a client in the higher courts. So called because such lawyers have been called to the bar, which is the area in a court room that separates the judge and Queen's or King's Counsel from the other lawyers and the public.

Battle of Maldon. A battle fought in Essex in 991. It was commemorated by an anonymous poet around 1000 in a poem of 325 lines.

Beak. Magistrate or J.P.

Beardsley, Aubrey (1872–1898). English illustrator who worked almost entirely in black and white. His work, witty and sensual, appeared in special editions of plays and poems and was associated with the popular but ill-fated *Yellow Book, q.v.*, of which he was art editor. He wore his hair rather long and parted in the middle.

"Beauty lives with kindness." A line from Shakespeare's *Two Gentlemen of Verona*, Act IV. It is informally known as "Who Is Sylvia." We will give you the first two of three verses.

> Who is Sylvia? What is she?
>   That all our swains commend her?
> Holy, fair, and wise is she;
>   The heaven such grace did lend her,
> That she might admirèd be.
>
> Is she kind as she is fair?
>   For beauty lives with kindness:
> Love doth to her eyes repair,
>   To help him of his blindness;
> And, being help'd, inhabits there.

Becket, Thomas à (1118–1170). A brilliant and courageous Archbishop of Canterbury. He came into serious conflict with the establishment and excommunicated much of it. The king, Henry II, who had been in conflict with Becket for years, said, or is thought to have said, "Will no one rid me of this troublesome prelate?"—or words to that effect. Four days later Thomas was murdered by four of the king's knights. The murder shocked the country. Becket was canonized by 1173. His burial site in the cathedral became a popular goal of pilgrimages, including the one described by Chaucer in *The Canterbury Tales.*

Beeton, Mrs. In 1861 she published a book on domestic management and cookery that made her a household word for generations.

Beggar my neighbor. A card game for two players. The deck is divided into two piles. Each player turns over one card at a time, in turns, and can demand from the other four cards for an Ace, three for a King, two for a Queen, and one for a Jack. The object is to collect all the cards.

Begum cooker. A play on Aga cooker: a kitchen range that comes in various sizes, with two or three ovens, each providing a different temperature, and with a varying number of burners. It is heated with coal, wood, or gas; the heat is always on.

La Belle Dame Sans Merci. *French.* Lovely lady without mercy; the title of a poem by Keats, but the title embodies a romantic concept that pervaded the culture at the time, so the phrase was often used.

Belt. This undergarment is known in the U.S. as a girdle.

Bench. The personification of a magistrate or Justice of the Peace, one of a few unpaid officials who sit at a bench, or something like it, and deal with minor local misdemeanors. Sam Adams, Frederick Belton Sr., and the Dowager Lady Lufton were all J.P.'s.

Benedick. A happy bridegroom, especially one who has always sworn he would never marry. From Shakespeare's *Much Ado about Nothing.*

Bergère. *French.* An armchair designed for comfort, large and deep.

Bevan, Aneurin. Welshman born to a poor miner's family, who rose to become Minister of Health in the Labour government. He introduced the National Health Service in 1948.

Beveridge, William Henry. A British economist who published a report in 1942 called the "Beveridge Report," or to give it its full title, *Report on Social Insurance and Allied Services.* It was significant in forming the National Health Insurance and other bulwarks of the welfare state.

Bézique. A game similar to pinochle. Six pack bézique is played with a deck of 192 cards—six each of the Ace, King, Queen, Jack, Ten, Nine, Eight, and Seven in each suit. The game is further described in *Hoyle Up-to-Date* or any other edition of Hoyle's official rules for card games.

Bickerstaff, Isaac. A person created by Jonathan Swift as the supposed writer of a set of predictions for the year 1708. The name was spelled without the final "e." There was an Isaac Bickerstaffe, an ex-Irish playwright who had for a while a successful career in London. A scandal linking him with David Garrick caused him to flee to France where he died in obscurity around 1808.

Bijou. *French.* It means jewel. When used to describe a house it means one that is small, elegant, and charming.

Billycock. A derby hat.

Bissell. The brand name of a non-motorized carpet sweeper.

127

Bist du bei mir. *German.* Stay near me.

Blake, William (1757–1827). English poet, painter and engraver. He was also a mystic who believed himself to be in touch with the spiritual world. Blake's frontispiece to *Europe, a Prophecy,* 1794, shows a kneeling Urizen, the god of Reason. He has a long beard blowing away to the side, perhaps swept by cosmic winds.

The Black Arrow. An 1888 novel by Robert Louis Stevenson. It is set in the time of King John.

Blackleg. A strikebreaker, usually known in the U.S. as a scab.

Bleeding Heart Yard. From Dickens' *Little Dorrit.* It was the yard of the Bleeding Heart Inn in Charles Street, Hatton Garden, a depressed area of several mean dwellings owned by the slum landlord Christopher Casby.

"Bliss it was. . . . " A line from "French Revolution," an 1809 poem by William Wordsworth. The first eight lines are

> Oh! Pleasant exercise of hope and joy!
> For mighty were the auxiliars which then stood
> Upon our side, we who were strong in love!
> Bliss was it in that dawn to be alive,
> But to be young was very heaven! — Oh! times,
> In which the meagre, stale, forbidding ways
> Of custom, law, and statute, took at once
> The attraction of a country in romance!

Blondin (1824–1897). A famous French acrobat whose greatest feat was crossing Niagara Falls on a tightrope blindfolded, while pushing a wheelbarrow, carrying a man on his back, and brandishing an umbrella.

Bloomsbury. The residential area around the British Museum, made famous by Virginia Woolf, Clive Bell, Vanessa Bell, Desmond McCarthy, Duncan Grant, J.M. Keynes, Roger Fry, Lytton Strachey, and the other artists and writers known as the Bloomsbury Group. To Barsetshire, Bloomsbury was a hotbed of degeneracy, immorality, and depraved aesthetic values. Geoffrey Harvey lived in Bloomsbury.

Blue. The Oxford or Cambridge equivalent of what in the U.S. is called a letter man.

Blue Ribbon. This refers to the Blue Ribbon Army, a temperance society, and by extension to all teetotalers.

Boadicea. Also Boudicca. A warrior queen living in the first century A.D. When in 60 A.D. her husband died, her daughters were raped and she was whipped by the occupying Roman army. She took her revenge by rousing local tribes and burning Colchester, St. Albans, and parts of London. Just before her capture she took poison and died.

Boat race. An annual rowing competition held each summer. The course is the Thames between Putney Bridge and Mortlake. The contestants are the champion rowing teams of eight from Oxford and Cambridge. It is one of the main sporting events of the year. It is also known as the University Boat Race.

Boiler suit. A one-piece garment worn for dirty jobs; Americans call this garment a coverall.

Bonté de coeur. *French.* Goodness of heart.

Bornée. *French.* Limited, narrow.

Borough English. An ancient English custom providing that the youngest son be the heir, or failing that, the youngest daughter. It had not the status of law and was not widely used.

Borrow, George (1803–1881). A writer of vivid travel literature, partly fictional. He made studies of the Spanish gipsies.

"Bosom's lord sitting sadly on his throne. . . . " A line from Wordsworth's "Apology," a defense of the Roman Catholic martyrs.

> . . . and therefore to the tomb
> Pass, some through fire — and by the scaffold some —
> Like saintly Fisher, and unbending More.
> 'Lightly for both the bosom's lord did sit
> Upon his throne;' unsoftened, undismayed
> By aught that mingled with the tragic scene. . . .

Boswell, James (1740–1795). A Scottish writer remembered for being the friend and biographer of Samuel Johnson. Boswell's own life was full of events, as far as that goes.

Bouche bée. *French.* Agape with wonder or shock.

Bovril. The trade name of a beef-and-vegetable concentrate, flavored with herbs and spices. It can be spread on something such as toast, added to sauces and soups, or diluted with hot water to make a consommé.

Bowdler, Thomas, M.D. (1754–1825). In 1818, Bowdler brought out his edition of *Family Shakespeare*, from which all "profanity and obscenity" had been removed. A similarly expurgated edition of Gibbon's *Decline and Fall of the Roman Empire* appeared some years later. Thus Bowdler's name has come to be synonymous with prudishly edited versions of the work of other authors.

Boy's Own Paper. A popular periodical for boys, published from 1879 to 1967. It began as a penny weekly. Combining breezy stories of school or adventure with occasional poems or puzzles, it was popular with middle-class boys and their parents. The standards, both literary and artistic, were high, but as the years passed it was less and less able to compete with cheaper papers that had a more stirring content.

Bracebridge Hall. The title of a collection of stories and sketches about English life. It was written by Washington Irving during the time he was living in England, and was published in 1824.

Bradshaw. *Bradshaw's Railway Guide*, a railway timetable published from 1839 to 1965.

Brass, Sally. An unlovely but rather interesting character from Dickens' *Old Curiosity Shop*. She was her brother's law clerk, and a good one, who sustained him in his business.

"Brave new world." A quote from Shakespeare's *The Tempest*, Act V, scene i, made famous as the title of Aldous Huxley's 1932 novel. Miranda says

> O wonder! How many goodly creatures here!
> How many beauteous mankind is! O brave new world,
> that has such people in it!

Brawn. Pork that has been preserved by being pickled or jellied.

Brian Bois de Gilbert. A character from *Ivanhoe*, by Sir Walter Scott. Bois de Gilbert was an intense and fierce Knight Templar, affiliated with King John; he died of conflicting emotions when on the verge of fighting a duel with Ivanhoe.

Briareus. (Pronounced bri-AR-e-us.) A giant from Greek Mythology. He had fifty heads and one hundred hands.

"Brightness falls from the air." From a poem by Thomas Nashe (1567–1601) called "Adieu, Farewell Earth's Bliss" or "In Time of Pestilence." The entire verse is

> Beauty is but a flower
> Which wrinkles will devour;
> Brightness falls from the air;
> Queens have died young and fair;
> Dust hath closed Helen's eye;
> I am sick, I must die—
> > *Lord, have mercy on us!*

British. This word was not liked in Barsetshire, where it smacked of Newthink and Political Correctness. Barcastrians such as Sir Edward Pridham saw nothing wrong with things English.

British Restaurants. Restaurants established by the London County Council during the years of rationing, meant to provide nutritious, low-priced meals not requiring the use of ration books. They were eventually to be found throughout the country.

British warm. A short heavy overcoat worn over their uniforms by army officers.

Brother Ass. The body, according to St. Francis of Assisi.

Brother Lawrence. *See **Soliloquy in a Spanish Cloister**.*

Browdie, Mr. and Mrs. From Dickens' *Nicholas Nickelby*. The Browdies were a simple, warm-hearted Yorkshire couple.

Browning, Robert. Apart from being the romantic hero of an idyllic marriage, and the same in a drama based on his courtship of Elizabeth Barrett, Robert Browning (1812–1889) was a prolific and occasionally famous and renowned Victorian poet. Some of his well-known works are *Men and Women, Dramatis Personae, The Ring and the Book,* and *Asolando.* The poem referred to by Lydia Merton in her conversation with Roddy Wicklow about keeping riches after death is *Gold Hair.*

The reference to music in chapter five of *Threescore and Ten* can be found in *Abt Vogler*, which is about the miracle of music and composition. Here we quote from verses VII and XI.

> VII.
> But here is the finger of God, a flash of the will that can,
> > Existent behind all laws, that made them, and lo, they are!
> And I know not if, save in this, such gift be allowed to man,
> > That out of three sounds he frame, not a fourth sound, but a star.
> Consider it well: each tone of our scale in itself is naught;
> > It is everywhere in the world — loud, soft, and all is said:
> Give it to me to use! I mix it with two in my thought,
> > And, there! Ye have heard and seen: consider and bow the head!

And what is our failure here but a triumph's evidence
 For the fullness of the days? Have we withered or agonized?
Why else was the pause prolonged but that singing might issue thence?
 Why rushed the discords in but that harmony should be prized?
Sorrow is hard to bear, and doubt is slow to clear,
 Each sufferer says his say, his scheme of the weal and woe:
But God has a few of us whom he whispers in the ear;
 The rest may reason and welcome; 't is we musicians know.

(Her) Brow was sad, her speech was low. From *Lays of Ancient Rome, Horatius* (1842), by Thomas Babington Macaulay. Here is the relevant verse.

But the Consul's brow was sad,
 And the Consul's speech was low,
And darkly looked he at the wall,
 And darkly at the foe.

Brunel, Isambard (1806–1859). A British engineer employed by the Great Western Railway to construct bridges, tunnels and viaducts as the line was expanded.

Buchan, John, 1ˢᵗ Baron Tweedsmuir (1875–1940). Scottish politician and author, remembered primarily for his action-packed thrillers, the most famous of which is *The Thirty-Nine Steps.*

Bullingdon. An Oxford club comprised of about a dozen of the wealthier undergraduates. Its apparent purpose was to give good dinners to its members and to keep alive a vigorous tradition of practical jokes.

Bump Supper. A dinner held in conjunction with a bumping race. These were races held on the rivers at Oxford or Cambridge in which one boat tried to catch up to and bump another.

Mrs. Bun, Miss Bun. From the card game Happy Families, *q.v.*. They were the wife and daughter of the baker, Mr. Bun.

Bunyan, John (1628–1688). A nonconformist lay preacher, who spent many years in jail. He wrote several books; by far the most famous is *The Pilgrim's Progress,* which appeared over the years from 1674 to 1684.

Burke, John. Publisher of an annual book, *Burke's Peerage,* that gives information about members of the peerage. *See* **Debrett.**

Lord Burleigh's nod. William Cecil, Lord Burleigh, was secretary of state in the reign of Queen Elizabeth I. He was enormously honest, capable, and powerful. "Lord Burleigh's nod" refers to what happens in a play by Richard Sheridan. During the action of this play, *The Critic,* a farce called *The Spanish Armada* is being produced. In this comic piece, the character representing Lord Burleigh is too busy during the crisis of the naval battle to do more than nod or shake his head whenever he is pressed for answers.

Burnt Njal. The full title is *The Story of Burnt Njal, or Life in Iceland at the End of the Tenth Century.* Not surprisingly this is often known as *Njal's Saga.* It was made available to the English-speaking world in a translation by George W. Dasant in 1861. It is a classic tale, written about 1280 and set in the year 1000, an epic of duels, murders, feuds—the full complement of blood and excitement, including encounters with the law courts of the day.

Butlin's Holiday Camps. A series of self-contained holiday camps for the working classes, established in 1936 by Billy Butlin. They are often near the sea, and include all amenities and facilities for entertainment.

C

Calories are rot. No one knows what they are. What father's men on the place want is good beer and fat bacon and plenty of bread and cheese. That's what Barchester has lived on and everyone wants.

— Lucy Marling

Cairngorm. A yellow or greyish brown form of quartz crystal, named for Mt. Cairngorm in Scotland. Specimens found there are abundant and of high quality.

Caligula. One of the most degenerate of the Roman emperors, Caligula was born Gaius Caesar Augustus Germanicus (A.D. 12–41). He was assassinated, not a minute too soon, at the age of twenty-nine.

Cameron, Julia (1815–1879). An early Victorian photographer whose work is considered of great value. She was, incidentally, the maternal aunt of Virginia Woolf.

Cami-knickers. A teddy—a one-piece undergarment for women, comprising both camisole and knickers (underpants).

Camorra. A secret criminal society that originated in the jails of Naples in the early 19th century. It grew to have considerable political influence and some of its members were knowingly hired as policemen. It bears resemblance to the Mafia.

Canning, George (1770–1827). Politician and writer, known for founding *The Anti-Jacobin* in 1797 and writing clever literary parodies.

Canon. A clergyman on the staff of a cathedral who helps with the various services and with maintenance.

Capable du tout. *French.* Capable of anything, usually in the sense of being unpredictable.

Captain Reece. The subject of one of the Bab Ballads, by W.S. Gilbert.

Captain Reece

Of all the ships upon the blue
No ship contained a better crew
Than that of worthy CAPTAIN REECE
Commanding of *The Mantelpiece.*

He was adored by all his men,
For worthy CAPTAIN REECE, R.N.,
Did all that lay within him to
Promote the comfort of his crew.

133

> "By any reasonable plan
> I'll make you happy as I can;
> My own convenience counts as *nil;*
> It is my duty and I will."

"The captains and the kings depart." From the second verse of Kipling's famous "Recessional." The poet says that after a battle when things have died down and the captains and kings have departed, the sacrifice of a humble and contrite heart still stands.

Mother Carey. A figure from folk tradition, made into a character in Charles Kingsley's *The Water Babies.* Originally she was a sailor's invention, similar to but lesser than Mother Nature. To sailors, the stormy petrels are Mother Carey's chickens and the fulmars are Mother Carey's geese. If it were snowing they would say that Mother Carey was plucking her chickens. In *The Water Babies* Mother Carey lived alone near the North Pole. She was a grand lady of ice in the midst of the Peace Pool, where the good whales went. All day she made sea creatures from sea water, but it was a quiet process, for she sat without moving and got them to make themselves.

Carmen. *Latin.* Song.

Carton, Sydney. A character from Dickens' *Tale of Two Cities.* Carton was a dissolute young law clerk who did his best work at night, steadily drinking, with his head draped in a damp towel. He attained grace and heroism by sacrificing himself for the happiness of the woman he had loved but never won. His famous last words here, "It is a far, far finer thing I do than I have ever done; it is a far, far better rest I go to than I have ever known."

Casabianca. A poem by Felicia Dorothea Hemans. It appeared in 1829 and celebrated the heroic Corsican naval officer and his son who both went down with their ship during the Battle of the Nile in 1798. It begins

> The Boy stood on the burning deck,
> Whence all but him had fled;
> The flame that lit the battle's wreck
> Shone round him o'er the dead.
> . . . .
> The flames rolled on; he would not go
> Without his father's word;
> That father, faint in death below,
> His voice no longer heard.

Casanova (1725–1798). An Italian remembered almost exclusively for his numerous affairs. He needed the twelve volumes of his *Memoirs* to describe them all.

Casterbridge. The Wessex town that is the setting for *The Mayor of Casterbridge,* by Thomas Hardy.

Cast her shoe. From Psalm 60, verse 8: "Moab is my washpot; over Edom I will cast out my shoe: Philistia, triumph there because of me." Which is to say, I will march and I will prevail.

Castle puddings. Individual steamed sponge cakes, served with a jam or custard sauce.

Catechumen. One who is taught not with books, but in dialog. "Catechism" is derived from this word.

Catullus, Gaius Valerius (c. 84 –54 B.C.). Roman poet. He was ardently in love with a married woman he called "Lesbia" who inspired some of his best work.

The Cat Who Walked by Himself. From Rudyard Kipling's *Just So Stories* (1902). To this cat all places were the same. However, he noticed that three of his friends went into the cave of the Man and the Woman, and did not come out.

Cavaletto, John Baptist. From Dickens' *Little Dorritt. See* **Mr. Baptist.**

Cela n'empêche pas. French. That won't stop me.

Célibataire. French. An unmarried man.

The Cenci. A play written in 1819 by Percy Bysshe Shelley. It was about the corrupt and evil Count Cenci, whose atrocities toward his own daughter drove the poor young woman to murder him. Her brother and mother-in-law were involved in the cover-up, but they all were tried and punished by death in 1599.

Century. A cricket term meaning 100 runs. We Americans will have to take it that this is a Good Thing and then put the matter by. To do otherwise, to try to explain what a run is, for instance, and then to explain a popping-crease, would involve us in a morass of cricket terms, and we would rue the day.

Cerberus. From Greek and Roman myth: the three-headed dog that stands guard over the gates of Hades.

Chanctonbury Ring. Once an ancient Roman military camp, but now a clump of ash and beech trees atop a hill of 783 feet. It is, as Mrs. Brandon said, visible from much of West Sussex.

Chadband. From Dickens' *Bleak House.* Mr. Chadband would describe himself as a vessel of the Lord, and "in the ministry," though he was not formally associated with any denomination. He ate prodigiously, being a hollow vessel, and spoke in great gusts, being a wind-driven one. He was an oily fellow, and big as a bear.

Chankly Bore. A faraway region in such poems as "The Jumblies" and "The Dong with the Luminous Nose," by Edward Lear. The Jumblies went to sea in a sieve,

> And in twenty years they all came back,
> In twenty years or more,
> And everyone said, 'How tall they've grown!
> For they've been to the Lakes, and the Torrible Zone,
> And the hills of the Chankly Bore!'

Chariots of fire. From the preface to Blake's *Milton,* written in 1809.

> Bring me my bow of burning gold,
> Bring me my arrows of desire,
> Bring me my spear — O clouds, unfold!
> Bring me my chariots of fire!
> I will not cease from mental flight,
> Nor shall my sword sleep in my hand,
> Till we have built Jerusalem
> In England's green and pleasant land.

135

Chapel. A Protestant church that isn't Anglican. A class distinction is often implied when "church" and "chapel" are mentioned. Thus, in Barsetshire, the Leslies go to the parish church, while some of their servants attend chapel.

Chatham House. The home of the Royal Institute of International Affairs, located in St. James Square, London.

Chelsea Flower Show. A renowned annual flower show sponsored by the Royal Horticultural Society. It has been held each May since 1913 on the grounds of the Royal Hospital in Chelsea. The scions of *Palafox borealis* certainly have been exhibited there.

Cheerfulness Breaks In. This title is drawn from a remark made by Oliver Edwards in 1778, quoted by James Boswell in his *Life of Samuel Johnson:* "I have tried too in my time to be a philosopher; but I don't know how, cheerfulness was always breaking in."

Chee serra serra. Mr. Pilward's rendering of *che sarà sarà*.

Che gelida manina. *Italian.*   "What an icy hand." These words are the first in a famous and beautiful tenor aria from a famous and beautiful opera, Puccini's *La Boheme*.

Che sarà sarà. *Italian.* What will be, will be. Fat lot of good it does to know that.

Cheval de harrue et cheval pur sang. *French.* Plow horse and thoroughbred.

Chevaux-de-frise. *French.*   Literally, "horses of the Fresians" and used in English untranslated. It is a military barricade consisting mainly of spikes, sometimes threaded with barbed wire.

Children of the New Forest. A very popular children's novel by Captain Frederick Marryat, published in 1847. It was still being read in the early decades of the twentieth century.

Chips, Mr. The carpenter from the Happy Families game. It is also the nickname of the old classics master Mr. Chipping in the novel *Good-bye, Mr. Chips* by James Hilton. Mr. Chips has retired and is reminiscing about his many years of service at Brookfield School as his life gently runs down and he dies a peaceful death.

Chi va sano va lontano. *Italian.* He who goes safely goes far.

"(There are)Chords in the human mind. . . ." Mr. Guppy's characteristic remark. What he meant by this pseudo-profundity is unclear, because he never completed the sentence. *See* **Mr. Guppy.**

Christian. From John Bunyan's *Pilgrim's Progress*. He was the pilgrim whose journey to the Celestial City is described.

Church. In Barsetshire, this means the Church of England, or Anglican Church, the church that resulted from the exodus of Henry VIII from the Roman Catholic Church, and which retains to varying degrees some elements of the old religion. The church may be "high" or "low," depending on the complexity or simplicity of the ritual and accoutrements, or the degree to which these resemble those of the Roman Catholic Church. A priest who has "high" preferences, like Father Fewling, will have as part of his services incense or candles and may hear confessions.

A brief sketch of the organization of the Anglican Church may be helpful to American readers.

The head of the Church of England is the sovereign. Below him or her in descending order of rank are the Archbishop of Canterbury, the Archbishop of York, and the bishops of all the other dioceses, which numbered forty-two in 1977. Every diocese comprises a group of parishes; each parish has a patron, lay or ecclesiastical, which may be a single person or a body such as a college. This patron may appoint, but not remove, the vicar—for each parish is under the care of a rector, vicar, or perpetual curate.

The cathedral is the center of the ecclesiastical life in the diocese. Its services and upkeep are overseen by the chapter, from the chapter house. The head of the chapter is the dean, and his assistants are called canons. The bishop oversees the diocese, assisted by an archdeacon. His residence is called the "palace," he is addressed as "My Lord," and he is entitled, if there is a seat for him, to sit in the House of Lords. Bishop, dean, and canons live in the cathedral close.

Bishops are elected in a roundabout way, via the Sovereign, the Prime Minister, the Archbishop of Canterbury, and the local chapter.

Churchill, Sir Winston (1874–1965). Renowned English statesman, writer, and occasional artist. Mentioned in many of the Barsetshire novels, always with admiration, Sir Winston was Prime Minister during the war, when he inspired the nation with his hard work and eloquent speeches. After his defeat in 1945 he was sorely missed, as we all know, and the joy was great when he made a transit of the Barsetshire Agricultural Show and Conservative Rally at Staple Park in 1947.

Churchwarden. An assistant to the local rector or vicar, who is responsible for the upkeep of the church and who acts as a lay representative in parish matters. As a rule every parish had two wardens, one elected by the vestry (*q.v.*) and one appointed by the vicar.

Churchill, Frank. A character in Jane Austen's *Emma*. He was a rather slick out-of-town man with a worldly manner and attractive bearing who was quite a singer. He set local girls aflutter—until it was revealed that he had been secretly engaged all the time to a visitor among them.

Cicisbeo. Italian. The escort of a married woman. This was an acceptable arrangement made in 18th century Italy, when men did not often accompany their wives in public. Thus it came to mean a pretty boy, a fop, an epicene character who might devote himself to an unobtainable woman.

Ci-devant. French. Formerly called.

Circumlocution Office. From Dickens' *Little Dorritt*. It is a satiric portrayal of everything bad about bureaucracy.

> If another Gunpowder Plot had been discovered half an hour before the lighting of the match, nobody would have been justified in saving the Parliament until there had been half a score of boards, half a bushel of minutes, several sacks of official memoranda, and a family-vault full of ungrammatical correspondence, on the part of the Circumlocution Office.

The cities of the plain. A reference to Sodom and Gomorrah; also the title of one of the novels by Marcel Proust in his *Remembrance of Things Past*, now being translated as *In Search of Lost Time*. The original phrase is from Genesis 13:12

> Abram dwelled in the land of Canaan, and Lot dwelled in the cities of the plain, and pitched his tent toward Sodom.

City. More formally known as the City of London, this refers to the ancient walled part of London that has in recent centuries been the center of commercial and financial activity. It is roughly a mile square in area and has its own government.

"City of Brass." A prophetic poem by Rudyard Kipling. Written in 1909, it seems to predict, in the opinion of Barsetshire, what was happening in England in the 1950's—the rise to power of small, mean-spirited, lazy, feckless bureaucrats who will rob the hard working toilers of what is rightfully theirs.

Clara Gazul. Title of a novel by famed courtesan Harriette Wilson. AT wrote a biography of Wilson.

Claret. Originally, this meant any red table wine. Now it usually designates Bordeaux.

Clergy. A clerical career was one of the traditional occupations of younger sons.

Cloakroom. A room on the first floor of a large house for storing coats and outdoor gear. It often incorporated a toilet, and is sometimes a euphemism for those facilities.

Cloche. *French.* Bell. To gardeners, it is a heavy glass bell-shaped jar used by gardeners to cover and protect tender young plants in cool climates.

Clumsy, Sir Tunbelly. A character from Vanbrugh's play *The Relapse* and from Sheridan's musical version of the story, *A Trip to Scarborough.* Sir Tunbelly is a jolly country squire.

Clusium. One of twelve cities of ancient Etruria. It is now called Chiusi, in Sienna. See **Lars Porsena.**

Coat and skirt. Americans would call this a suit.

A cock and a bull, story of. From Laurence Sterne's *Tristram Shandy.* It comes at the end of a longish tale of woe delivered by the Shandys' manservant, Yorick. In sum, it seemed that the Shandys' bull had failed to impregnate Yorick's cow. Mrs. Shandy broke in with

> L—d! said my mother, what is all this story about?—
> A Cock and a Bull, said Yorick—And one of the best of its kind, I ever heard.

That, by the way, is the last line of the book.

Cocqcigrues. Characters from Charles Kingsley's *The Water Babies, q.v.* They were beings heralded but not present, whose arrival would cause all of life's mysteries to be revealed.

Cocteau, Jean, and Anouilh, Jean. Modern dramatists. Cocteau (1889–1963) wrote poetry as well as drama and was also a film director. Anouilh (1910–1987) wrote *Waltz of the Toreadors, Beckett,* and *Antigone.*

Cold Comfort Farm. A novel by Stella Gibbons that appeared in 1932. It is a parody of the novels depicting rural life with overheated romance, magic, and earthiness by authors such as D.H. Lawrence and Mary Webb. Jasper Margett could have stepped right out of the pages of any of those novels.

Collins letter. A bread-and-butter letter. The name seems to have come from *Pride and Prejudice,* in which Mr. Collins writes to thank the Bennets for their hospitality.

Colney Hatch. A mental hospital established in 1851.

The Colonel's Lady and Judy O'Grady. From Kipling's poem "The Ladies," which at first glance seems a bit out of place in Barsetshire. The speaker in the poem has led a carefree and boisterous love-life, and is giving it as his learned wisdom that all women, whether well-placed or humble, are "sisters under the skin."

"Come here Charlotte, and I'll kiss yer." From Dickens' *Oliver Twist*. In the home of the undertaker, Sowerby, Charlotte was the maidservant. Noah Claypole, who spoke the words, the only kind words he ever uttered to anyone, was Mr. Sowerby's assistant. His charm worked miracles: Charlotte was enticed to rob the till and run away with Noah to lead a life of petty crime in London.

Comes Pontefractus. Latin. Comrade Pontefract. This is the only indication that the name Pomfret was originally, as we suspected, Pontefract, which of course would be pronounced "Pomfret."

"Come then, Sorrow. . . ." A line from Keats' *Endymion*. It begins "A thing of beauty is a joy forever" and continues for many pages. The verse in question is

> Come then, Sorrow!
> Sweetest Sorrow!
> Like an own babe I nurse thee on my breast:
> I thought to leave thee
> And deceive thee,
> But now of all the world I love thee best.

Coming out. This refers to the somewhat ritualistic presentation to the Court and to London society of a young woman of marriageable age. It was accomplished during the few months of the London season (springtime). While it doesn't seem to have figured in the lives of our Barsetshire friends, it is occasionally referred to.

Commination service. A church service read after the litany on Ash Wednesday. It confesses to a state of sinfulness and is a plea for mercy.

Congé. *French.* Time off. It signifies a dismissal.

Consols. Short for Consolidated Annuities. These were government securities, a type of investment paying three percent.

Constable, John (1776–1837). Perhaps the most famous of the English landscape painters. Over twenty of his paintings hang in the National Gallery, and several more hang in the Tate.

Consultant. A medical specialist. In the legal world, a consultant is a lawyer connected with a firm, but not a partner.

Contrariwise. From *Alice in Wonderland* by Lewis Carroll. "Contrariwise" was Tweedledee's catchword.

> "I know what you're thinking about," said Tweedledum; "but it isn't so, nohow."
> "Contrariwise," continued Tweedledee, "if it was so, it might be; and if were so, it would be; but as it isn't, it ain't. That's logic."

Copper. A large vessel in which laundry was boiled. Or, in the kitchen, large pots used for heating water or making soups or stocks.

The Coral Island. An 1857 adventure novel for boys by R.M. Ballantyne.

Corday, Charlotte (1768–1793). A excitable young French woman of Royalist sympathies. Hearing that the revolutionary Jean Paul Marat planned the execution of 200,000 more people, she went to his house and, finding him at his bath, stabbed him even as he bathed. This dramatic act not only cost her life but led to measures being taken that ensured the survival of the republic.

Cordelia. From Shakespeare's *King Lear.* Cordelia was one of three daughters; the other two were Regan and Goneril. Although Lear did not believe her, Cordelia was the only one who loved him.

Cothornus. From Greek drama. A thick-soled boot worn by actors in tragic dramas, heaven knows why. The word has to do with the (literally) stilted and stylized quality of ancient drama.

Cottage hospital. Small hospitals in villages or rural areas. They were often housed in several cottage-like buildings.

Cottage Orné. *French.* An artistically rustic cottage built mostly to be decorative. These were part of a taste for the picturesque that was part of the Romanticism of the late 18ᵗʰ and early 19ᵗʰ centuries.

Coulisse. A theatrical term referring to action on the side of the stage.

Count of Paris. *See* **Paris, Count.**

County. As an adjective, this denotes the landed gentry, the upper crust of rural society. The people in Barsetshire are aware of who is and who is not county. The Marlings, Pallisers, Dales, Keiths, Hallidays, Beltons, Leslies, Sowerbys, and Wickhams are county by virtue of having been landowners in Barsetshire for many generations. The Bartons, Sam Adams, Laura Morland, the Brandons, the Fieldings, the Perrys, and the Deans are recent additions and know that they aren't county. Whether or not this matters we really cannot say, and neither could they.

Couperin, François (1668–1733). French organist and Composer in Ordinary to Louis XIV.

Court curtsey. A very deep curtsey made by women being presented at Court. *See* **Presented.**

Cousin(e) germain(e). *French.* First cousin.

Coventry. To send to Coventry is to punish by treating cooly or ignoring. Coventry is a city of around 500,000, eighteen miles east-southeast of Birmingham.

Crabbe, the Reverend George (1754–1832). Author of both poetry and prose, although it is the poetry for which he is most remembered. In it he tells tales of rural life in realistic, unromantic terms.

Creating. Slang for creating a scene or throwing a fit: having hysterics.

Cretonne. A heavy unglazed cotton fabric used for covering furniture, or for curtains.

Crew of the *Hot Cross Bun.* From one of the Bab Ballads, *The Bumboat Woman's Story.* The bumboat woman fell in love with Lieutenant Belaye of the *Hot Cross Bun.* She disguised herself as a sailor, slipped on board, and easily passed as part of his peculiar crew.

When Jack Tars meet, they meet with a "Messmate, ho! What cheer?"
But here, on the *Hot Cross Bun*, it was "How do you do, my dear?"
When Jack Tars growl, I believe they growl with a big big D—
But the strongest oath of the *Hot Cross Bun* was a mild "Dear me!"

Yet, though they were all well bred, you could scarcely call them slick:
Whenever a sea was on, they were all extremely sick;
And whenever the weather was calm, and the wind was light and fair,
They spent more time than a sailor should on his back back hair.

But no wonder! They were all women, all in love with Lieutenant Belaye, and all heartbroken when he married Another.

Cri de coeur. *French.* A cry from the heart — a spontaneous, intense cry of deep feeling.

Cripps, Sir Stafford. Labor statesman. He was on the Board of Trade in 1945. In 1947, as Chancellor of the Exchequer, he instituted the austerity policies which created so much resentment in Barsetshire.

Croix de Guerre. French military honor—literally, "cross of war."

Crock. A physical wreck, not necessarily of a human being.

Crocket. An ornamental projection incorporated into the sloping edge of a gable, conveniently placed so as to give young boys a plausible rationale for climbing.

Crossed letters. To save postage in the early days of mail service, letters would be written, then the paper turned ninety degrees and the next lines written at right angles over the first. If that were done a second time, with a third set of lines over the first two, the result could be confusing.

Crown. A coin worth five shillings. *See* **Money.**

Cruft's. An important dog show established in 1886 by Charles Cruft. It is held every February in London

Mrs. Crummles. A character from Dickens' *Nicholas Nickleby.* She was the wife of Vincent Crummles, the manager of a company of itinerant actors. She was "a stout portly female, apparently between forty and fifty; in a tarnished silk cloak, with her bonnet dangling by the strings in her hand, and her hair (of which she had a great quantity) braided in a large festoon over each temple."

Cubbing. Less formal than the regular fox-hunting season, cubbing is a way to teach hunt skills to all the participants: young hunters go after fox cubs on horses that may be novices; included in the mix are some equally inexperienced hounds. This may seem like a recipe for disaster, or possibly a three-ring circus in the making, but it was tradition.

"The cuckoo of a joyless June. . . . " From Tennyson's "Prefatory Poem to My Brother's Sonnets" (1879). The lines are contained in these verses:

I.
Midnight—in no midsummer tune
The breakers lash the shores;
The cuckoo of a joyless June
Is calling out of doors.

And thou hast vanish'd from thine own
To that which looks like rest,
True brother, only to be known
By those who love thee best.

II.
Midnight—and joyless June gone by,
And from the deluged park
The cuckoo of a worse July
Is calling thro' the dark;

Cul-de-poule. *French.* Chicken's bottom.

Curate. An ordained priest who does not have a living and who then becomes an assistant to one who can afford to pay him.

Curfew Must Not Ring Tonight. The title and frequent refrain of a very romantic poem by Rose Hartwick Thorpe. The hero is condemned by Cromwell to die when the church clock strikes the hour for curfew. Bessie, the heroine, prevents the clock from striking by climbing into the bell tower, leaping out and grabbing the clapper. She shows her torn and bruised hands to Cromwell when he rides into town for the execution and he issues the pardon.

Wide they flung the massive portal; led the prisoner forth to die—
All his bright young life before him. 'Neath the darkening English sky
Bessie comes with flying footsteps, eyes aglow with love-light sweet;
Kneeling on the turf beside him, lays his pardon at his feet.
In his brave, strong arms he clasped her, kissed the face upturned and white,
Whispered, "Darling, you have saved me—
"Curfew will not ring tonight!"

Cuttle, Captain Edward. From Dickens' *Dombey and Son.* He was a one-handed sea-going gentleman, who had been a pilot and the skipper of a privateer. He was a friend of Solomon Gills, who kept a nautical instruments shop, and was devoted to Solomon's nephew Walter and to Florence Dombey.

Cymric. (Pronounced SIM-rik or KIM-ric.) The Welsh form of Celtic.

Dainty rogue in porcelain. A well-known phrase from *The Egoist* by George Meredith. The heroine, Clara Middleton, is thus described by Mrs. Mountstuart Jenkinson. This was before Clara had second thoughts about her engagement and finally broke it. Clarissa Graham is described as a dainty rogue in porcelain several times.

Daisy-chainish. Like something familial from Charlotte Yonge's 1856 novel *The Daisy Chain.*

Dame of the British Empire. An honor awarded to women. According to her biographer Margot Strickland, AT had hoped for a DBE in 1959 and was disappointed.

Damon and Pythias. From classical Rome. Damon and Pythias were two devoted friends. Pythias was condemned to death by the god Dionysius. He requested leave to go home and settle his affairs; Damon had agreed to take his place if he didn't return. But Pythias did return, and Dionysius was so impressed by this selflessness that he freed them both.

Danae. From Greek myth. Danae was the daughter of Danaus, the king of Argos. Danaus took to heart a prophecy that he would be killed by his grandson, so he locked his daughter in an impenetrable tower. This plan was foiled by Zeus, who penetrated Danae's aerie as a shower of gold. Danae afterward bore a son, Perseus, who did as it happened, kill his grandfather, although it was an accident.

Danegeld. A land tax levied during the time of Ethelred II (978–1016). It was paid to the Danes in return for peace, but was continued beyond the time when it was needed. Kipling wrote a contemptuous poem about it.

Dantes, Edmund. The hero of Alexandre Dumas' *Count of Monte Cristo.* Edmund was imprisoned on false charges and kept for many years in a cell that was solitary until the Abbé Faria tunnelled into it and began teaching Edmund history, chemistry, mathematics, and four languages. When the Abbé died, Edmund escaped and began a long and satisfying course of revenge.

Darby and Joan. An elderly devoted couple, inspired by a poem by Henry Woodfall, published in *The Gentleman's Magazine* in 1735. Supposedly Woodfall knew the originals of Darby and Joan, and described them in his poem, "The Joys of Love Never Forgot."

> Old Darby with Joan by his side,
> You've often regarded with wonder.
> He's dropsical, she's sore-eyed,
> Yet they're never happy asunder.

Darkness made visible. A line from John Milton's *Paradise Lost.*

> A dungeon horrible, on all sides round
> As one great furnace flam'd; yet from those flames
> No light, but rather darkness visible
> Served only to discover sights of woe,
> Regions of sorrow, doleful shades. . . .

Dartle, Rosa. From Dickens' *David Copperfield.* Rosa was sharp-edged and intense. She worked entirely by indirection, casting doubts by asking questions, and excusing the questions by saying "I only want to know."

Darvinchy; Renwar. Mr. Scatcherd's rendering of Leonardo Da Vinci (1452–1519), the Italian painter of the *Mona Lisa* and *The Last Supper,* among many other works of genius, and the French Impressionist Pierre Auguste Renoir (1841–1919).

Dashwood, Marianne. From Jane Austen's *Sense and Sensibility.* Marianne represented the "sensibility," having apparently no sense at all. She went into hysterics after having been jilted by a man who trifled with her affections. So assaulted were her sensibilities that she spent page after page in various agonies, until she came to her senses and accepted a reasonable proposal from an old family friend.

Dastard in war. *See* **laggard in love.**

"a Daughter—she left us at a very tender age. . . . " A daughter, Mary, had been born to AT and her husband James McInnes in March, 1917. This was their third child, born at a time when the marriage had disintegrated. AT took the three children to her parents' home soon after Mary's birth. The baby was frail and died of pneumonia the following February. AT makes no mention of her at all until this line appeared in *Three Score and Ten.*

Dead for a ducat. This is a quotation from *Hamlet.* "How now! A rat? Dead, for a ducat, dead!"

D-Day. June 6, 1944. This was the day of a massive Allied offensive launched on the beaches of Normandy. "D" means "undetermined" and can be used for any big event for which the date has not been selected. The date for the D-Day invasion remained unknown until the weather could reasonably be relied upon to be favorable.

"The dead they cannot rise. . . . " From Rudyard Kipling's poem "Soldier, Soldier." It is a dialog between a young woman, asking for news of her lover, and a returning veteran, breaking the news of his death. In the last verse and the refrain the veteran advises her that as the dead cannot rise, she would be well advised to dry her eyes and take a new love when it is offered.

Deal. Pine or fir boards of a specified width, such as seven inches.

Death of Chatterton. A romantic painting by Henry Wallis. It shows the young man gracefully disposed on a narrow bed beneath a double casement window in what is obviously an attic. Somehow we doubt that the victims of arsenic poisoning look so calm and clean—but it is a lovely picture.

Debrett, John. Publisher of *Peerage of England, Scotland and Ireland,* a social register. It first appeared in 1802, but since 1926 has been updated annually under the title *Debrett's Peerage, Baronetage, Knightage, and Companionage. See* **Burke.**

The Decameron. A collection of tales retold by Giovanni Bocaccio (1313–1375). The device used is a situation in which seven young ladies and three young men have left Florence to escape the plague and are staying at various villas in the country. To pass the time, each tells ten stories. They range from the bawdy to the suspenseful, the romantic to the clever, the funny to the poignant.

Decline and Fall of the Roman Empire, the History of the. Lydia Keith Merton's favorite reading, *Decline and Fall* was written by Edward Gibbon (for whom the chameleon was named) and published in three volumes in 1776, 1781 and 1788. It is famous for the elegance of its language and the superiority of its scholarship. *See* **Gibbon.**

Dedlock, Volumnia. From Dickens' *Bleak House.* Spinster cousin of the wealthy Sir Leicester Dedlock. She spent several weeks in the year at his house, adding zest and sparkle, or a facsimile thereof, to the house parties at Chesney Wold. She was sprightly though far from young, she danced well, she asked French riddles, and she always agreed with Sir Leicester.

"Deep as a well. . . . " From *Romeo and Juliet.* This bit of dialog gives the ironic flavor of the words spoken by Mercutio, who has just received a mortal wound:

> Mercutio: I am hurt. A plague on both your houses! I am sped. Is he gone, and hath nothing?
> Benvolio: What, art thou hurt?
> Mercutio: Ay, ay, a scratch, a scratch; marry, 'tis enough.
> Romeo: Courage, man; the hurt cannot be much.
> Mercutio: No, 'tis not so deep as a well, nor so wide as a church-door; but 'tis enough, 'twill serve. Ask for me tomorrow and you will find me a grave man.

De Farge, Madame. From Dickens' *Tale of Two Cities,* a Frenchwoman who was consumed by the wish to avenge her family. She was a watchful woman and a revolutionary, and as such, a pitiless tigress. She was also quite a knitter, and incorporated into the pattern of her work a coded record of the enemies of the Republic. While on a murderous errand she was killed by her own pistol during a struggle.

Defendant's song from *Trial by Jury.* This song from the Gilbert and Sullivan operetta is sung by a young man defending a breach of promise suit.

> Of Nature the laws I obey,
>   For nature is constantly changing;
> The moon in her phases is found,
>   The time and the wind and the weather,
> The months in succession come round,
>   And you don't find two Mondays together.
>   Consider the moral I pray,
>   Nor bring a young fellow to sorrow,
>   Who loves this young lady to-day,
>   And loves that young lady tomorrow.

De Gaulle, Charles (1890–1970). French general, leader of the Free French in England during World War II. He was later head of the provisional government and was elected president in 1958.

Dégringolade. *French.* A fall or tumble; decadence or downfall; descent into decadence or squalor.

De gustibus non est disputandum. *Latin.* There's no arguing with taste.

Démarches. *French.* Steps.

"Dem'd moist unpleasant body." *See* **Mr. Mantalini.**

Demon in the House. This title is a take-off on *The Angel in the House,* a long poem celebrating married love, by Coventry Patmore. It appeared over the years 1854, 1856, 1860, and 1861. Its sentimentality was mocked by more sophisticated writers, and Virginia Woolf said that women writers must "kill the angel in the house."

De mortuis nil nisi bonum. *Latin.* Of the dead (say) nothing but good.

De musique tout confit. *French.* Steeped in music.

Dennet. A light, open two-wheeled sort of gig. It was popular from around 1820 to 1830.

Desideratum lectum. *Latin.* Desired bed.

Mr. Deuceace. A character from Thackeray's *Pendennis.*

Deus ex machina. Latin. Literally, "god out of a machine;" in Greek drama, one of the gods would arrive at a critical moment, suspended from overhead by a piece of equipment. The conflict would then be resolved and all would be well. Thus the phrase has come to mean someone who appears out of the blue to solve a problem. This is wonderful when it happens in real life, but is considered a cheap shot in fiction.

Devil's tattoo. An irritating repetitive movement, such as drumming the fingers or tapping a foot.

Dew pond. A shallow pond carved out of a chalk or limestone substratum. It catches rain and provides water for livestock.

"O Diamond, Diamond." The full line is "O Diamond! Diamond! Thou little knowest the mischief done!" It was uttered by Isaac Newton to his dog Diamond, when the poor creature had tipped over a candle and burned some important papers.

Diane Chasserasse. *French.* Diana the Huntress. Diana was a Roman goddess associated with the moon, and also with hunting.

Dick, Mr. An amiable lunatic, a character from Dickens' *David Copperfield.* He lodged with Miss Trotwood, but at the end was revealed to have been her husband. He had had a breakdown soon after their marriage.

Dido. *See* **Aeneas.** The queen of Carthage.

Disraeli, Benjaman, 1ˢᵗ Earl of Beaconsfield (1804–1881). Author and statesman, prime minister off and on between 1868 and 1880. Even more than most, his career was a struggle and he is known for an admirable perseverance. He is famous also for the relationship he was able to establish with Queen Victoria. His novels include *Vivian Grey, Sybil, Tancred,* and *Henrietta Temple.*

Distemper. Paint with a base of pore-filling size, as distinguished from oil based paint.

Divers et ondoyant. *French.* Varied and flowing.

Divorce. There was no divorce, either.

Dochandorus. Scottish, and spelled various ways. One for the road; a drink before leaving—a wee drap, that's a'.

"Does the truth sound bitter. . . . " *See* **"The Lost Mistress."**

Dolly Foster. Title character in *The Dolly Dialogues*, published in 1894 by Anthony Hope. At the time of her engagement Dolly's grandfather wrote, congratulating her on her "most suitable alliance."

Dombey, Edith and Mr. Carker. Edith Dombey and James Carker; Clara Newcome and Lord Highgate; and Clara Mowbray and Francis Tyrrel—all were couples from 19th century fiction who were, or appeared to be, in carnal relationships unsanctified by marriage vows.

Dombey, Florence. From Dickens' *Dombey and Son*. Florence was devoted to her small brother Paul and to her father, although he neglected her.

Dombey, Mrs. Also from *Dombey and Son*. Fanny Dombey, never robust, and dying from some complication of childbirth, lacked entirely the strength to "make an effort," as her husband, doctors and sister-in-law heartily commanded her to do. She died at the end of the first chapter.

Domine defende nos/contra hos motores bus. *Latin*. God protect us from the motor bus.

Don. Any member of the teaching faculty at the old universities such as Oxford or Cambridge. A don could be a teacher, tutor, or the head of a college. The word comes from the Latin *dominus* which means "lord," or, by extension, "leader."

Donne, John (1572–1631). A major figure in English letters, a poet and writer of memorable sermons. He entered upon his church career in midlife, and became dean of St. Paul's in 1621. He is the author of the familiar lines "Death be not proud," "Go and catch a falling star," and "No man is an island . . . . never send to know for whom the bell tolls."
  George Herbert was a poet and friend of Donne's. **Henry Vaughan** was inspired by Herbert, but was younger; **Richard Crashaw**, much the same age as Vaughan, was a Roman Catholic poet.

Donneurs de seranades. *French*. Serenaders. *Belles ecouteuses:* beautiful listeners.

Doré, Gustav (1832–1883). French artist and engraver, best known today for his illustrations of such dramatic works as Dante's *Inferno*. His steel-cut engravings conveyed every nuance of the sombre and grotesque.

Dormouse. A character from Lewis Carroll's *Alice in Wonderland*. The dormouse was a guest at the mad tea party, as were Alice, the Mad Hatter, and the March Hare. As the dormouse kept nodding off, the Hatter and the Hare tried to stuff it into the tea pot—the obvious thing to do.
  The real dormouse, *Muscardinus avellanarius*, is a small creature something like a chipmunk, but smaller, being only about five inches long, including the tail. It is nocturnal and hibernates. Victorian children kept dormice as pets.

Douceur de vivre. *French*. Sweetness of life.

Douceur. *French*. Something to sweeten a transaction; a tip or bribe.

Douglas, James, 2nd Earl of Douglas and Mar (1358–1388). A Scottish earl involved in the border wars of the time. At Newcastle he defeated but did not kill Sir Henry Percy. Some months later, again fighting the Percys, he himself was killed—which no doubted gratified Earl Percy, Sir Henry's father.

Dowager. A widow entitled to property. Dower is a complicated subject involving the various rights or lack thereof of a widow to her deceased husband's property, especially when a title is involved.

Dower house. A house on a large estate set aside for the use of the dowager. Upon the death of the lord, the heir would take possession of the house and the dowager would obligingly go somewhere else, most conveniently the dower house. *See* **The widow's lot.**

Down. University lingo. Universities "come down" or "go down" for vacation, and, logically enough, "go up" when the term opens. Being "sent down" is being expelled.

Downs. Uplands; rolling hills. The word is etymologically related to "dune," meaning "hill."

Doyen. The respected older member of a group. The feminine of this is doyenne.

Drag. A scented bag that is dragged over the field to excite and guide the hounds when there are no foxes.

The Drink that cheereth. Wine, from Psalms 104:15: "And wine that maketh glad the heart of man . . . "

Druids. A class of scholar-priests among pre-Roman Celts in Europe, England, and Ireland. There is very little reliable information about them, but they are associated with human sacrifices made in oak groves hung with mistletoe.

Duckboard. Wood strips nailed across long boards to make a safe and dry flooring or walkway.

Dulce ridentum, dulce loquantum Lalagen. *See* **Lalage.**

Du mal qu'un amore ignoré / Nous fait souffrir. *French.* From the pain of unrequited love we are made to suffer.

Du Maurier, George (1834–1896). British artist, cartoonist, and author of *Peter Ibbetson* and *Trilby.* He spent his early years in London and Paris, returning to England in 1860. He is the father of Gerald Du Maurier, and the grandfather of Daphne Du Maurier. As an artist he portrayed the ideals of contemporary beauty for both sexes just as Charles Dana Gibson did a generation later.

Dux Omnium. Latin. The Duke of Omnium

"Each glance of the eye so bright." From Browning's "The Lost Mistress," *q.v.*

Eagle. In a church, the more or less eagle-shaped brass or wood lectern.

Earth. A fox's den.

Écarté. A French card game for two, played with a pack of thirty-two cards, *i.e.*, a regular deck from which the sixes and below have been removed. The remaining cards have point values, and the goal is to accumulate tricks. In casinos écarté is played for stakes.

Eccomi. Italian. Here I am.

Echo du temps passé. French. An echo of past times.

Écrasez l'enfâme. French. Crush the abomination—a cry made famous by Voltaire, who by *l'enfâme* meant the establishment of pre-revolutionary France.

Edgeworth, Maria (1768–1849). The daughter of a large Anglo-Irish family and esteemed author of the first English historical novels and regional novels, although many had contemporary settings. *Patronage* (1814) was about the English society of the time. Edgeworth also wrote novels about Irish life and a series for parents and children.

Mrs. Edmonstone. *See **The Heir of Redclyffe**.*

Education. Among our Barsetshire friends, this most often meant schooling at home with a governess until the age of eight. Then the child, if male, was sent to a preparatory school until he was thirteen or so. After that came a school, such as Eton or Southbridge, which occupied him until he was around eighteen. If the boy wanted and was suited for higher education, he went to university at Oxford, or perhaps Cambridge. Other universities, "redbricks," were new and therefore unthinkable. Girls went from their governesses (at home) to a school such as Barchester High School, if their parents deemed it suitable. Only rarely did they attend university—Betty Dean went to Oxford, and Clarissa Graham went to Cambridge for technical training in engineering draughtmanship.

It is obvious to the meanest intellect that the content of our friends' education was very high in quality. Children were expected to learn Latin and often Greek and other modern European languages as well. They were well-versed in literature and experienced in the writing of essays. They knew history and mathematics, biology and physics. Activities at schools included dramatics, writing for publications, debates, and singing.

E finita la commedia. *Italian.* So ends the play.

Egeria. This name is often used in reference to Miss Pemberton and is, not surprisingly, from classical sources. Egeria was a nymph believed to have given wise counsel to the emperor Numa Pompilius, the second king of Rome (753–673 B.C.), and thus the word means an advisor or counselor. The term was in fairly common use during the age of classical education.

Ego et rex meus. *Latin.* My king and I. Words made famous by Cardinal Wolsey (1475–1530), whose partially realized aim was to be the power behind the throne. As the throne at the time was sat in, or on, by Henry VIII, it was a dicey proposition, and it ended badly for him.

Eights Week. The high point of the Oxford social calendar. It comes at the end of the Trinity term, after schools (final exams). "Eights" refers to the teams of eight who compete in bumping each other in rowing boats on the Cherwell. The successful college holds a Bump Supper. There are other dinners, dances, and lawn parties. Visiting friends and relatives swell the crowds. As it is early summer, the river and campuses are their loveliest, as well as their liveliest.

Eisel. Vinegar.

Eldon, Lord (1751–1838). English lawyer and politician whose distinguished career included a famous decision made during his tenure as Lord Chancellor. This pertained to the Leeds Grammar School Case (1805), which denied the school the use of its endowment for teaching such modern subjects as French and German. It should be noted that he did not deny the school the right to change its statutes; he was only interpreting the existing statutes.

Elisha. An old testament prophet, the heir to the prophet Elijah. Elisha encountered some resistance at the time of the transition after Elijah's death; his encounter with the children and the she-bears is described in II Kings 2: 23–24.

> 23 And he went from thence to Beth-el: and as he was going up by the way, there came
> forth little children out of the city, and mocked him and said unto him, Go up, thou bald
> head: go up, thou bald head.
> 24 And he turned back, and looked on them, and cursed them in the name of the Lord.
> And there came forth two she bears out of the wood, and tare forty and two children
> of them.

Éminence grise. *French.* "Gray eminence;" subtle or secret influence; a power behind the throne.

Emma. The main character in Jane Austen's *Emma,* published in 1816. During the course of the novel a ball is held at one of the village inns. It is exceedingly like the ball held at the Nabob just after Christmas in *Happy Return.*

Empedocles under Etna. Empedocles was a Sicilian of great and varied talents, a scientist, philosopher, seer, statesman, healer and poet. There is a story that he jumped into the crater of Mt. Etna in order to enhance his reputation as a divinity. This story was rendered in poetry by Matthew Arnold in "Empedocles on Etna."

Encaenia. (en.SEE.nee.a) From a Greek word meaning "commemoration," Encaenia was a ceremony in June at Oxford at which various awards were given. Ancillary parties were given as well, and a good time was had by all.

Encaustic tile. A tile on which a pattern is formed by inlaying a different color of clay and firing both together.

Enceladus. From Greek myth. A powerful giant with one hundred arms, who was rash enough to plot against Zeus. For this he was thrown into Mt. Etna, from whence his enraged breathing causes flames to rise to this day.

En disponibilité. *French.* At your disposal.

English Fairy Tales and More English Fairy Tales. Collections of tales by folklorist Joseph Jacobs. "Mouse and Mouser" is one of the stories. Others are "Mr. Miacca," about a cannibalistic neighbor, "Johnny Cake," and "Titty Mouse and Tatty Mouse." There are also poems, such as "Lawamercyme."

Enoch Arden. The subject of a long poem by Tennyson, published in 1864. It concerns a love triangle. Enoch marries the girl, Annie, but is compelled to go to sea, where he is shipwrecked and is considered drowned. When he finally does return after having been rescued ten years later, he finds Annie happily married to his rival. He resolves his return shall not be revealed until after his death.

Eno's Salts. A tonic made by mixing the aforesaid salts in water with satisfying fizzy results.

Engadine. The Swiss portion of the sixty-mile-long valley of the Inn River.

England Expects. Just before the battle of Trafalgar in October 1805, Nelson sent a signal to his fleet which, with a couple of amendments made by his subordinate officers, read "England expects every man will do his duty." Every man did, for as our readers may know, the battle was won, Nelson was killed, and England was far safer than before. Every British schoolchild knows the words of the signal.

Entail. This is a legal term. An entailed piece of property, while it may be inherited, cannot be sold, given away or mortgaged, but must pass through a line of heirs. It was the combination of primogeniture and entailment that enabled the formation of a great landed gentry.

Entbehren sollst du! Sollst du entbehren. *German.* Refrain you must! You must refrain. From Goethe.

Entrechats gris. *French.* Dreary dance capers.

Épris. *French.* Taken with, or in love with.

Erda. The earth-goddess from Richard Wagner's *Ring* cycle of operas. Erda rises from the earth to dispense advice and then gracefully sinks back into whatever abyss from whence she arose.

Esquire. This title, ever more vague in meaning, designates a social rank just lower than a knight, and when applied to a landowner with no other title is often shortened to "Squire." In days of yore, an esquire was a young gentleman who served a knight while awaiting the time when he himself would be a knight. In more recent times, "Esquire" has sometimes been used to designate a young man in certain professions, especially those related to the law.

Esther. A saintly young woman, the ward of Mr. Jarndyce, from Dickens' *Bleak House.* She took a benign interest in Peepy and his little brothers and sisters, the small children of the busily philanthropic Mrs. Jellyby.

Est modus in rebus. *Latin.* There is a proper measure in things. Horace, *Satires,* I.

Etanswill. From Dickens' *Pickwick Papers.* Mr. Pickwick happened to be visiting Etanswill at the time an election was being contested. *See* **Slumkey, Samuel,** and **Smorltork.**

Eton suit. From 1798 until 1967 the junior boys at Eton wore a waist-length square-cut jacket with wide lapels and a small turned-down collar. Underneath was a white shirt with a wide, rounded detachable starched collar and a waistcoat. The trousers had narrow stripes. Following the death of George III the entire suit was black, including the tie; only the shirt was white. There were variations on this for older boys, and for different occasions.

Euclid. Mathematician from 4th century Greece. His thirteen-volume *Elements of Geometry* was a classic, still in use in the early 20th century.

Eugene Aram. Both Thomas Hood, the poet, and Bulwer–Lytton, the novelist, wrote about this character, a poor schoolmaster driven by despair to commit a murder, who later repented.

Euripides (c.482–406 B.C.). Greek dramatist. Author of *Hippolytus, Medea, Electra,* and *Hecuba,* among other plays.

Europa. From Greek mythology. Europa, a king's daughter, was taken for a ride on the back of a bull. This energetic beast plunged into the sea and carried her away to Crete, where he revealed himself to be Zeus. King Minos was her son, and Europe was named after her.

Evacuees. According to her biographer Margot Strickland, Mrs. Thirkell was advised by Alfred Knopf, her American publisher, to paint a more positive picture of the evacuee children. She refused, saying that she had already done so. The reality, she said, was far, far worse.

"Even the ranks of Tuscany. . . ." Lines from the *Horatius* section from Lord Maculay's *Lays of Ancient Rome.* See *Horatius.*

The Eve of St. Agnes. A romantic poem by John Keats, written in 1819. We quote the last verse.

XLII

And they are gone: aye, ages long ago
These lovers fled away into the storm.
That night the Baron dreamt of many a woe,
And all his warrior-guests, with shade and form
Of witch, and demon, and large coffin-worm,
Were long be-nightmared. Angela the old
Died palsy-twitch'd, with meagre face deform;
The Beadsman, after thousand aves told,
For aye unsought-for slept among his ashes cold.

"Even tenor of her way. . . . " *See* **Gray, Thomas.**

"Every day's most quiet need. . . . " A line from Elizabeth Barrett Browning's Sonnet XLIII, from the Portugese. We quote the entire sonnet because it is so often mentioned.

XLIII

How do I love thee? Let me count the ways.
I love thee to the depth and breadth and height
My soul can reach, when feeling out of sight
For the ends of Being and ideal Grace.
I love thee to the level of every day's
Most quiet need, by sun and candle-light.
I love thee freely, as men strive for Right;
I love thee purely, as they turn from Praise.
I love thee with the passion put to use
In my old griefs, and with my childhood's faith.
I love thee with a love I seemed to lose
With my lost saints,— I love thee with the breath,
Smiles, tears, of all my life!— and, if God choose,
I shall but love thee better after death.

Exhibition. A scholarship to a university college which is given for a fixed term of years.

Experto crede. _Latin._ Believe someone who speaks from experience.

"Eyeless in Gaza in the mill with slaves. . . . " A line from Milton's _Samson Agonistes._

Face-à-main. *French.* A lorgnette; an aid to vision held in the hand rather than worn on the face, like a pair of spectacles on a stalk, without ear-pieces. Nobody asked us, but we think it odd that someone who objected to a word like *fiancée* because it seemed affected and Frenchified, would then insist upon a *face-à-main.* Not that *lorgnette* didn't start out as a French word. Oh dear.

Fairservice, Andrew. A character from Scott's *Rob Roy,* published 1817. Fairservice was a gardener at Osbaldistone Hall. His name was ironic, as he was disloyal and generally a royal pain; he was loquacious, cowardly, and self-righteous.

Fait accompli. *French.* An accomplished fact; a deed that has irrevocably been done.

Faits divers. *French.* News items.

Falernian. A famous Italian wine.

Falstaff, Sir John. A character from Shakespeare's *King Henry IV*, parts I and II, and also from *The Merry Wives of Windsor.* Falstaff appears in several variations, but in general may be considered to be a roistering, hard-drinking, clever fellow, companion to Prince Hal, wooer of women, slick in his dealings, somewhat buffoonish, but overall, endearing.

A Farewell to Arms. A poem by George Peele, written in 1590. Parts of it are given here.

> His golden locks Time hath to silver turn'd;
>   O Time too swift, O swiftness never ceasing!
> His youth 'gainst time and age hath ever spurn'd,
>   But spurn'd in vain; youth waneth by increasing:
> Beauty, strength, youth, are flowers but fading seen;
>   Duty, faith, love, are roots, ever green.
>
> His helmet now shall make a hive for bees;
>   And, lovers' sonnets turn'd to holy psalms,
> A man-at-arms must now serve on his knees,
>   And feed on prayers, which are Age his alms:
> But though from court to cottage he depart,
>   His Saint is sure of his unspotted heart.

Farthingale. A petticoat stiffened with a series of hoops of cane, wire, or whalebone, worn during the 16th century. Fifty yards of whalebone might be used. A French farthingale was wide from side to side, and is perhaps what we think of when imagining the court of Queen Elizabeth I.

"The fault was mine. . . ." *See* **Maude.**

Feeder. A bib.

Félibristes. *French.* Provençal writers belonging to a society called the Félibrige, founded in 1854 to revive interest in Provençal writing.

Felo-de-se. *Latin.* A legal term meaning to commit the felony of self-destruction; suicide.

"The female of the species. . . ." The title and refrain of a poem by Rudyard Kipling. All of the thirteen witty verses give examples and end with the refrain, "The female of the species is more deadly than the male."

Femgericht. *German.* A member of a secret tribunal.

Fences. Expressions such as "take your fences" or "plunge my fences" will be familiar to any reader who may have ridden to hounds or learned the style of riding intended for the hunt. A fence in this context is any obstacle that must be jumped, and the rider needs a certain amount of planning, skill, and courage each time. Obviously this term has trickled out into general figurative usage.

Fender. A metal structure placed before a fireplace to keep the coals or wood in the grate, and to keep the inhabitants of the room out of the fire. Sometimes fenders were high and wide enough to sit on, or just the right height to prop one's feet on.

Festina lente. *Latin.* Make haste slowly.

Fiancée. *French.* AT takes exception to this word as vulgar—presumably because the use of French was affected and thus a genteelism. Mr. Fowler shares her opinion. The word he prefers is *betrothed*, but he admits that it is out of fashion and cannot be used without self-consciousness. Thus neither Fowler nor AT has left us with a suitable term other than *affianced*, equally bulky. Luckily, "fiancée" has by now passed into general English usage and we need no longer be troubled.

Fifth columnist. A secret sympathizer working for the enemy, who may go so far as to aid and abet him. The term came into being during the Spanish Civil War (1936–39), when General Mola said he had a fifth column of supporters in Madrid.

"Fill high the cup with Samian wine. . . ." From Lord Byron's poem "The Isles of Greece." In the sixteen verses the line appears four times, and the theme appears to be "eat, drink and be merry." But in the last line he changes his mind. Here are the last two verses.

> Fill high the bowl with Samian wine!
>   Our virgins dance beneath the shade —
> I see their glorious black eyes shine;
>   But gazing on each glowing maid,
> My own the burning tear-drop laves,
> To think such breasts must suckle slaves.
>
>
> Place me on Sunium's marbled steep,
>   Where nothing, save the waves and I,
> May hear our mutual murmurs sweep;
>   There, swan-like, let me sing and die:

155

A land of slaves shall ne'er be mine—
Dash down yon cup of Samian wine!

First. Designates the quality of achievement at the time of commencement from a university. A **first** equates to a *summa cum laude*, a **second** or **third** correspondingly lower.

Floddin Field. Site of a terrible battle in Northumberland, 1513. James IV of Scotland with 30,000 men met the forces of Thomas Howard, earl of Surrey, whose army numbered 20,000. Despite smaller forces, Howard prevailed. James was killed, with 10,000 of his men.

"The floor of heaven is thick inlaid. . . . " Lines from Act V of Shakespeare's *Merchant of Venice*. Lorenzo is speaking to Jessica.

> How sweet the moonlight sleeps upon this bank!
> Here will we sit, and let the sounds of music
> Creep in our ears; soft stillness and the night
> Become the touches of sweet harmony.
> Sit, Jessica: look, how the floor of heaven
> Is thick inlaid with patines of bright gold:
> There's not the smallest orb which thou behold'st
> But in this motion like an angel sings
> Still quiring to the young-eyed cherubins:
> Such harmony is in immortal souls;
> But, whilst this muddy vesture of decay
> Doth grossly close it in, we cannot hear it.

Florin. A coin worth two shillings. Its use has been discontinued.

Flowers of the Forest. Any of several poems mourning the dead of Flodden Field, *q.v.* These are lines from the last verse of one by Jane Elliot, written in 1765.

> We'll hear no mair lilting at the ewe-milking
> Women and bairns are heartless and wae:
> Sighing and moaning on ilka green loaning —
> The flowers of the forest are a' wede awae.

Fons et orrigo. *Latin*. Source and origin.

Forms. Schoolroom benches. Also, it is roughly the equivalent of the American "grade," although sixth graders in America are eleven-year-olds, and the sixth form in England would be seventeen- or eighteen-year olds.

Fortunatos nimium, sua si bona norint, Agricolas! *Latin*. O farmers! Excessively fortunate if only they realized their blessings! — Virgil.

Fosco, Count. From Wilkie Collins' *The Woman in White*, 1860. Count Fosco, an Italian, was a villain charming as a snake might be charming—superficially smooth, but with a deadly intent.

Fowler, Henry Watson (1858–1933). English writer and lexicographer, known as the author of *Modern English Usage*, 1926. It is a successful handbook of the highest standard of English usage. Now in a third edition, it is used by those who need a final arbiter in these matters.

Frankie and Johnny. An almost interminable American traditional ballad, concerning the lovers Frankie and Johnny. They had sworn to be true, but somehow or other he was not, and, to cut a long story short, Frankie "done him in." She shot him and was taken away to jail.

"Free from stain. . . . " Lines from "A Jacobite's Epitaph," by Lord Macaulay.

> Courage and faith; vain faith and courage vain—
> For him I threw lands, honours, wealth away,
> To my true king I offer'd free from stain
> And one dear hope that was more prized than they.

Freemason. A member, literally or figuratively, of a secret brotherhood. Thus a freemasonry would be a secret or perhaps tacit brotherhood, or sisterhood.

French. In the sense of something to mix with gin, this would be French vermouth, such as Noilly Prat.

"A Fresh generation that knows not Joseph. . . . " *See* **Joseph.**

Friday, Man. A character from Daniel Defoe's 1719 novel *Robinson Crusoe*. Crusoe was shipwrecked for many years on an island in the mouth of the Orinoco off the coast of Venezuela. Friday was a native whom Crusoe rescued from cannibals. Crusoe taught Friday to speak a sort of pidgin English, and Friday was much given to saying "O!" when excited or impressed.

Friday to Monday. To say "weekend" was considered vulgar. The actual names of the days were used.

"Friends of the merest. . . . " *See* **"The Lost Mistress."**

Frietchie, Barbara. The heroine of the poem of the same name by American poet John Greenleaf Whittier. Barbara flew the American flag (or, if you prefer, the Union flag) from her upstairs window. When Stonewall Jackson marched his men into Frederick, Maryland, she defied his order to take it down. He ordered it fired upon but she held it up in her hands:

> "Shoot, if you must, this old grey head,
> But spare your country's flag," she said.

The Frog and the Ox. One of Aesop's fables. The ox crushed one of the frog's children underfoot. The mother frog tried to inflate herself to the size of the monster who had done this deed. Then another of her froglets said, "Let it pass, Mother, rather than burst yourself in imitation."

Fry, Elizabeth (1780–1845). A Quaker reformer who worked to better conditions in prisons and asylums, and who founded hostels for the homeless.

But Gladstone was dreadful. He chewed thirty-two times and jumped on his bath sponge.

— Laura Morland

Gaily the Troubadour. The name of a saccharine song, popular during the early decades of this century. It featured a troubadour gaily strumming his guitar, announcing that he was home from battles in Palestine and entreating his lady love to welcome him home. In linking professor Gawky with this song, AT has given us an idea of the level of scholarship in her book.

Gaiters. When used to refer to what we Americans call a drugstore, Gaiters corresponds to the big English chain, Boots. This is because, in one sense of the word, gaiters are boots, an old-fashioned type with a canvas upper that buttons up well over the ankle. In yet another meaning, gaiters are zipped or buttoned cloth or leather coverings for the leg between foot and knee; as such they are part of a of a bishop's ecclesiastical dress. To return to Boots: For many years the chain incorporated in its premises a small subscription library called "Boots Booklovers Library." There are several references to the Gaiters' library in the series.

Galop. A vigorous dance in 2-4 time. Sometimes it was part of a set of quadrilles.

Gamboge. A brilliant reddish-yellow, saffron color.

Gamp, Sarah. A character from Dickens' *Martin Chuzzlewit*. She was a colorful character, a nurse, midwife, and layer-out-of-the-dead who saw life in the basic terms that resulted in employment for her. She could not see a bride without a gleam coming to her eye as she speculated when the first confinement would be. It was her habit, when a job took her to an upper story, to look out the window and gauge her chances of escape in case of fire. The falling out with Mrs. Prig took place in Mrs. Gamp's room in a very vinegary and winey atamosphere, as each insulted the other.

Gandhi, Mohandâs (Mahatma) (1869–1948). Leader of the Indian struggle for independence, using to maximum effect techniques of civil disobedience such as non-violent confrontation and fasting.

Garden. In general usage, "garden" in England refers to all ornamental property attached to a house: lawns, flower gardens, rock gardens, even uncultivated areas. A "yard" is a paved service area.

Garden party. In addition to other obvious meanings, this refers to the annual party given by the sovereign in the gardens of Buckingham Palace for the kingdom's current leaders.

Gargery, Joe. A character from Dickens' *Great Expectations*. Pip, an orphan, was raised "by hand" by his sister and her husband, Joe. A simple blacksmith, Joe was the only source of kindness in Pip's early life, as his sister was a harpy. Joe remained faithful and devoted through all the vicissitudes of Pip's early adulthood.

Garibaldi biscuits. A type of cookie studded with dried currants. Looked at one way, for instance with the eyes of a school-boy, these currents look like squashed flies; hence the name, fly-biscuits. They were named for the Italian patriot Giuseppe Garibaldi (1807–1882) who was visiting in England at the time the biscuits were introduced by the McVities baking company.

Garrick, David (1717–1779). Great British actor who excelled in both comic and tragic roles. He was celebrated in print by the writers of the day, and painted by Reynolds, Hogarth, and Gainsborough, among others. The Garrick Club, one of London's most brilliant, is named for him. It is for authors, actors and playwrights—Trollope was one of its members.

Gas and gaiters. From Dickens' *Nicholas Nickleby*. "Gas and gaiters" was the expression of joy uttered by the gentleman in smallclothes when he saw Miss LaCreevy. "She is come at last—at last—and all is gas and gaiters!" He was a cheerful madman who was next-door neighbor to the Nickelbys. Smallclothes are knee-breeches.

Gatto. Mr. Tozer's rendering of the French word for cake, *gâteau.*

Gaudy. A grand annual commemorative dinner at a college.

Gavelkind. An early system governing property and inheritance rights. It is complicated, but one of its stipulations was that land be divided equally among the sons if the father died intestate. After the Norman conquest, gavelkind was replaced by the custom of primogeniture, which made the eldest son heir to the titles and family seat.

Gay, John (1685–1732). Poet and dramatist whose greatest success was *The Beggar's Opera*, 1728, from which comes the line about the Turk surrounded by his doxies.

Genesis 19:30–38. Mrs. Trapes mentioned this interesting passage when she came to Marling Hall to dress Lucy for her wedding. To save you the trouble of looking it up, here it is.

> 30. And Lot went up out of Zoar, and dwelt in the mountain, and his two daughters with him; for he feared to dwell in Zoar: and he dwelt in a cave, he and his two daughters. 31. And the firstborn said unto the younger, Our father is old, and there is not a man in the earth to come in unto us after the manner of all the earth: 32.Come, let us make our father drink wine, and we will lie with him, that we may preserve seed of our father. 33. And they made their father drink wine that night: and the firstborn went in, and lay with her father; and he perceived not when she lay down or when she arose. 34. And it came to pass on the morrow, that the firstborn said unto the younger, Behold, I lay yesternight with my father: let us make him drink wine this night also; and go thou in, and lie with him, that we may preserve the seed of our father. 35. And they made their father drink wine that night also: and the younger arose, and lay with him; and he perceived not when she lay down, nor when she arose. 36. Thus were both the daughters of Lot with child by their father. 37. And the firstborn bare a son, and called his name Moab: the same is the father of the Moabites unto this day. 38. And the younger, she also bare a son, and called his name Benammi: the same is the father of the children of Ammon unto this day.

Geneva bands. White lawn strips hanging at the neck of a clerical gown.

A Gentle girl and boy. A line from "Stanzas," by John Keats.

> In a drear-nighted December,
> Too happy, happy tree,
> Thy branches ne'er remember
> Their green felicity.

The north cannot undo them,
 With a sleety whistle through them;
Nor frozen thawings glue them
 From budding at the prime.

Ah! Would 'twere so with many
 A gentle girl and boy!
But were there ever any
 Writh'd not at past joy?
To know the change and feel it,
When there is none to heal it,
Nor numbed sense to steel it,
 Was never said in rhyme.

Gentelman's Relish. Otherwise known (in almost-Latin) as Patum Peperium, this was a spicy anchovy paste used as a spread for sandwiches and toast. It has been made since 1828 at Elsenham from a secret recipe still in use.

George VI (1895–1952). George VI came to the throne in 1936, upon the abdication of his brother, Edward VIII. He was educated at Dartmouth Naval College and at Trinity College, Cambridge. During World War I he served with the Grand Fleet at the Battle of Jutland. His moments of greatest popularity were during World War II, when he remained in Buckingham Palace even after it was damaged by bombs. He toured bombed areas and spoke to the people in several radio addresses. He was the father of Elizabeth II and Princess Margaret Rose.

Ghost's Walk at Chesney Wold. From Dickens' *Bleak House*. Chesney Wold was the country house of Sir Leicester and Lady Dedlock. The terrace, from an old family story, was known as the Ghost's Walk, and in bad weather it was cold and drear in the extreme.

Giddy harumfrodite. From Kipling's "Soldier an' Sailor Too." The poet sees a worker on a man of war who was dressed as a soldier but doing the work of a sailor—he is neither, but slaves away doing the work of both.

Gibbon, Edward. Author of *The Decline and Fall of the Roman Empire*. Thirkell's work abounds with references and allusions to Gibbon. She often plays with his famous remark, from his *Autobiography*, made when his father had forbidden him to pursue his love of Suzanne Churchod: "I sighed as a lover, I obeyed as a son."

In *Before Lunch* John Middleton "sighed as a worker, but obeyed as a husband." In *Private Enterprise* Mrs. Brandon "sighed as a hostess and obeyed as a mother," and in *The Old Bank House* Francis Brandon "sighed as a father and obeyed as a friend." George Halliday "sighed as one who felt that Edith was a nice kid and not bad looking, and obeyed as a prospective land-owner." And finally, in *A Double Affair*, Dr. Crawley remembered to "spoil as a grandfather, and command as a Dean."

Gilbert and Sullivan. W.S. Gilbert (1836–1911) and A.S. Sullivan (1842–1900) collaborated and gave the world several light comic operas, of which the best known are probably *H.M.S. Pinafore* and *The Mikado*. Gilbert, the librettist, also wrote and illustrated *The Bab Ballads;* Sullivan, the composer, is known for "The Lost Chord" and "Onward, Christian Soldiers," as well as for other music and the scores of the operettas.

Gilpin, John. The subject of the poem *The Diverting History of John Gilpin*, by William Cowper, (1731–1800).

> John Gilpin was a citizen
>   Of credit and renown,
> A train-band captain eke was he
>   Of famous London town.
>
> John Gilpin's spouse said to her dear,
>   'Though wedded we have been
> These twice ten tedious years, yet we
>   No holiday have seen.

The Gilpins made a plan to have dinner with their extended family at an inn in a nearby town, and to drive there in a chaise. Mrs. Gilpin was a modest soul, and certainly didn't want the neighbors to think she was putting on airs.

> The morning came, the chaise was brought,
>   But yet was not allowed
> To drive up to the door, lest all
>   Should say that she was proud.
>
> So three doors off the chaise was stayed,
>   Where they did all get in;
> Six precious souls, and all agog
>   To dash through thick and thin.

Alas, they were too many for the chaise, and John was to borrow a horse and ride there. The poem goes on to relate how they were unable to meet at the inn because Gilpin's borrowed horse kept running away with him. One reason the horse was so nervous was that John was carrying two stone bottles of wine on a belt, which not only clanked together and made a noise, but cracked and broke, drenching the animal with wine. Then, too, John's cloak flapped about and finally flew off. These are the sorts of things horses can't stand.

Prince Giglio. From Thackeray's *The Rose and the Ring*, a fairy story with appeal to both adults and children. The prince was the subject of a spell that made him irresistibly attractive. This caused some problems from which he was rescued by Fairy Blackstick. *Giglio* is Italian for lily.

Girton. A women's college at Cambridge, founded in 1869 at Hitcham and moved to Cambridge in 1875.

"Glad confident morning. . . ." *See* **never glad confident morning.**

Godiva. A poem by Tennyson which tells the story of the courageous countess who saved her townspeople in Coventry from a burdensome tax imposed on them by her husband, the earl. We quote the introduction.

> *I waited for the train at Coventry;*
> *I hung with grooms and porters on the bridge,*
> *To watch the three tall spires; and there I shaped*
> *The city's ancient legend into this: —*

Gog and Magog. Mentioned in the Bible, but in England, Gog and Magog are legendary giants. They are just two of a huge family of creatures. They were the offspring of Diocletian's thirty-three daughters and some local English demons. All the others were killed, but Gog and Magog were captured and taken to London, where they lived in semi-slavery as porters in the king's palace.

161

Golden boots and silver underclothing. *See* ***The Periwinkle Girl.***

"Golden lads and lasses. . . . " From *Cymbelline*, Act IV, scene ii.

> Fear no more the heat o' the sun,
> Nor the furious winter's rages;
> Thou thy worldly task hast done,
> Home art gone, and ta'en thy wages.
> Golden lads and girls all must,
> As chimney-sweepers, come to dust.

"Golden locks time hath to silver. . . . " *See* **"A Farewell to Arms."**

Goldbeaters' skin. A very strong yet thin membrane prepared from ox intestines. It is used to separate leaves of gold foil for making gold-leaf.

The Gondoliers. A light opera by Gilbert and Sullivan, first performed in December of 1889. The line about being condescending is the refrain, with variations, of one of the quintets, part of which is quoted here.

> MARCO AND GIUSEPPE: Let us combine a pose imperious
> With a demeanor nobly bland.
> DUKE: That's, if anything, *too* unbending —
> Too aggressively stiff and grand;
> Now to the other extreme you're tending —
> Don't be so deucedly condescending!

"Gone, alas, like our youth, too soon." A line from "The Kerry Dance", a popular Irish song by James Lyman Malloy (1837–1909). The singer longs for the days of the Kerry dancing, the song of the piper's tune, for even one of those happy hours to come again, but alas they are gone, like our youth, too soon.

Goodwood Park. A park near Chichester with tracks for horse and auto racing. There is also an airfield and a golf course.

Gooseberry. An unwanted third person in what would otherwise be a romantic opportunity.

"Gosh, he will but say. . . . " *See* **"The Lost Mistress."**

Gotha Almanack. Correctly known as the *Almanach de Gotha*, an annual French publication begun by Justus Perthes de Gotha in 1763. It lists genealogical, diplomatic and statistical information, and has helped to keep track of European aristocracy and royal families.

Governess cart. A two-wheeled vehicle drawn by a pony or small horse. It had facing seats along the sides.

Graiae. From classical mythology. The Graiae were three sisters of the Gorgons. They were born gray-haired, and rapidly grew even more elderly. Before too long they had but one tooth and one eye among them, which they passed from one to the other. Perseus stole the eye to get them to tell him the way to the Gorgons, and after achieving his ends, threw it away.

Gray, Thomas (1716–1771). A famous English poet, whose most well known work is "Elegy (written in a country church-yard)." These are the verses from which lines are quoted.

162

> The curfew tolls the knell of parting day,
> The lowing herd winds slowly o'er the lea,
> The ploughman homeward plods his weary way
> And leaves the world to darkness and to me.
>
> . . . .
>
> Let not Ambition mock their useful toil,
> Their homely joys and destiny obscure;
> Nor Grandeur hear with a disdainful smile
> The short and simple annals of the poor.
>
> . . . .
>
> Far from the madding crowd's ignoble strife
> Their sober wishes never learn'd to stray;
> Along the cool sequester'd vale of life
> They kept the noiseless tenour of their way.

Great Anarch. From Alexander Pope's *Dunciad.*

> *Religion* blushing veils her sacred fires,
> And unawares *Morality* expires.
> Nor *public* Flame, nor *private*, dares to shine;
> Nor *human* Spark is left, nor Glimpse *divine*!
> Lo! Thy dread Empire, CHAOS! is restored;
> Light dies before thy uncreating word:
> Thy hand, great Anarch! Lets the curtain fall;
> And universal Darkness buries All.

Great-heart. A noble character from the second book of *The Pilgrim's Progress* who escorts Christiana on her pilgrimage. Along the way he defeats monsters and overcomes obstacles.

Greats. An Oxford term. It refers either to a course of study that includes classical literature, philosophy, and history, or to the final examinations in these subjects.

Greenery-yallery. From Gilbert and Sullivan's comic opera *Patience.*

> "A pallid and thin young man —
> A haggard and lank young man —
> A greenery–yallery, Grosvenor Gallery,
> Foot-in-the-grave young man!"

The words, those of Bunthorne, are generally taken to be a spoof of Oscar Wilde, and *Patience* is considered to be a lampoon of the far too languid young men of the Aesthetic Movement.

"A Green thought in a green shade. . . . " A line from Andrew Marvell's poem "The Garden."

> Meanwhile the mind from pleasure less
> Withdraws into its happiness;
> The mind, that ocean where each kind
> Does straight its own resemblance find;
> Yet it creates, transcending these,
> Far other worlds, and other seas;
>
> Annihilating all that's made
> To a green thought in a green shade.

163

Grimes, Tommy. Hero of the fairy story "Mr. Miacca." Tommy was captured by the evil Mr. Miacca, who planned to have him stewed for dinner. In fact Tommy was caught often, but always escaped.

"Grow old along with me. . . ." Famous lines from "Rabbi Ben Ezra," by Robert Browning (1812–1889).

> Grow old along with me!
> The best is yet to be,
> The last of life, for which the first was made:
> Our times are in his hand
> Who saith "A whole I planned,
> Youth shows but half; trust God: see all, nor be afraid!"

Mrs. Grundy. A character in Thomas Morton's 1798 play, *Speed the Plough*. She was rigidly proper and conservative, and has become the symbol of prudish morality.

Mrs. Gummidge. From Dickens' *David Copperfield*. The widow of Mr. Peggoty's partner. The saintly Mr. Peggoty was good enough to offer her a home, but she, a dismal, self- pitying sort of soul, wasn't terribly appreciative. Very often she reminded everyone that she was "a lone, lorn creetur" who felt things more than other people did. When these moods came on her Mr. Peggoty said, "She's thinking of the old 'un."

Mr. Guppy. From Dickens' *Bleak House*. An unprepossessing law clerk with many failings, he nonetheless played a key role in the events of the story. His mother had decidedly odd quirks which he pardoned, knowing she was thinking entirely of his welfare. He felt that there are chords in the human mind—chords—there are chords— but the conclusion of this sentence can only be imagined as he never expanded at all on the nature of these chords, or what might be expected from them.

Mrs. Guppy. Mr. Guppy's rather curious mother. He said of her, "She has her failings—as who has not?— but I never knew her to do it when company was present; at which time you may freely trust her with wines, spirits, or malt liquors." Mrs. Guppy was very energetic with her elbows. However peculiar she might appear to others, all had to agree that she always had Mr. Guppy's interests uppermost.

Gurth. A Saxon swineherd in Sir Walter Scott's *Ivanhoe*.

Guster. A character from Dickens' *Bleak House*. Guster was the well-intentioned but simple servant of the law-stationer Snagsby and his wife.

Guy. The effigy burned in the bonfire on Guy Fawkes' Day. By extension, it's any scarecrowish or silly looking man, and has come in America to refer to absolutely anyone.

Guy Fawkes Day. November 5. The day commemorates the Gunpowder Plot, which was an attempt on November 5, 1605, to blow up King James I and the entire Parliament by placing explosives underneath the chamber where Parliament assembled. Although Guido (Guy) Fawkes was not the only person in the conspiracy, he was caught in the gunpowder room. He was tortured into revealing the names of the other members of the group. He was then tried and subsequently executed in the way usual for traitors: hanged, drawn, and quartered. Guy Fawkes has been burned in effigy every November 5 since, and children go about requesting "a penny for the old Guy."

Guy's Hospital. A London hospital established in 1724 by Thomas Guy and still in use.

H

The historian of the future may look upon these as the good old times, living as he will under a totally totalitarian state, or in other words under the unmitigated and petty tyranny of fourth-rate minds.
— Charles Fanshawe

Habakkuk. An Old Testament prophet. He said some curious things, but if indeed he was *capable du tout*, it is not for us to say. Readers wishing to know more are referred to the Book of Habakkuk.

Ha-ha. An unobtrusive border to a garden, that delineates without blocking the view. Often it is a sunken wall of stone placed in a trench, with the far side of the trench sloping away.

Haggai. A sixth-century B.C. prophet who helped inspire the Jews returned from Babylonian exile to re-build the Temple of Solomon in Jerusalem.

Half. One of the terms at some public schools, such as Eton, even though there were three terms in the school year. Originally, however, there had been only two, so out of habit all were called halves.

Half-crown. A coin worth two shillings and sixpence, or, in 1933, about $6.10 by contemporary standards. *See* **Money.**

Hall. When a butler or other servant refers to the Hall, he or she means the servants' hall, in which all their meals were taken and all their views expressed. At times the upper servants dined in the house keeper's room—*see* **Room.**

   In another meaning, "hall" refers to a large reception room, perhaps also an entry area, in a really large house. Such a hall had a fireplace and furniture and was often used for entertaining. This room is the architectural descendant of the great hall which was almost the entire house, in which all the household ate, slept, and carried out their daily activities.

   At the universities, "hall" was the dining hall.

Halma. A board game very like checkers, in that there is a board with pieces, and play is advanced by jumping one piece over another.

Lady Hamilton: a Lady Hamilton attitude. Prior to becoming established as Nelson's mistress, Lady Hamilton had entertained by posing in "attitudes" or *poses plastique*, depicting famous personages.

Hampden, John (1594–1643). A gentleman who practiced civil disobedience in the matter of a certain outrageous tax, and as a result became famous and popular. However, he did help precipitate the Civil War, during which he was mortally wounded.

Hanger. Trees clinging to the steep side of a hill or bank.

Hannay, Richard. Hero of *The Thirty-nine Steps* and four other thrillers by John Buchan.

Hannay, Mary. She was just what Hannay's wife should be, a spy. She was beautiful, courageous, and resourceful.

Happy Families. A children's card game for at least three players. The pack consists of forty-eight cards, divided into twelve families of four each. These families represent different trades, each with two parents, a son and a daughter. The Bung family were brewers, the Pots were painters, the Chips carpenters, and so on. The goal for each player is to collect as many complete families as possible.

"Happy the family that has no history. . . . " A twist on this line from *The Mill on the Floss* by George Eliot: "The happiest women, like the happiest nations, have no history."

Happy Thoughts. A series of literary sketches by Sir Francis Cowley Burnand. They appeared in *Punch* in 1866.

Mrs. Harris. Mrs. Gamp's particular friend and client, whose many babies had been delivered by Mrs. Gamp, and to whose exemplary life Mrs. Gamp referred with predictable regularity. Mrs. Harris turned out to be a figment.

Hatches. Floodgates; sluices.

Hatto, Bishop. A 10th Century Bishop of Mainz, remembered for his remarkably uncharitable views—or so it is said. According to legend, he sought to solve the problem of the poor by saying they were like mice. To exterminate them he set fire to a barn in which they were gathered.

"Having put his hand to the plough. . . . " Luke 9:61-62.

> And another also said, Lord, I will follow thee; but let me first go to bid
> them farewell, which are at home in my house.
> And Jesus said unto him, No man, having put his hand to the plough, and
> looking back, is fit for the kingdom of God.

Miss Havisham. From Dickens' *Great Expectations.* She had been traumatized many years before the opening of the story by having been left at the altar on her wedding day. She stopped the clocks at that hour and dressed henceforth in her bridal gown. The wedding feast, including the cake, was left on the table to be carried off in bits by mice, and become festooned in cobwebs. The windows were shrouded and very few guests penetrated her solitude. And yet she did become the guardian of the child Estelle.

Captain Hawdon. A character from Dickens' *Bleak House.* Twenty years before the story opens, he had been the lover of Lady Dedlock. Since then he had drifted downward in life, ending his days as an opium addict and law copier who used the alias "Nemo." Captain Hawdon was the father of Esther Summerson.

Haw-Haw, Lord. William Joyce, who broadcast anti-English propaganda from Germany during the war. In 1946 he was hanged for treason.

Hay box. A simple device used for slow cooking and keeping stews and casseroles warm. It was a wooden box stuffed with newspaper or hay, with a hollowed place in the middle for the vessel—some sort of large dutch oven—that would be put into it. An insulated lid was placed over it and the slow cooking would be expected to take several hours.

"Heaven pity all poor wanderers. . . . " A line from a sentimental song sung by Becky Sharp in Thackeray's *Vanity Fair*. It was calculated to have an effect on Joseph Sedley, and it did, temporarily. It is about an orphan boy.

> They mark'd him as he onward prest,
> With fainting heart and weary limb;
> Kind voices bade him turn and rest,
> And gentle faces welcomed him.
> The dawn is up—the guest is gone,
> The cottage hearth is blazing still;
> Heaven pity all poor wanderers lone!
> Hark to the wind upon the hill!

Hebe. From mythology: a cup-bearer to the gods; she who had the power of restoring youth.

The Heir of Redclyffe. A novel by Charlotte Yonge, published in 1853. The plot is summarized by Laura Morland in chapter six of *Close Quarters,* but for those who haven't read it we'll give our version. At the center of the novel is the Edmonstone family, father, mother, son Charles, and daughters Laura and Amy. They have two cousins who are themselves cousins, Guy and Philip Morville. Guy and Philip are in love with Laura and Amy, but never mind the consanguinity—that is the last of anyone's concerns. Guy is the heir to Redclyffe; he grows up into an engaging and honorable fellow despite a family tendency to hot-headedness. Philip has given up an academic career and gone into the military to support his sister and widowed mother, and is a humorless, self-righteous, jealous menace—but nice in his way. Philip tries unsuccessfully to prevent Guy's marriage to Amy. In Italy on their honeymoon, Guy and Amy hear that Philip is ill in a nearby town, and go to him. Guy nurses Philip to health, only to fall ill of the same fever and die. Deeply affected by this, Philip is transformed into a new and better man, and now, as the heir to Redclyffe, can marry Laura. Amy, with her infant daughter, Mary Verena, vows never to abandon her mourning.

Incidental to the plot, but occasionally mentioned in Barsetshire, is the fact that Mrs. Edmonstone had a small sitting room, a former dressing room, which was the center of family life.

"He either fears his fate too much. . . . " A line from a poem by James Graham, Marquis of Montrose (1612–1650). The title is variously "I'll Never Love Thee More" or "My Dear and Only Love." This is verse two.

> Like Alexander I will reign,
> And I will reign alone;
> My thoughts did evermore disdain
> A rival on my throne.
> He either fears his fate too much,
> Or his deserts are small,
> That dares not put it to the touch,
> To gain or lose it all.

Heeltaps. What remains in the glass after most of the contents have been drunk.

Heep, Uriah. From Dickens' *David Copperfield.* Heep was first a clerk to the lawyer Mr. Wickfield and later Mr. Wickfield's partner. He professed to being very, very 'umble, and was forever wringing his damp hands. He humbly edged himself into Mr. Wickfield's business to the extent that he reduced that gentleman to a pawn, and was on the way to a lucrative career as a thief, forger, and general defrauder when his crimes were discovered and he was sent to jail under a life sentence.

Heine, Henrich (1797–1856). German poet and essayist, one of the last of the romantics. He was read by all educated people.

"Helmet for a beehive. . . . " *See* **"A Farewell to Arms."**

Hengist and Horsa. They were (possibly legendary) leaders of the ancient Germanic tribe of Jutes, and were said to have led the German invasion of Britain in the fifth century. They were given the Isle of Thanet to live on. Horsa was killed in battle and Hengist sired a line of Kentish kings. It is thoughts of such random outcomes that make us want to stay home from battle altogether.

Heptarchy. The supposed confederation of seven kingdoms of Angles and Saxons in early England.

Heriot. Property given or restored to the lord of the manor upon the death of a tenant, or money given in its place.

Herod (the Great) (73–4 BC). Among other unlovely activities, Herod ordered the slaughter of all male infants in Bethlehem under the age of two. In this he was seeking to protect himself from the rivalry of a rumored new-born king. Horrible as this deed was, it was occasionally thought of wistfully in Barsetshire by those, such as Dean Crawley on Christmas Day, who felt beset by swarms of children.

Hereward. A Lincolnshire outlaw squire who is thought to have led a rebellion against William the Conquerer in 1070. In 1866 Charles Kingsley published a novel, *Hereward the Wake,* based on his exploits.

Hervé Riel. A ballad by Robert Browning based on the true story of a young sailor who piloted the French ships into a dangerous harbor and saved them from destruction by the English during a battle in 1692. When Riel was asked what he wanted for a reward, he answered

> "Since 't is ask and have, I may —
>   Since others go ashore —
> Come! A good whole holiday!
>   Leave to go and see my wife, whom I call the Belle Aurore!"
> That he asked and that he got,— nothing more.

Hic jacet. Latin. Here lies.

High tea. A light evening meal, served when for some reason both tea and dinner are not possible. For that reason it is often associated with a working class lifestyle.

High School. This usually is a day school for girls, although we know Barchester High School took some weekly boarders. In England, the term "high school" does not have a definite meaning as it has in the United States.

High Tide on the Coast of Lincolnshire 1571. A short ballad by Jean Ingelow, thought to be her best work.

Hildebrand, St. (Pope Gregory VII) (c.1020–1085). Hildebrand became Pope in 1073 and waged ceaseless battle against certain practices that he felt led to corruption. This brought him to excommunicate many European bishops, and finally the emperor, Henry IV. The Diet of Worms was held to debate these matters in 1076. Henry made an appearance of repentance, but there were further struggles. Hildebrand escaped to Salerno and died there.

Hill Difficulty. From Bunyan's *The Pilgrim's Progress*. Difficulty was the name of a path on the hill up which Christian had to make his way in order to reach the Celestial City. The other two paths were Danger and Destruction; Christian wisely chose Difficulty.

Hippolytus. The son of the legendary Theseus and his wife Hippolyta. *Hippolytus* is also the name of the play by Euripides which tells the story of Phaedra, another wife of Theseus. She fell in love with her step-son, which led to Theseus' curse on Hippolytus, Hippolytus' death, and the death as well of Phaedra.

Hiram's Trust. *See* **Hiram's Hospital** in the index of places.

Hire purchase. Also referred to as the Never Never. Known in the U.S. as buying on time, buying on credit or the installment plan.

Hitler, Adolph (1889–1945). German political figure before and during World War II. He rose from non-descript origins to become chancellor of Germany in 1933. He and his associates undertook the re-arming of Germany and began seizing territory, thus beginning the war. He developed a network of concentration camps for political enemies, Jews, and anyone not eugenically correct, and was responsible for the loss of 30,000,000 lives, in the camps, in gas chambers, on battlefields, and in bombed cities world-wide.

Hob. A part of the back or side of a fireplace, having a level surface parallel with the grate but higher, upon which kettles and pots could be set to keep them warm.

"The Hobyahs." Eponymous little characters in one of the grimmest of fairy tales. Hobyahs were horrid grinning imps who marauded by night. They began to come to the house in the story at night. Each night the little dog Turpie barked to warn the family, but the father saw nothing, and on the first night cut off little dog Turpie's tail. On successive nights the Hobyahs came, aroused little dog Turpie into a fit of barking, and left, and on each night, annoyed at having been awakened apparently for nothing, the farmer cut off more of Turpie's parts until after a week or so Turpie was dead. The night after that, the Hobyahs came, destroyed the house, killed the farmer and his wife, and carried off their little girl. She was saved the next day by a neighbor's dog, who obligingly ate all the Hobyahs.

     For the rather colorless Eleanor Grantly to choose this of all stories to tell to the Foster children, who adored it, perhaps once again shows Angela Thirkell hiding currents of feeling, revealed in allusion, behind a bland exterior. Or possibly it is just amusing irony which one familiar with "The Hobyahs" would understand.

Hogmannay. In Scotland, this is New Year's Eve, with attendant feasting, drinking, and celebrating.

Horace (Quintus Horatius Flaccus) (65–8 B.C.). Roman poet, author of four books of *Odes*, some collections of *Epistles*, and two books of *Satires*. He was poet laureate from around 38 BC until his death. The passage referred to by Lydia Merton on the first page of *Private Enterprise* is from the *Odes*, Book III, poem VI.:

Damnosa quid non imminuit dies?	What do the ravages of time not injure?
Aetas parentum peior avis tulit	Our parents' age (worse than our grandparents')
Nos nequiores, mox daturos	Has produced us, more worthless still, who will soon
Progenium vitiosiorem.	Give rise to a yet more vicious generation.

Horatius. Properly, Publius Horatius Cocles (530–500 B.C.), a Roman soldier who held a bridge over the Tiber against the advancing army of the Etruscan ruler Lars Porsena.

Horatius is also the name of a section of *Lays of Ancient Rome* by Lord Macaulay. It describes the above event.

Hornby. A well-known manufacturer of model railway cars and equipment.

Hors concours. *French.* Out of the competition; without equal.

"The horsemen and the footmen are pouring in amain." A line from *Horatius.*

Hosiers. In the City of London, one of several City Livery Companies. These are societies descended from medieval craftsmen's guilds. Membership is usually hereditary, but can be attained by apprenticeship or bought. Some of the oldest companies are the Carpenters, the Drapers', the Fishmongers', the Goldsmiths', the Mercers', and the Grocers' Companies. Often they have considerable wealth and undertake charitable or educational projects. There is no Hosiers' Company, but the Mercers' Company could be the model. That Company, which began as importers of silk and velvet, administers both a boys' and a girls' school, among many other charities.

Hotspur. A character in Shakespeare's *Henry IV, part I*. Hotspur, based on Sir Henry Percy (*q.v.*) was eager for war and was a hearty companion for the prince. He was also bored by his father-in-law, who was extremely tiresome on the subject of mystical matter.

> . . .Sometimes he angers me
> With telling me of the moldwarp and the ant,
> Of the dreamer Merlin and his prophecies,
> And of a dragon and a finless fish,
> A clip-wing'd griffin and a moulten raven,
> A couching lion and a ramping cat,
> And such a deal of skimble-skamble stuff
> As puts me from my faith.

Houyhnhnms. From *Gulliver's Travels*. The Houyhnhnms were a race of intelligent, honest, and civilized talking horses encountered by Gulliver on one of his last travels.

Hovis flour. The patent name for a type of flour used to make whole wheat bread.

"How happy could I be with either, Were other dear charmer away." Lines from *The Beggar's Opera,* by John Gay.

Hunt, Holman. English painter (1827–1910). One of the Pre-Raphaelite painters, along with Dante Gabriel Rosetti, Everett Millais, Ford Maddox Brown, and Edward Burne-Jones, AT's grandfather. He has painted several famous pictures, among which are *Isabella and the Pot of Basil* and *The Lady of Shalott.*

Hymen (Hymenaeus). The Roman god of marriage.

Hypatia. An Alexandrian, the daughter of the mathematician Theon. She was herself a learned mathematician, an astronomer, and an eloquent Neoplatonist. For this last the bishop (Cyril) had her torn to pieces by a mob of Christians in the year A.D. 415.   Charles Kingsley wrote an 1851 novel, *Hypatia*, about this woman.   It emphasized her nakedness in the mob scene, and it was perhaps this that amused Mr. Johns when he considered Mrs. Rivers in the role of Hypatia—or it might have been the difference in their intellects.

ℱ

Doesn't do to have a family if you're an invalid.
Bad for the stock.

— Lord Stoke

"I am not fit to loose the latches of their shoes." From Mark I:vii.

> There cometh one mightier than I after me, the latchet of whose
> shoes I am not worthy to stoop down and unloose.

Ice. Ice cream.

Ice Hell of Pitz Palu. A rendering of the title of a German film of the silent era, *The White Hell of Pitz Palu.* The later-famous director Leni Riefenstahl was a member of the cast.

Ich bin sehr leicht beleidigt. *German.* I am very easily offended.

"The idle singer of an empty day." From "Prologue of the Earthly Paradise," by William Morris. The line is a sort of refrain, variations of which are repeated at the end of each verse.

> 1
> Of Heaven and Hell I have no power to sing,
> I cannot ease the burden of your fears,
> Or make quick-coming death a little thing,
> Or bring again the pleasure of past years,
> Nor for my words shall ye forget your tears,
> Or hope again for aught that I can say,
> The idle singer of an empty day.

"If hate killed men, brother Lawrence. . . . " *See **Soliloquy in a Spanish Cloister.***

"If it prove a girl, the boy will have plenty." From Tennyson's **Maud**, *q. v.*

"If pressed for time, omit Cambridge." A nice condensation of Baedeker's actual words, which were,

> Oxford is on the whole more attractive than Cambridge to the ordinary visitor; and the
> traveller is therefore recommended to visit Cambridge first, or to omit it altogether if
> he cannot visit both.   *Baedeker's Great Britain,* 1887

Ignorance. A character from Bunyan's *Pilgrim's Progress.* He was not only denied entrance to the Celestial City, he was bound hand and foot, put through a door in the side of the hill, and sent down a chute straight to hell.

"I kissed Maud's hand. . . . " *See **Maud**.*

172

"I lie so composedly. . . . " Lines from Poe's poem, "For Annie."

> And I rest so composedly,
>   Now, in my bed,
> That any beholder
>   Might fancy me dead —
> Might start at beholding me,
>   Thinking me dead.

I know where I'm going. First line of an old English folk song made famous in our day by the Weavers.

"*Impavidium ferient ruinae. . . .* " A quote from Horace, which in full is

Si fractus illabatur orbis	If the world would break and fall on him,
Impavidium ferient ruinae.	Its ruins would not dismay him.

Impayable. *French.* Priceless.

The Importance of Being Earnest. An 1895 play by Oscar Wilde, full of sparkling wit and delightful stock characters. Lady Bracknell is one of those formidable mothers and/or aunts who abound in such comedies.

Incubus. An evil spirit supposed to have sexual intercourse with sleeping women at night, or simply to lie on sleepers. A succubus is a demon, especially one in female form, that steals upon men in their sleep and forces herself on them. But either word can simply mean a loathsome burden that cannot be gotten rid of.

Infang. Shortened form of infangthief, an ancient English law having to do with the right of a lord to conduct a trial and to levy punishment against thieves who are his own tenants, if they are caught in the act. This dates back to the twelfth century at least. **Outfang** (outfangthief) is similar, with the difference that the thief, if the lord's tenant, committed the crime away from the lord's demesne. Outfang gives the lord the right to retrieve the miscreant for trial and punishment.

In forma pauperis. *Latin.* As a poor person.

Ingans (ING . uns). *Scottish dialect.* Onions.

Ingelow, Jean (1820–1897). English writer of stories and poems for children. One of the best-known is "High Tide on the Coast of Lincolnshire."

Ingoldsby Legends. Popular humorous rhyming versions of certain medieval legends by Richard Harris Barham, first published in 1837. He used the pen name Thomas Ingoldsby. The legend described in chapter three of *Love at All Ages* is *A Lay of St. Gengulphus*, a merry tale of the murder of a crusader who returned from the Holy Land far too soon. His wife and her lover the clerk did the obvious thing, and murdered him. They then, making one of those spur-of-the-moment decisions, sawed and nipped his body into pieces and stuffed his beard into a chair cushion. However, his body began to reassemble itself and became the source of miraculous cures—but of course, murder will out.

> The Chair!—at that word—it seems really absurd,
>   But the truth must be told,—what contortions and grins
> Distorted her face! —She sprang up from her place
>   Just as though she'd been sitting on needles and pins!

> . . . .
> She shriek'd with the pain, but all efforts were vain;
> In vain did they strain every sinew and muscle, —
> The cushion stuck fast! —From that hour to her last
> She could never get rid of that comfortless 'Bustle'!

"I know their tricks and their manners." From Dickens' *Our Mutual Friend.* It is a remark frequently made by the dolls' dressmaker, Jenny Wren, who had no doubt suffered the tricks—and the manners.

In petto. Italian. Secretly.

In posse. Latin. Possibly, potentially.

"In the spring. . . . " A couplet from Tennyson's *Locksley Hall.*

> In the spring a livlier iris changes on the burnish'd dove;
> In the spring a young man's fancy lightly turns to thoughts of love.

"Into my heart an air that kills." See ***The Land of Lost Content.***

"Into the breast that gave the rose/Shall I with shuddering fall?" From George Meredith's 1862 poem *The Spirit of the Earth in Autumn.*

"In vain did St. Dunstan. . . . " A line from *The Lay of St. Dunstan,* one of the Ingoldsby Legends. The verse tells the legend of St. Dunstan, whose broomstick had a spell laid on it by the devil. As a result, vast amounts of beer flooded the monastery. (This story was told by Walt Disney in *Fantasia* using Dukas' symphonic poem *The Sorcerer's Apprentice* as a background, with Mickey Mouse as the main character.) Some of this beer, by the way, was **Audit Ale.**

> When they open'd the door out the malt-liquor flowed,
> Just as when the great Vat burst in Tot'n'am Court Road;
> The lay-brothers nearest were up to their necks
> In an instant, and swimming in strong double-X;
> While Peter, who, spite of himself now had drank hard,
> After floating awhile, like toast in a tankard,
>   To the bottom had sunk,   And was spied by a monk,
> Stone-dead, like poor Clarence, half drown'd and half drunk.
> In vain did St. Dunstan exclaim, '*Vade retro*
> *Strongbeerum! —discede a Lay-fratre Petro!* —

"In youth it sheltered me. . . . " From the 1830 poem by George Pope Morris, "Woodman, Spare that Tree."

> Woodman, spare that tree!
> Touch not a single bough!
> In youth it sheltered me,
> And I'll protect it now.

Io. From Greek myth. Io was one of Juno's priestesses. When Juno discovered that Jupiter was in love with Io, she transformed Io into a heifer. In this guise Io wandered the world, coming at last to Egypt, where her own form was returned to her.

"Iron sleet of an arrowy shower." A line from *The Fatal Sisters,* by Thomas Gray.

"It's my own invention." *See* **White Knight.**

Irving, Sir Henry (1838–1905). English actor. The Clovers named their son for him.

It. Short for Italian vermouth, possibly a product of the firm of Martini and Rossi. This is why when an unsuspecting American asks for a martini in England, envisioning a cold frosty glass of almost pure gin, he may get a glass of warm Italian vermouth seasoned with a large dash of disappointment.

"It is a beauteous evening. . . . " From an 1802 sonnet by William Wordsworth, "Evening on Calais Beach."

> It is a beauteous evening, calm and free,
>> The holy time is quiet as a Nun
>> Breathless with adoration; the broad sun
> Is sinking down in its tranquility;
> The gentleness of heaven broods o'er the sea:
>> Listen! The mighty Being is awake,
>> And doth with his eternal motion make
> A sound like thunder — everlastingly.

"Its bosom did so heave. . . . " *See* **"the silence grows."**

"It was the azalea's breath. . . . " From "The Azalea," by Coventry Patmore.

> At dawn I dream'd, O God, that she was dead.
> And groan'd aloud upon my wretched bed,
> And waked, ah, God, and did not waken her,
> But lay, with eyes still closed,
> Perfectly bless'd in the delicious sphere
> By which I knew so well that she was near,
> My heart to speechless thankfulness composed.
> Til 'gan to stir
> A dizzy somewhat in my troubled head —
> It *was* the azalea's breath, and she *was* dead!

"I waited for the train at Coventry. . . . " *See* **Godiva.**

"I was adored once. . . . " From Shakespeare's *Twelfth Night.* The line is spoken by Sir Andrew Auguecheek, a reedy, pitiful knight.

"I will hold your hand as long as all may. . . . " *See* **"The Lost Mistress."**

𝒥

Other people's holidays are of no interest at all.
— Angela Thirkell

Jack Ketch. *See* **Ketch, Jack.**

Jacquerie. *French.* An uprising of peasants. The term is based on the original *Jacquerie* in France in 1358.

Janissary. A soldier hand-picked for special duty in the Turkish army of the 14ᵗʰ century. Thus any member of a group of loyal supporters.

Jarndyce v. Jarndyce. From Dickens' *Bleak House*. Jarndyce v. Jarndyce was a protracted law-suit which finally collapsed when the contested funds were consumed in legal fees.

Mrs. Jellyby. From Dickens' *Bleak House*. Her life was entirely taken up with unworthy charities while her large brood of children was neglected.

Jellybolee. The waters of the Jellybolee and the shores around it are the home of the Scroobious Pip in Edward Lear's poem of the same name.

Jenkinson, Mrs. Mountstuart. From George Meredith's 1879 novel *The Egoist*. She was a widow of a certain age, with a gift for summing up a situation, or a person, with a perfect image—such as "a racing cutter" for one beautiful woman, or "a dainty rogue in porcelain" for another.

"Jenny kissed me. . . . " A poem by Leigh Hunt, written in 1838.

> Jenny kiss'd me when we met,
>   Jumping from the chair she sat in;
> Time, you thief, who love to get
>   Sweets into your list, put that in!

"Je pense donc je suis. Je suis donc le monde exist." *French.* A great thought of René Descarte (1596 – 1650): "I think, therefore I am. I am, therefore the world exists." This has also been given as "Cogito ergo sum"— "I think, therefore I am."

Jephtha's daughter. This complicated story is told in Judges II. Jephtha made a very silly vow to God, that if He would let Jephtha prevail in battle, he, Jephtha, would make a burnt offering of whatever came first out of the door of his house. We hate to think what Jephtha expected, but through the door, dancing and drumming to welcome him home, came his daughter. Her very reasonable response to this crisis was to ask to take some of her friends into the mountains for two months, so that they could bewail their virginity. This they did, and she returned and he carried out his vow. It thus became the custom that the daughters of Israel went into the mountains for four days a year to lament Jephtha's daughter.

176

Jerboa. One of several Old World mouse-like leaping rodents, family Dipodidae. They are capable of horizontal jumps of from five to ten feet, and vertical jumps of three feet, which makes them ideal contestants in competitive events.

Jerusalem the Golden. A hymn much beloved in Barsetshire. The words and music are by Alexander C. Ewing and can be found in many hymnals.

Jinglia Tinkettlia. One of the plants from Edward Lear's Nonsense Botany. It is a member of the lily family, with a flowering stalk rising from a bulb and topped by a raceme of tiny tin kettles, gradually increasing in size from 3 mm. at the tip to 1 cm. at the beginning of the spike. The leaves, no more than two in number, are basal, glabrous, narrow, and clasping. Flowers bloom daily in the late afternoon, throughout the year.

Jo. From Dickens' *Bleak House.* Jo was a homeless boy who swept a street-crossing and was an important witness in an investigation. This brought him to the attention of several people and led to considerable "chivying," or orders to him to move on. At last the poor child died of malnutrition and exposure.

Jobling, Toby. From Dickens' *Bleak House.* A friend of Mr. Guppy's. Mr. Jobling was in embarrassed circumstances and had to lodge at Krook's Rag and Bottle Warehouse in the room made available by Nemo's death. Like Nemo, he too, used an alias; his was Weevle, an obvious choice. It was to Mr. Jobling/Weevle that Mr. Guppy was wont to mention the chords in the human mind.

Johnny Cake and Fox. Characters from the story "Johnny Cake," in Joseph Jacobs' *English Fairy Tales.* The story is a variation of "The Gingerbread Man." Johnny Cake ran away from the Old Man, Old Woman, Bear, and Wolf. But Fox pretended to be weak and deaf, and when Johnny Cake drew close and shouted in Fox's ear, Fox snapped him up in a twinkling.

Johnson, Samuel (1709–1784). Renowned lexicographer, writer, and conversationalist. On the subject of claret, Johnson said that it was so weak that "a man would be drowned by it before it made him drunk. . . . Claret is the liquor for boys; port for men; but he who aspires to be a hero must drink brandy." For the quotation "toil, envy, etc." *See* **"toil, envy, want, etc. . . . "**

Jointure. There are several meanings of this, but the one most common in Barsetshire has to do with a property settlement made upon a wife for her use during her lifetime.

Jorrocks. Farcical sketches of sporting life by Robert Smith Surtees. They first appeared in 1838 as *Jorrock's Jaunts and Jollities.*

Jorum. A large cup or goblet.

Joseph. An Old Testament patriarch. As a child he had been given by his jealous older brothers to a passing band of Ishmaelites and carried into Egypt. Years later, in a season of drought, these same brothers appeared before him in Egypt to ask for grain. We quote from Genesis 42:8.

> And Joseph knew his brethren, but they knew him not.

Joseph Vance. A novel by William de Morgan, published in 1906. Joseph, the hero, is the son of a builder. He is befriended by a middle-class family who, among other things, help him through Oxford; he becomes an engineer.

Jude the Obscure. An 1895 novel by Thomas Hardy. It is the story of a promising but poor young man, Jude Fawley, who sets his heart on going to the university. However, he is waylaid by his relationships with two very different women, both of whom bear him children. By the end, Jude is dead, both children are dead, one of the women is married to a man she does not love, and the other is already taking on a new lover.

Judy. *See* **Punch.**

Jument de la nuit, ombre sombre. *French.* Nightmare, dark shadow.

Jung, Karl (1875–1961). Swiss psychiatrist, one of the associates of Freud who broke away from him. Jung's rather complicated ideas do not lend themselves to a brief description, so we will just say that he brought to the study of human behavior such terms as "collective unconscious," "archetype," "introvert and extrovert," and "anima and animus."

Jupiter Pluvius. The Roman god Jupiter, in his function as the bringer of rain and wielder of thunderstorms.

Juste milieu. *French.* The perfect balance or golden mean.

Justice of the Peace. A magistrate. *See* **bench.**

Jutland. A large peninsula comprising most of Denmark and part of Germany. Its west coast was the scene of a famous naval battle fought May 31–June 1, 1916. British losses were heavier, but the result was a victory for Britain, for its ships prevented the German navy from leaving their ports for the rest of the war.

J'y suis, j'reste. *French.* Here I am; here I stay. These words are attributed to General MacMahon when he took Sebastopol in 1855.

*No good trying to compete with you
bloated businessmen. Kamerad!*
— George Halliday

Kamerad. *German.* Comrade; used by the Germans in World War I as an appeal for surrender, and so more or less equates to "uncle," or "you win."

Keats, John (1795–1821). One of the renowned poets of the Romantic movement, whose most admired poems include "Ode on a Grecian Urn" and "The Eve of St. Agnes." His "Ode to Autumn" begins

> Season of mists and mellow fruitfulness,
> Close bosom-friend of the maturing sun;
> Conspiring with him how to load and bless
> With fruit the vines that round the thatch-eaves run;
> To bend with apples the moss'd cottage-trees,
> And fill all fruit with ripeness to the core;
> To swell the gourd, and plump the hazel shells
> With a sweet kernel; to set budding more,
> And still more, later flowers for the bees,
> Until they think warm days will never cease;
> For summer has o'erbrimmed their clammy cells.

"Keep the Home Fires Burning." As we know, this was the song sung to such great effect by Cora Palliser as the finale of the little performance at the Conservative Do in *County Chronicle*. It came out in 1915 during the First War and describes all the places from which the brave young men were called. Those left at home are told not to add to the soldiers' hardships by letting the young men see tears. Even as their hearts are breaking these mothers, fathers, sweethearts and wives should sing a cheery song and, yes, keep the home fires burning. The words are by Lena Ford and the music is by Ivor Novello.

Kensal Green. A very large London cemetery covering fifty-four acres. Anthony Trollope is buried there.

Ketch, Jack. There was a real Jack Ketch, a well-known executioner and hangman. His name has come to stand for all hangmen, and he was incorporated as a character into the *Punch and Judy* puppet show.

Kilmeny. A long narrative poem by Scottish poet James Hogg. It is about a girl, Kilmeny, "pure as pure could be," who vanishes and is given up for dead. Then she reappears, full of an other-worldly ecstasy. After a month and a day among her old friends, she returns to the land of love, light, and thought.

King Charles' Head. Charles I was beheaded in 1649, during the Civil War. In Dickens' novel *David Copperfield*, the harmless lunatic Mr. Dick is obsessed with King Charles' head, and finds that no matter what he thinks he is writing, it always turns out to be about King Charles' head. The term has come to be used for any obsession.

Kingsley, Henry (1830–1876). English author whose novels include *Geoffrey Hamlyn* (1859), *Ravenshoe* (1862), *Austin Elliott* (1863), and *The Hillyers and the Burtons* (1865). He was the brother of Charles Kingsley, who wrote *The Water Babies*.

Kipling. Thirkell refers frequently to Kipling. We could understand if she had done it even more, for Rudyard Kipling was her second cousin, the son of her grandmother's sister Alice Macdonald Kipling. Born in 1865, he was AT's senior by twenty-five years, and spent much of his life away from England. It appears that for those reasons she did not know him well. Yet she had spent some time with him and such an impressive connection apparently had some influence on her.

"Kipling poem about Jane Austen." This is "Jane's Marriage," in which Kipling imagined Jane, upon entering heaven, happily joined at last with the man who had been the model for Captain Wentworth in *Persuasion*.

Kirchwasser. *German.* Cherry brandy.

Kitchener, Horatio Herbert (1850–1916). Brilliant and popular British general, a veteran of service in Palestine, Egypt, the Sudan, South Africa, and India. He was influential in raising a large army of volunteers in 1914. His famous words are from a message to soldiers of the British Expeditionary Force in 1914, a copy of which each man was to keep in his pay book. We quote from its few sentences.

> In this new experience you may find temptations both in wine and women. You must entirely resist both temptations, and, while treating all women with perfect courtesy, you should avoid any intimacy.

Lord Kitchener was killed when the ship in which he was a passenger was struck by a German mine in 1916. **Sir Redvers Buller** (1839–1908) was another English career soldier. He served in China, South Africa, Egypt and the Sudan. He was Commander-in-Chief of the army during the second Boer War and was succeeded by **Lord Roberts** (1832–1914), a British soldier, veteran of campaigns in India, Afghanistan, and South Africa. Lord Roberts was Commander-in-Chief of the army, and died while visiting the troops in France in 1914.

The Knight of the Burning Pestle. A comedy written by Sir Francis Beaumont and first performed in 1607. It was a spoof of serious plays featuring knights and chivalry.

Krafft–Ebbing, Richard (1840–1902). German psychiatrist whose studies focused on sexual pathology. That Krafft-Ebbing was known in the popular culture of the time is illustrated by this famous limerick:

> There was a young girl of East Anglia
> Whose loins were a tangle of ganglia.
> Her mind was a webbing
> Of Freud and Krafft-Ebbing
> And other erotic new-fanglia.

Krook, Mr. A character from Dickens' *Bleak House*. Mr. Krook was the proprietor of Krook's Rag and Bottle Warehouse. But the name was misleading, for a sign also advertised that Mr. Krook dealt in Marine Stores, and several placards announced that he bought bones, kitchen stuff, waste paper, and ladies' and gentlemen's wardrobes. All these items, and more, lay in heaps on the floor or hung like bats from the beams and walls. Mr. Krook was a victim of spontaneous combustion.

Never economize on luxuries, my pet.
— Lady Cora Palliser

Lac du Cygnes. *French. Swan Lake*, a ballet by Tchaikovsky.

The lads who will never grow old. Words from poem number XXIII from *A Shropshire Lad*, by A.E. Housman (1858–1936). It was published in 1896.

> The lads in their hundreds to Ludlow come for the fair,
> There's men from the barn and the forge and the mill and the fold,
> The lads for the girls and the lads for the liquor are there,
> And there with the rest are the lads that will never be old.
> . . . .
> But now you may stare as you like and there's nothing to scan;
> And brushing your elbow unguessed-at and not to be told
> They carry back bright to the coiner the mintage of man,
> The lads that will die in their glory and never be old.

La Fontaine, Jean (1621–1695). French poet and author, known for his retelling in poetic form of fables from various cultures.

"a laggard in love. . . . " A line from the romantic poem *Lochinvar*, by Sir Walter Scott. In the poem, Lochinvar is hurrying to interrupt a wedding.

> He stayed not for brake and he stopped not for stone,
> He swam the Eske River where ford there was none,
> But ere he alighted at Netherby gate
> The bride had consented, the gallant came late;
> For a laggard in love and a dastard in war
> Was to wed the fair Ellen of young Lochinvar.

La joie fait peur. *French.* Joy frightens.

Lalage. A woman beloved by Horace in ode 22 from Book I.

> *Dulce ridentem Lalagen amabo,*   I will go on loving Lalage, who
> *Dulce loquentum.*   Laughs so sweetly, talks so sweetly.

Lambeth degree. An academic degree in arts, law, music, medicine, or divinity, conferred by the Archbishop of Canterbury, whose London residence is in Lambeth, south of the Thames. The right to do this was conferred on the Archbishops of Canterbury in 1533.

L'ami de maison. *French.* A friend of the house (family).

Mr. Lammle and Fascination Fledgeby. Two characters from Dickens' *Our Mutual Friend*, both opportunists looking for any way to reap a little harvest of pounds, shillings, and pence. It was Lammle's idea to arrange a meeting between young Fledgeby and the wealthy Georgianna Podsnap. As it happened, neither young person cooperated. Fledgeby's singular ineptitude so moved Mr. Lammle to fury later that he shouted, "Give me your nose!" and tried to wring it off Fledgeby's face, and would have except that Fledgeby dodged, evaded, and finally calmed Lemmle's wrath.

L'amour fait passer le temps, le temps fait passer l'amour. *French.* Love makes time pass; time makes love pass.

Lancers. A form of quadrille, a lively dance in which four couples are arranged in a square and execute five figures. Lancers is so called because it was made popular by a type of cavalry soldier who carried a lance. It dates back to 1836.

Land Girls. Young women enlisted for a stint during the war as agricultural laborers. *See* **Women's Land Army.**

Land of lost content. Words from poem XL in *A Shropshire Lad,* by A.E. Housman.

> Into my heart an air that kills
> From yon far country blows:
> What are those blue remembered hills,
> What spires, what farms are those?
>
> That is the land of lost content,
> I see it shining plain,
> The happy highways where I went
> And cannot come again.

Langtry, Lily (1853–1929). English actress and famous beauty. She was one of the many mistresses of the Prince of Wales, who later was Edward VII. She was from Jersey, which was why Mr. Middleton named his beautiful Jersey cow for her.

Lantern. In the architectural sense, a lantern is a small glass-sided turret built into the roof over a large entry hall in order to let in light.

Laocoön. From Greek mythology. Laocoön was a priest of Apollo, whom he offended in some way. His punishment was that he and his two sons were set upon by huge boa constrictors and crushed to death; a statue depicting this is now on display in the Vatican. The word is sometimes used to describe complex situations with tortuously intertwining elements.

L'appetit vient en mangeant. *French.* Appetite comes from eating.

Lara. Hero of a poem by Byron. Lara is actually named Conrad, but is travelling incognito. When recognized, he is drawn into fighting between rival groups and is killed.

Lars Porsena (6th century B.C.). Ruler of the Etruscan city of Clusium. His march on Rome was held back by Horatius at the bridge over the Tiber. This account is from *Lays of Ancient Rome, Horatius,* 1842.

> Lars Porsena of Clusium
> By the nine gods he swore
> That the great house of Tarquin

Should suffer wrong no more.
By the Nine Gods he swore it,
And named a trysting day,
And bade his messengers ride forth
East and west and south and north,
To summon his array.

"The Last Chantey." The title of a poem by Kipling published in 1892. Using the line from the Book of Revelation, "And there was no more sea," the poet imagines such a thing happening on Judgment Day. After hearing pros and cons from some that love and use the sea, and others that were killed by it and fear it, the Lord decides that the sea is worth keeping

The Last of England. An 1883 painting by Ford Maddox Brown. It shows a young husband and wife on the deck of a ship. They are obviously emigrants, and are staring very soberly at the vanishing shore of their homeland. The picture now hangs in the Birmingham (England) Museum and Art Gallery.

Latitudinarian. One who attaches little importance to dogma or correctness. The name comes from Church of England history; it was used for clergy who held such views.

Laudator temporis acti. Latin. One who praises the good old days.

"Lawkamercy on me, this is none of I !" This is from a poem collected in *More English Fairy Tales* by Joseph Jacobs entitled "Lawkamercyme." The subject is an old woman who went to market to sell her eggs, but grew drowsy on her way and fell asleep by the highway. A peddler happened along to whom it seemed a good idea at the time to cut off her skirts up to her knees :

When this old woman first did wake,
She began to shiver and shake;
She began to wonder, and she began to cry —
"Lawkamercyme, this is none of I !"

"Lay low, said nothing. . . . " From Joel Chandler Harris' *Uncle Remus and His Friends*, published in 1892: "Tar Baby, he ain't sayin' nothin', en Br'er Fox, he lay low."

Law Lord. A peer in the House of Lords who sits on the highest court of appeal.

Lear, Edward (1812–1888). English zoological draughtsman, water colorist, and writer of travel articles. However, he is remembered chiefly for his nonsense stories, drawings, and poems for children.

Leads. Sheets of lead used as roofing material on large old houses.

Lear's "Never." From Shakespear's *King Lear,* Act V, scene iii.

And my poor fool is hanged! No, no, no life!
Why should a dog, a horse, a rat have life,
And thou no breath at all? Thou'lt come no more,
Never, never, never, never, never!

"Leather boots and cambric underclothing." *See The Periwinkle Girl.*

Le ciel est padersoo le twah. Miss Crowder's rendition of a line of poetry by the French poet Verlaine (1844–1896). Here is the first verse.

Le ciel est par dessus...	The sky above the roof...
Le ciel est, par-dessus le toit,	The sky, above the roof,
Si bleu, si calme!	Is so blue, so peaceful!
Un arbre, par-dessus le toit,	A tree, above the roof,
Berce sa palme.	Waves its branches.

Legree. A character from *Uncle Tom's Cabin,* by Harriet Beecher Stowe and published in 1851. Simon Legree was a cruel plantation owner who beat his slave, Uncle Tom, to death.

Le peintre qui voit d'une certaine façon et peint comme il voit. *French.* The artist who sees in a certain style and paints as he sees.

Leporello's catalog. From an aria in Mozart's *Don Giovanni.* In Act I, Leporello, the servant of Giovanni, reads a long tally of women whom the Don has dishonored. The list is categorized by nationality.

Lesbia. The name by which the Roman poet Catullus (84–54 B.C.) called his mistress Clodia. She was an important influence in his life, bringing to him every permutation of love, from joyful discovery to the anguish of disillusionment.

"Les gens du monde se représentent volontiers les livres comme une espèce de cube dont une face est enlevée, si bien que l'auterr se dépêche de 'faire entrer' dedans les persones qu'il recontre."
This somewhat enigmatic quotation from Proust is the prefatory note to *The Duke's Daughter.* The Meaning is, roughly, this: "People see books as a cube with one side emphasized, so much that the author hurries to enter into the characters whose stories he tells." We are certain that the connection between this lucid comment and the events and characterizations of *The Duke's Daughter* will be at once understood by our readers.

"Les grandes jets d'eau sveltes. . . ." From a poem by Paul Verlaine. This is the last verse.

Claire de lune	Moonlight
Au calme clair de lune triste et beau	The calm moonlight, sad and lovely,
Qui fait rêver les oiseaux dans les arbres	That makes the birds in the trees to dream
Et sangloter d'extase les jets d'eau,	And the jets of water from the fountain sob with ecstasy,
Les grands jets d'eau sveltes parmi les marbres.	The tall jets of water are slender among the statues.

Les pieds ronds. *French.* Round feet.

"lesser breeds. . . ." These words are drawn from verse four of Rudyard Kipling's famous "Recessional," 1897, reminding us that we should not forget the lesser breeds beyond the law.

"Let contemplation with extensive viewgia. . . ." A parody of some lines by Samuel Johnson. We do not know the rest of the parody, but we can give you some of Dr. Johnson's original verse. It is called "The Vanity of Human Wishes," and was written in 1749.

> Let observation with extensive view,
> Survey mankind, from China to Peru;
> Remark each anxious toil, each eager strife,
> And watch the busy scenes of crowded life.

Lime tree. *Tilia*, probably *Tilia* x *vulgaris*. This is the common lime, a member of the linden family, and seen frequently in England. It is a tall, stately tree, frequently planted in avenues.

Li-lo. An air mattress. Li-lo was a brand name that became generic.

Little-ease. Any of several ways of confining a prisoner uncomfortably, such as in a narrow cell. A chamber in the Tower of London was known as Little Ease.

"Little liar." Possibly a quotation from Hilaire Belloc's children's verse, "Matilda, Who told Lies and was Burned to Death." Matilda was a child who told outrageous lies. She lived with her aunt, an excellent woman who tried to believe these stories. One day, for a lark, Matilda summoned the fire department; her aunt had to pay them to get them to leave before they did a lot of damage. Later, on an evening when her aunt was at the theater, the house did catch fire, and Matilda screamed from the window. The people passing in the street assumed she was lying, so both the house and Matilda were burned.

Living. A benefice; the position or post of vicar, rector, or perpetual curate in the Church of England.

(Ladies of) Llangollen. They were Lady Eleanor Butler (c.1739–1829) and Miss Sarah Ponsonby (c.1735–1831). They are known partly for their independence in leaving their homes in Ireland to set up housekeeping together in Wales, and partly for their house itself, a marvel of Gothic-romantic style at Plas Newydd in Llangollen Vale. It is pronounced "hlan.GA.hlen". Do not try to say this by yourself at home.

Lloyd George. David Lloyd George, 1st Earl Lloyd-George of Dwyfor, was a Welsh Liberal statesman, and Prime Minister from 1916 to 1922. Although he did much that was admirable and was a stunning orator, he was implicated in an honors-selling scandal. Ninety-one new lords were created between 1917 and 1923. The elder Lord Norton definitely was a Lloyd George peer, and Sir Ogilvy Hibberd was often described as one.

Locus standi. *Latin.* The place to stand; a recognized position.

Lodore. A waterfall in the Lake District.

Lohengrin. The legendary son of Percival (or Parsifal). His is a long story, but among other things Lohengrin journeyed from Montsalvat to Antwerp and returned, making the round trip in a boat drawn by a swan. The story is told in the *Parzifal* of Wolfram von Eschenback (c.1205) and retold in grand operatic form by Wagner in his opera *Lohengrin*.

Longfellow, Henry Wadsworth (1807–1882). American poet. His "The Song of King Olaf" is contained in *Tales of a Wayside Inn*.

Long Vacation. A school holiday of about eight weeks, occurring sometime from July to September. The Law Court calendar is similar.

"Looked on the wine when it was red. . . . " From Proverbs 23: 29-32.

> 29. Who hath woe? who hath sorrow? who hath contentions? who hath babbling? who hath wounds without cause? who hath redness of eyes?

185

30. They that tarry long at the wine; they that go to seek mixed wine.
31. Look not thou upon the wine when it is red, when it giveth his colour in the cup, when it moveth itself aright.
32. And at the last it biteth like a serpent, and stingeth like an adder.

Loose box. An enclosed area in a barn or stable in which a horse is confined but not tied; a box stall.

"The Lord of Burleigh." A poem by Tennyson in which a titled landscape painter living incognito woos a simple village lass. After their marriage he takes her for a walk; when they stroll through the gates of the county's finest manor and into the great hall itself, he reveals that he is Lord there—and she must be Lady. Her spirits sink, for she feels she doesn't deserve the honor, but she tries. She bears three children and then dies.

"The Lost Chord." An impressive religious song by Arthur S. Sullivan. It begins, "Seated one day at the organ, I was weary and ill at ease . . . "

"The Lost Mistress." This poem by Robert Browning is quoted from so often, and is so short, that we include all of it.

THE LOST MISTRESS

I.
All's over, then: does truth sound bitter
  As one at first believes?
Hark, 't is the sparrows' good-night twitter
  About your cottage eaves!

II.
And the leaf-buds on the vine are woolly,
  I noticed that to-day;
One day more bursts them open fully:
  You know the red turns gray.

III.
To-morrow we meet the same then, dearest?
  May I take your hand in mine?
Mere friends are we, — well, friends the merest
  Keep much that I resign:

IV.
For each glance of the eye so bright and black,
  Tho' I keep with heart's endeavour, —
Your voice, when you wish the snowdrops back,
  Tho' it stay in my soul forever! —

V.
Yet I will but say what mere friends say,
  Or only a thought stronger;
I will hold your hand but as long as all may,
  Or so very little longer!

Love among the Ruins. A poem by Robert Browning. Its theme of the triumph of love in a place once made noisy by warfare is similar to that of AT's novel of the same name, and probably inspired her use of the title. To deepen the meaning, she was possibly also thinking of the ruins of the society

186

she had known, which was being destroyed by the bloodless revolution then occurring. There was an unrelated film of the same title made in 1975.

Love in the Valley. A long poem by George Meredith (1828–1909), quoted from now and then by one or two Barsetshire mothers.

> When her mother tends her before the laughing mirror,
> Tying up her laces, looping up her hair,
> Often she thinks, were this wild thing wedded,
> More love should I have, and much less care.

Loveliest of Trees. Poem II in AE Housman's collection, *A Shropshire Lad.* The title for *Three Score and Ten* appears in this poem, though its origin is Biblical. We quote it all.

> Loveliest of trees, the cherry now
> Is hung with bloom along the bough,
> And stands about the woodland ride
> Wearing white for Eastertide.
>
> Now, of my threescore years and ten,
> Twenty will not come again,
> And take from seventy springs a score,
> It only leaves me fifty more.
>
> And since to look at things in bloom
> Fifty springs are little room,
> About the woodlands I will go
> To see the cherry hung with snow.

Loves of the Triangles. A parody by Canning and Frere, written in 1789. It spoofed a long botannical poem by Erasmus Darwin, *The Loves of the Plants,* also published in 1789. Here is a sample verse.

> But chief, thou NURSE of the DIDACTIC MUSE,
> Divine NONSENSIA, all thy soul infuse;
> The charms of *Secants* and of *Tangents* tell,
> How LOVES and GRACES in an *Angle* dwell;
> How slow progressive *Points* protract the *Line,*
> As pedant spiders spin the filmy twine;
> How lengthen'd *Lines,* impetuous sweeping round,
> Spread the wide *Plane,* and mark its circling bound;
> How *Planes,* their substance with their motion grown,
> Form the huge *Cube,* the *Cylinder,* the *Cone.*

Lucina. From Roman mythology; the goddess of childbirth.

Lucus a non lucendo. *Latin.* Literally, called a grove (or dark place) because it isn't light, *lucus* being the word for grove or wood. A paradoxical or absurd explanation.

Luke and Huxley's. This stands in for Marks and Spencer's, a chain of department stores. Mark and Luke are both Gospel writers. Herbert Spencer and T. H. Huxley were both 19th century scientists and philosophers. By the way, Herbert Spencer was not connected with the store—that was a Thomas Spencer.

Lych gate. A roofed gateway into a churchyard. It is a place where a coffin may be rested while the pall-bearers wait out of the weather for the priest.

Macaulay, Thomas Babbington (1800–1859). Lord Macaulay was a writer, politician, and historian, author of *Lays of Ancient Rome*, of which *Horatius* is just one part.

Macdonald, Flora (1722–1790). A heroine of the Jacobite struggles in Scotland. When Charles Edward Stewart (Bonnie Prince Charlie) was fleeing the English soldiers, she conducted him, dressed as her Irish maid, from the island of Benbecula to Skye and from there to the island of Portree. It was a forty-mile journey by open boat (rowed by five men), and it took fifteen hours.

Macheath. A character from *The Beggar's Opera*, by John Gay (1685–1732). Polly and Lucy were both in love with Macheath, who was a handsome outlaw. He married Polly, was sent to jail, and there met Lucy. He loved them both, but thanks to the generosity of Lucy, he was reunited with Polly.

Madame Recamier (1777–1849). A Frenchwoman famous for her charm and beauty, the friend of many literary celebrities of the day. She was painted half-lying on a day bed by the French neo-classical painter Jacques Louis David.

"Mad, bad, and dangerous to know." Written by Lady Caroline Lamb in her journal after her first meeting with Lord Byron in 1812. She was for nine months one of Byron's lovers, so the words were prophetic.

Maeterlinck, Maurice (1862–1949). Belgian playwright. He used themes from fairy tales or the classics and the mood of his plays was haunting, mysterious, and romantic. Among his works are *Pelléas and Mélisande*, *The Princess Maleine*, and *The Blue Bird*.

Mafeking Day. Mafeking is a South African town that was besieged for 217 days during the Boer War, from October 12, 1899, to May 17, 1900. The celebration in London on May 18, 1900, was said to be greater than that at the end of the war in 1918.

Magic. Belief in magic flourished in Barsetshire, at least among the working class. Many cooks read tea leaves, for instance. Jasper Margett said that his old grandmother, long dead, would occasionally reappear as a black hare. He also knew that snakes had a charm in them which could be transferred to anyone who ate either the snake's head or tail. Ed Pollett believed that it was bad luck to visit a newborn bull calf twice. Dorothy Simnet believed that when glass was accidentally broken, two more pieces should be broken for good luck. It was generally believed among pigmen that no good comes if a pig is killed when the moon was past full. Stirring the butter with a twig from Hangman's Oak was sure to make it good, and the farmer who ate live snails would be told by the snails when it was time to plant. Mrs. George Panter believed she could tell the weather by the clothes line. Of it all, the tea leaves seemed to have been the most reliable, as so many events of any given day had been clearly foretold in the morning's tea.

Magistrate. A Justice of the Peace, or J.P. *See* **bench.**

Magnall's Questions. The short title of an instructive book by Richard Magnall, more properly known as *Historical and Miscellaneous questions, for the use of young people.*

Magnus, Peter. A character from Dickens' *Pickwick Papers.* He started as a casual fellow-traveler with Pickwick in the coach to Ipswich, and ended challenging Mr. Pickwick to a duel. This was because during the night Mr. Pickwick had accidentally gone into the room of Miss Witherfield, who turned out to be the very woman whose hand in marriage Mr. Magnus had gone to Ipswich to seek.

Mains. The power or water lines belonging to the utility company.

Malvoisie. Malmsey. A sweet wine made in southern Europe from the malvoisia grape.

"A man of words." From a nursery rhyme of the same name.

> A man of words and not of deeds
> Is like a garden full of weeds.
> For when the weeds begin to grow,
> Then doth the garden overflow.

Manfred. From Byron's poetic drama of the same name, published in 1817. Manfred is a Faustian character who endures many torments and then dies anyway.

Mangold. Short for mangel-wurzel. It is a type of coarse beet used as food for cattle.

Mantalini, Alfred. A character from Dickens' *Nicholas Nickleby.* Mr. Mantalini was the utterly useless, foppish, ruinous husband of the dressmaker, Madame Mantalini. He was one of those who control their loved ones with threats of suicide. When Madame Mantalini stated her intention of putting him on a (very generous) allowance, Alfred leapt for the door, saying he would drown himself in the Thames, exclaiming, "She calls me cruel—me—me—who for her sake will become a dem'd damp, moist, unpleasant body!"

Manypeeplia Upsidedownia. A plant from Edward Lear's 1871 *Nonsense Botany.* From a whorl of sparse basal leaves, a single scape rises to about eighteen inches, bearing on its end a raceme of eight to ten small humans, depending head down with their feet attached to short pedicels.

March hare. As March is the breeding time for hares in England, the expression "mad as a March hare" has an obvious meaning.

Marchioness. The wife or widow of a marquis.

Martha. The patron saint of housewives. Martha was the sister of Mary Magdalen, and is associated with domestic activities.

Mary Rose. A play by James M. Barrie.

Marryat, Captain Frederick (1792–1848). An author who published sixteen novels of the sea between 1829 and 1840. His well-known children's books appeared between 1841 and 1847. The most famous of them was *Children of the New Forest*.

Matchboard. Wooden tongue-in-groove paneling.

Maud. A very long poem by Alfred, Lord Tennyson. In it the narrator tells a tale of love, duplicity, death, remorse, and salvation by war. A few excerpts, often referred to, are quoted here:

PART I
II.

All that I saw (for her eyes were downcast, not to be seen)
Faultily faultless, icily regular, splendidly null.
Dead perfection, no more; nothing more. . . .

VII
1
Did I hear it half in a doze
    Long since, I know not where?
Did I dream it an hour ago,
    Asleep in this armchair?
2
Men were drinking together,
    Drinking and talking of me;
"Well, if it prove a girl, the boy
    will have plenty: so let it be."

VIII
She came to the village church,
And sat by a pillar alone;
An angel watching an urn
Wept over her, carved in stone;
And once, but once, she lifted her eyes,
And suddenly, sweetly, strangely blush'd
To find they were met by my own;
And suddenly, sweetly, my heart beat stronger
And thicker, until I heard no longer
The snowy-banded dilettante,
Delicate-handed priest intone;
And thought, is it pride?

XII
4
I kiss'd her slender hand,
    She took the kiss sedately;
Maud is not seventeen,
    But she is tall and stately.

PART II

I

"The fault was mine, the fault was mine" —
Why am I sitting here so stunn'd and still,
Plucking the harmless wild-flower on the hill? —
It is this guilty hand! —
And there arises ever a passionate cry
From underneath in the darkening land —
What is it, that has been done?

V 3

And another, a statesman there, betraying
His party-secret, fool, to the press. . . .

Maud Muller. A narrative poem by American poet John Greenleaf Whittier, published in 1854. It tells of a young judge who, out riding, was given water by a farmer's lovely daughter. They went their separate ways and each married appropriately, but both were haunted for years by thoughts of what "might have been."

Alas for the maiden, alas for the Judge,
For rich repiner and household drudge!

God pity them both and pity us all,
Who vainly the dreams of youth recall.

For of all the sad words of tongue or pen,
The saddest are these: "It might have been!'

Maxime debetur. *Latin.* Much indebted.

Mead. Since Anglo-Saxon times, mead has been a fermented drink made of honey, water, yeast, and malt.

Mèche. *French.* Short for *mèche de cheveux,* a lock of hair. *Mèche* itself means a wick, fuse, or tassel.

Medmenham Abbey. A restored abbey which was the home of the Hell-fire Club, founded in 1755 by Sir Francis Dashwood. Members of this club were known as the Monks of Medmenham Abbey, and probably we are better off not knowing what they did. Their motto was *"Fay ce que voudras"* —Do what you wish.

"The merchant, to secure his treasure. . . . " These lines from Chapter Eight of *Love among the Ruins* are from a poem by Matthew Prior variously titled "Song" or "Ode." In its four verses the poet describes trying to please two women and making a bad job of it. Here are the first and third verses.

The merchant, to secure his treasure,
    Conveys it in a borrow'd name:
Euphelia serves to grace my measure;
    But Chloe is my real flame.
. . . .
My lyre I tune, my voice I raise;
    But with my number mix my sighs:
And while I sing Euphelia's praise,
    I fix my soul on Chloe's eyes.

192

"Mere friends are we. . . . " *See* **"The Lost Mistress."**

Merriles, Meg. A character from Scott's *Guy Mannering,* published in 1815. Meg was an old gypsy who sacrificed herself in an effort to thwart a plot that would have unseated Harry Bertram, the rightful heir to Ellangowan.

Merrythought. Wishbone.

Mesmer, Doctor (1734–1815). An Austrian physician who pioneered the use of what he called animal magnetism and what is today, broadly speaking, hypnotism.

Mr. Miacca. A character from the story "Mr. Miacca" in *English Fairy Tales,* collected by Joseph Jacobs. Mr. Miacca was a cannibal who lived at the end of the street and would catch and eat children who wandered too from home.

Micawber, Wilkins. A character from Dickens' *David Copperfield.* Mr. Micawber was a man of great good will and considerable fecklessness, whose descent into debtors' prison in no way estranged him from his wife, who said she would never desert him. His advice about managing money was very good:

> Annual income twenty pounds, annual expenditure
> nineteen nineteen six, result happiness. Annual income
> twenty pounds, annual expenditure twenty pounds ought
> and six, result misery.

Middle classes. In *Love at All Ages* AT voices her pleasure at being middle class, with "no need to fear a fall nor be proud about anything in particular."

Middlemarch. A novel by George Eliot, published in 1872. In the novel a young woman, Dorothea Brooke, married a much older scholar and soon came to regret it. She remained loyal to him but her love had changed to pity.

Midgard Worm. In Scandinavian mythology, Midgard is the abode of man, and the Midgard Worm was a huge serpent that was thrown into the sea by Odin. So large was the serpent that he could encircle the earth holding his tail in his mouth.

Miggs, Miss. From Dickens' *Barnaby Rudge.* Miss Miggs was Mrs. Varden's sharp-tongued maid, and later a turnkey at Bridewell.

Milestones — "There are milestones on the Dover Road." From Dickens' *Little Dorrit.* This was one of Mr. F's Aunt's mysterious pronouncements.

Mills, Julia. From Dickens' *David Copperfield.* Julia was a kind and sensible friend of Dora Spenlow, the young woman David married. When Miss Mills found Dora prostrated with shock at the news of David's poverty, she thought David and Dora had quarreled and were "verging on the Desert of the Sahara." Her wise counsel kept them together.

Military careers. The basis of many titles was military action, when a title and property would be awarded for bravery and success on the battlefield. Thus there is a tradition of military service in the upper classes. Military service was also a usual career for younger sons.

Milton, John (1608–1674). English poet of great renown, most famous as the writer of *Paradise Lost, Paradise Regained,* and *Samson Agonistes.* He was twice a widower and was blind after 1652.

Mi piace tanto. Italian. It pleases me very much.

Moddle, Augustus. A character from Dickens' *Martin Chuzzlewit.* He was a lodger at Todgers' who escaped marriage to the eager and unlovely Charity Pecksniff by departing for Tasmania on the morning of the wedding.

Money. All the Thirkell novels took place before the introduction of the new decimal currency in 1969, 70, and 71. The currency in use, and its value, was as follows:

		What a pound in 1933 would be worth in 1998 and the dollar equivalent	1943	1953	1960
(21 shillings	= 1 guinea)				
20 shillings	= 1 pound	£30 or $50.00	£21 or 35.25	£15 or $25.20	£12 or $20.15
5 shillings	= 1 crown	$12.50	$8.75	$6.25	$5.00
2 ½ shillings	= 1 half crown	$6.25	$4.35	$3.15	$2.50
12 pennies	= 1 shilling	$2.50	$1.75	$1.25	$1.00
4 farthings	= 1 penny	.20	.15	.11	.08

Information provided by Sam Rahman of Barings Assets, January, 1998.

Monkey puzzle tree. *Araucaria araucaria.* Also known as the Chile pine, because it was introduced into England from South America in the eighteenth century. Growing to 150 feet, it seems to be composed entirely of droopy or sprangly leafless branches. Upon close examination, one sees that each branch is in fact covered with green needles that hug it somewhat like scales. The bark is rough. The monkey puzzle is a curiosity that might be attractive in some landscapes, but it is not appropriate in a small garden or next to a house. In the U.S. it is seen occasionally in the Pacific Northwest.

"The Monkey's Paw." A tidy little tale of horror by W.W. Jacobs, published in 1902. It tells the story of a simple and kindly family almost destroyed by a monkey's paw to which a magical spell had been attached. It could grant three wishes. But when they wished for £200 to pay off the mortgage, the money came in the form of compensation for their son's having met a hideous death in the machinery at the mill where he worked. When the wife wished for their son to be alive again, the husband knew that it would be in an agonized and mutilated form, so he spent the third wish rescinding the second.

Monks and friars of Rheims. This is from one of *The Ingoldsby Legends,* "The Jackdaw of Rheims." The clever jackdaw stole the cardinal's ring when no one was looking. A great uproar ensued, and the cardinal uttered terrible curses upon the thief—to no avail, it seemed. Then:

> The day was gone, The night came on,
> The Monks and the Friars they search'd till dawn;
>   When the sacristan saw, On crumpled claw,
> Come limping a poor little lame Jackdaw!
>   No longer gay, As on yesterday;
> His feathers all seem'd be be turn'd the wrong way; —
> His pinions droop'd—he could hardly stand,—
> His head was as bald as the palm of your hand;
>   His eye so dim, So wasted each limb.
> That, heedless of grammar, they all cried, "THAT'S HIM!"

Monna Vanna. The heroine of a 1902 play by Maurice Maeterlinck, and the title of an opera by Henri Ferrier. A dramatic painting of Monna Vanna by D.G. Rosetti (a close friend and colleague of AT's grandfather, Sir Edward Burne–Jones) was well-known to admirers of the Pre-Raphaelites. Monna Vanna was the central figure in an intrigue, during a war between Pisa and Florence, that pitted her husband against her former lover.

Monstrous Regiment of Women. From the title of a pamphlet by John Knox: *The First Blast of the Trumpet Against the Monstrous Regiment of Women*, published in 1558, in which he objected to women in positions of power, such as being Queen Mary (Tudor), Queen Mary (Stuart, of Scotland), or Queen Elizabeth I. In this sense *regiment* means *rule*.

Monthly nurse; from the month. When a baby was imminent, a monthly nurse was engaged to care for mother and child for the first month. The nanny would then be hired to take the baby "from the month," and the monthly nurse would go on to another confinement.

Mopsa. Mopsa was a foolish young woman, a character in *The Arcadians* by Sir Philip Sidney, the first version of which was completed in 1581. In another incarnation, Mopsa was a creation of Jean Ingelow, whose *Mopsa the Fairy* was published in 1869. Mopsa, a baby fairy, was escorted to Fairyland by Jack, a mortal boy. During various picaresque adventures he watched her grow up into a lovely fairy queen. At the end Jack was returned to the mortal world and a double took his place.

Morland, George (1763–1804). English painter best known for rural scenes—cows standing in water meadows, pigs, other farm animals, or charmingly rustic cottages. One of his most famous is *The Interior of a Stable* (1791).

Morn or Morm. The author Lt. John Fairweather was referring to in *Cheerfulness Breaks In* was Somerset Maugham, who in addition to several famous novels (*Of Human Bondage* comes to mind) published a collection of short stories called *The Casuarina Tree*. A casuarina tree, for the curious, is a strange affair with leafless jointed branches, like a giant horsetail. It is a native of Australia and the Indian archipelago. Apparently John was confusing casuarina with ocarina.

Morton's Fork. A pretty piece of logic, the creation of John Morton (1420–1500), Archbishop of Canterbury and minister of Henry VII. In collecting forced loans—called benevolences—from subjects, Morton argued, if they seemed rich, that they could obviously afford to pay. If they lived modestly he argued that they must have money saved. Therefore everyone was caught by one side or the other, and all could afford to pay. (Forks in those days had two tines.)

Mot juste. French. The right word, the one that perfectly suits the occasion.

Moss Bros. A famous London second-hand clothing and rental shop established in 1850. It grew and grew over the decades to its present site at 21 Bedford Street. It is known for all sorts of clothes, including uniforms and formal wear, and is patronized by people attending such gala occasions as coronations. (Usually pronounced "Moss Bross.")

Mouth of the lion. This is from Psalm 22, a long catalog of afflictions and a plea for help:

> 19. But be not far from me, O Lord: O my strength, haste thee to help me.
> 20. Deliver my soul from the sword; my darling from the power of the dog.
> 21. Save me from the lion's mouth: for thou hast heard me from the horns of the unicorns.

Mr. F's Aunt. From Dickens' *Little Dorrit* She was the aunt of the departed Mr. Finching, a crazed and terrifying old lady. From out of a hostile stillness she would hurl meaningless but menacing pronouncements.

Mules, mention of in Genesis. Not a very rich reference for our mule-loving readers. However, here it is, such as it is, from Genesis 36:24.

> And these are the children of Zibeon; both Ajah, and Anah: this was that
> Anah that found the mules in the wilderness, as he fed the asses of Zibeon
> his father.

Mulier com non olet tum bene olet. *Latin.* Roughly translated: For a woman the only good odor is no odor.

Muniment Room. A storage room for family records, documents, and other memorabilia.

Murdstone, Edward. From Dickens' *David Copperfield.* Mr. Murdstone was David's beautifully whiskered but cruel stepfather. He beat David with a cane and sent him away to a terrible school.

Mussolini (1883–1945). Known to his admirers as *il duce* (the leader), Mussolini was the Fascist leader of Italy from 1922–45. He defeated the socialists and became a dictator and an ally of Hitler. He suffered terrible defeats during the war and was executed, along with his mistress, at the end of the war by leaders of the Italian majority.

Mutatis mutandus. *Latin.* Necessary changes having been made; with due attention to details.

Muzzle the ox. "Thou shalt not muzzle the ox when he treadeth out the corn." From Deuteronomy 25: 4. In other words, do not grudge a worker whatever little bits or privileges he can pick up.

"My helmet has become a hive for bees. . . ." *See* **"A Farewell to Arms."**

Nannies always know everything.
— Nannie Allen

Naboth's vineyards. This story is from I Kings, chapter 21. It was Naboth's misfortune to have a fine vine-yard and to be a neighbor of Ahab, the king. The vineyard was coveted by Ahab, whose wife Jezebel schemed to get it taken away from Naboth. The rest is a shocking and sad tale, ending with Naboth's being stoned to death.

Nancy brig. From W.S. Gilbert's *The Yarn of the Nancy Bell,* one of the Bab Ballads. In twenty-three verses the story is told by an elderly naval man of his ship having been stuck on a reef for so long that the crew began drawing lots and each time eating the loser. The sole survivor was the narrator who felt he could justifiably claim to be ten different people, as he had eaten the other nine.

> 'Twas on the shores that round our coast
>   From Deal to Ramsgate span,
> That I found alone on a piece of stone
>   An elderly naval man.
>   . . . .
> "Oh, I am a cook and a captain bold
>   And the mate of the *Nancy* brig,
> And a bo'sun tight and a midshipmite,
>   And the crew of the captain's gig."

Nanny. "they were . . . brought up by a proper nanny, without which no civilization is possible. . . . " Mrs. Thirkell makes this comment about the children in the Marling and Watson families in 1941, but it is implicit in every one of her novels. The nanny did indeed make a gentle and pleasant life possible. She took almost complete care of the children, including doing their laundry. She gave them their meals and baths, taught them manners, and took them for their outdoor walks. The parents saw their children often, but only when convenient, and only as a sort of luxury, for they were free of the onus of discipline and the drudgery of constant care.

Nasser, Gamal Abdel (1918–1970). President of Egypt in 1956, and instigator of the seizure of the Suez Canal from England. In 1958 he was elected first president of the United Arab Republic, which he had been instrumental in organizing. *See* **Suez.**

Nasticreechia Krorlupppia. From Edward Lear's *Nonsense Botany.* This plant sends forth a long naked scape on the end of which are several paired wormlike excrescences which creep up the stem as the plant matures.

Neck, Earl P. A character from Stella Gibbons' *Cold Comfort Farm.* Neck is a Hollywood producer, and never as bad as you think he's going to be.

Neep. *Scottish dialect.* Turnip.

Neither wife nor maid. . . . From the poem "Elena's Song," by Sir Henry Taylor (1800–1886).

> Quoth tongue of neither maid nor wife
> To heart of neither wife nor maid—
> Lead we not here a jolly life
> Betwixt the shine and shade?

Nel mezzo del cammin di nostra vita. *Italian.* The first line from Dante's *Inferno*: "Midway in the journey of our life. . . . "

Nem. con. *Latin.* Short for *nemine contradicente:* no one contradicting; unanimously.

Nelson, Horatio, Viscount Nelson (1758–1805). English naval commander and hero, who during the Napoleonic War won the Battle of the Nile, the Battle of Copenhagen, and the Battle of Trafalgar, during which he was killed. *See* **England Expects**.

Nelson pension. A stipend to be paid in perpetuity to the descendents of Admiral Nelson. It was terminated by the Labour Government after World War II.

"Never glad confident morning. . . . " From Robert Browning's 1875 poem "The Lost Leader," about a leader who has deserted a cause he had formerly embraced.

> Life's night begins: let him never come back to us!
> There would be doubt, hesitation and pain,
> Forced praise on our part — the glimmer of twilight,
> Never glad confident morning again!

The Newcomes. A novel by William Makepeace Thackeray which appeared in 1855. It is the story of a large family. Some marry unhappily and some lose their money and some do both. Clive Newcome is the central character. His wife fortuitously dies.

Newgate frill. A style of beard in which the lower face is outlined in hair while the face itself is clean-shaven.

New Look. A style introduced by Christian Dior in the spring of 1947. It featured longer flared skirts, narrow shoulders, and a fitted waist.

Mrs. Nicholas Nickleby. From Dickens' *Nicholas Nickleby*. She was a widow, the mother of Nicholas, and rather a nit-wit. Her discourse tended to run on and on, not always very sensibly.

Nickleby, Ralph. The brother of the deceased Nicholas Nickleby, and uncle of young Nicholas. He was a thoroughly unpleasant character, a misanthropic moneylender, a plotter and schemer who betrayed his own family.

Nightmare Abbey. This is both the name of the 1818 novel by Thomas Love Peacock, and the location of all the action, such as it is. It was a grim mansion located on a bare strip of dry ground between the sea and the fens. The owner, Mr. Glowery, chose all his domestics for their gloomy and silent demeanors.

Niobe. From classical myth. Niobe was the daughter of Tantalus, the wife of the king of Thebes, and the mother of fourteen. All the children were destroyed by Latona, whom Niobe had taunted for having a small family of only two. Inconsolable at her loss, Niobe wept until she died, and is considered the personification of bereaved mothers.

Nkrumah, Kwame (1909–1972). Ghanian political leader. In 1957 he was the first prime minister of the independent Commonwealth State of Ghana, and led his country to their status as a Republic in 1960.

Noblesse Oblige. French. Literally, this means an obligation by the nobility to behave generously and responsibly to those less fortunate. We include it here so that we may reflect upon the selflessness with which so many of Barsetshire's landlords carried out their duties. Being an earl, a baronet, a duke, or just a squire carried with it a set of obligations that all visitors to Barsetshire can see is a full-time occupation. In this no doubt we are seeing an idealized version of reality. Landlords could and often did shirk their duties; no law existed to make them conscientious. But in Barsetshire there was no shirking: young Lord Pomfret worked himself to a frazzle, and his more robust wife was always busy as well. Lord Stoke, Mr. Marling, and Sir Edmund Pridham were constantly caring for their property and their tenants and are outstanding examples of *noblesse oblige.*

Noiseless tenour of its way. *See* Thomas Gray.

Nomen et praetera nihil. Latin. A name and nothing more.

No name, no pack drill. If no names are mentioned, the punishment cannot be carried out, as the identity of the offender remains unknown. *See* **Pack drill.**

No, never. If the reader is familiar with Gilbert and Sullivan's *H.M.S. Pinafore,* he, or more likely she, will at once understand the laughter that greeted Sir Cecil Waring's "No, never" when asked by Dr. Gus Perry if he had certain revolting skin symptoms. Here is an excerpt from the exchange in *Pinafore:*

> CAPTAIN: I am never known to quail
> At the fury of a gale,
> And I'm never, never sick at sea!
> ALL: What, never?
> CAPTAIN: No, never!
> ALL: What, *never?*
> CAPTAIN: Hardly ever!
> ALL: He's hardly ever sick at sea!

"No bigod nonsense about her." From Dickens' *Little Dorrit.* A remark made by Edmund Sparkler (*q.v.*) about Fanny Dorrit. As if he were such a judge of nonsense—he was pretty chuckle-headed himself.

Non più andrai. . . . A bouncy aria from Mozart's *Marriage of Figaro.* You will recall that Modestine was humming it at the end of *August Folly.* The words were addressed to Gunnar, but perhaps they are a happy summary of the events that occurred that week at Lamb's Piece.

Non più andrai, far fallone amoroso,	No more, you amorous butterfly,
Notte e giorno d'intorno girando,	Will you go fluttering around night and day,
Delle belle turbando il riposo,	Disturbing the peace of every maid,
Narcisetto, Adoncino d'amor.	You pocket Narcissus, you Adonis of love.

Norna of the Fitful Head. From Scott's *The Pirate*. Norna of the Fitful Head was usually known as Ulla Troil. She was a half-crazed woman who, despite having psychic and magical powers, was still unable to tell which of two of the main characters was her son.

Mrs. Norris. A character from Jane Austen's *Mansfield Park*. Mrs. Norris was far, far worse than Mrs. Tebben. Mrs. Norris was vain, snobbish, hypocritical, officious, and deeply unkind.

Nothing common or mean/Upon that memorable screen. Thus AT describes the television coverage of the coronation of Elizabeth II. She has made use of these words of Andrew Marvell (1621-1678) in his poem *Upon Cromwell's Return from Ireland*.

> He nothing common did or mean
> Upon that memorable scene.

"Nous avons changé tout cela." *French*. We have changed all that.

"Now folds the lily all her sweetness up. . . . " These lines are from Tennyson's *The Princess* and are the most open and frank avowal of sexual love in the annals of Barsetshire. They are said by Anne Fielding to Robin Dale shortly before their wedding.

> Now lies the Earth all Danaë to the stars,
> And all thy heart lies open unto me.
>
> Now slides the silent meteor on, and leaves
> A shining furrow, as thy thoughts in me.
>
> Now folds the lily all her sweetness up,
> And slips into the bosom of the lake.
> So fold thyself, my dearest, thou, and slip
> Into my bosom and be lost in me.

"Now this wild thing is wedded. . . . " *See **Love in the Valley**.*

Lord Nuffield.   William Richard Morris, 1ˢᵗ Viscount Nuffield (1877–1963). Remember the MG? Lord Nuffield, when he was still William Morris (not to be confused with the arts-and-crafts William Morris), started the creatively named Morris Group, which developed mass-produced and inexpensive autos at Cowley, in Oxford. The Morris Group has had significant success.

Nunc dimittis. . . . Latin. The full line is *Nunc dimittis servum tuum, Domine, secundum verbum tuum in pace.* Lord, now lettest thou thy servant depart in peace: according to thy word.

Nupkins, George. A character from Dickens' *Pickwick Papers*. Mr. Nupkins was the mayor of Ipswich, and as grand a personage as could be seen for miles around. He referred all decisions from the bench to his clerk, who was an imposter, and, failing that, to his wife. It was Mr. Nupkins who adjudicated in the noisy matter of Miss Witherfield's complaint against Mr. Pickwick, which was conducted at the mayoral residence. The crowd, shut out, kicked at the gate and rang the bell for an hour afterwards. *See* **Magnus, Peter.**

Nuremburg Trials. Trials held in Nuremburg, Germany, in 1945, to assess guilt and mete out punishment to the European war criminals after World War II.

But how much ought one to ask? I mean what I'd like to ask—
I mean what I've have liked to ask before the election—was
Please kill all the government. Perhaps that isn't a real prayer?
—Delia Grant

Obiter dicta. *Latin.* Incidental or offhand remarks.

Ochiltree, Edie. A character from Scott's *The Antiquary*. Ochiltree was the bedesman of Joathan Oldman, The antiquary. As a bedesman, Ochiltree was maintained by the charity of Oldbuck and in theory was expected to say prayers for him. He was a kindly man, and did say the prayers, but also cleverly expressed his views which were not calculated to be pleasing.

Odi et amo. *Latin.* I hate and I love. Catullus.

Offices. That part of a house in which servants' tasks are carried out, such as the kitchen, pantry, scullery, laundry, stillroom, or stables.

O fortunatos nimium, sua si bona norint. *Latin.* O how happy they, if they but knew their blessings.

Often I think were this wild thing wedded . . . " See *Love in the Valley*.

Old boy, old girl. An alumnus or alumna, usually of a public school.

Old Moore. An astrologer named Francis Moore (1657–1714). He began publishing *Old Moore's Almanac.* in 1700. It is still being published.

Old Mother Slipper Slopper. A character in the folk song *The Fox*. The words were known as a nursery rhyme in the eighteenth century, and were set to music in print in a Scottish publication in 1832.

"The old order changeth . . . " A line from Tennyson's *The Passing of Arthur*.

> And slowly answer'd Arthur from the barge:
> 'The old order changeth, yielding place to new,
> And God fulfils himself in many ways,
> Lest one good custom should corrupt the world.
> Comfort thyself; what comfort is in me?

Old person of Sheen. A limerick by Edward Lear.

> There was an Old Person of Sheen,
> Whose expression was calm and serene;
> He sate in the water, and drank bottled porter,
> That placid Old Person of Sheen.

"O love, O fire!" A line from Tennyson's poem "Fatima." This is the third of six verses:

> Last night, when some one spoke his name,
> From my swift blood that went and came
> A thousand little shafts of flame
> Were shiver'd in my narrow frame.
> O Love, O fire! Once he drew
>   With one long kiss my whole soul thro'
>   My lips, as sunlight drinketh dew.

Ombra mai fu. *Italian.* Shadow never dying.

Omphale. In Greek myth, she was the original henpecker. She was quite masculine, and while Hercules was enslaved to her she wore his lion skin and he was made to wear her garments.

"Oh, Naughty Naughty One Mayfair." See **Arcadians.**

"One must not look into people's eyes." This is based on Poem XV in *A Shropshire Lad,* by A. E. Housman. There are two verses; here is the first:

> Look not in my eyes, for fear
>   They mirror the true sight I see,
> And there you find your face too clear
>   And love it and be lost like me.
> One the long nights through must lie
>   Spent in star-defeated sighs,
> But why should you as well as I
>   Perish? gaze not in my eyes.

One of Our Conquerors. A novel by George Meredith, published in 1897. In *The Headmistress* Mr. Carton speaks of Sam Adams as "One of our Conquerors"—a rather dark comparison. The hero of Meredith's novel, Victor Radnor, rose from obscurity to have the appearance of worldly success, in which he is like Sam Adams. But Radnor married for money, was living with a woman not legally his wife, his daughter was illegitimate—his life was laid on a foundation of quicksand, and he died a lunatic.

Onesiphorus. (On.e.SIF.o.rus) Onesiphorus appears in II Timothy, I:16: "The Lord give mercy unto the house of Onesiphorus; for he oft refreshed me, and was not ashamed of my chain."

"One word is too often profaned . . . " First line and title of a poem by Percy Bysshe Shelley, written in 1821. This is the first of two verses:

> One word is too often profaned
>   For me to profane it,
> One feeling to falsely disdain'd
>   For thee to disdain it.
> One hope is too like despair
>   For prudence to smother,
> And Pity from thee more dear
>   Than that from another.

"Only the actions of the just . . . " From a poem, "Death the Leveller," by James Shirley (1596–1666)

The garlands wither on your brow;
    Then boast no more your mighty deeds!
Upon Death's purple alter now
    See where the victor-victim bleeds.
        Your heads must come
        To the cold tomb:
Only the actions of the just
Smell sweet and blossom in their dust.

Oratio obliqua. *Latin.* Indirect speech.

Oratio recta. *Latin.* Correct or proper speech.

Orlando. A character from Shakespeare's *As You Like It. See* **Rosalind.**

Oscar. This refers to an exchange between J.M. Whistler and his younger friend, Oscar Wilde. Although Wilde was clever, he admired Whistler and was accused of stealing witticisms from him. On one occasion when Whistler had said something clever Wilde said, "I wish I'd said that," to which Whistler replied, "You will, Oscar, you will."

O tempi passati! *Latin.* O times past!

Othello and Desdemona. Characters from Shakespeare's play *Othello.* Othello, a renowned general, wooed Desdemona by telling her stories of his travels. When Iago contrived to make Othello jealous, and further contrived proof of Desdemona's infidelity, Othello smothered her.

Others abide our question. . . a line from Matthew Arnold's poem "Shakespeare".

Others abide our question. Thou art free.
We ask and ask: Thou smilest and art still,
Out-topping knowledge.

Don Ottavio, etc. Characters from Mozart's opera *Don Giovanni.* Donna Anna and Donna Elvira have both suffered from Don Giovanni's behavior, but Donna Elvira has appeared at a small supper party given by the Don to beg him to save himself before it is too late. As she leaves, she encounters the statue of Donna Anna's father, whom Don Giovanni had killed in a sword fight. The statue, miraculously come to life, had been invited to the dinner, but when it appears the servant, Leporello, trembling with fright, tries to hide under the table. When Giovanni refuses any repentance, the statue grasps him by the hand, lets go, and sinks into the floor as flames shoot up. With a horrifying cry Don Giovanni is enveloped in flames and the scene ends. An epilogue follows, in which Don Ottavio and his betrothed, Donna Anna, appear accompanied by Donna Elvira and three other characters. They sing a sextet the gist of which is that Don Giovanni got what he deserved.

Overall. A loose-fitting tunic or smock worn over other clothes to protect them. A wrap-around apron.

Oxford frame. A picture frame in which the sides extend slightly beyond the corners, in some cases carved to give the impression of small branches crossed and bound.

Thought all you publishers drank like fishes. You do publish, don't you? I mean books and so on.
— Old Lord Pomfret

P. Slang. Short for pious.

Pack drill. A form of military punishment. The offender must march for a given time in full military pack: uniform, weapons, ammunition, knapsack, and overcoat. In everyday speech, "no pack drill" meant nothing formal or complicated, perhaps something with no strings attached.

Palladian. A style of architecture imported to England in the 18th century from Italy, where it was developed by Andrea Palladio a hundred years earlier. It is characterized by "harmonic proportions" and gracefully repeated simple symmetrical elements. Palladian windows have three openings, the central one larger than the other two and surmounted by an arch.

Pardiggle, Mrs. From Dickens' *Bleak House*. Mrs. Pardiggle was the formidably philanthropic neighbor of Mr. Jarndyce. She was a bully, first of all to her five young sons, and secondly to the neighboring poor, whom she would badger about going to church while overlooking their real needs. She was quite pleased with all her efforts and never tired of telling about them.

Paris. From classical mythology. A golden apple was to be awarded to the fairest among three fair goddesses, Hera, Athena, and Aphrodite. A comely shepherd, Paris, was invited to be the judge. Each goddess tried to bribe him to choose in her favor: Hera offered him power, Athena offered him military prowess, and Aphrodite promised him a beautiful woman as his wife. Not surprisingly Paris chose Aphrodite, instantly making powerful enemies of Hera and Athena. He took Aphrodite away to Sparta were they were guests of King Menelaus and his wife Helen. You can probably see what is coming: Aphrodite helped Paris to win the love of Helen and take her away to Troy—and the Trojan war had been ignited. A thousand ships were launched. Paris and Helen were married in Troy, which makes her a bigamist. Paris was killed during the combat and Helen and Menelaus were reunited after Troy fell, so things worked out very nicely at least for some of them.

Paris, Count. From *Romeo and Juliet*. Count Paris was a kinsman of Prince Escalus. In Act I, scene ii, Paris says of the thirteen-year-old Juliet, "Younger than she are happy mothers made."

Partington, Mrs. During a great storm at Sidmouth in 1824, Mrs. Partington tried to keep the Atlantic out of her house with a mop; that at any rate was the story making the papers. It was included in a speech by Sydney Smith in which he compared the efforts of the House of Lords to stop the reform bill to Mrs. Partington's attempt with the mop.

Patch-and-powder dramas. Restoration drama, in which the actors wore small silk patches as beauty spots on their faces or (if female) bosoms, and powder on their faces and wigs.

Patmore, Coventry (1823–1896). A poet associated with the Pre-Raphaelites. Patmore's poetry manifested all the aspects of Victorian sentimentality, although some of his later work transcended it. His most famous work is *The Angel in the House*, a tribute in four volumes to married love. (AT's *The Demon in the House* is a take-off on this title.) Patmore's tribute was inspired by his first wife Emily, who died in 1862, leaving him with six children. "The Azalea" refers to her death. He married twice again; his third wife survived him.

Peacockian vein. A reference to Thomas Love Peacock (1785–1866). He was the author of *Nightmare Abbey, Crotchet Castle, Headlong Hall,* and several other novels. Many are satirical and include long scenes in which several men, each a caricature of a poet, writer, or thinker of the day, sit drinking and discussing weighty issues.

Pebbledash. Also known as roughcast, pebbledash is an exterior finish for houses. It is made by throwing pebbles at a coating of wet cement where they stick and give a rough finish.

Pecksniff, Seth. From Dickens' *Martin Chuzzlewit.* Pecksniff was an architect and a treacherous hypocrite, who took Martin as a pupil and did everything he could to bring about his ruin. He was at last exposed and ended his career as a writer of begging letters.

Peer. A member of the titled nobility. Dukes, marquises, earls, and barons are entitled to sit in the House of Lords; baronets and knights are not.

Pelagianism. Belief in the ideas of the British monk Pelagius (c.360–c.420), who rejected the concepts of original sin and predestination.

Pelléas and Mélisande. A play by Maurice Maeterlinck adapted for opera by Claude Debussy. It is a legend of a very young woman, Mélisande, married to a much older man, Golaud. Golaud has a handsome younger half-brother, Pelléas. Inevitably, Pelléas and Mélisande fall in love and just as inevitably both end up being killed by Golaud.

Pendennis. A novel by Thackeray, published in 1850. It is the coming-of-age story of young Arthur Pendennis and all his misguided attachments before he finally marries a suitable young woman and realizes his true vocation as a writer. His uncle is Major Pendennis, an unmarried and worldly gentleman who outlived his social set and realized, almost, that he was lonely.

Percy, Sir Henry. Known as Harry Hotspur for his enthusiasm for battle—*see* **Douglas**. The earl referred to by AT in *Love among the Ruins*, chapter 7, would have been Sir Henry's father.

"Perhaps it was right to dissemble your love, but—why did you kick me downstairs?" A line from the play *The Panel,* by John Philip Kemble (1757–1823). Kemble was primarily an actor; later he became a manager of Covent Garden Theatre. *The Panel* was an adaptation of a play by Isaac Bickerstaff entitled *'Tis Well It's No Worse.* Kemble was the brother of the famous actress Sarah Siddons.

Peri. A creature from Persian Myth. A female sprite or fairy, she was originally a mischief-maker who could be blamed for anything that went wrong. She evolved into a plurality of gentle loving spirits who directed fallen souls into heaven.

The Periwinkle Girl. The title of one of the Bab Ballads by W.S. Gilbert. The periwinkle girl was quite a beauty; her favors were sought by two dukes and an earl. Of its twenty-one verses, we quote these.

Both high and low and great and small
    Fell prostrate at her tootsies,
They all were noblemen, and all
    Had balances at COUTTS'S.

Dukes with the lovely maiden dealt,
    DUKE BAILEY and DUKE HUMPHREY,
Who ate her periwinkles till they felt
    Exceedingly uncomfy.

DUKE BAILEY greatest wealth computes,
    And sticks, they say at no-thing,
He wears a pair of golden boots
    And silver underclothing.

DUKE HUMPHREY, as I understand,
    Though mentally acuter,
His boots are only silver, and
    His underclothing pewter.

A third adorer had the girl,
    A man of lowly station —
A miserable grov'ling Earl
    Besought her approbation.

This humble cad she did refuse
    With much contempt and loathing,
He wore a pair of leather shoes
    And cambric underclothing!

. . . .

Her views of earldoms and their lot.
    All underwent expansion —
Come, Virtue in an earldom's cot!
    Go, Vice in ducal mansion!

Perpetual Curate. The equivalent of a vicar.

Perrine et le pot au lait. *French.* Perrine and the milk pail. This seems to refer to the fable of the farmer's daughter who was carrying a pail of milk on her head and making far-reaching plans for what she would do with the money it would bring—when the bucket slipped and fell. The milk ran into the ground and her dreams vanished with it.

Peter Ibbetson. A novel by George Du Maurier, published in 1891. It is the story of a man, the Peter Ibbetson of the title, whose life is spent in a love affair that occurs in his dreams. What is interesting to us about this novel is that it is the source of the Harcourt family. The Duke of Towers (the family name is Harcourt) is transplanted directly into Barsetshire at the end of *A Double Affair.* In *Peter Ibbetson* the duke is a dissolute fellow who dies fairly young. He had come into the title unexpectedly after a number of deaths and was unable to cope sensibly with its privileges and responsibilities. His wife was Peter's childhood sweetheart, Mimsey Seraskier. They were the parents of one son, a mindless cripple who died at an early age. The current duke's father came into the title when that young duke died, as is more or less explained in *Love at All Ages.*

Petersham ribbon. A heavy gros-grain silk ribbon used for decorative trim or for waistbands.

Petra. An historic site in southwest Jordan, a city carved into the colored rock walls of a deep gorge. It was inhabited for several centuries before going into decline in the 7th century. By the 12th century it was used only as a way-station by those passing through. Many structures in Petra have the façades of buildings but are really only elaborate tombs.

Petruchio. From Shakespeare's *Taming of the Shrew*. Petruchio is the husband of the ill-tempered Katerina, whom he has married for her dowry. By some clever ploys he brings her to loving submission.

Philips, Stephen (1864–1915). A poet and playwright. His most successful play was *Paolo and Francesca*, performed in 1902.

Phantastes. An allegorical fantasy for adults by Scottish author George Macdonald (1824–1905). It involves a search for the spirit of the earth, and is full of fairies, sprites, and shadows.

Philosopher's stone. A substance in which alchemists believed, and for which they searched over the centuries. It was supposed to enable the conversion of base metals to gold. This, alas, never happened, but along the way much was discovered about chemistry and physics.

Piano nobile. Italian. Noble level. It is that floor of a house containing the principal reception rooms. It has higher ceilings than the floors below or above.

Pickwick's trial scene. *See* **Bardell vs. Pickwick.**

The Pilgrim's Progress. A long allegory by John Bunyan about the difficulties and rewards of Christian life—Christian is the name of the pilgrim who is the central figure. The book was enormously popular, was translated into a hundred languages, and was part of every child's life up to the end of the 19th Century. Many of the landmarks of the pilgrimage have passed into the general culture, such as the Slough of Despond, Vanity Fair, and the Celestial City. In a sequel to the first book Bunyan wrote of the similar pilgrimage made by Christian's wife Christianna.

"Piljian's projess of a mortal wale. . . ." Words uttered by Mrs. Gamp, *q.v.* She meant pilgrim's progress, of course.

Pinch, Tom. A character from Dickens' *Martin Chuzzlewit.* Tom was the assistant of Mr. Pecksniff, the Salisbury architect and surveyor. Tom was of an indeterminate age, stooped and clumsy, bald and thin, with shrunken clothing. But his character had the beauty lacking in his person. He was loyal, honest and hard-working, sweet, mild, and gentle. Tom and his sister Ruth set up housekeeping together after he left Mr. Pecksniff. This is why they were buying beefsteak together and being advised that "Meat must be humored, not drove."

Pinero, Sir Arthur (1855–1934). English playwright, author of comedies and dramas on the theme of the double standard for men and women, and innovator of a more modern style of drama. His well-known plays include *Lady Bountiful* (1891), *The Second Mrs Tanqueray* (1893), and *Trelawny of the 'Wells'* (1898).

Pip emma. *Post meridian*, or after noon.

Piquet. A card game for two players, with variations for three and four, using a deck of 32 cards. It is five hundred years old, and has always been popular in Europe.

"Pity his ignorance and despise him." A remark made by Fanny Squeers in Dickens' *Nicholas Nickleby*. She was referring to Nicholas in a letter to her uncle; Nicholas had not only been uninterested in certain overtures made by Fanny, he had attacked and beaten her father.

Pleonasm. A redundancy, especially of words.

Plimsoll line. A line on the side of a ship above which the ship should never sink, because it indicates the maximum load the ship can safely carry. It is named for its sponsor, Samuel Plimsoll (1824–1898), a reformer interested in marine matters who was instrumental in the passage of the Merchant Shipping Act of 1876, at which time a load-line, quickly dubbed the Plimsoll line, became mandatory.

Plornish, Mr. From Dickens' *Little Dorrit*. A plasterer who lived in Bleeding Heart Yard, Mr. Plornish was capable of so distorting a sentence as to wring all communication from it.

Plum-pudding Flea. The flea is the subject of a little verse contained within "The History of the Seven Families of Lake Pipple Popple," by Edward Lear. It is quoted in *Miss Bunting*, near the end of chapter 2. But if that is not the book you are reading, here it is:

> Plum-pudding Flea,
> Plum-pudding Flea,
> Wherever you be,
> O come to our tree,
> And listen, O listen, O listen to me!

The flea in the illustration is perfectly round, with one long stick of a leg, a bird-looking head, and two tiny wings.

Podsnap, John. From Dickens. A character from *Our Mutual Friend* who was above all things self-satisfied. He had both inherited and married a comfortable fortune, and there could be no greater reason for self-satisfaction than that. He was the father of Georgianna Podsnap, described by Dickens as a "young rocking-horse," and by her father as a "young person."

Poe story. The story referred to in *Love at All Ages* in the luncheon conversation between Giles Foster and Mrs. Morland is "The Facts in the Case of M. Waldemar." The narrator describes an attempt to mesmerise M. Waldemar at the very point of death. This was done. A further experiment to revive M. Waldemar seven months later had the unsatisfactory result described by Mrs. Morland.

Policy. A walled, planted, or otherwise embellished part of an estate.

Porridge's. A stand-in for Claridge's, a London hotel famous for its ability to provide discreet service to the most discriminating tastes, which is why it is patronized by members of the royal family.

Porthos. From Alexandre Dumas. Porthos was one of the *Three Musketeers*, the other two being Athos and Aramis. Porthos was a dashing, swashbuckling fellow, much admired by his servant Mousqueton.

Pose plastique. French. A pose that is taken by a costumed actor. The pose is to illustrate a figure from history, the classics, or a celebrity of the day.

Post hoc ergo propter hoc. Latin. After which therefore because of which. A useful piece of logic, but of course not always true—in fact it is one of the major fallacies.

The Potteries. The six Staffordshire towns that have been famous for the production of pottery and fine china. They were Hanley, Longton, Fenton, Burslem, Tunstall, and Stoke-on-Trent. In 1910 all were incorporated into Stoke-on-Trent. Burslem was the birthplace of Josiah Wedgewood.

Prebendary. A cleric with the title of canon, but who does not get the land or stipend formerly granted.

Precentor. The cleric in charge of music at a cathedral.

Prefect. A student monitor.

Preferment. Any post, but usually an ecclesiastical one, which puts the occupant in a position to be noticed and advanced.

Premier cru. *French.* First growth, said of French wine. It indicates a good but not a great wine.

Present. Usually seen as a past participle, "presented." It refers to the very formal ritual of being presented at court in St. James Palace. It was part of "coming out" for young women, although young men and older people of both sexes could be presented.

Press. A large cupboard with shelves, often made to fit into a recess in the wall.

The Princess. A seventy-two page narrative poem by Tennyson, published in 1847. It is a medley containing several famous "song" sections. In this romantic fantasy of long ago, Ida, the princess, and an early feminist, has made a vow not to marry. But inevitably she does. Gilbert and Sullivan satirized this story in their operetta *Princess Ida.*

Princess Ida. *See* above. Gilbert and Sullivan's operetta was first performed in 1884.

Princesse Lointaine. *French.* A faraway princess. In general usage the term refers to a remote and perhaps entirely unobtainable love.

The Prisoner of Zenda. A novel by Anthony Hope, published in 1894. The swashbuckling story involves the hero, Rudolph Rassendyll, in a plot to save the King of Ruritania from an attempted coup.

"Proie sanglante d'une fière et mâle rage,/ Dieu châtré des chrétians, je crache à ton visage." *French.* "Bloody prey of a fierce and manly fury, /God castrated by Christians, I spit in your face." *Châtre* means to castrate, spay, or neuter; *châtié* is punished or chastised.

"Proputty, proputty, proputty. . . . " An often-repeated line in Tennyson's *Northern Farmer, New Style.* The "proputty" is property. Here is the first verse.

> Dosn't thou 'ear my 'erse's legs, as they canters awaäy?
> Proputty, proputty, proputty — that's what I 'ears 'em saäy.
> Proputty, proputty, proputty — Sam, thou's an ass for thy païns;
> Theer's moor sense i' one o' 'is legs, nor in all thy braïns.

Proteus. According to Greek legend, Proteus was Neptune's herdsman. He was able to change his shape and is thus identified with versatility.

Proust, Marcel (1871–1922). Renowned French author best known for the seven-part novel cycle *A la re cherche du temps perdu,* translated as *Remembrance of Things Past,* or more recently as *In Search of Lost Time.*

Puggaree. A type of headgear imported from India; the word is related to the word for turban. It is a type of light scarf wound around a topee or other hat to protect the wearer from the sun and blowing sand; or, by extension, any similar headgear. Also spelled puggree or puggry.

Pumblechook, Mr. From Dickens' *Great Expectations.* He was the uncle of Pip's brother-in-law, Joe Gargery, and as such felt free to criticize Pip, to remind him that he was a varmint that his sister had brought up by hand, and to catechize him on mathematical concepts. When Pip came unexpectedly into property, Uncle Pumblechook could not be kind enough; he became obsequious and begged over and over to shake hands, saying, "May I? *May* I shake your hand?"

Punch, Mr. The main character in the famous puppet drama, *Punch and Judy.* This is a highly eventful and allegorical story involving beatings, death, and destruction. Jealous of the attention paid his and Judy's babe-in-arms , Mr. Punch kills it, whereupon Judy beats him and he retaliates by killing her as well as the baby. The plot thickens when Punch goes to prison, escapes, and manages to engage and defeat Disease, Ennui, Death, all in disguises, and the Devil. In the end he is hanged after all, in some versions; in others, it is the hangman who is hanged. As you can see this show makes inspiring entertainment for children, especially at Christmas.

Punch. English humor magazine which as been published weekly since 1841.

We all know the false heartiness we put on when we have a smile on our lips and great annoyance in our hearts on account of our mothers' behavior.
— Angela Thirkell

Quangle-Wangle. One of the creations of Edward Lear. In the story of "The Four Little Children Who Went Round the World," the Quangle-Wangle was the cook on their large boat. There were various adventures, and after one awful set-to "the Quangle-Wangle's foot was so knocked about that he had to sit with his head in his slipper for at least a week."

Quantocks. A range of hills in northwest Somerset. The highest has an altitude of 1,262 feet.

Quarterdeck. This stands for the ship's officers and the admiral, if he's aboard. For the academically inclined among our readers, this is an example of metonymy.

Queen Victoria's coronation, a book about, by someone with a name like Turtle. A reference to AT's own *Coronantion Summer*, a fictionalized account of the coronation of 1838. The book is well researched and highly recommended.

Quickly, Dame. A character in Shakespeare's *Henry IV*, parts I and II, and *The Merry Wives of Windsor*. Usually known as Mistress Quickly, she is semi-respectable as the hostess of the Boar's Head Tavern in Eastcheap. She is a comic character, pushful, noisy, and canny.

Qui facit per alium facit per se. Latin. He who acts through another does the deed himself.

Quinquegesima Sunday. The Sunday before Lent, from the Latin word for fiftieth.

Quis custodiet ipsos custodes? Latin. Who will guard the guards? From Juvenal's *Satires*.

*Now a rain-butt, she's like a man's innards. Needs filling, she
does. It stands to reason if a man's innards aren't filled that
man's no use, and no more is a rain-butt.*

— Jim Snow

Rabbi Ben Ezra. A poem by Robert Browning. There are thirty-one verses; this is the first.

> Grow old along with me!
> The best is yet to be,
> The last of life, for which the first was made:
> Our times are in His hand
> Who saith "A whole I planned,
> Youth shows but half; trust God; see all, nor be afraid!"

Race. *French.* Family; "one of us."

Rag. To tease; as noun, a joke or stunt.

Ragnarok. From Scandinavian mythology. It equates to the *Gotterdamerung* or Twilight of the Gods, when all creation was destroyed and a peaceful new world was born.

Ramp. Slang. A racket; a scam; a dishonest arrangement.

Rape of Europa. *See* **Europa.**

Rating. A naval term referring to an enlisted man or able-bodied seaman.

Rationing. A complex system of allocating food and goods in times of crisis. During World War II, there was rationing in England, Germany, the Soviet Union, and the United States. In England, rationing continued from 1940 until 1954. The purpose was to control access to scarce goods, to ensure equitable distribution, to provide industry with food and raw materials for military priorities, and to control prices. Nearly all food was rationed for "points," the value of which changed with circumstances such as availability and the time of year. The details are voluminous, but Thirkell's pared-down descriptions give a good idea. With eggs at times rationed at one per week per person, it is easy to see why Joyce Smith made such an effort to annex a chicken or two for herself.

Ravenshoe. A novel by Henry Kingsley, published in 1862. Probably the best known of his twenty-one novels, it features a hero, Charles Ravenshoe, who is the embodiment of all that Kingsley considered ideal in the English gentleman. Lord Saltire is an older friend of the family.

The readiness is all. From *Hamlet*, Act 5, scene 2:

> HORATIO. If your mind dislikes any thing, obey it: I will forestal their repair hither, and say you are not fit.

> HAMLET. Not a whit, we defy augury: there's a special providence in the fall of a sparrow. If it be now, 'tis not to come; if it be not to come, it will be now; if it be not now, yet it will come: the readiness is all: since no man has aught of what he leaves, what is't to leave betimes? Let be.

Rector. A parish priest. Because both the church and the parish were in many cases the property of one person or body, that person or body had a right to the tithes. A rector got all the tithes, while a vicar, who represented the rector, had to share the tithes with the owner of the property.

Reculer pour mieux sauter. French. Moving back the better to jump ahead.

Redbrick. This refers to all the new universities; it may even, depending on the usage, refer to any university other than Oxford or Cambridge. In some circles, including that of our Barsetshire friends, it is pejorative, implying inferior facilities, instruction and social milieu.

The Rehearsal. A farce attributed partially to George Villiers, written around 1672. It spoofs the great tragic dramas of the time but possibly what was intended, when this play was mentioned in *Love at All Ages* in reference to Lord Burleigh's nod, was the rehearsal scene in Sheridan's *The Critic*. See **Burleigh.**

Rejected Addresses. In 1812, when its managers were preparing an opening celebration for the new Drury Lane Theatre, they announced a competition for an inaugural address. James and Horatio Smith answered the call with several entries, each purporting to be from a well-known writer of the day: Wordsworth, Byron, Coleridge, and Sir Walter Scott were among them. Some of these were better than others, but all were good, and were collected and published that year as *Rejected Addresses.*

Rennie, John (1761–1821). A Scottish engineer famous as a bridge-builder and designer of dockyards. One of his pupils built the bridge at Northbridge.

Repton, Humphrey (1752–1818). A landscape architect of the Regency period.

Rere-. A prefix (pronounced *rear*) meaning subsequent or additional. AT uses it creatively, as in rere-tea, meaning a second tea taken by someone who has already had a first one.

"The rest to some faint meaning made pretence." A line from John Dryden's *Mac Flecknoe*, published in 1682.

> The rest to some faint meaning made pretense,
> But Shadwell never deviates into sense.
> Some beams of wit on other souls may fall,
> Strike through and make a lucid interval;
> But Shadwell's genuine night admits no ray,
> His rising fog prevails upon the day.

The Revenge. See **"Ship after ship. . . . "**

Revelation. In the book of Revelation a reference is made to no more sea. This is Revelation 21: I.

> And I saw a new heaven and a new earth: for the first heaven
> and the first earth were passed away; and there was no more sea.

Richard III; Richard Crookback. The novel advancing arguments exonerating Richard III from arranging the murder of his nephews is *The Daughter of Time*, by Josephine Tey, *q.v.* Using contemporary sources, Tey shows how and why the blackening of his reputation occurred.

Ride. A wide swath cut in woodlands to provide space for horses to go two or three abreast.

Riderhood, Miss Pleasant. From Dickens' *Our Mutual Friend.* She was the daughter of the disreputable boatman Rogue Riderhood, and to add to her woes she had hair that refused to stay in a tidy knot. It slipped down at the least bit of excitement.

Riding the whirlwind. A phrase from *The Campaign*, by Joseph Addison.

> And, pleased the Almighty's orders to perform,
> Rides in the whirlwind and directs the storm.

Risorgimento. *Italian.* Literally, resurrection. It applies to a revival of learning in Italy in the 14th and 15th centuries. Also it may refer to the resurgence of Italian nationalism in the 1860's.

R.L.S. Robert Louis Stevenson (1850–1894), the original owner of a donkey named Modestine, which, or whom, he tells about in *Travels with a Donkey in the Cevennes*, written in 1879. He is the author of *Treasure Island, Kidnapped, The Black Arrow*, and *A Child's Garden of Verses.*

Roaring girl. The original of this phrase was Roaring Boys, used to describe the rowdy young men of the 17th century. Then in 1611 Dekken and Middleton wrote a play called *The Roaring Girle.* Its heroine was Moll Cut-Purse, who used her sword in self-defense.

Robinson, Heath (1872–1944). English illustrator and cartoonist. Many of his cartoons depict fanciful contraptions somewhat along the lines of a Rube Goldberg creation.

Ronsard, Pierre de (1524–1585). French poet. His verse consisted primarily of poems of love. Ronsard's work passed out of favor, but was revived with the romantic movement of the late 18th and early 19th centuries. The 6th earl of Pomfret had translated one of these sonnet cycles.

Room. The housekeeper's room, a place for high-level meetings and occasional meals of the upper servants.

Mr. Root and Mr Crow. Racine and Corneille. Naso and Locusta are the Latin for nose and locust or crab.

Rosalind. A character from Shakespeare's *As You Like It.* Rosalind, dressed as a young man, meets her lover in the Forest of Arden. As is usual in such circumstances, he cannot penetrate her disguise, but enjoys some badinage on the subject of time. Rosalind opines that time trots hard for a bride between the date of her engagement and the wedding; it ambles for a priest who has no Latin, because he need not study. And, she says, time gallops for the thief between his sentencing and its execution but does not move at all for lawyers during vacations because they are asleep.

Rumours of Peace. A takeoff on Matthew 24:6: "And ye shall hear of wars and rumours of wars: See that ye be not troubled: for all these things must come to pass, but the end is not yet."

Rum-ti-Foo. One of the Bab Ballads, by W.S. Gilbert. The missionary Bishop of Rum-ti-Foo was loved by his flock, who objected to his temporary return to England for a Synod meeting:

> His flock, I've often heard him tell,
> (His name was PETER) loved him well,
> And summoned by the sound of bell,
>   In crowds together came.
> "Oh, Massa, why you go away?
> Oh, Massa PETER, please to stay."
> (They called him PETER, people say,
>   Because it was his name.)
> . . . .
> Another game the dancer planned —
>   "Just take your ankle in your hand,
> And try, my lord, if you can stand —
>   Your body stiff and stark.
> If, when revisiting your see,
> You learnt to hop on shore — like me —
> The novelty would striking be,
>   And must attract remark."

Rusticated. To be suspended from university for a prescribed time and then readmitted.

Mustn't be sick in front of ladies.
— Lord Stoke

St. John Ambulance Brigade. Volunteers providing nursing care or first aid to patients at home, in various facilities, or on a standby basis at public events.

Sachet. In a rather obsolete meaning, a sachet is a (perhaps padded) wallet or, by extension, folder.

Sack. A sort of dry sherry.

Sacré tas d'imbéciles. *French.* Holy heap of imbeciles.

Sal volatile. (sal vo-LA-ti-lay) A mixture of ammonium carbonate in alcohol and ammonia water, in varying combinations. It was highly aromatic and was used to revive the faint. Smelling salts.

Sampson, George. The betrothed of the irrepressible Lavinia Wilfer in Dickens' *Our Mutual Friend.* George, who was usually something of a cipher, found himself in the midst of a family scene of seismic proportions. When Lavinia went into hysterics he delivered his greatest line, addressed to her truly horrible mother: "Demon— with the highest respect to you—behold your work!"

Sanford, Harry. A character from *The History of Sanford and Merton,* by Thomas Day (1748–1789). It is a moralistic but popular children's book about the rich and unpleasant Tommy Merton, and the poor but sterling farmer's son, Harry Sanford. Their tutor, Mr. Barlow, one of those rare inspired teachers, helps them learn and grow.

Sandhurst. The Royal Military Academy in Sandhurst, Berkshire.

Sarah Siddons (1755–1831). A British actress, famous for her lovely voice and great success in tragic roles.

Sartor Resartus. The Latin title means "the tailor re-tailored." It is a work by Thomas Carlyle published in 1834, and inspired by the German Romanticism then current. The argument is that all one knows of life intellectually or spiritually is a form of "clothes" and is thus temporary. The text is full of exclamation points and capital letters; there are extravagant prophecies, satiric passages, and addresses to the reader. Few could be surprised that a boy of seventeen would use the book as a football.

Sartre, Jean-Paul (1905–1980). French novelist, political activist, and philosopher; he was the leader of Existentialism in France, expounded in such books as *L'Être et le Néant* (*Being and Nothingness*). He also wrote several relentlessly grim novels and plays, the titles of which indicate their general themes: *La Nausée* (*Nausea*), *Les Mains Sales* (*Dirty Hands*), and *Huis Clos* (*No Exit*).

Sassenach. A somewhat pejorative Scottish term for the English.

Sauf contre-ordre. *French.* Unless told otherwise.

Savoir-vivre. *French.* Literally "how to live." Tact or good manners.

Savoy Hill. The first studios of the BBC were located here in 1922, and Savoy Hill remained the headquarters of the BBC until 1932.

Sawyer, Bob. From Dickens, a character in *The Pickwick Papers.* Sam is a medical student suffering from an excess of *joie de vivre.* He is brash, irresponsible, and well on his way to being an alcoholic.

Sbirri. Italian police officers.

Scenes of Clerical Life. Three long stories by George Eliot, published in 1858. All have to do with difficulties faced by three different clergymen. Their titles are *Amos Barton, Mr. Gilfil's Love Story,* and *Janet's Repentance.*

Schools. An Oxford term, meaning the final examinations for a bachelor of arts degree.

Scotch, Scots, Scottish. What is the proper way to refer to those who live in Scotland? Mrs. Moreland and her friends never came to any conclusion that we know of. However, they all had, and used, their copies of H. W. Fowler's *Modern English Usage.* Had they had the book with them at the time of the discussions, they might have settled on *Scots,* that being the form preferred in modern Scotland. All the uses are time-honored—and no one will refer to a bottle of Scots.

Scott, Sir George Gilbert (1811–1878). English architect, a leading proponent of the Gothic revival. It was he who designed St. Pancras Station, the inspiration for Pomfret Towers.

Scott, Sir Walter (1771–1832). Prolific Scottish author. His poetic works include *The Lady of the Lake, The Lay of the Last Minstrel,* and *Rokeby.* Among his many novels are *Waverly, Rob Roy, The Pirate, Ivanhoe,* and *Kenilworth.* In addition, he wrote plays, biographies, encyclopedia entries, and letters to the editor.

Scout. A male servant at Oxford. The scout, shared by a few students, brought in breakfast, kept the room tidy, waited at table, ran errands, brushed clothes, and so on. The same type of servant at Cambridge and Durham is called a gyp.

Scratch meal. A meal scratched or cobbled together out of whatever is handy.

Season. The months May through July in London, when the prominent families were in town and many dinners, parties, and balls were given. Débutantes would be presented to the sovereign and "brought out" during the season.

Seccotine. The brand name of an adhesive, and thus a general term for all household glue.

Secondary school. A state-supported secondary school intended to provide a general education. The academically talented (to use the current jargon) attended grammar school if boys and high school if girls.

Se débrailler. *French.* To bare their breasts. Figuratively, we hope.

Seisin. A legal term meaning possession or token of possession.

Sentimental Tommy. A somewhat autobiographical novel by J.M. Barrie, published in 1896. His play *Peter Pan* was first performed in 1906.

Shadowy third. From Robert Browning's *By the Fireside*, 1855, stanza 46.

> But you spared me this, like the heart you are,
>   And filled my empty heart at a word.
> If two lives join, there is oft a scar,
>   They are one and one, with a shadowy third;
> One near one is too far.

Shaftesbury Avenue. The heart of London's theatre district.

Shagreen. Untanned leather covered with granules and usually dyed green. It was considered a luxurious material and at the height of its popularity during the Art Deco period was used for personal and domestic items such as desk blotters, tobacco boxes, and cosmetic cases.

Shakespeare on "time." *See* **Rosalind.**

Shalott, the Lady of. A character from Arthurian legend who suffered a hopeless love for Sir Lancelot. In the Tennyson poem of the same name we find the Lady weaving in her tower room, and occasionally glancing in the mirror, in which she at last sees the flash of Lancelot's armor as he rides by:

> She left the web, she left the loom,
> She made three paces thro' the room,
> She saw the water lily bloom,
> She saw the helmet and the plume,
>   She looked down to Camelot.
> Out flew the web and floated wide;
> The mirror cracked from side to side;
> 'The curse is come upon me!' cried
>   The Lady of Shalott

Distraught at being ignored by Lancelot, the Lady went to the river, found a boat, wrote her name on it, and floated away in it. She arranged herself carefully, so her corpse would make a good impression, sang a while, and then died of romantic causes. The penultimate verse is:

> Under tower and balcony,
> By garden-wall and gallery,
> A gleaming shape she floated by.
>   Silent into Camelot.
> Out upon the wharfs they came,
> Knight and burgher, lord and dame,
> And round the prow they read her name,
>   *The Lady of Shalott.*

Mr. Shandy's Brother. Toby Shandy, a character from Laurence Sterne's *Tristram Shandy*. Toby was Tristram's uncle, a kindly and practical man whose career was in the army and whose especial interest was fortifications.

Shape. Any dessert (pudding) made by chilling and moulding, such as a cream, jelly, or blanc-mange. Shapes were held in low esteem.

Sharp, Becky. One of the main characters from Thackeray's *Vanity Fair.* Becky was pretty, blonde, resourceful, intelligent, and self-seeking. She absorbed no pieties from her girlhood training, and declared herself no angel. She made the most of her attractiveness to men.

Shavian. An adjective referring to George Bernard Shaw; *see* below. The adjective so tastefully omitted from the final chapter of *Three Score and Ten* was spoken boldly in Shaw's *Pygmalion* by Eliza Doolittle. The occasion was her first appearance as a lady speaking a lady's English. Her performance was mixed; the accent was good but the content pure gutter. When asked by Freddy Eynsford–Hill if she will walk across the park, her devastating reply, in perfect diction, was, "Walk! Not bloody likely! I am going in a taxi."

To understand the explosive power of this, one must know that the word "bloody" was never spoken in polite society.

Shaw, George Bernard. Irish playwright, creator of some of the finest plays of his age, including *Pygmalion, Candida,* and *Man and Superman.* Shaw's work is witty, intelligent, and full of ideas challenging much that was dear to Victorian sensibilities. He was also a vegetarian and a socialist.

"Shayderve." This is Mr. Scatcherd's rendering of *chef-d'oeuvre,* a French word meaning masterpiece, and pronounced shay.DUHV.ruh, with all the proper French inflections and management of the "r" that perhaps Mr. Scatcherd had not got.

Sheepshanks. A play on the name of Woolworths.

"She's the darling of my heart. . . . " A line from "Sally in Our Alley," a poem by Henry Carey (1693–1743) who also wrote the words to "God Save the King." Here's the first verse of "Sally."

> Of all the girls that are so smart
> There's none like pretty Sally;
> She is the darling of my heart,
> And she lives in our alley.
> There is no lady in the land
> Is half so sweet as Sally;
> She is the darling of my heart,
> And she lives in our alley.

She Stoops to Conquer. A comedy by Oliver Goldsmith, first produced in 1773.

"She walks in beauty. . . . " First line and title of a poem by Lord Byron.

> She walks in beauty, like the night
> Of cloudless climes and starry skies;
> And all that's best of dark and bright
> Meet in her aspect and her eyes:
> Thus mellow'd to that tender light
> which heaven to gaudy day denies.

"Ship after ship. . . . " This quotation, found in *Jutland Cottage,* is from "The Revenge" by Tennyson. The verse finishes with these two lines.

> For some were sunk and many were shattered and so could fight us no more—
> God of battles, was ever a battle like this in the world before?

"Short and simple annals of the poor. . . . " *See* **Gray, Thomas**.

"Short, brutish and nasty. . . . " Taken from Thomas Hobbes' description of the life of man in a state of nature in *The Leviathan* (1651). It was, he said, was "solitary, poor, nasty, brutish and short."

Shrunk shanks. From Shakespeare's *As You Like It*. The phrase is from Jacques' "All the world's a stage" speech.

> His youthful hose, well-saved, a world too wide
> For his shrunk shank . . . .

Sic itur ad astra. Latin. Thus do we reach the stars.

"sighed . . . obeyed. . . . " See **Gibbon, Edward**.

"The silence grows. . . . " Another line from Browning's *By the Fireside* found in verse thirty-two.

> But at afternoon or almost eve
>   'T is better; then the silence grows
> To that degree, you half believe
>   It must get rid of what it knows,
> Its bosom does so heave.

Silent Noon. A sonnet by Dante Gabriel Rosetti, the last four lines of which we quote here:

> So this wing'd hour is dropped to us from above.
> O! clasp we to our hearts, for deathless dower,
> This close-companioned inarticulate hour
> When twofold silence was the song of love.

Silk. To take silk is to become a King's or Queen's Counsel and wear a silk gown and, on ceremonial occasions, a full-bottomed wig. This is an honor for a barrister, and is often the prelude to becoming a judge. Only a barrister can take silk, and judges are rarely appointed from any other source than from among KC's or QC's.

Silver, Miss. The sleuth in a long series of detective stories by Patricia Wentworth. Maud Silver is a deceptively mild-looking ex-governess with a chronic cough and unflagging nerve. She's also a great knitter.

Simony. Buying an ecclesiastical position.

Sine die. Latin. Without a day (having been named).

Sintram. A tale by the German writer Friedrich de la Motte Fouqué. Sintram was the Greek hero.

"Sirène, fange, boue, immondices, ordure. . . . " *French.* Siren, mire, mud, foulness, sewage . . . .

Siren suit. This was a prettier version of a boiler suit—a one-piece garment made to pull on over pajamas in the event of an air raid, to make the wearer warm and presentable in the air raid shelter.

Sir John Soane's Museum. Sir John Soane (1753–1837) was an architect who took delight in the antique and the unusual. To this end he amassed a large and eclectic collection, which he stored at his home at 13 Lincoln's Inn Fields and was kind enough to open to the public. Included in the displays are busts, paintings, manuscripts, cork models of classical buildings, the sarcophagus of Seti I, a large fungus from Sumatra, and a reconstructed monk's parlor.

Sisyphus. From Greek myth. Sisyphus was condemned to an eternity of rolling a large stone to the top of a hill, watching as it rolled back down, and then rolling it up again. What he must have felt will be familiar to anyone who has had to keep the laundry done.

Skraelings. A Norse word for Eskimos or American Indians.

Skiffins, Miss. From Dickens' *Great Expectations*. Miss Skiffins was a good soul who visited Mr. Wemmick on Sunday evenings. She brewed the family tea and as they drank it she removed Mr. Wemmick's arm from around her waist at regular intervals. Eventually she became his bride.

Slime-draught. An arcane medical term for a preparation used occasionally as a laxative or at other times, curiously, to induce sleep. In *Great Expectations* Pip was given a slime-draught when he was ill; it was this novel that Lord Mellings had read.

Sloppy. From Dickens' *Our Mutual Friend*. Sloppy was a sweet orphan boy with lots of buttons who had been taken in by Betty Higden. He turned the mangle for her in a most devoted way, but when Betty left town he worked for Mr. Boffin. Later he studied carpentry and we think he may eventually have married Jenny Wren.

Slough of Despond. A place described in *Pilgrim's Progress*. It was one of the first of Christian's trials, a gloomy, dispiriting swamp or fen. Figuratively, it means a period of depression.

Slumkey, The Honourable Samuel. From Dickens' *Pickwick Papers*. He was a candidate for Parliament. While campaigning in Etanswill he showed great aptitude for kissing babies and shaking hands. Oddly enough these were successful ploys, and he was elected.

Smalls. As you may have thought: underwear.

Smallweed, Mr. From Dickens' *Bleak House*. Mr. Smallweed was a canny, grasping, and crippled old money-lender. He and his wife were ending their days in a pair of porter's chairs on either side of the fireplace in their home. When Mrs. Smallweed screeched, her husband's invariable response was to throw a pillow at her, along with a vituperation or two. He would then call upon the nearest person to shake him back into position.

Smallweed, Mrs. Wife of the above, far advanced in her second childhood. Her only comments were shrill, senseless shrieks. She was the sister of Mr. Krook, of the Rag and Bottle Warehouse, and fully exemplified the adage that it's not what you know but who you know.

Smike. From Dickens' *Nicholas Nickelby*. Smike is a pitiful, rather simple boy who bears the brunt of the cruelty of Wackford Squeers, headmaster of Dotheboys Hall. As Smike had been abandoned to the mercy of Mr. Squeers, he of course had no clothes that fit.

"Smiling, put the question by. . . . " A line from *The Daydream* by Tennyson. It tells the legend of the Sleeping Beauty. The entire court had been asleep until the beauty was kissed by the fairy Prince. At that moment the spell snapped and everyone rumbled into action, unaware that they had been asleep for years.

'. . . we have slept, my lords.
    My beard has grown into my lap.'
The barons swore, with many words,
    'Twas but an after-dinner's nap.
'Pardy,' return'd the king, 'but still
    My joints are somewhat stiff or so.
My lord, and shall we pass the bill
    I mention'd half an hour ago?'
The chancellor, sedate and vain,
    In courteous words return'd reply,
But dallied with his golden chain,
    And, smiling, put the question by.

Smorltork, Count. From Dickens' *Pickwick Papers.* The count was a well-bewhiskered and possibly Russian gentleman attending a fancy-dress breakfast at The Den, the Etanswill home of Mrs. Leo Hunter. He was gathering material for his great book on England. Most of what he heard he misunderstood, but at least he took a lot of notes. When Mr. Pickwick said, "The word politics, sir, comprises in itself a difficult study of no inconsiderable magnitude," the Count put in his notes: "Politics. The word politics surprises by himself—"

Snakes and Ladders. A children's board game, known in the U.S. as Chutes and Ladders.

Snapdragon. A lively pastime for a group. It calls for the participants to snatch raisins from a dish of flaming brandy and pop them still blazing into their mouths.

Snorri Sturlasson (1179–1241). The most respected of the Icelandic historians. He was also a chieftain and poet.

Snow, Lucy. From Charlotte Brontë's *Villette.* Lucy was in love with Dr. John Bretton, but he was not in the least interested in her.

Solicitor. A lawyer whose services include wills, contracts, trusts, domestic matters, and advice on legal matters of all sorts.

Soliloquy of the Spanish Cloister. A poem by Robert Browning, published in 1842, in which a mean-spirited monk reflects in an angry way upon what he sees as the disgusting simplicity of his mild-mannered, nature-loving brother monk.

I.
Gr-r-r – there go, my heart's abhorrence!
    Water your damned flower pots, do!
If hate killed men, Brother Lawrence,
    God's blood, would not mine kill you!
What? Your myrtle-bush wants trimming?
    Oh, that rose has prior claims –
Needs its leaden vase filled brimming?
    Hell dry you up with its flames!

"Solitaire et glacé. . . . " Lines from a romantically grim poem, *"Colloque Sentimental,"* by Paul Verlaine. It is in eight couplets, of which this is the third.

Dans le vieux parc solitaire et glacé	In the old park, lonely and frozen,
Deux spectres ont évoqué le passé.	Two ghosts are recalling the past.

Somne, quies rerum, placidissime, somne. *Latin.* Sleep, most gentle sleep. From Ovid's *Metamorphoses*, Book II.

Song of Solomon, 2:15. "Take us the foxes, the little foxes, that spoil the vines: for our vines have tender grapes."

"So she went into the garden to cut a cabbage leaf. . . . " From a little nonsense tale, allegedly written by Samuel Foote in 1854 to test the memory of the actor Charles Macklin. This is the entire thing:

> So she went into the garden to cut a cabbage-leaf, to make an apple pie; and at the same time a great she-bear, coming up the street, pops its head into the shop. 'What! No soap?' So he died, and she very imprudently married the barber; and there were present the Picninnies, and the Joblillies, and the Garyalies, and the grand Panjandrum himself, with the little red button on top, and they all fell to playing the game of catch as catch can, till the gun powder ran out at the heels of their boots.

"So the quiet was. . . . " From Matthew Arnold's "Bacchanalia; or, The New Age."

> Shepherd, what ails thee, then?
> Shepherd, why mute?
> Forth with thy joyous song!
> Forth with thy flute!
> Tempts not the revel blithe?
> Lure not their cries?
> Glow not their shoulders smooth?
> Melt not their eyes?
> Is not, on cheeks like those,
> Lovely the flush?
> — *Ah, so the quiet was!*
> *So was the hush!*

Sotto voce. *Italian.* In an undertone.

Soubrette. *French.* A chambermaid—a stock character in 19th century comedy who survived into the 20th as a saucy or humorous domestic.

Souffre douleur. *French.* A butt or scapegoat.

Spade guineas. Golden coins issued in 1787. Although "guinea" designates the source of the gold, the origin of the name "spade" is obscure.

Spang rod. We believe this to be a flexible tool used for reaching far into difficult places, but can find no source for a reliable definition.

Spanner. A monkey wrench, though why "monkey" we cannot say.

Sparkler, Edmund. A character from Dickens' *Little Dorrit*. He was Mrs. Murdles' son from her first marriage. He was a bit dim, but amiable. He married Fanny Dorrit, admiring her because she was "a woman with no bigod nonsense about her."

Special license. A way to avoid the prolonged procedure of reading the banns in the parish church was to get one of three kinds of special license that would allow an immediate marriage.

Spillikins. Usually called jackstraws. Spillikins are used for what in the U.S. is called Pick-Up-Sticks.

Spread eagle. Also called "blood eagle" and now thought to be apocryphal, the result of a mistranslation. It was, if it existed, a cruel and unusual form of punishment carried out by the ancient Norsemen. The victim was pinioned and a deep incision made in two curving lines under the ribs (in the form of the wings of an eagle in flight). Then someone reached in and pulled out his heart. Apocryphal or not, when Mr. Tebben wishes this fate on someone, it is eloquent.

Spud. Any long-handled digging tool, especially the sort with three or four heavy prongs, known in the U.S. as a garden fork (as opposed to a pitchfork).

Spurlos versenkt. *German.* Sunk without a trace.

Squeers, Mr. and Mrs. Wackford, Wackford Junior, and Fanny. From Dickens' *Nicholas Nickleby*. There is nothing good to be said for any of the Squeers. Mr. Squeers was headmaster of Dotheboys School, and the family combined every unpleasant quality available to ordinary mortals to make the school a miserable place and each student in it wretched.

Squire. *See* **Esquire.**

Starkadder, Seth. A character from Stella Gibbons' *Cold Comfort Farm, q.v.* Seth was a simmering hunk of rustic manhood—in short, the "local irresistible bounder." Mr. Neck knew at first glance, as Seth stood bathed in a shaft of sunlight, that he had found the next box office hit.

The Statue and the Bust. A poem by Robert Browning. It recounts the legend of Duke Ferdinand I, who placed an equestrian statue of himself at a site from which it was looking forever at a certain window in the old Riccardi palace. Gazing out of the window, also forever, would be the shade of his lady love, whose husband had imprisoned her there, very selfishly wanting to keep her for himself.

Sterne, Laurence (1713–1768). Irish author, most memorably of *Tristram Shandy*. Sterne was educated at Cambridge, took Holy Orders, and had a prebendary stall at York. He traveled widely on the Continent, writing about his impressions in *A Sentimental Journey through France and Italy.*

Stew Ponds. Small ponds in which fish were kept alive while awaiting their fate in the kitchen.

Stillroom. One of the offices in a large house. Originally used for the distillation of cordials and perfumes, it came to be used for the storage of cakes, preserves, and liqueurs, and for the preparation of coffee and tea.

Stone. A unit of measure the value of which has changed occasionally. In 1953 it was fourteen pounds.

Story of a cock and a bull. *See* **A cock and a bull.**

Stranger in a strange land. From Exodus 2:22.

> 21. And Moses was content to dwell with the man: and he gave Moses Zipporah his
> daughter. 22. And she bare him a son, and he called his name Gershom: for he said,
> I have been a stranger in a strange land.

Strophe and antistrophe. Terms from classical Greek drama indicating the actions of the chorus. At strophe, the chorus moved to the left, and at antistrophe to the right. AT uses these words in a very general way, usually to indicate the contributions of two people to the enlightenment of a third.

Struldbrugs. From *Gulliver's Travels,* by Jonathan Swift. The Struldbrugs were inhabitants of Luggnagg. Though they had neither intellect nor vigor, they were condemned to eternal life.

Stud book. Informally, either Burke's *Peerage* or DeBrett's *Peerage, q.v.*

Styx. According to classical mythology, the River Styx was a river of hate that flowed nine times around the underworld.

Sub rosa. Latin. Literally, under the roses. The usual meaning, however is secret or clandestine.

"Suddenly, sweetly, strangely. . . . " *See* **Maud.**

Suez. An area of northeast Egypt where the Gulf of Suez is joined to the Mediterranean by the Suez Canal. The canal was built in 1859 through 1869 by the French. The British gained control in 1875 and established a protectorate in 1882. The canal was nationalized in 1956 by the Egyptians, who retain control to this day. *See* **Nasser.**

Sultan cooker. *See* **Begum.**

Summer Pudding. A favorite dessert in summer, when black currants and other red fruit are ripe. It is unbaked, delicious, and enjoyed by those with lots of raspberries, strawberries, currants, and plums.

Summer Pudding

| 1 ½ lb. mixed soft red fruit, the freshest possible | 1 cup water |
| slices of good bread, crusts removed | sugar to taste |

Place the fruit in a saucepan, having first removed any inedible parts. Add water and sugar. Taste. Simmer until tender. Strain through a fine sieve, retaining the juice.

Line a buttered bowl with the bread slices. Use a circle for the bottom and fingers or triangles for the sides—just make sure there are no very large gaps in the bread.

Fill the bowl with the fruit, then pour in the juice. Cover with another round of bread, and cover that last piece of bread with a small plate, and place upon it a weight. Refrigerate overnight. Turn it out on a plate to serve it. Decorate with flowers, maybe, and accompany with cream, whipped cream, or a custard sauce.

"A sunset touch. . . . " Lines from Robert Browning's *Bishop Bloughman's Apology,* a long discussion about faith, doubt, and realistic acceptance of what is. We start with line 181.

> . . . . how can we guard our unbelief,
> Make it bear fruit to us? — the problem here.
> Just when we are safest, there's a sunset-touch,
> A fancy from a flower-bell, some one's death,

> A chorus-ending from Euripides, —
> And that's enough for fifty hopes and fears
> As old and new at once as nature's self . . . .

Suovetaurilia *Latin*. A Roman rite of purification involving the sacrifice of a pig, a sheep, and a bull.

Surtees, Robert Smith (1805–1864). Author of successful sketches of sporting life and other comic novels dealing primarily with fox-hunting. *See* **Jorrocks.**

Suttee. From India. The ritual cremation of a widow at her husband's funeral. The practice was never widespread and is definitely uncommon now.

Swede. Rutabaga.

Swift, Jonathan (1667–1745). Dean of St. Patrick's, Dublin. He was a prolific writer in all prose forms and in poetry. He is best known to the casual reader as the author of *Gulliver's Travels* (1726), and such satirical essays as *A Modest Proposal.*

Swinburne, Charles Algernon (1837–1909). A writer and critic associated with the Pre-Raphaelites, Swinburne was known for his various excesses. He was a leading figure in the aesthetic movement, parodied by Gilbert and Sullivan in *Patience* as a greenery-yallery, Grosvenor-gallery young man. In any case, Swinburne was a very influential critic.

Swiveller, Richard, and Sally Brass. From Dickens' *Old Curiosity Shop.* Richard Swiveller was a law clerk for Sally's brother—as she was herself, unofficially. Neither Richard nor Sally was a very pleasant person, but they gradually developed enough of a friendship for him to slap her on the back now a and then.

Sybil. In classical mythology, she was a prophetess.

Sybil, or The Two Nations. A novel by Benjamin Disraeli dealing at some length with the conditions of the poor.

Sybo (or sybow). *Scottish.* Spring onions.

I say, Colin. What is real; Now or Then?
— Lydia Merton

Taglioni, Maria (1804–1884). Italian ballerina famous for her performance as La Sylphide.

Take Up the White Man's Burden. A poem by Rudyard Kipling, published in 1899. In *The Duke's Daughter* Cora Palliser mentions this poem in connection with the involvement of the Americans in Korea, but it is clearly more about the sacrifices associated with being a colonial power, as it delineates the nature of the responsibilities involved. The best men, it says are sent out to do hard work for their strange subjects, "half-devil and half-child."

Tantalus. A stand built to hold two or three decanters. They were kept in place by a grooved bar which had to be unlocked before the bottles could be withdrawn. The name comes from the myth of the Lydian king Tantalus, who was confined in such a way that food and drink were always just out of reach. The verb *tantalize* is derived from the same source.

Tare. The weight of the package or packing in which something is sold. "Tret" is an allowance of four pounds out of each 104 pounds, or 1/26, on merchandise after the deduction for the tare. According to the OED the reason for all this was already obscure in the 17ᵗʰ century, but it boils down to being an allowance for a certain amount of wear and tear on goods during shipping.

Tarquin. Properly, Lucius Tarquinius Superbus—the last Roman king. This rather monstrous character, who may or may not have existed, and may or may not have been what legend has said, was finally overthrown after his son Sextus raped Lucretia, the beautiful and virtuous wife of Lucius Tarquinius Collatinus. Driven out of Rome, Tarquin sought the support of Lars Porsena in trying to reconquer his throne. The attempt failed and Tarquin died in exile; we think it served him right.

Tarsus. A city in southern Turkey, the birthplace of St. Paul. As a boy he left it as Saul, a devout Jew. Several years later he returned, not only grown up, but as the even more devout Christian, Paul. Lady Lufton perhaps knew what his mother must have felt like.

Tas de cochons. *French.* Heap of swine—or, if you prefer, pile of pigs.

Tea. There is a class distinction here, which we have seen in Barsetshire. China tea, which is pale and subtle, is drunk by the gentry. India tea, which is dark and hearty, is preferred by the working class. This is, of course, a generalization.

"Teach the orphan boy to read, teach the orphan girl to sew. . . . " Lines from Tennyson's poem, "Lady Clara Vere de Vere." The theme of the poem is stated in one of its lines, "Kind hearts are more than coronets." Clara had trifled with the heart of a man below her in station. This is the last verse.

Clara, Clara Vere de Vere,
    If time be heavy on your hands,
Are there no beggars at your gate,
    Nor any poor about your lands?
O, teach the orphan-boy to read,
    Or teach the orphan-girl to sew;
Pray Heaven for a human heart,
    And let the foolish yeoman go.

"Tears, idle tears. . . . " A line from one of the songs in *The Princess*, by Tennyson. This is the first verse.

'Tears, idle tears, I know not what they mean,
Tears from the depth of some divine despair
Rise in the heart, and gather to the eyes,
In looking on the happy autumn-fields,
And thinking of the days that are no more.

Tea tasters. Two characters from the W. S. Gilbert's Bab Ballad titled "Etiquette." This poem is fully described in the text of *Love at All Ages*.

How they wished an introduction to each other they had had
When on board the *Ballyshannon!* And it drove them nearly mad
To think how very friendly with each other they might get,
If it wasn't for the arbitrary rule of etiquette!

Teetotum. A small top-like fortune-telling device, similar to a dreidl, with letters on its sides. It would be spun and then fall. The uppermost letters would reveal, or indicate, the fortune of the spinner.

Tell, William. Legendary Swiss patriot who defied the Austrian governors of his canton. He was made to shoot an apple off the head of his small son. This scene has been recorded in various paintings and murals—it is impossible to say which one Swan saw.

Temple; Inner Temple. In London, the Middle Temple and Inner Temple are buildings in the historic complex of buildings known as the Inns of Court, located in the City of London. For centuries young men aspiring to the legal profession resided here. The Inns of Court contain students, law offices, and flats that are let to anyone who wants one whether or not he is a member of the bar, such as Alister Cameron.

Tempora mutantur et nos mutamur in illis. *Latin*. Times change and we change with them. Attributed to the Emperor Lothar I (795–855).

Tennyson, Alfred, 1st Baron (1809–1892). A beloved poet during his lifetime, Tennyson was made Poet Laureate in 1850. He was popular with the whole nation, beginning with Queen Victoria. The most famous of his works are *In Memoriam, Poems, Maud, Enoch Arden, Idylls of the King, The Lady of Shalott*, and his last poem, "Crossing the Bar."

Terence, Publius Terentius Afer (c.195–159 B.C.). Roman author of six comic plays. His work influenced dramatists for centuries to come.

Tess of the D'Urbervilles. A novel by Thomas Hardy, published in 1891. The Derbyfields, simple farmers, find they are descended from the old aristocratic family of D'Urbervilles. Tess is seduced and her life ruined by a scion of that family, Alec D'Urberville.

Tey, Josephine. A pen name, as was her other *nom de plume,* Gordon Daviot, of Elizabeth Mackintosh (1896–1952). She was the author of several good mysteries including *The Daughter of Time.*

"That little face of yours." Swan's remark to Justinia Lufton in the course of proposing to her. It was inspired by a poem by Robert Browning, called *A Face,* from *Dramatis Persone,* 1864. It begins,

> If one could have that little head of hers
> Painted upon a background of pale gold,
> Such as the Tuscan's early art prefers!

Themis. A Roman goddess who, with Jupiter, presided over law and order, hospitality, and the oppressed.

"Thinking of the old 'un." From Dickens' *David Copperfield.* When Mrs. Gummidge waxed morose, Mr. Peggotty said she was "thinking of the old 'un." *See* **Mrs. Gummidge.**

The Thirty-nine Articles of Religion. Thirty-nine statements, with explanations, of the basic beliefs of the Anglican Church. They are found in the last pages of the Book of Common Prayer.

"This close-companioned inarticulate hour." *See* **"Silent Noon."**

"Those behind cried forward. . . . " From *Horatius,* by Lord Macaulay. He was describing the scene on the bridge over the Tiber, where Horatius was defending the passage with just a few men against an onslaught of Lars Porsena's army. It is delightful of AT to describe a drinks party in these words. The line is found in verse 50.

> Was none who would be foremost
>   To lead such dire attack:
> But those behind cried 'Forward!'
>   And those before cried 'Back!'
> And backward now and forward
>   Wavers the deep array;
> And on the tossing sea of steel,
> To and fro the standards reel;
> And the victorious trumpet-peal
>   Dies fitfully away.

"Three whole days together." A phrase from the first verse of Sir John Suckling's poem "The Constant Lover."

> Out upon it, I have loved
>   Three whole days together!
> And am like to love three more,
>   If it prove fair weather.

"Thrift, thrift, Horatio. . . . " From *Hamlet.* Hamlet's friend Horatio is speaking to him.

> HORATIO. My lord, I came to see your father's funeral.
> HAMLET. I pray thee, do not mock me, fellow-student;
>   I think it was to see my mother's wedding.
> HORATIO. Indeed, my lord, it followed hard upon.
> HAMLET. Thrift, thrift, Horatio! The funeral baked meats
>   did coldly furnish forth the marriage tables.

Through a glass darkly. From I Corinthians, 13:11-12.

> 11. When I was a child, I spake as a child, I understood as a child, I thought as a child:
> But when I became a man I put away childish things.
> 12. For now we see through a glass, darkly: but then face to face: now I know in part;
> but then shall I know even as also I am known.

"Through caverns measureless. . . ." From the poem "Kubla Kahn," by Samuel Taylor Coleridge. We give the line in the first verse.

> In Xanadu did Kubla Khan
>   A stately pleasure-dome decree:
> Where Alph, the sacred river, ran
> Through caverns measureless to man
>   Down to a sunless sea.

"the thrush who will sing each song twice over. . . ." From Browning's "Home Thoughts from Abroad." The line is in the middle of the poem.

> Hark, where my blossomed pear-tree in the hedge
> Leans to the field and scatters on the clover
> Blossoms and dewdrops — at the bent spray's edge —
> That's the wise thrush: he sings each song twice over
> Lest you should think he never could recapture
> The first fine careless rapture!

Thule. An island or point of land considered by the ancient Greek navigator Pytheas (4th century B.C.) to be the northernmost limit of the habitable world. He reached it by sailing six days north from the Orcades (Orkneys), probably to Iceland or Norway. "Ultima Thule" therefore means the farthest away, the last possible place, the ultimate land.

Tied house. A public house that, by arrangement with a particular brewery, sells only that brewery's beer. The brewery may own the house.

Tilbury. An open two-wheeled carriage popular in the early 1800's. It was named for its creator.

Tiles. As in "on the tiles" which means, figuratively, roof tiles. Out on the town, living it up, in high spirits, no doubt drinking—a time-honored form of getting high.

"Time, like an ever-rolling stream. . . ." A line from "Psalm," by Isaac Watts, written in 1719.

> Time, like an ever-rolling stream,
> Bears all its sons away;
> They fly forgotten, as a dream
> Dies at the opening day.

Time-serving. Temporizing; suiting oneself to circumstances, probably insincerely or perhaps obsequiously.

Tite Barnacle. A character in Dickens' *Little Dorrit*. He was a pompous government official from the "Circumlocution Office." The last thing he wished was to be helpful.

Titles. Duke: If you are a peer yourself, you may address a duke or duchess as "Duke" or "Duchess." Otherwise the correct form is "Your grace" to either one. The eldest son of a duke is a marquess, earl, or viscount, addressed as "Lord." The other children are "Lord" or "Lady."

Marquise, earl, and viscount: Except on formal occasions, these are referred to and addressed as "Lord." The eldest son of a marquise or earl is a viscount. The wife of a marquise is a marchioness; the wife of an earl is a countess. The sons and daughters are referred to as, but not addressed in person as, "Honorable."

Baron, baronet, and knight: All are referred to and addressed as "Sir," and their wives as "Lady." The children of barons are "Honorables."

Toad, Mr. From Kenneth Grahame's *The Wind in the Willows.* Toad was a satirical representation of the effete gentleman, personifying everything reprehensible about the stereotype. Yet he was loveable in his foolishness. In one escapade he escaped from prison and in his wanderings encountered a kindly gypsy who gave him some hot stew in exchange for his horse. Later Toad held a grand celebration at Toad Hall, recaptured from the weasels and stoats, and prepared a long poem extolling the virtues of no one but himself. (His friends, although loyal, did not allow him to carry out this plan.)

Todgers's. From Dickens' *Martin Chuzzlewit.* Todgers's was the familiar name of the Commercial Boarding House, kept by Mrs. Todgers. When the occasion demanded, Mrs. Todgers could produce a bang-up dinner. "Oh, Todgers's could do it when it chose!"

"To him who hath. . . . " Matthew 25:29.

> For unto everyone that hath shall be given,
> and he shall have abundance:
> but from him that hath not shall be taken away
> even that which he hath.

"Toil, envy, want. . . . " From "The Vanity of Wishes," by Samuel Johnson. This is the relevant passage.

> Deign on the passing world to turn thine eyes,
> And pause awhile from letters to be wise;
> There mark what ills the scholar's life assail,
> Toil, envy, want, the patron, and the jail.
> See nations slowly wise, and meanly just,
> To buried merit raise the tardy bust.

Tolpuddle Martyrs. Heroes of the labor movement. The "martyrs" were six men from the Dorsetshire town of Tolpuddle. In 1834 they were arrested, tried, and sentenced to seven years of servitude in an Australian penal colony for organizing the local agricultural laborers. There was a public outcry and they were returned to England in 1836.

Mr. Toobad. A character from Thomas Love Peacock's *Nightmare Abbey.* Mr. Toobad was a millenarian and had only one opinion—that the devil was abroad in the land and evidence of his work was everywhere.

Touché. French. A fencing term. It means "touched," and announces a hit. By extension, in conversation it means that the speaker is aware of the other having scored a point.

Touchstone. A clown from *As You Like It.* His line is from Act II, scene iv.

> Ay, now I am in Arden; the more fool I;
> when I was at home I was in a better place:
> but travellers must be content.

Tout pétrie d'esprit de grâce. *French.* Entirely steeped in the spirit of grace.

Traire les Vaches. *French.* Milk the cows.

"Travellers must be content." *See* **Touchstone.**

Treue Schwesterliebe. *German.* Loyal sisterly affection.

Trilby. A novel by George Du Maurier, published in 1894. It is the story of an artist's model, Trilby O'Ferrall, who falls under the spell of the charismatic musician, Svengali. He trains her to be a singer, and has such great power over her that when he dies she languishes and eventually dies as well. Little Billie was one of her artist friends from her modeling days; he was, in fact, deeply in love with her.

Tripos. A Cambridge term referring to the honors examination.

Trivium and ***quadrivium.*** *Latin. Trivium* is language, grammar, logic, and rhetoric. *Quadrivium* is mathematics, astronomy, and music.

Trollope, Anthony (1815–1882). Post Office employee and prolific novelist, who introduced England to the pillar box and the serial novel. *The Warden* was his fourth novel, followed by the remainder of his Barsetshire series. In the political novels, perhaps known to some contemporary Americans as the Palliser series, video-taped sets of which have recently been reissued, Trollope established the family of the Duke of Omnium in Barsetshire for its country seat and pocket borough. All in all, Trollope wrote forty-seven novels, many short stories, and two plays.

Trooper George. A character from Dickens' *Bleak House.* He was the owner of a shooting gallery and one of Mr. Smallweed's clients. He had been a friend of Captain Hawdon, *q.v.* Dickens describes him in a paragraph that could answer as well for the physical training master at Southbridge School as described in Chapter Eight of *High Rising.*

> He was a swarthy man of fifty; well-made and good
> looking. . . . He sits forward on his chair as if he were,
> from long habit, allowing space for some dress or
> accoutrement, that he has altogether laid aside.

Trotwood, Betsy. From Dickens' *David Copperfield.* Miss Trotwood was David's gruff but kind aunt. She became his guardian, after which his fortunes began to improve. So amazed was she when he appeared at her garden gate that she sat right down on the path and said. "Oh, Lord!"

Trunk call. A long distance call.

Tu Marcellus eris. *Latin.* The full quotation from Virgil's *Aeneid* follows.

> Heu, miserande puer, si qua fata aspera rumpas,
>
> Tu, Marcellus eris. Manibus date lilia plenis.

> Alas, pitiable boy—if only you might break your cruel fate!
>
> —you are to be Marcellus. Give me lilies in armfuls.

The Two Ogres. One of the Bab Ballads by W.S. Gilbert. The two ogres were brothers. The wicked ogre James ate good boys. His brother Bland, the kindly ogre, ate only bad boys. So for punishment, James

> "Secured by fetter, cramp, and chain,
>   And gagged securely — so —
> You shall be placed in Drury Lane,
>   Where only good lads go.

> "Surrounded there by virtuous boys,
>   You'll suffer torture wus
> Than that which constantly annoys
>   Disgraceful Tantalus.

And a reward for the good ogre:

> "But as for Bland who, as it seems,
>   Eats only naughty boys,
> We've planned a recompense that teems
>   With gastronomic joys.

> "Where wicked youths in crowds are stowed
>   He shall unquestioned rule,
> And have the run of Hackney Road
>   Reformatory School!"

Two on a Tower. A novel by Thomas Hardy, published in 1882. It is the complex story of star-crossed lovers, both astronomers, and was intended to show the paltriness of human affairs when seen against the backdrop of the vast and eternal cosmos.

Perhaps it is rather like that in heaven, which I am sure will be a most confusing place, though perfectly delightful, rather like going abroad only worse. How we are to know who anyone is I don't know, but I am sure it will all be arranged perfectly.

— Agnes Graham

Under Two Flags. A popular novel by Ouida (Marie Louise de la Ramée), published in 1867. Ouida's heroes tended to be idealized but a bit languid.

Undine. A water nymph who first appears in the story *Undine*, written in 1811 by Friedrich de la Motte Fouqué. This story was the basis for musical works by Hoffman in 1816 and Lortzing in 1845. A play entitled *Ondine* was written by Jean Giraudoux in 1939. As a nymph Undine was without a human soul, but she acquired one by marrying a mortal. When he fell in love with Another, her watery relatives snatched her back into the river. She returned just once, to kill him on his wedding day with a kiss.

Universal dovetaildness. Eric Swan pleased Mr. Belton in *Happy Return* by recognizing this quotation from *Nicholas Nickleby*.

> "The unities, sir . . . are a completeness — a kind of universal dovetaildness with regard to place and time."

Usher. A member of the teaching staff in a school, as distinguished from the headmaster.

Utility clothes. During the war the Board of Trade came up with a scheme for clothing production which would ensure efficient use of resources and more egalitarian distribution. The fabrics and designs were limited and there resulted an unpopular standardized look. Men will never understand that women do indeed want to look like everyone else—but in their own way.

Vache-en-Écurie. *French.* Cow in the stable.

Vache-en-Étable. *French.* Cow in the cowshed.

Vache-en-Foin. *French.* Cow in the hay.

Vanderhum. Properly, *Van der Hum..* A South African liqueur made aromatic by the addition of a pungent mix of fruit, bark, and seeds, but flavored chiefly with mandarin oranges. It might be compared to curaçao.

Varium et mutabile semper femina. *Latin.* Even Virgil knew this (*see* **Utility clothes**) over two thousand years ago when he said, "Woman is always changeable."

V-E Day. Victory in Europe: May 8, 1945, the day of Germany's surrender in World War II.

Vehmgericht. *German.* A medieval tribunal for administering justice in the German kingdoms, although administered differently in each. The tribunals grew to be more and more secret, repressive, and corrupt. Eventually they fell into disuse.

Vendeuse. *French.* A saleswoman.

Venerable Bede. Originally Baeda. The Bede (673–735) was an Anglo-Saxon scholar and teacher who wrote an ecclesiastical history of England which has proved to be of great value. He wrote many other works on natural science and biblical subjects.

Vera incessu patuit dea. *Latin.* By her walk a true goddess was revealed. Virgil.

Verb. sap. *Latin.* An abbreviation of *verbum sat sapienti.* A word to the wise is sufficient.

Verger. This could refer to one whose duty it was to care for the interior of the church, or, in another sense, to assist the bishop or dean by carrying a rod or similar symbol of office during ceremonies before church or university dignitaries.

Vergilius. The original Latin spelling of the Roman poet Virgil, whose full name was Publius Vergilius Maro. He was renowned in his lifetime and his works have been studied through the centuries. Virgil featured in medieval literature and folklore as a magician.

Verlorner Posten in dem Freiheitskriege. *German.* "Lost Positions in the Fight for Freedom," a poem by Heine.

Vestry. The robing room of a church. Also, a church governing body, comprised of parishioners that meet in the vestry. The vestry's churchwarden is elected by this group; the vicar's is appointed by the vicar.

Verte nouveauté. French. Fresh novelty.

Vicar. *See* **Rector.** Mr. Villars was a rector, Mr. Miller a vicar. For all practical purposes the distinction has vanished.

Vie intérieure. French. Inner life.

Villegiatura. *Italian.* A holiday spent at a villa or country residence.

Virelais. French. The plural of *virelai,* a type of short song that originated in 14th century France.

V-J Day. Victory over Japan: August 14, 1945, the day the Japanese declared surrender. The formal surrender was signed on September 2, 1945.

Volte face. French. A reversal of attitude or policy; an about face or turnaround.

"Vous pouvez serrer un peu plus fort," dit le penguine. French. "You can tighten a little more strongly," said the lady penguin.

Vox humana. Latin.   Human voice. An organ stop that produces a sound like the human voice.

In England warmth is, on the whole,
even more important than food.
— Angela Thirkell

Wahlverwandtschaft. *German.* Congeniality; affinity that is chosen.

Walpole, Horace (1717–1797). Writer and renowned correspondent. He had a press on which he printed his own works and those of his friends.

Wardour Street. A London street in which reproduction antique furniture was sold in the 1880's. Thus "Wardour Street" came to signify the cloyingly pseudo-ancient in speech or style. More recently Wardour Street was a center for the film industry, and now equates roughly to "Hollywood," with all attendant implications of the sham and the fake.

Warrington, George. A character from Thackeray's *Pendennis* and *The Newcomes.* Arthur Pendennis shared chambers with Warrington while reading for the bar. Warrington was able to dissuade him from an ill-advised marriage by revealing his own unhappy marriage at eighteen to an enticing older woman. She was a farmer's daughter who had been happy to snare a young gentleman. He soon found that not only was she a boor and unable to share any of his interests, but she was in love with someone else. They lived apart, but he was of course not free to marry.

Wash leather. Chamois.

The Water Babies. A children's story of enduring popularity written by Charles Kingsley (1819–1875), published in book form in 1863. It recounts the adventures of Tom, a chimney sweep's boy, whose adventures began when he went down the chimney of a manor house, landed in the daughter's bedroom, and ran away when the maid raised a cry. He found himself in a river, changed into a water baby, a tiny humanoid with exterior gills. In this form Tom encountered many creatures, both real and imaginary, in and near the river and in the sea. The book is full of natural history and palatable moral lessons.

Water meadow. A meadow inundated with flowing water during winter in order to keep the grass growing and thus to provide early forage for grazing animals.

Wave offering. A sacrificial object—often a part of some unfortunate and innocent animal—that is both elevated and moved from side to side. It is mentioned in Exodus 29:22–26, of which we quote only verse 26.

> And thou shalt take the breast of the ram of Aaron's consecration, and
> wave it for a wave offering before the Lord: and it shall be thy part.

Wear the willow. Going into mourning for a love lost through rejection, death, or separation.

Wedding Guest. A character from *The Rime of the Ancient Mariner* by the romantic poet Samuel Taylor Coleridge, published in 1798. The wedding guest was simply trying to get to his brother's wedding when he was waylaid by the ancient and ranting mariner who kept him captive while he related the equivalent of a dozen shaggy dog stories—the account of a fatal voyage of which he was the only survivor. A changed and newly religious man, the mariner felt compelled to recount the tale every so often. The opening verses set the scene:

> It is an ancient Mariner,
> And he stoppeth one of three.
> "By thy long grey beard and glittering eye,
> Now wherefore stoppest thou me?
>
> The bridegroom's doors are opened wide,
> And I am next of kin;
> The guests are met, the feast is set:
> May'st hear the merry din."
>
> He holds him with his skinny hand,
> "There was a ship," quoth he.
> "Hold off! Unhand me, grey-beard loon!"
> Eftsoons his hand dropt he.
> . . . .
> He holds him with his glittering eye —
> The Wedding-Guest stood still,
> And listens like a three years' child:
> The Mariner hath his will.

"Wee, sleekit, cow'rin' tim'rous beastie." From the poem "To a Mouse" (1786) by Robert Burns.

Wegg, Mr. From Dickens' *Our Mutual Friend.* Mr. Wegg was a great quoter of songs because he was in business as a peddler of songs and ballads. He was also scheming, treacherous, and a would-be blackmailer.

Welshman. In Barsetshire in the late 1940's, this refers to radical Labour politician Aneurin Bevan.

Weller, Sam. A character from Dickens' *Pickwick Papers.* Sam is Mr. Pickwick's personal servant. He dropped and added aitches marvellously.

Weltschmertz. *German.* World-weariness; world-weary melancholy.

Wemmick, John. A character from Dickens' *Great Expectations.* He was a law clerk with the original post office mouth (*see* **Mr. Winthrop** in the list of Barsetshire characters). At work he was dutiful and discreet, but at his home his fanciful life imitated the routines of a sailing ship. He kept a pig, he cared for his Aged Parent, and he wooed and won Miss Skiffins. These worlds he kept rigidly separate.

"We musicians know. . . . " *See* **Browning.**

West India sugar broker. In one of his Bab Ballads, the broker in Gilbert's drawings is round indeed, and according to the verse gets rounder and rounder until he turns into a ball, whereupon his peace of mind is completely wrecked.

"Westward the land may be bright. . . . " A line from "Say Not the Struggle Naught Availeth" by Arthur Hugh Clough (1819–1861).

> And not be eastern windows only,
> When the daylight comes, comes in the light;
> In front the sun climbs slow, how slowly!
> But westward, look, the land is bright!

"We were two sisters of one race. . . . " The opening line of a rather grisly poem, "The Sisters," by Tennyson. The first few lines are those relevant in describing Grace and Jane Crawley.

> We were two sisters of one race;
> She was the fairest in the face.
>   The wind is howling in turret and tree.
> They were together, and she fell;
> Therefore revenge became me well.
>   O, the earl was fair to see!

White City. A sports complex in West London in which various athletic contests, including show-jumping contests, are held.

Whitehall. A London street near the Houses of Parliament, also known as the Palace of Westminster. Whitehall is filled with government offices.

White Knight. From *Through the Looking Glass* by Lewis Carroll, published 1871. In the course of traversing a life-sized chess board on her way to becoming a queen, Alice met the White Knight. Dressed in tin armor, which seemed to fit him very badly, he had a queer-shaped little deal box fastened across his shoulders, upside down, and with the lid hanging open. Alice looked at it with great curiosity. "I see you're admiring my little box," the Knight said in a friendly tone. "It's my own invention—to keep clothes and sandwiches in. You see I carry it upside down, so that the rain can't get in."

The knight was a mild and gentle man with many inventions like the little box. Behind his saddle he had a bee hive in place of a helmet (*see* **"A Farewell to Arms"**) Despite much experience he was a terrible horseman and couldn't keep his seat.

Whitlow. Also known as a felon, a whitlow is a suppurating inflamation of a finger or toe, usually near the nail.

"Whose service is perfect freedom. . . . " Words from "A Collect for Peace" in *The Book of Common Prayer."*

> Oh God, who are the author of peace and lover of
> concord, in knowledge of whom standeth our eternal
> life, whose service is perfect freedom; Defend us thy
> humble servants in all assaults of our enemies; that we
> surely trusting in thy defence, may not fear the power
> of any adversaries, through the might of Jesus Christ,
> *Amen.*

Mr. Wickfield. A character from Dickens' *David Copperfield*. He was a Canterbury lawyer with whom David boarded while attending Dr. Strong's school. His daughter Agnes became David's second wife.

Widdershins. Counter-clockwise.

The Widow's Lot. Unless significantly wealthy in her own right, a woman might find her circumstances markedly altered upon the death of her husband. This is true in all walks of life and always has been, but it was true in a certain way for the landed and propertied classes. If there were a male heir, the house the new widow lived in automatically became his, and she lived there at his sufferance. Traditionally she was expected to remain in the house if he were under age, or until he married—that is, if he were her son. In any case, she would sooner or later be expected to make other arrangements. On large properties provision was made for this circumstance. A smaller house, called a dower house, was usually part of the estate, and she would move into it.

One reason this moving of widows was taken for granted was that the house was usually not the widow's to begin with, but was the property of her husband and his family.

It is this system of hereditary acquisition of land that, as we have noted, made possible a sizable class of landed gentry, and it was just this system that heavy death duties were designed to dismantle.

Interesting are the several happy widows who were not burdened with properties, and whose widowhood liberated them from tiresome or destructive husbands. We think of Mrs. Brandon, Mrs. Turner, Mrs. Arbuthnot, and of course Mrs. Morland. Only she held out for the single life until the end. If we think of her as an alter ego of Angela Thirkell we understand why no remarriage occurred: Angela Thirkell was never divorced from George Thirkell and was therefore not at liberty to remarry.

Wigs on the green. An old Irish expression, meaning a conflict of the sort that might lead to a public donnybrook.

Wilfer, Mrs., Bella and Lavinia Wilfer. Characters from Dickens' *Our Mutual Friend*. Mrs. Wilfer was proud, foolish, and unpleasant in equal degrees. Bella and Lavinia were her two daughters, the last of a large family. Bella was markedly beautiful, and Lavinia markedly spirited. Neither could endure their mother, although they were kind to her.

William Rufus. Otherwise known as William II, son of William the Conqueror, and king from 1087–1100. In that year he was shot and killed by a Norman knight named William Tyrell (or Tirel) while both were hunting in the New Forest. It was presumably an accident, but possibly intentional, with the connivance of William's younger brother Henry, who was suspiciously ready to assume power.

William Whiteley (1831–1907). Whiteley opened London's first department store in 1863 and referred to himself as the "Universal Provider," supplying "from a pin to an elephant at short notice."

Window, French. In America this architectural feature is usually known as French doors—glazed double doors which open in the middle and are set in an exterior wall.

Witch of Endor. A woman described in I Samuel 28:7–25. She was sought by King Saul because she was able to communicate with the spirits of the dead, and he wished to contact the dead prophet Samuel. Indeed, she temporarily raised Samuel from the dead, whereupon he correctly foretold Saul's defeat and death.

Witenagemot. *Anglo-Saxon.* An assembly of the *witan,* a council of wise men who elected and advised the king. It acted as a general governing body, combining the functions of the judicial and legislative branches.

Witatterly, Mrs. Julia. From Dickens' *Nicholas Nickleby.* The hypochondriacal, social-climbing woman who employed Kate Nickelby as a companion. She had problems with her large and troublesome soul.

"Wittles is up." From Dickens' *Martin Chuzzlewit.* Bailey Junior, page at Mrs. Todgers' lodging house, summoned the company to dinner with these heartening words.

Woad. A blue dye of ancient usage, made from the leaves of *Isatis tinctoria,* or common woad. Julius Caesar reported that the Britons of his day painted their bodies with woad to enhance their ferocious appearance during battle. Woad was used to dye policemen's uniforms as recently as the 1930's. It is now rarely seen except on a few inland cliffs.

Wodehouse, Pelham Grenville (1881–1975). For the very few who have not heard of this writer we will say that he is the author of at least ninety-five novels, many of which were humorous and far-fetched accounts of English country house escapades. Wodehouse is the creator of Jeeves, the perfect manservant, and a list of other delightful characters. Bertie Wooster, Psmith, Pongo Twistleton, Lord Emsworth, Aunt Agatha, and Mr. Mulliner come immediately to mind. AT was one of his admirers, and, to a lesser degree, he was one of hers. He was also very close to her brother, Denis Mackail.

Women. Barsetshire is no place for feminists. Even those who can hold elastic views will wince and be appalled at the occasional references to women needing beating, or, if true women, "licking the hand that holds the whip." Frequent disparaging references are made to university education for women. Whatever problems are presented by girlhood are solved by marriage, just as in Jane Austen's day. Women look terrible in trousers. How much of this is simply Thirkell's giving her public what she thought it wanted, we cannot say.

Although it is clear that in Barsetshire married women of the gentry class are not expected to have careers, a surprising number of them do. The fact that all households had at least a small staff to do the cooking, cleaning, child care, and laundry might have left the lady of the house with leisure to pursue her fancy. Lisa Bedale, Mrs. Barton and Mrs. Rivers fall into that category; their time was used productively and must have added significantly to the family coffers. Miss Hampton and Mrs. Morland wrote from economic necessity. Several women worked very hard with their husbands, such as Amy Birkett, Kate Carter, Ella Miller, Leslie Winter, Anne Dale, Clarissa Belton, and Justinia Swan, who ended up as the wife of the headmaster of Southbridge School. *Noblesse oblige* obliged the wives and daughters of the landed gentry to keep a busy schedule of activities, to be available to tenants, and even to take, in more recent times, a fairly active part in farming and husbandry. Emmy Grantly, Sylvia Leslie, Lucy Marling, and Margot Phelps come immediately to mind. Most salient here is that the married women did not leave home on a daily basis and were not, excepting the authors, receiving paychecks. That in turn may derive from the tradition that gentlemen did not handle large amounts of money, let alone work for wages. But surely enough these women were working. Yet in no case did the activities of any woman in Barsetshire (except Mrs. Rivers) detract her from her primary focus—her family—in which they resemble most working women.

Not a single working woman is described as dull. That epithet is reserved for married but not working women such as Mary Preston Leslie, Dierdre Marling, and Edith Fairweather Keith.

The picture is not a clear one, but seems to be in Barsetshire, as elsewhere, a mix of attitudes and a muddle of situations.

Women's Land Army. Farm work was one of the options available to women during World War II. By 1943, 70,000 women were members of the Women's Land Army. Some were country girls, but many were not, and had to learn everything from scratch. Not all did heavy work such as ditching, plowing, and hedging; some did pruning and disbudding, or worked in dairies. They were informally but almost universally known as Land Girls.

Wood, John (c.1705–1754). English architect, who designed most of the buildings in Bath. When he died, his son, also John, finished the work and then designed the Royal Crescent.

Woodstock. An 1826 novel by Sir Walter Scott, about the English Civil War.

Woolton, Frederick James, Marquis, 1st Baron (1883–1964). He became well known while serving at the ministry of food during the war. Later he gathered the Conservative forces and helped the party to victory in 1951.

Wopsle's *Hamlet.* From Dickens' *Great Expectations.* Mr. Wopsle was from Pip's home village; he became a member of a theatrical troupe that came to London with a production of *Hamlet.* For the performance his queen sported a curious metal band that attached her crown to her chin.

Wordsworth, William (1770–1850). Romantic poet, author of "My Heart Leaps Up," "The Daffodils," "The World is Too Much with Us," and many others. The lines quoted by Eric Swan and recognized by Margot Phelps are from "Lucy Gray," an account of a young girl's disappearance. These are verses four and five:

> "To-night will be a stormy night—
> You to the town must go;
> And take a lantern, Child, to light
> Your mother through the snow."
>
> "That, Father! Will I gladly do:
> 'Tis scarcely afternoon—
> The minster-clock has just struck two,
> And yonder is the moon!"

Worthing. Seaside resort in west Sussex, on the English Channel on the south coast of England. It is 47 miles south of London.

"W! X! Y! Z!" A line repeated in every verse from Lear's poem "Mr and Mrs Discobbolos." Here's the first verse:

> Mr and Mrs Discobbolos
> Climbed to the top of a wall.
> And they sate to watch the sunset sky
> And to hear the Nupiter Piffkin cry
> And the Biscuit Buffalo call.
> They took up a roll and some Camomile tea,
> And both were as happy as happy could be —
> Till Mrs Discobbolos said,
> 'Oh! W! X! Y! Z!

Wykehamist. (WIK.em.ist) An alumnus of or student at the old public school, Winchester. It was founded by William of Wykeham, Bishop of Winchester, in 1382.

Xanthippe. The wife of Socrates. Convention has it that she was unbearably shrewish and carping. We think, however, that any woman whose circumstances in life have been controlled by a husband whose idea of work is to stroll around the Agora nattering about abstractions while the larder is empty and the children hungry and barefoot, will sympathize.

Yahoos. Creatures from Jonathan Swift's *Gulliver's Travels.* They had human bodies but the behavior of beasts. Gulliver was shocked to be mistaken for one because of his appearance.

The Year. The landmarks of the English year are based almost entirely upon church dates.

Twelfth Night . . . . January 5
Epiphany . . . . January 6
Hilary Term (law courts or universities) . . . . Begins in January
Lady Day (a quarter day) . . . . March 25
Easter Term (law courts or universities) . . . . Begins in March or after Easter
Easter . . . . In March or April
Rogation Sunday . . . . The fifth Sunday after Easter

Whitsunday (Pentecost) . . . . Fifty days after Easter
Midsummer (a quarter day) . . . . June 24
Trinity Term (law courts) . . . . Begins after Whitsunday
Trinity Term (Oxford) . . . . Begins in June
Michelmas (a quarter day) . . . . September 29
Michaelmas Term (law courts or Cambridge) . . . . Begins in October
Michaelmas Term (Oxford) . . . . Begins in November
Guy Fawkes Day . . . . November 5
Martinmas . . . . November 11
Christmas (a quarter day) . . . . December 25
Boxing Day . . . . The first weekday after Christmas

Bank Holidays: . . . . New Year's Day (or first weekday thereafter)
Good Friday
Easter Monday
The first Monday in May (May Day holiday)
The last Monday in May (Spring Bank Holiday)
The last Monday in August (August Bank Holiday)
Christmas Day (or the next working day thereafter)
Boxing Day (or the next working day after Christmas)

(Boxing Day was traditionally the day on which boxes of food or gifts of money were given to servants, tenants, or tradesmen.)

The Yellow Book. A short-lived but culturally influential publication, begun in 1894 and cut short—although it is a long story—by the difficulties and trial in 1897 of Oscar Wilde, who had nothing at all to do with the magazine. *The Yellow Book*—with art work by Aubrey Beardsley (among others) and writing by Walter Crane, Henry James, Maurice Baring, Arnold Bennett and Charlotte Mew—definitely signaled the end of the Victorian era.

Yellow-crowned imperials. *Fritillaria imperialis.* A member of the lily family, this tall fritillary, 3 ½–4 feet tall, has broad, shiny leaves ascending the stem. It is topped by a showy cluster of up to ten drooping yellow bells, and above that, a tuft of leaves. It is a native of the western Himalayas.

Yonge, Charlotte M. (1823–1901). English author who lived all her life in Oterbourne in Hampshire. She is the author of such popular novels of her day as *The Heir of Redclyffe, The Daisy Chain,* and others, all full of detail about family and clerical life and social change—in short, she was an early version of Angela Thirkell.

You Can't Take It with You. A comedy by American dramatists George S. Kaufman and Moss Hart. It is about a large, unconventional family each member of which—save one staid soul—believes in wringing every possible joy from life, no matter what the results.

"You never lost the childlike. . . . " From Tennyson's poem *The Princess.*

Woman is not undeveloped man,
But diverse. Could we make her as the man,
Sweet love were slain; his dearest bond is this,
Not like to like, but like in difference.
Yet in the long years liker must they grow;

244

The man be more of woman, she of man;
He gain in sweetness and in moral height,
Nor lost the wrestling thews that throw the world;
She mental breadth, not fail in childward care,
Nor lost the childlike in the larger mind;
Till at last she set herself to man,
Like perfect music unto noble words;
And so these twain, upon the skirts of Time.
Sit side by side. . . . .

"Your voice could wish the snowdrops back . . . " *See* **'The Lost Mistress."**

Part Five

Family Trees of Several Barsetshire Families

I can't think why people ever have babies.
— Maria Lufton, The Duke's Daughter

The Leslie Family in 1933

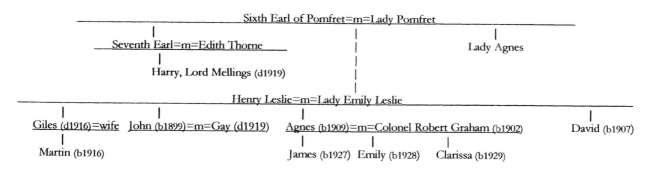

Sixth Earl of Pomfret=m=Lady Pomfret

Seventh Earl=m=Edith Thorne   Lady Agnes

Harry, Lord Mellings (d1919)

Henry Leslie=m=Lady Emily Leslie

Giles (d1916)=wife   John (b1899)=m=Gay (d1919)   Agnes (b1909)=m=Colonel Robert Graham (b1902)   David (b1907)

Martin (b1916)   James (b1927)   Emily (b1928)   Clarissa (b1929)

The Dean Family in 1935

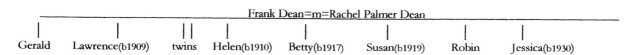

Frank Dean=m=Rachel Palmer Dean

Gerald   Lawrence(b1909)   twins   Helen(b1910)   Betty(b1917)   Susan(b1919)   Robin   Jessica(b1930)

The Keith Family in 1936

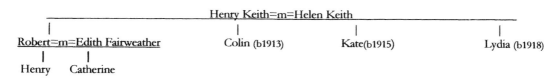

Henry Keith=m=Helen Keith

Robert=m=Edith Fairweather   Colin (b1913)   Kate(b1915)   Lydia (b1918)

Henry   Catherine

The Marling Family in 1941

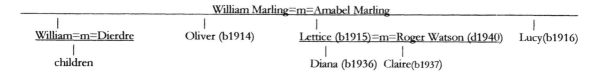

William Marling=m=Amabel Marling

William=m=Dierdre   Oliver (b1914)   Lettice (b1915)=m=Roger Watson (d1940)   Lucy(b1916)

children   Diana (b1936)   Claire(b1937)

The Leslie Family in 1960

Sixth Earl of Pomfret=m=Lady Pomfret

Seventh Earl=m=Edith Thorne

Harry, Lord Mellings (d1919)

Lady Agnes

Henry Leslie (dec.1939) =m1898= Lady Emily Leslie (dec. 1948)

Giles (dec) = wife

John =1.Gay (dec.) m1934= 2. Mary
(b1899)

Martin =m1946= Sylvia Halliday
(b1916)   (b1923) | | ||
Eleanor, George, two others

James
(b1910) ||| Henry, John, Clive

Agnes = Sir Robert Graham
(b1909)   (b1902)

Emily=m1950=Tom Grantly
(b1920) (b1928) |||| four

Clarissa=m1952=Chas. Belton
(b1929) |||| four

John
(b1921)

Robert
(b1932)

Edith=m1957=Wm. Harcourt
(b1935) (b1937) |
Gwendolyn Sally

David =m1945= Rose
(b1907)   (b1915) ||
Dorothy, Henry

The Dean Family in 1960

Frank Dean = Rachel Palmer Dean

Gerald

Lawrence =m1933=Marg. Tebbens
(b1909)   (b1917) |
children

Helen = m1935=Charles Fanshawe
(b1910)   (b1895) |
children

twins

Betty =m1939=Woolcot vanDryven
(b1917) |
children

Susan=m1947=Freddy Belton
(b1919)   (b1909) |
children

Robin

Jessica=m1948=Aubrey Clover
(b1901) |
Sarah Siddons (b1949) Henry (b1953)

The Keith Family in 1960

Henry Keith (d1940)= Helen Keith (d.1942)

Robert=m.1934= Edith Fairweather
(b1911)   (b. 1913) ||||
Henry, Catherine, two others

Colin=m.1948= Eleanor Grantly
(b.1925) |
children

Kate=m.1936=Everard Carter
(b.1915)   (b.1899) |
Robert, Angela, Philip
(b.1937) (b.1938) (b.1939)

Lydia=m.1940=Noel Merton
(b1918)   (b.1903)

Lavinia=m1961=Ludovic Foster
(b.1943)   (b.1939) |
Harry, Jessica
(b.1946)(b1947)

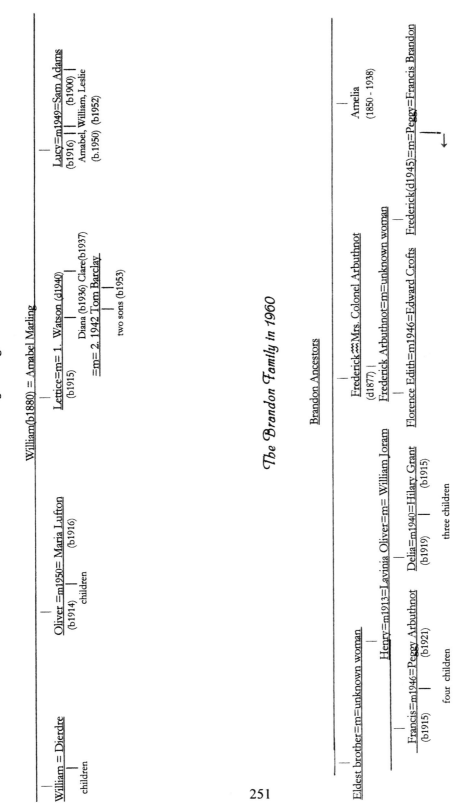

The Marling Family in 1960

William(b1880) = Amabel Marling

Oliver =m1950= Maria Lufton
(b1914)   (b1916)
    children

Lettice=m= 1. Watson (d1940)
(b1915)
=m= 2. 1942 Tom Barclay

   Diana (b1936) Clare(b1937)
       two sons (b1953)

Lucy=m1949=**Sam Adams**
(b1916)   (b1900)
   Amabel, William, Leslie
   (b.1950) (b1952)

William = Dierdre
  children

The Brandon Family in 1960

Brandon Ancestors

Frederick∽∽**Mrs. Colonel Arbuthnot**
(d1877)
Frederick Arbuthnot=m=unknown woman

Florence Edith=m1946=**Edward Crofts**

Frederick(d1945)=m=Peggy=Francis Brandon

Amelia
(1850 - 1938)

Eldest brother=m=unknown woman

Henry=m1913=Lavinia   Oliver=m= William Joram

Delia=m1940=Hilary Grant
(b1919)   (b1915)
    three children

Francis=m1946=Peggy Arbuthnot
(b1915)   (b1921)
    four children

A Barsetshire Chronology

Winter, 1932-33

George V is King

High Rising
Engaged and later married: George Knox and Anne Todd.
Adrian Coates and Sybil Knox.
Routed: Una Grey.

Summer, 1933

Wild Strawberries
Fêted: Martin Leslie on his seventeenth birthday.
Engaged and later married: John Leslie and Mary Preston.
Departed: David Leslie, to Argentina.

1934

The Demon in the House
Born: June, 1933, to Adrian and Sybil Coates, a daughter, Laura.
Engaged: Dr. James Ford and Sylvia Gould. They married thirty years later.

Summer, 1935

August Folly
Engaged and later married: Lawrence Dean and Margaret Tebben.
Helen Dean and Charles Fanshawe.
Life affected: Richard Tebben goes to work for Mr. Dean.

Summer, 1936
George V dies.
Edward VIII ascends and abdicates.
George VI becomes king.

Summer Half
Engaged and later married: Kate Keith and Everard Carter.
Dis-engaged: Philip Winter and Rose Birkett.
Life affected: Colin Keith decides to read law with Noel Merton.

January, 1938

Pomfret Towers
Engaged and later married: Giles Foster and Sally Wicklow.
In love and later married: Roddy Wicklow and Alice Barton.
Died: Major Foster.

Summer, 1938
September: the
Munich agreement.

The Brandons
Engaged and later married: Justin Miller and Ella Morris.
Delia Brandon and Hilary Grant.
Died: Amelia Brandon.

Summer, 1938

Before Lunch
Thwarted: Lord Aberfordbury, in his wish to turn Pooker's Piece into a garage.
Engaged and later married: Daphne Stonor and C.W. Bond.
Lilian Stonor and Alister Cameron.
Life affected: Denis Stonor leaves England, his ballet financed by Lord Bond.

Fall, 1939; winter & spring, 1940 England prepares for war. September 3: war is declared Spring: Dunkirk evacuation	### *Cheerfulness Breaks In* **Married:** Rose Birkett and John Fairweather. **Engaged and later married:** Tommy Needham and Octavia Crawley. Geraldine Birkett and Geoffrey Fairweather. **Married:** Lydia Keith and Noel Merton. **Died:** Mr. Keith. **Died:** Lord Pomfret. Giles Foster becomes 8th Earl. **Life affecting:** The Hosiers' Boys' Foundation School is evacuated to Southbridge School.

Autumn, 1940; winter 1941
Rationing is started.
Roosevelt is re-elected.
Churchill is Prime Minister.
Holland, Belgium, France fall.
The Blitz begins.
The Battle of Britain is fought.
Italy enters the war.
	### *Northbridge Rectory*
	Life in wartime: Work parties, parachute spotting, caring for evacuees, living
	        among military personnel.
	News of friends: Noel and Lydia Merton are living in Scotland.
	Failed romance: Poppy Turner decides she can live without Mr. Downing.
	Engaged and later married: Edie Pover and Corporal Jackson.
	        Mrs. Turner's nieces to Tommy Greaves and Captain Topham.
	Passing through: Major and Mrs. Spender.

1941
 	
Pearl Harbor
The U.S. Enters the war.
Heavy fighting in North Africa.
Germany invades Russia.
	### *Marling Hall*
	Enlarged families: Agnes and Robert Graham now have six children.
	        Lord and Lady Pomfret have two: Ludovic and Emily.
	        Kate and Everard Carter have three: Bobby, Angela and Philip.
	Honored: Robert Graham is knighted.
	Failed romances: Lettice Watson and David Leslie.
	        Lucy Marling and Tom Barclay.
	        Frances Harvey and Oliver Marling.
	Engaged and later married: Lettice Watson and Tom Barclay.
	Passing through: Geoffrey and Frances Harvey.

Autumn, 1942; winter 1943 Japan captures Singapore. The Beveridge Report published.	### *Growing Up* **Casualty:** Tommy Needham has lost an arm in North Africa. **Engaged and later married:** Selina Crockett and Sergeant Hopkins. Leslie Waring and Philip Winter. **Still engaged and soon to be married:** Octavia Crawley and Tommy Needham. **Life affected:** Tommy is given the living at Lambton. **Pregnant:** Lydia Merton.

Autumn, 1943
Winter, 1944
	### *The Headmistress*
	Lives affected: The Beltons have had to let their big house to a school and move
	        to a smaller one in the adjacent village of Harefield.
	        Sam Adams meets the Beltons.
	Born: Lavinia Merton.
	Engaged and later married: Elsa Belton and Christopher Hornby.
	        Madeleine Sparling and Sidney Carton.

1944	*Miss Bunting*
Allied troops storm Anzio.	**Casualty:** Robin Dale is home in Hallbury, adjusting to the loss of a foot in the Anzio offensive.
	Lives affected: Francis Gresham is missing in the Far East. Jane, his wife, waits. Gradka, the Myxo-Lydian refugee, learns from Miss Bunting. Robin Dale returns to Southbridge School as Junior Classical Master. Francis Gresham returns home.
	Died: Maud Bunting.
D Day.	**Nearly romance:** Sam Adams and Jane Gresham.
	Budding romance: Anne Fielding and Robin Dale.

Summer, 1945	*Peace Breaks Out*
	Home from the war: George and Sylvia Halliday.
Death of Hitler	**Enlarged family:** John and Mary Leslie have two sons.
	Lives affected: Martin Leslie has returned to Rushwater with a serious leg injury suffered
VE DAY	at Anzio.
VJ Day	Robin Dale is Housemaster of the Junior House at Southbridge School.
Government resigns	**Nearly romance:** David Leslie and Sylvia Halliday. David Leslie and Anne Fielding.
General election; Churchill	**Engaged and later married:** Robin Dale and Anne Fielding.
defeated, Atlee elected.	Martin Leslie and Sylvia Halliday.
Beginning of Labour Party's	David Leslie and Rose Bingham.
sweeping changes	**Died:** Robin's father, Dr. Dale. Henry Leslie

Summer, 1946	*Private Enterprise*
	Family enlarged: Noel and Lydia Merton have a second child, a son, Harry.
Rationing continues.	**Failed romance:** Colin Keith and Peggy Arbuthnot.
	Lives affected: Noel Merton takes silk, and has a flirtation with Peggy Arbuthnot.
	Mr. Birkett retires and moves to Winter Overcotes.
	Everard Carter is new Headmaster; he, Kate and family move to
	Headmaster's house.
The Welfare State unrolls.	**Engaged and later married:** Effie Arbuthnot and Edward Crofts.
	Peggy Arbuthnot and Francis Brandon.

Summer, 1947	*Love among the Ruins*
A bad winter.	**A wedding:** Anne Fielding and Robin Dale.
	A birthday party: Lady Emily Leslie's eightieth, at Rushwater.
Sir Stafford Cripps is	**Engaged and later married:** Richard Tebben and Petrea Krogsbrog.
Chancellor of the Exchequer	Freddy Belton and Susan Dean.
	Failed romance: Oliver Marling and Jessica Dean.
Indian independence	**Budding romance:** Charles Belton and Clarissa Graham.
	Families enlarged: Martin and Sylvia Leslie have a daughter, Eleanor.
	Lawrence and Margaret Dean have at least one child.
	David and Rose Leslie have two: Catherine and Henry.
	Christopher and Elsa Hornby have two: Catriona and Freddy.
	John and Mary Leslie have a third son.
	Lives affected: Lucy Marling will farm for Sam Adams on land he has bought from
	her father.
	Beliers Priory now houses a preparatory school run by Philip Winter.
	Miss Holly is now headmistress of Hosiers' Girls' Foundation School.
	Passing through: Winston Churchill.

Summer, 1948	**The Old Bank House**
	Lives affected: Sam Adams buys The Old Bank House in Edgewood from Miss Sowerby.
	Miss Merriman moves back to Pomfret Towers to help Lord Pomfret.
	Henry Grantly leaves for his National Service in the Far East.
	Family enlarged: Noel and Lydia Merton have a third child, a daughter, Jessica.
	Freddy and Susan Belton have a son, Freddy.
	Died: Lady Emily Leslie.
	Marriage revealed: Jessica Dean and Aubrey Clover.
	Engaged and later married: Eleanor Grantly and Colin Keith.
	Lucy Marling and Sam Adams.

Autumn & winter, 1948	**County Chronicle**
Spring, 1949	**Married:** Heather Adams and Ted Pilward.
	A wedding: Lucy Marling and Sam Adams.
	Born: to Robin and Anne Dale, twin daughters.
	to Peggy and Francis Brandon, twins, their second and third children.
	to Jessica and Aubrey Clover, a daughter, Sarah Siddons Clover.
	Died: Mrs. Dale, Isabel Dale's old mother and Robin Dale's aunt.
	Engaged and later married: Isabel Dale and Lord Silverbridge.
	Mrs. Brandon and Bishop Joram.
	Charles Belton and Clarissa Graham.
	Lives affected: Mr. Miller goes to St. Ewold's and Mr. Parkinson comes to Pomfret Madrigal.
	Robin Dale has inherited the Great House at Allington.

Autumn, 1949	**The Duke's Daughter**
Spring & Summer, 1950	**Died:** Sir Harry Waring and Lady Harriet Waring, a few weeks apart.
	Mr. Macpherson, at Rushwater.
	Lives affected: Jeff and Isabel Palliser rent The Lodge in Silverbridge.
	Mr. Marling gives The Cedars to Oliver Marling.
	The Priory School will move to Harefield House.
	Tom Grantly tries being a bureaucrat.
	Cecil Waring will use Beliers Priory as a home for naval orphans.
	Freddy and Susan Belton move to Dowlah Cottage.
Gasoline is no longer rationed.	**Births:** Ted and Heather Pilward have their first child, a son.
	Sam and Lucy Adams have their first child, a daughter, Amabel.
	Preganant: Isabel Palliser (Lady Silverbridge).
	Engaged and later married: Cora Palliser and Cecil Waring.
	Tom Grantly and Emmy Graham .
	Again: Charles Belton and Clarissa Graham.
	Oliver Marling and Maria Lufton
	Marigold Smith and Geoffrey Coxon.

Autumn, 1951	**Happy Return**
Early winter, 1952	**Failed romance:** Eric Swan and Grace Grantly.
	Married: Charles Belton and Clarissa Graham, on January 1, 1952.
Election: Conservatives returned.	**Families enlarged:** Mavis and Ted Parkinson have their third, a son, Josiah.
	Cora and Cecil Waring have their first, a son, Plantagenet Cecil
	Maria and Oliver Marling have their first, a daughter, Mora.
	Engaged and later married: Lord Lufton and Grace Grantly.

Jutland Cottage

Winter, through summer, 1952

Lives affected: Tubby Fewling made an honorary Canon; he moves to Greshamsbury.
He has received a substantial inheritance from an aunt.
Margot Phelps is treated to a make-over, and her book is sent to a publisher.

February 6,
Death of King George IV
Ascension of Elizabeth II

Mr. Wickham inherits £600 a year.
The Priory School moves, becomes Harefield House School.
Hosiers' Girls' Foundation School moves to a nearby campus.

Family enlarged: a second son is born to Lord and Lady Silverbridge (the Pallisers).

Failed romance: Tubby Fewling and Margot Phelps.

Engaged and later married: Margot Phelps and Donald Macfadyen.
Justinia Lufton and Eric Swan.

What Did It Mean?

February – June, 1953

Lives affected: Noel Merton is knighted.
Ludovic Foster performs at the Northbridge Coronation Ceremony.

Coronation of Elizabeth II

Miss Pemberton is ill.
A cook/housekeeper has been engaged for the Phelpses, allowing the marriage of Margot and Mr. Macfadyen.
Poppy Turner returns to Northbridge.

Sir Edmund Hillary
conquers Everest

Family enlarged: Aubrey and Jessica Clover have a second child, a son, Henry.

Engaged and later married: Poppy Turner and Harold Downing.

Enter Sir Robert

Summer, 1954

Pregnant: Sylvia Halliday Leslie, with her third child.
Clarissa Graham Belton, with her first.

Life affected: The Hatch End bank vacates the Old Manor House.
Sir Robert Graham retires.
Leonard Halliday is ill.
Edith Graham leaves to visit New York with the David Leslies.

Never Too Late

Summer, 1955

Died: Miss Pemberton. Leonard Halliday.

Lives affected: Mr. and Mrs. Carter rent the Old Manor House.
Edith Graham goes to Pomfret Towers to learn estate management.
Mrs. Halliday goes to Rushwater for a long visit after Mr. Halliday's death.

Failed romance: Mrs. Morland turns aside Lord Crosse's rather tepid proposal.

Pregnant: Sylvia Halliday Leslie, with her fourth.

Engaged: Dorothea Merryman and Herbert Choyce.

A Double Affair

Autumn, 1955
January, 1956

A wedding: Dorothea Merryman and Herbert Choyce.

Lives affected: Edith Graham has visited the U.S. again for several months.
Mrs. Halliday rekindles a friendship and winters in France.
Miss Dunsford cuts the apron strings and also winters in France.

Engaged and married: George Halliday to Jane Crawley.
John-Arthur Crosse to Grace Crawley.

Budding romance: Edith Graham and Lord William Harcourt.

Summer and autumn, 1957

Close Quarters
(Married: Edith Graham and Lord William Harcourt.)
Died: Donald Macfadyen. Mrs. Phelps. Admiral Phelps.
Lives affected: Tubby Fewling becomes a resident Canon and takes Acacia House.
    Gregory Villars retires, vacates The Rectory and moves to the Close.
Engaged and later married: Tubby Fewling and Margot Phelps Macfadyen.

Spring through summer, 1958

Love at All Ages
Born: to Edith Graham Harcourt and William Harcourt, a daughter, Gwendolyn Sally.
Engaged; a wedding: Gwendolyn Harcourt and Caleb Oriel.
Lives affected: Elaine Harcourt decides to break free a bit and visit in the U.S.
    Dow decides to visit Lady DeCourcy in Mentone.
    Everard Carter has retired and is living in the Old Rectory, Northbridge.
Budding romance: Ludovic Foster, Viscount Mellings, and Lavinia Merton.

July and August, 1961

Wedding of Princess Margaret and Antony Armstrong–Jones

Threescore and Ten
Lives affected: Laura Morland's seventieth birthday and party.
    Eric Swan is Headmaster of Southbridge School.
Family enlarged: Octavia Crawley Needham and Tommy Needham have twins, their
    seventh and eighth children.
Thwarted: Lord Aberfordbury in his scheme to buy Wiple Terrace and put up a factory
    in its place.
Engaged: Dr. Ford and Sylvia Gould.
    Ludovic Foster, Viscount Mellings, and Lavinia Merton.

1962

(adumbrated)
A wedding: James Ford and Sylvia Gould.
And: Ludovic Foster, Viscount Mellings, and Lavinia Merton, just after Easter.

BARSETSHIRE SERIES

The Warden, 1855

Septimus Harding, an engaging widower with two daughters, is the Precentor at the Cathedral in Barchester. His elder daughter, Susan, is married to Archdeacon Theophilus Grantly, son of the Bishop. The younger daughter, Eleanor, is engaged to John Bold, a surgeon. Part of Mr. Harding's income comes from his duties as warden of Hiram's Hospital, a home for twelve impoverished old men. The funds to support this home derive from certain properties in the area which had been modest enough in the fifteenth century, when the home was established, but which generate an unseemly large income for the warden in the nineteenth. For such was the nature of the covenant under which the hospital was administered, that after its expenses had been met, the remaining money was properly the warden's. This situation looks fishy to John Bold, who, with surprising disregard for his future happiness in this family, brings it to public attention. A large flap ensues. Mr. Harding is found to be blameless, but he decides that perhaps after all he is receiving too much money. He gives up his position as warden to become rector in the small parish church of St. Cuthbert's. Eleanor and John Bold marry after all.

Barchester Towers, 1857

Various power struggles lie at the heart of this novel. Bishop Grantly has died, and his son, Theophilus, husband of Susan Harding Grantly, has been passed over to succeed his father. Instead, that unlovely couple the Proudies are installed in the Palace, bringing with them the even more unlovely Obadiah Slope, who is their domestic chaplain but who wishes to be made Dean of the Cathedral. In the power struggle with his wife, the unprepossessing Bishop has been vanquished long before. Mrs. Proudie herself is vying with Mr. Slope for control of the diocese. In this he might have some success should he marry one of the Proudie daughters, as Mrs. Proudie intends. The Proudies and Mr. Slope oppose a church faction that seeks to reinstall Mr. Harding at Hiram's Hospital, but Mr. Slope switches sides when he begins to pursue Eleanor Harding Bold, by now a widow with a handsome income. Mr. Slope also is instrumental in recalling from Italy Dr. Vesey Stanhope, who reappears in Barchester with his family of grown children, one of whom is the beautiful Madeline Neroni. Having been rebuffed by Susan Bold, Mr. Slope turns his attentions to Madame Neroni. This infuriates Mrs. Proudie and spells the end of Barchester for Mr. Slope. Susan marries Mr. Arabin, the brilliant Vicar of St. Ewold's; it is he who is made Dean of the Cathedral.

Doctor Thorne, 1858

Set in Greshamsbury, this story entwines the fates and fortunes of the Greshams, the Scatcherds, and the Thornes. Dwindling fortune dictates that young Frank Gresham marry a woman with money, but he is in love with Mary Thorne, not aware that she is the illegitimate daughter of Mary Scatcherd and Henry Thorne. The Scatcherds are a family of rising fortune. Roger Scatcherd, a coarse stone mason, had killed Henry Thorne to avenge the honor of his sister Mary. After serving a prison term, he has made a fortune as a contractor, becoming a baronet, lending money to Frank Gresham's father, and buying Boxall Hill, one of the loveliest properties on the Gresham estate. Mary Thorne has been raised by her uncle, Thomas Thorne, the local doctor, a man of genteel upbringing but no fortune to speak of. As luck would have it, both Sir Roger Scatcherd and his son are alcoholics, dying of drink in timely fashion and leaving all their money to Mary, who is then able to marry Frank. Frank Gresham's mother is from the DeCourcy family. Many critics have considered *Dr. Thorne* to be one of Trollope's most satisfying and pleasing novels.

Framley Parsonage, 1861

Mark Robarts, a young clergyman from a modest background, has been given the living of Framley through the auspices of Lady Lufton, widowed mother of his friend Ludovic, the young Lord Lufton. He takes up his life in Framley parsonage with his wife Fanny and makes friends in the neighborhood. In particular he becomes acquainted with the M.P., Nathaniel Sowerby of Chaldicotes, a charming fellow but known to be dodgy in his financial dealings. Sowerby sets about a sort of seduction of Mark, inviting him to affairs at Chaldicotes and to the Duke of Omnium's Gatherum Castle, with the result that Mark signs notes totaling £900. (Readers of Trollope will learn, if nothing else, *never* co-sign a promissory note.) When payment came due, and Sowerby smoothly leaves Mark to face the creditors, he throws him the sop of a prebendial stall at Barchester Cathedral. When the Duke of Omnium, who holds mortgages on Chaldicotes, presses Sowerby for payment, Sowerby makes a try for the hand in marriage of the wealthy Martha Dunstable. She has better sense than to marry him, but she buys the mortgages, thus acquiring Chaldicotes. She and Doctor Thorne are married and live there happily ever after.

In the meantime, Mark Robert's father has died and his lovely sister Lucy has arrived to visit him. Lord Lufton falls in love with her, but his mother disapproves of the match, desiring that her son should marry the cool and stately Griselda Grantly, daughter of Theophilus and Susan. However, Lady Lufton is eventually won over by Lucy's fine character and the strength she shows in caring for Grace Crawley, the gravely ill wife of the impoverished perpetual curate of Hogglestock. A glittering match is made for Griselda with Lord Dumbello—and if you think his name was meant to indicate his intelligence, you are right.

The Small House at Allington, 1864

At the center of this novel are the sisters Lilian and Isabella Dale, always known as Lily and Bell. They live with their widowed mother in the Small House at Allington, provided by the generosity of Mrs. Dale's brother-in-law, Squire Christopher Dale of Allington Great House. Christopher wishes for his nephew and heir to marry Bell. Lily is loved by her childhood friend the penniless Johnny Eames, but she falls in love with Adolphus Crosbie, a self-seeking cad, although of course she doesn't know of his feet of clay. They become engaged, but shortly afterward, on a visit to Courcy Castle, Adolphus proposes to Lady Alexandrina de Courcy. For reasons of her own she accepts. Lily is devastated, but tries not to show it. Johnny Eames renews his suit, but Lily is determined to marry no one. Meanwhile, Johnny just happens to be passing by when a bull charges Lord de Guest, saves Lord de Guest's life, and is thereafter a favored friend at Guestwick, receiving a substantial legacy when the old Lord dies. Bell marries a local doctor, James Crofts. The Crosbie marriage is a disaster; soon after the ceremony Adolphus and Lady Alexandrina separate, she going with her mother to stay at Baden-Baden.

The Last Chronicle of Barset, 1867

Remember the perpetual curate, Mr. Crawley, at Hogglestock? He is accused of stealing a check and spends much time and anguish getting his name cleared. Major Henry Grantly, son of Archdeacon Theophilus Grantly and his wife Susan Harding Grantly, is a widower with a daughter, Edith. He is in love with Mr. Crawley's daughter Grace His father opposes the marriage as financially disadvantageous but eventually relents. Johnny Eames continues to press his suit with Lily Dale, unsuccessfully. Mrs. Proudie, who has cast her evil shadow over the matter of Mr. Crawley and the check, is defeated by him. She then dies, and a sigh of relief goes up all over England, as she was as much a popularly loathed character and as Lily Dale was a much loved one.

PARLIAMENTARY SERIES

Note: These novels are even more complex than the preceding ones. Only the aspects that concern Barsetshire or characters whose descendants are known in Barsetshire are mentioned.

Can You Forgive Her? 1864

Gatherum Castle in West Barsetshire is the seat of the Duke of Omnium. His heir, Plantaganet Palliser, has reluctantly been married to the equally reluctant heiress, Glencora Palliser. Both are dutiful, although Glencora can not forget her lover, Burgo Fitzgerald (you can tell by his name that he is no good) and Plantaganet can scarcely think of anything but politics. At a ball Glencora attracts attention by dancing with Burgo, who has counted on persuading her to elope with him. Plantaganet, summoned from home, arrives and takes her away. The next morning she confesses that she still loves Burgo, but Plantaganet, saying that he loves her, decides to take her to Europe, even turning down in order to do so something he had wanted for years, the office of Chancellor of the Exchequer. The trip gradually becomes a success as Glencora slowly realizes her husband's many fine qualities. She returns pregnant and later, at Matching Priory, their Yorkshire home, she gives birth to a son and heir, Lord Silverbridge.

Phineas Finn, 1869

Primarily the account of the career of a young Irish M.P., Phineas Finn, this novel has little to do with Barsetshire. The Pallisers are in the background; Lady Glencora has mounted a series of entertainments designed to further Plantaganet's career; he is again offered the position of Chancellor of the Exchequer and loses no time accepting it.

The Eustace Diamonds, 1873

This novel, about Lizzie Eustace and a diamond necklace belonging to her late husband's family, has only slight connection with Barsetshire. The Duke of Omnium is by this time very old and increasingly infirm; Lady Glencora keeps him up to date on all the gossip about the diamonds and Lizzie.

Phineas Redux, 1874

Phineas returns to London after an absence of seven years, and resumes his political career, encouraged and aided by his friend Madame Max Goesler. His career runs into a snag when he is arrested and tried for murder. Thanks to some investigation on the part of Madame Max, he is acquitted. While all this is going on, the old Duke of Omnium dies and Plantaganet assumes the title.

The Prime Minister, 1876

Plantaganet Palliser, now the Duke of Omnium, is Prime Minister following the fall of the Liberal government, furthered in his career by the ever more energetic social affairs organized by Lady Glencora. After three years the government falls, and the Duke retires from politics. He and Lady Glencora spend little or no time at Gatherum Castle, because she loathes it. Their marriage is workable, even satisfying, but not blissful, as each has to endure in the other the essential qualities that have been present since the beginning. The Duke is cool, intellectual, benign, and detached; the Duchess warm, witty, willful, impulsive, and outspoken. She is one of Trollope's most successful and memorable heroines.

The Duke's Children, 1880

      Several months after leaving office, the entire family of the Duke of Omnium goes on an extended European tour. A week after their return to Matching Priory, the Duchess is dead of, perhaps, influenza. The three children provide the focus of the novel: The are Lord Silverbridge, Lord Gerald, and Lady Mary, and they give the reader a run for his money. Lord Silverbridge is sent down from Oxford for a prank, and then falls in with a shady fellow, buys a large share in a race horse, and loses £70,000, which the Duke pays. Lord Gerald, who has done indifferently at Cambridge, is also sent down, and runs up gambling debts of £3400. These the longsuffering and fortunately very wealthy Duke also pays. Lord Gerald then goes up to Oxford to turn over a new leaf. Lady Mary, who has been engaged to Frank Tregear with her mother's consent, but without her father's knowledge, runs into trouble with the Duke when he hears of it. At the end, Silverbridge marries the rich American, Isabel Boncassen, Lady Mary and Frank are wed after all, Gerald is still at Oxford and the Duke has returned to political office.

Note: In the mid-1970's the Parliamentary series was dramatized by the BBC as *The Pallisers*. These videotapes have now been reissued in two sets of four tapes each.

A Chronology of Events in the Life of Angela Thirkell

1890, January 30	Angela was born to Doctor and Mrs. John Mackail of 27 Young Street, Kensington, London. Her mother was the daughter of Edward Burne–Jones, her father a respected Dante scholar. Rudyard Kipling and Stanley Baldwin were second cousins.
1898	Edward Burne–Jones died. The Mackails moved to #6, Pembroke Gardens.
1901	During a childhood illness, Angela's mother began reading *Barchester Towers* to her. Angela later finished the Trollope Barsetshire series on her own.
1904	Angela left the Froebel Institute in Kensington and entered St. Paul's school in Hammersmith. In her late teens Angela spent six months at a pension in Paris. She studied dressmaking and perfected her French. The next year she lived for several months in Gotha, Germany, studying music and German.
1911, May 5	Angela and James McInnes, a professional singer with a fine baritone voice, were married by special license. He was sixteen years her senior.
1912, January	Angela's son Graham was born.
1914, August	Angela's son Colin was born.
1917, March	Angela's daughter Mary was born.
1917, May	Angela returned, with her children, to her parents' home. She was no longer able to tolerate McInnes' drunkenness, his savage temper, his physical abuse, or his flagrant infidelities. She spent time with the Wyndhams at Clouds House in Wiltshire, and with their daughter, Mary, Lady Elcho (later Lady Wemyss) at Stanway House in the Cotswolds.
1917, May	A divorce was granted on uncontested grounds of cruelty and adultery. Although Angela was innocent, divorce under any conditions was at the least an embarrassment, because she was inevitably considered guilty of being at fault in some way.
1918, February	Mary died of pneumonia.
1918, December	Following a brief but romantic courtship, Angela was married to the Tasmanian George Lancelot Thirkell. He had been in Scotland recuperating from wounds received at Gallipoli, and was posted to a training depot in Wiltshire when they met at a house party. He was an engineer.
1919	The Thirkells lodged in the village of Totley, Yorkshire. George had an engineering job in Darlington, and Angela began learning to cook. She took her sons for walks and picnics on the moors and no doubt observed village life at first hand.
1920, January	The Thirkells set sail for Australia on a reconditioned troopship. She told the story of this mad voyage in *Trooper to the Southern Cross*. The ultimate destination was

Hobart, Tasmania; they reached it in March after several other stops and set up housekeeping at 405 Elizabeth Street.

1920, June	George and Angela moved to Melbourne, Australia, where George worked as an agent for a steel company.
1921, January	Angela's son Lancelot George Thirkell was born.
1923	Angela's parents visited her. By this time she was terribly homesick. She had made a heroic effort to adapt to Australian life, but simply couldn't be happy there. She had, however, begun writing, and had had some sketches and essays published in Australian newspapers. She began painfully to realize the cultural disparity between herself and George Thirkell. Angela's cousin Stanley Baldwin became Prime Minister.
1928	Angela returned to England for a visit that lasted nearly a year. It included visits to country houses, the excitement of London, and falling in love. (She wrote about this affair in *Ankle Deep*, 1933.)
1929	After a brief reunion with George in Melbourne, Angela left Australia. She had begged passage money from James M. Barrie, and used it to buy tickets for herself and her son Lance. She left everything in Australia, and never saw George Thirkell again. Colin joined her in England a few weeks later. Angela lived with her parents in Pembroke Gardens; Colin was sent to Switzerland and Lance to a prep school.
1930	A piece Angela wrote for the BBC was never aired. Whether she rejected the BBC or they her is not clear. She continued to write.
1931, December	*Three Houses* was published by Oxford University Press. It was a marked success.
1932	Angela gained support from old friends E.V. Lucas and Graham Robertson, who introduced her to James Hamilton, the young man who was the principal in Hamish Hamilton, Ltd. He accepted *Ankle Deep*. That Christmas Angela and Lance spent with friends at the Old Vicarage in Tirley, Gloucestershire. This holiday formed the basis of *High Rising*.
1933	*Ankle Deep* came out in January, on Angela's 43rd birthday. *High Rising* came out in September. That summer Angela was again invited to Stanway by Lady Wemyss. *Wild Strawberries* was inspired by the visit, and the character of Lady Emily Leslie by Lady Wemyss.
1934	Three books were published: *Trooper to the Southern Cross, Wild Strawberries,* and *The Demon in the House.* It was in the last that Barchester was first mentioned. As a Trollope revival was occurring at the time, readers took easily to the extension of Barsetshire life into their present.
1935	Angela spent time in Buxton, in the Midlands; in August she was in Ambleside in Cumberland. She and her father were in Scotland in September as guests of Lady Wemyss at Harestanes in East Lothian. She read books for Hamilton at the rate of £1 per book.

We cannot detail all of Angela's visits in England or on the continent, nor can we detail the publication of all her books, as they are in any case listed on a following page. Suffice it to say that over the years she was a guest in many houses in many parts of England. Only those that have some bearing on her Barsetshire novels are noted among the other entries here.

1937	Angela made her first trip to the United States and Canada, visiting New York, Boston, Washington, Ottawa, Montreal, and Quebec. She preferred The United States, finding it warm and cheerful.
1938	Graham McInnes was married in London. He and his wife lived in Canada.
1939	Angela and her parents left London. They stayed at a hotel in Chipping Camden; she went as a paying guest to a Miss Dorothy Collins at Top Meadow in Beaconsfield. It was this village in wartime that inspired her next few books. Lance was an undergraduate at Magdalen College, Oxford. While living in Beaconsfield, Angela met C.A. Lejeune.
1940	Angela got her first taste of political correctness when Alfred Knopf asked that she modify some portions of *Cheerfulness Breaks In*. She changed the Warburgs to Warburys to avoid offending her Jewish public (Knopf was Jewish), but would not change the strong portrait of the evacuees, feeling that her picture of them was if anything too pallid. (The English children that had come to the U.S. were all attractive and civilized children from upper- and middle-class families.) (For a seriously politically incorrect picture of wartime evacuees, read Evelyn Waugh's novel *Put Out More Flags*.)
1945	Angela reopened the house in Pembroke Gardens and moved back into it to care for her parents, who were very ill. Dr. Mackail died just before Christmas.
1946	Lance Thirkell was married in the village of Aldbourne near Salisbury. Angela's mother was a permanent invalid. The postwar Labour Government began to dismantle much that Angela held dear.
1974	Angela was invited to the wedding of Princess Elizabeth and Philip Mountbatten. She attended.
1948	Angela moved to a flat in Cheyne Walk, facing the Thames.
1949	In April Angela visited the U.S. for the third time, speaking at Harvard, Princeton, and Yale about Dumas père. She visited Graham and his family in Canada.
1950	Margaret Bird began to do secretarial work for Angela. Angela gave frequent talks throughout England, to various groups, guilds, and university audiences. Colin McInnes' first book came out that year. Angela did not like that nor any of his books, which seemed designed to shock her. An antagonism had developed between them—not surprisingly. Few are the mothers who are serene in the face of wholesale rejection of their values, who find that their sons are sexually unorthodox and frequently drunk and in trouble with the police. Each loathed everything the

other stood for; their relationship broke down completely and she omitted any mention of him in her will.

1951   During the Festival of Britain Angela gave a televised interview for the BBC. In May she signed a lease for a three-story house in Shawfield Street. A fall on the steps there left her with a permanent limp.

1953   Margaret Mackail died. The task of closing her family's home exhausted Angela and she spent some time in a nursing home. She felt that she never fully recovered from the strain.

1955   Another trip to America: New York, Boston, Chicago, Minneapolis. She had booked numerous speaking engagements.

1957   Angela was increasingly unwell from an undiagnosed condition. However, she kept up her schedule, wrote introductions to reissues of *The Warden* and *Barchester Towers,* and produced *Close Quarters* on schedule.

1958   Graham, by now Deputy High Commissioner for Canada, visited London. Her relationship with him, as well as that with Colin, was deteriorating. He too disagreed with her politics and her conservative social attitudes. During this year she began to be unable to write, and struggled to make her dead-lines. Her work was often a confused muddle.

1960   She was admitted to St. Thomas Hospital, diagnosed with aplastic anemia. Later she was transferred to Hyde–Style, a nursing home, where she was given a blood transfusion every two weeks. These gave no lasting benefit. She was lonely, continually cold, and longing for rum, to which she had become addicted.

1961   Angela died in the hospital in January, one day before her 71st birthday. C.A Lejeune finished her final novel, *Three Score and Ten.*.

The above biographical information has been taken from *Angela Thirkell, Portrait of a Lady Novelist,* by Margot Strickland. For those with a real interest in the Barsetshire books, we recommend this biography. It has abundant detail about the events and relationships that found their way onto the pages of the novels.

A List of the Novels

Barsetshire novels are starred, and abbreviations used in the text are given

1931 Three Houses
1933 Ankle Deep
1933 High Rising*   HR
1934 Wild Strawberries*   WS
1934 Trooper to the Southern Cross
1934 The Demon in the House*   DH
1935 O, These Men, These Men!
1935 The Grateful Sparrow
1936 The Fortunes of Harriet
1936 August Folly*   AF
1937 Coronation Summer
1937 Summer Half*   SH
1938 Pomfret Towers*   PT
1939 The Brandons*   B
1939 Before Lunch*   BL
1940 Cheerfulness Breaks In*   CBI
1941 Northbridge Rectory*   NR
1942 Marling Hall*   MH
1943 Growing Up*   GU
1944 The Headmistress*   H
1945 Miss Bunting*   MB
1946 Peace Breaks Out*   PBO
1947 Private Enterprise*   PE
1948 Love Among the Ruins*   LAR
1949 The Old Bank House*   OBH
1950 County Chronicle*   CC
1951 The Duke's Daughter*   DD
1952 Happy Return*   HaRe
1953 Jutland Cottage*   JC
1954 What Did It Mean?*   WDIM
1955 Enter Sir Robert*   ESR
1956 Never Too Late*   NTL
1957 A Double Affair*   ADA
1958 Close Quarters*   CQ
1959 Love at All Ages*   LAA
1961 Three Score and Ten*   TST

Sources

Addison, Paul. *Now the War Is Over.* London: British Broadcasting Company and Jonathan Cape, 1985.

Aesop's Fables. New York: Vincent Dill, n.d.

Allen, Reginald. *The First Night Gilbert and Sullivan.* New York: The Heritage Press, 1958.

Arnold, Matthew, Poetry and Prose. John Bryson, ed. Cambridge: Harvard University Press, 1967.

Austen, Jane. *Pride and Prejudice.* London: The Folio Society, 1975.

_____ . *Sense and Sensibility.* Ibid.

_____ . *Mansfield Park.* Ibid.

_____ . *Emma.* Ibid.

_____ . *Northanger Abbey.* Ibid.

Automobile Association. *Book of the British Countryside.* London: Drive Publications Ltd., 1973.

Baedeker, Karl. *Great Britain* vol. I. New York: The Macmillan Company, 1966.

Barham, R.H. *The Ingoldsby Legends.* London: William Heinemann, 1909.

Beattie, John W., et al. *The Golden Book of Favorite Songs.* Chicago: Hall & McCreary Company, 1941.

Beauman, Nicola. *Cynthia Asquith.* London: Hamish Hamilton Ltd., 1987.

Belloc, Hillaire. *Cautionary Verses.* New York: Alfred A. Knopf, 1951.

Bickerton, Fred. *Fred of Oxford.* London: Evans Brothers, 1954.

Boccaccio, Giovanni. *Tales from the Decameron.* New York: Washington Square Press, Inc., 1961.

The Book of Common Prayer. New York: Oxford University Press, 1938.

Boswell, James. *Life of Samuel Johnson.* New York: Doubleday and Co., 1946.

Briggs, Susan. *The Home Front.* London: Weidenfield and Nicholson, 1975.

Bromhead, Peter. *Life in Modern Britain.* London: Longman Group Ltd., 1962.

Browning, Robert. *The Poems of Robert Browning.* Edited by Charlotte Porter and Helen Clark. New York: Thomas Y. Crowell, 1896.

Bryson, John, Ed. *Matthew Arnold, Poetry and Prose.* Cambridge, Massachusetts: Harvard University Press, 1967.

Bulfinch's Mythology. New York: Doubleday & Co., 1948.

Bunyan, John. *The Pilgrim's Progress.* New York: E.P. Dutton & Co., 1961.

Cannadine, David. *The Decline and Fall of the British Aristocracy.* New Haven: Yale University Press, 1990.

Carroll, Lewis. *Alice in Wonderland and Through the Looking Glass.* New York: Grosset and Dunlap, 1946.

Churchill, Winston. *The Birth of Britain.* New York: Dodd, Mead & Co., 1956.

Cross, Milton. *Complete Stories of the Great Operas.* New York: Doubleday & Company, 1952.

Cruden, Alexander. *Cruden's Complete Concordance to the Old and New Testament.* Grand Rapids: Zondervan Publishing House, 1968.

Dakers, Caroline. *Clouds, the Biography of a Country House.* London and New Haven: Yale University Press, 1993.

Defoe, Daniel. *Robinson Crusoe.* New York: Doubleday and Company, 1946.

Dickens, Charles. *Bleak House.* New York: Books, Inc., n.d.

_____ . *David Copperfield.* New York: Books, Inc., n.d.

_____ . *Dombey and Son.* New York: Books, Inc., n.d.

_____ . *Great Expectations.* Ibid.

_____ . *Little Dorrit.* Ibid.

_____ . *Martin Chuzzlewit.* Ibid.

_____ . *Nicholas Nickleby.* Ibid.

_____ . *Oliver Twist.* Ibid.

_____ . *Our Mutual Friend.* Ibid.

_____ . *The Pickwick Papers.* Ibid.

_____ . *A Tale of Two Cities.* Ibid.

Drabble, Margaret, ed. *The Oxford Companion to Englsih Literature.* Oxford: Oxford University Press, 1985.

Drotner, Kirsten. *English Children and their Magazines, 1751–1945.* New Haven: Yale University Press, 1988.

Du Maurier, George, *Peter Ibbetson.* New York: The Modern Library, 1932.

Eliot, Charles W., ed. *English Poetry,* vols. 1, 2, and 3. New York: P.F. Collier and Son, 1910.

Eliot, George. *Middlemarch.* New York: Clarke, Given & Hooper, n.d.

_____ . *Scenes from Clerical Life.* Boston: Estes and Lauriat, n.d.

Evans, Ivor. *Brewer's Dictionary of Phrase and Fable,* fourteenth edition. London and New York: Harper & Row, 1989.

Fleming, John, with Hugh Honor and Nikolaus Pevsner. *The Penguin Dictionary of Architecture 3d ed.* London: Penguin Books, 1980.

Fowler, H.W. *Modern English Usage 2d ed.* New York and Oxford: Oxford University Press, 1965.

Gascoigne, Bamber. *Encyclopedia of Britain.* New York and London: Macmillan Press, Ltd. 1993.

Gathorne–Hardy, Jonathan. *The Rise and Fall of the British Nanny.* London: Weidenfeld and Nicholson, 1972, 1993.

Gerould, Winifred G., and James T. Gerould. *A Guide to Trollope.* Princeton: Princeton University Press, 1948, 1976.

Gibbons, Stella. *Cold Comfort Farm.* New York: Penguin Books, 1977.

Gilbert, William S. *The Bab Ballads.* London: Macmillan & Co., Ltd., 1925.

_____. *More Bab Ballads.* London: George Routledge & Sons, n.d.

Graves, Charles. *Leather Armchairs.* New York: Coward McCann, 1964.

Graves, Robert, and Alan Hodge. *The Long Weekend, A Social History of Great Britain 1918–1939.* New York and London: W.W. Norton & Co., 1940.

Griffith, Paddy. *The Viking Art of War.* London: Greenhill Books, 1995.

Hardwick, Michael, and Mollie Hardwick. *The Charles Dickens Comopanion.* New York: Holt, Rinehart & Winston, 1965.

Hilton, James. *Good-bye, Mr. Chips.* Boston: Little Brown, and Company, 1935.

Horace. *The Complete Works.* New York: The Modern Library, 1936.

Housman, A.E. *A Shropshire Lad.* New York, The World Publishing Co., 1932.

Ingelow, Jean. *Mopsa the Fairy.* New York: E. P. Dutton & Co., 1964.

Jacobs, W.W. *The Monkey's Paw.* In *The Golden Argosy,* Van H. Cartmell and Charles Grayson, eds. New York: The Dial Press, 1955.

Jacobs, Joseph. *English Fairy Tales.* New York and London: G.P. Putnam's Sons, n.d.

_____. *More English Fairy Tales.* New York and London: G.P. Putnam's Sons, n.d.

Jerrold, Walter, and R.M. Leonard, eds. *A Century of Parody and Imitation.* New York: Oxford University Press, 1913.

Keats, John, and Percy Bysshe Shelley. *Complete Poetical Works.* Shelley's works edited by Mary W. Shelley. New York: The Modern Library, n.d.

Kermode, Frank, and John Hollander, eds. *The Oxford Anthology of English Literature,* vol. 2. New York: Oxford University Press, 1973.

Kingsley, Charles. *The Water Babies.* New York: William Morrow and Company, 1997.

Kingsley, Henry. *Ravenshoe.* Lincoln: University of Nebraska Press, 1967.

Kipling, Rudyard. *Rudyard Kipling's Verse.* New York: Doubleday, Doran & Co., 1928.

Knox, Bernard, ed. *The Norton Book of Classical Literature.* New York: W.W. Norton & Company, 1993.

Lear, Edward. *Complete Nonsense.* London: The Folio Society, 1996.

Legman, G., ed. *The Limerick.* New York: Bell Publishing Company, 1969.

Lomas, Roy. "Over the Sea to the Isle of Skye." *British Heritage* 2 (1998): 36-41.

Macaulay, Lord. *Lays of Ancient Rome.* London: T. Nelson & Sons, Ltd., n.d.

Magnusson, Magnus, KBE, ed. *Chambers Biographical Dictionary.* Edinburgh: Chambers Harrap Publishers, 1897, 1990.

Mavor, Elizabeth. *A Year with the Ladies of Llangollen.* New York: Viking Penguin, Inc., 1986.

Meredith, George. *The Egoist.* New York: The Modern Library, 1947.

_____ . *One of Our Conquerors.* New York: Charles Scribner's Sons, 1898.

Ministry of Information. *Front Line, 1940–41. The Official Story of Civil Defense in Britain.* London: His Majesty's Stationery Office, 1942.

Moore, David, and Alastair Fitter. *Trees.* London: Collins, 1980.

Morehead, Albert and Geoffrey Mott-Smith, eds. *Hoyle Up-to-Date.* New York, Grosset and Dunlap, 1970.

Ourselves in Wartime. London, Odhams Press Limited, n.d.

Patmore, Coventry. *The Poems of Coventry Patmore.* Edited by Frederick Page. London: Oxford University Press, 1949.

Peacock, Thomas Love. *Nightmare Abbey and Crochet Castle.* London: Hamish Hamilton, 1947.

Perrot, Roy. *The Aristocrats.* London: Weidenfield and Nicolson, 1968.

Poole, Daniel. *What Jane Austen Ate and Charles Dickens Knew.* New York: Simon & Schuster, 1993.

Porter, Charlotte, and Helen A. Clarke, eds. *The Poetry of Robert Browning.* New York: Thomas Crowell Company, 1924.

Redlich, Monica. *Everyday England.* London: Gerald Duckworth & Co., 1957, 1971.

Richard, Ivor. *We, the British.* Garden City, New York: Doubleday & Company, 1983.

Room, Adrian. *Dictionary of Britain.* Oxford: Oxford University Press, 1986.

Stansky, Peter. *England Since 1867: Continuity and Change.* New York: Harcourt, Brace, Jovanovich, Inc., 1973.

Schur, Norman W. *British English A to Zed.* New York: Facts on File Publications, 1987.

Sterne, Laurence. *Tristram Shandy.* New York: The Modern Library, n.d.

Stevenson, Robert Louis. *Novels and Stories.* London: Pilot Press, 1945.

Strickland, Margot. *Angela Thirkell, Portrait of a Lady Novelist.* London: Gerald Duckworth & Co., 1977.

Swift, Jonathan. *Gulliver's Travels.* New York: Alfred A. Knopf, 1991.

Tennyson, Alfred, Lord. *The Poems and Plays.* New York: The Modern Library, 1938.

Thirkell, Angela. *Ankle Deep.* Wakefield, Rhode Island and London: Moyer Bell, 1996.

_____ . *August Folly.* New York: Carroll & Graf, 1988.

_____ . *Before Lunch.* New York: Carroll & Graf, 1988.

_____ . *The Brandons.* New York: Alfred A. Knopf, 1939.

_____ . *Cheerfulness Breaks In.* New York: Alfred A. Knopf, 1941.

_____ . *Close Quarters.* New York: Alfred A. Knopf, 1958.

_____ . *County Chronicle.* New York: Alfred A. Knopf, 1950.

_____ . *The Demon in the House.* London and Wakefield, New Jersey: Moyer Bell, 1996.

_____ . *A Double Affair.* New York: Alfred A. Knopf, 1957.

_____ . *The Duke's Daughter.* London: Hamish Hamilton, 1951.

_____ . *Enter Sir Robert.* New York: Alfred A. Knopf, 1955.

_____ . *Growing Up.* Wakefield, New Jersey: Moyer Bell, 1996.

_____ . *Happy Return.* New York: Alfred A. Knopf, 1952.

_____ . *The Headmistress.* Wakefield, New Jersey: Moyer Bell, 1995.

_____ . *High Rising.* New York: Carroll & Graf, 1989.

_____ . *Jutland Cottage.* New York: Alfred P. Knopf, 1953.

_____ . *Love Among the Ruins.* London: Hamish Hamilton, 1948.

_____ . *Love at All Ages.* New York: Alfred A. Knopf, 1959.

_____ . *Marling Hall.* London, Hamish Hamilton, 1974.

_____ . *Miss Bunting.* Wakefield, New Jersey: Moyer Bell, 1996.

_____ . *Never Too Late.* New York: Alfred A. Knopf, 1956.

_____ . *Northbridge Rectory.* London: Hamish Hamilton, 1947.

_____ . *The Old Bank House.* New York: Alfred A. Knopf, 1949.

_____ . *Peace Breaks Out.* Wakefield, New Jersey: Moyer Bell, 1997.

_____ . *Pomfret Towers.* New York: Carroll & Graf, 1988.

_____ . *Private Enterprpise.* New York: Alfred A. Knopf, 1947.

_____ . *Summer Half.* London: The Hogarth Press, 1988.

_____ . *Three Score and Ten.* New York: Alfred A. Knopf, 1961.

_____ . *What Did It Mean?* New York: Alfred A. Knopf, 1954.

_____ . *Wild Strawberries.* New York: Carroll & Graf, 1989.

Thurber, James. *Fables for Our Time.* Garden City: Blue Ribbon Books, 1943.

Trollope, Anthony. *Barchester Towers and The Warden.* New York: The Modern Library, 1936.

_____ . *Dr. Thorne.* Ware: Wordsworth Editions Limited, 1994.

_____ . *Framley Parsonaage.* Ware: Wordsworth Editions Limited, 1994.

_____ . *The Last Chronicle of Barset.* Ware: Wordsworth Editions Limited, 1994.

_____ . *The Small House at Allington.* Oxford: Oxford University Press, 1980.

_____ . *Can You Forgive Her?* Oxford: Oxford University Press, 1977.

_____ . *Phineas Finn.* Oxford: Oxford University Press, 1977.

_____ . *The Eustace Diamonds.* Oxford: Oxford University Press, 1977.

_____ . *Phineas Redux.* Oxford: Oxford University Press, 1977.

_____ . *The Prime Minister.* Oxford: Oxford University Press, 1977.

_____ . *The Duke's Children.* Oxford: Oxford University Press, 1977.

Weinreb, Ben, and Christopher Hibbert. *The London Encyclopedia.* London: Macmillan, 1983.

Wemyss, Lady. *A Family Record.* Plaistow, London: The Curwen Press. 1932.

Willet, Cecil, and Phillis Cunningham. *The History of Underclothes.* New York, Dover Publications, Inc., 1992.

Williams, Oscar, and Edwin Honig, eds. *Major American Poets.* New York: New American Library, 1962.

Woodward, Marguerite. "Boots Booklovers Library." *Journal of the Angela Thirkell Society* 18 (1998): 19–20.

Wordsworth — Poetical Works. Thomas Hutchins and Ernest de Selincourt, eds. New York: Oxford University Press, 1969.

Yonge, Charlotte. *The Heir of Redclyffe.* London: Gerald Duckworth & Co., Ltd., 1964.

Ziegler, Philip. *London at War.* New York: Alfred A. Knopf, 1995.